Diane Telgen and *Jim Kamp* are accomplished editors who specialize in biography and multicultural studies. Previous works include *Hispanic Writers* and the award-winning *Contemporary Authors*® series, both published by Gale Research.

Born in Manhattan's *El Barrio*, foreword writer *Nicholasa Mohr* is an award-winning author and visual artist. Her published works for children and adults include: *Nilda* (1973), winner of the New York Times Outstanding Book Award in juvenile fiction; *El Bronx Remembered* (1975), also a winner of the New York Times Outstanding Book Award in juvenile fiction, the Best Book Award from School Library Journal, and a National Book Award finalist for the "most distinguished book in children's literature", *In Nueva York* (1977); *Felita* (1979); *Rituals of Survival: A Woman's Portfolio* (1985), a collection of short stories and a novella; *All for the Better: A Story of El Barrio* (1994); *The Magic Shell* and *The Song of El Coquí and Other Tales of Puerto Rico*, both published in 1995; and *Old Letivia and the Mountain of Sorrow*, an original fairytale, will be published in 1996. Her works have been translated into Spanish and Japanese.

ALSO AVAILABLE FROM
VISIBLE INK PRESS

The Hispanic Almanac: From Columbus to Corporate America

"Documents Hispanic achievements over the ages, from politics to business to art."—*Evansville Courier*

Through fascinating text and photos, take an intriguing look at the people, places, and events that shape Hispanic America. Includes hundreds of profiles of entertainers, artists, athletes, and other major figures from Ponce de León to Henry Cisneros, plus thoughtful discussion of current issues and topics.

Foreword by writer/director Luis Valdez, founder of the revolutionary theater company El Teatro Campesino.

By Nicólas Kanellos, 7 1/4" x 9 1/4", paperback, 644 pages, 200 photos and line drawings, ISBN 0-7876-0030-X.

¡LATINAS!
WOMEN OF ACHIEVEMENT

¡LATINAS!
WOMEN OF ACHIEVEMENT

DIANE TELGEN • JIM KAMP
EDITORS

Foreword by Nicholasa Mohr

DETROIT

NEW YORK

TORONTO

Latinas! Women of Achievement

Copyright © 1996 by Visible Ink Press

Published by **Visible Ink Press**™
a division of Gale Research
835 Penobscot Building
Detroit, MI 48226-4094

Visible Ink Press is a trademark of Gale Research

Most Visible Ink Press™ books are available at special quantity discounts when purchased in bulk by corporations, organizations, or groups. Customized printings, special imprints, messages, and exerpts can be produced to meet your needs. For more information, contact the Special Markets Manager at the above address. Or call 1-800-877-4253.

Art Director: Tracey Rowens

Library of Congress Cataloging-in-Publication Data

Latinas! : women of achievement / Jim Kamp and Diane Telgen, editors;
    foreword by Nicholasa Mohr.
        p.   cm.
    Includes bibliographical references and index.
    ISBN 0-7876-0883-1
    1. Hispanic American women—Biography—Dictionaries.   I. Kamp,
Jim.   II. Telgen, Diane.
E184.S75L354   1996
920.72′08968073—dc20   96-15651
[B]   CIP

CONTENTS

FOREWORD

When I was growing up female and Puerto Rican in New York City, I

would have thought any dream or ambition possible in my future had I

been able to read about the talented Latinas in this outstanding

collection of biographies.

In my barrio neighborhoods of Spanish Harlem and the South Bronx back in the 1940s and 50s, I grew up unaware that I had an extended Latino family living in the barrios of Chicago, Tampa, Los Angeles, and in a multitude of towns and cities all across this nation. I had no idea of the millions of other Latinos with whom we as Puerto Ricans shared a common culture.

Pride in my family and pride in my community were restricted to life in my barrio. Outside my neighborhood, self-esteem and loving who I was became challenges and acts of faith. The dominant society not only demanded that I exclusively embrace the Anglo-American culture, but I was also expected to reject my own Latino heritage. For example, I was taught that the United States had rescued Puerto Rico from the cruel Spaniards. The reality about the U.S. government's participation in the sinking of the U.S. battleship *Maine* in 1898, which resulted in the American invasion and colonization of Puerto Rico, was omitted from my history lessons. As Latinos, we were expected in turn to be grateful, speak only English, and strive toward total assimilation by rejecting our ancestry.

• *Searching for*

Role Models

There were no positive role models for me—out there in the dominant society—when I was growing up. When I looked and searched for successful Latinas to emulate, my efforts were futile. As a Puerto Rican and a female of color, my legacy was one of either a negative image or was invisible. I grew up with the stereotyping of Hispanic women in an era when there was no recognition of the Latinas who had prevailed in a vast array of disciplines. Instead, we were subjected to The Maria Syndrome, which equated Latinas with the sacrificing *Virgen Maria,* purity and motherhood, or *Maria de Magdalena,* the prostitute. In categories other than these, Latinas were invisible.

Yet I knew even at an early age that this typecasting was not the truth: Where were the valiant women I knew? Where were my mother, my aunts, and all the courageous females who had been forced to leave Puerto Rico out of necessity, arriving in the United States by themselves for the most part, bringing children to a cold and hostile environment? They had come ill-equipped, with limited education and few survival skills, and no knowledge of English. But they all were determined to give their children a better life—a future. This is where I came from and it was these women who became my heroes.

Many of the Latinas profiled in this edition are the daughters of these undaunted women, descendants of strong females who passed on the survival techniques they learned and bestowed upon us the strength and determination that pressed the next generation to continue to succeed.

"Racism is an epidemic, like AIDS. It permeates every aspect of our society. I continue to be an optimist—a cautious, sometimes suspicious, but still a vigilant optimist. What if we dialogue and learned about each other so as to lessen sensitivity and hostility? What if we gave each other the benefit of the doubt? What if we begin today?" These are the words of Elizabeth Martinez, Mexican American, who was born in the poorest part of the town of Pomona, California. Today she is the executive director of the American Library Association. Back in 1966, shortly after Martinez joined the Los Angeles County Public Library, a Hispanic girl brought her mother to meet Martinez. "See mom, she looks just like me," said the child. "You never understand how much of a role model you are until something like this happens," concludes Martinez.

Elizabeth Martinez is one of the seventy Latinas profiled in these biographies. Each one of these extraordinary women have excelled—in the disciplines of science, law, government, education, social activism, visual arts, music, fashion, literature, sports, media, and entertainment. Their backgrounds vary: some have come from privileged families while many have had to surmount modest beginnings and sometimes, extreme poverty. But these talented individuals share a common bond. They have triumphed over society's bias to exclude them by succeeding brilliantly in their professions and thus, have defied the stereotypes.

Carmen Zapata, actress, producer, and community activist, born in New York City to a Mexican father and an Argentine mother, first used the name Marge Cameron in a singing and comedy act she created. "At one time it was not 'in' to be Hispanic. I had a hard time getting club owners to hire me unless I shook my fanny and played the maracas." Eventually her film roles caused the producers to claim that Marge Cameron did not look 'All-American.' Zapata began using her real name. However, she was then stereotyped in roles of either a maid or a mother. Despite a successful career that earned her money, Zapata decided to delve further into her Latino roots. Today she is the president and managing producer of the Bilingual Foundation of the Arts, a successful, Los Angeles-based theatrical organization, which she co-founded. She states that the Foundation's goal is to "have everyone learn about, share and become part of our literature and tradition."

Astronaut Ellen Ochoa, born in California and of Mexican descent, understands her success may encourage young girls to achieve their goals because she is similar to them.

Antonia Novello, born in Puerto Rico, was both the first woman and first Hispanic to hold the position of Surgeon General of the United States. Novello claims she is for the people who deserve help, "I think that as a woman, as a Hispanic, as a member of a minority . . . I bring a lot of sensitivity to the job."

Other notable women in government are Katherine D. Ortega, U.S. Treasurer during President Reagan's administration, and Mari-Luci Jaramillo, ambassador and business woman serving during President Carter's administration. Both of these Latinas were born in New Mexico of Spanish heritage.

In 1992 three Latinas were elected to the U.S. Congress: Lucille Roybal-Allard, democrat, is the first woman of Mexican-American ancestry; Ileana Ros-Lehtinen, republican, is the first Cuban-born woman; and Nydia Margarita Velazquez, democrat, is the first Puerto Rican woman. Velazquez is dedicated to showing that Hispanic women can serve proudly in the political arena, fighting the notion that, "we are the ones who go out and collect signatures but when it comes to the final process, we were not good enough to run for office."

Rosie Perez, actress, dancer, and choreographer, was born in Brooklyn and grew up watching her Puerto Rican parents dance *salsa* on the weekends and holidays. Singer Linda Ronstadt reveals that "when we were little, we spoke Spanish at home, but the schools pounded it out of us pretty early." Ronstadt celebrated her paternal Mexican heritage with a successful album of *mariachi* songs that her father used to sing.

Nely Galán, television anchor and producer, born in Cuba, came here when she was an infant. As a popular television personality, Galán is determined to help shape the future of television produced for the U.S.-born Hispanics and warns that, "You damage a whole group of people because they're not seen anywhere, and that reflects badly on their self-esteem."

In this collection, you will discover the talented Cuban-born Tania León, composer, conductor, and musical director. In dance there are ballerina Lupe Serrano, born in Santiago, Chile, and Gracíela Daniele, choreographer originally from Buenos Aires, Argentina.

Christy Turlington, born in Caracas, Venezuela, whose mother was from El Salvador, is recognized world-wide as a top fashion model. Carolina Herrera, originally from Caracas, is internationally identified as one of the world's prime fashion designers.

Rosemary Casals, professional tennis player born in San Francisco of poor immigrants from El Salvador said that in her early years, "other kids had nice tennis clothers, nice white shoes and came in Cadillacs. I felt stigmatized because we were poor." Casals was a maverick because she dared to go on tour to play in amateur tournaments for pretty trophies and left the money to men.

Journalist Evelyn Nieves, whose parents were Puerto Rican, was raised in the Bronx. She is one of the first Latina journalists at *The New York Times* and is proud of her heritage. In an interview she said, "I get calls from people, and they say maybe you will want to do this story—and it's strictly from my name. You don't see many Hispanic journalist."

Critics have compared the work of poet Sandra María Esteves, born of a Puerto Rican father and a Dominican mother, to that of the late great Puerto Rican poet Julia de Burgos. Esteves's poems reflect the conflicts of living between two languages and two cultures as well as the problems of surviving as a Latina in a world dominated by Anglo males.

Pat Mora, poet and educator, born in El Paso, Texas, is well aware of the influence she has on minority youths and minority issues, "I write to try to correct these images of worth." Mora states her pride in being a Hispanic writer.

Writer Clarissa Pinkola Éstes, whose natural parents were Mexicans of Spanish and Indian descent, was adopted by immigrant Hungarians. A Jungian psychoanalyst, her book *Women who Run with Wolves: Myths and Stories of the Wild Woman Archetype*, received critical acclaim and is hailed as a "feminine manifestor for all women regardless of age, race, creed, or religion, to return to their wild roots."

Like Carmen Zapata and others portrayed in this wonderful collection, I too searched and eventually found the works and books that document the invaluable Hispanic contributions that are an indelible part of these United States. Now, *Latinas! Women of Achievement* is another welcomed addition to that documentation.

Nicholasa Mohr
1996

ACKNOWLEDGMENTS

Expressions •

of

thanks

When we began working on this book, the biggest challenge facing us was not who we should include, but rather who can we possibly leave out? Every notable Hispanic woman we read or heard about seemed worthy of inclusion—but, in these pages, we cannot tell every story. So here we have collected those of seventy Latinas, stories that may be familiar to some of our readers and others that are not because the woman profiled is someone whose achievements have not put her squarely in the spotlight—yet. The common thread among them? These are women of determination and strength.

With the help of Nicolás Kanellos, whose work as founder and publisher of Arte Público Press makes him singularly qualified to lend sound advice about editorial questions, and that of Isabel Valdés, businessperson/marketer and a notable Hispanic woman in her own right, we carefully put together a list of names, representing women from many different backgrounds and from across the spectrum of occupations. Before long, the list grew and became seventy full-length profiles, each chronicling the life of a Latina woman, and together, chronicling the accomplishments of Latina women.

More help came from Pamela Shelton, who, in her fact-checking, updating, and writing, became so close to these stories that upon finishing her part, she remarked that she missed these women. And we are indebted to editors Diane Telgen and Jim Kamp, whose larger work *Notable Hispanic American Women* (©Gale Research), a hefty volume published in 1993 for the library reference shelf, we have selected from, updated, and reprinted here.

Thanks also to Margaret Chamberlain for her assistance in securing photos; Pam Hayes for her help in cropping and sizing those photos; Andy Malonis for research assistance; Tracey Rowans for her page and cover design; and Casey Roberts for efficient typesetting.

Rebecca Nelson
Leslie A. Norback
Editors,
Visible Ink Press

PHOTO CREDITS

CONTRIBUTORS

D. D. Andreassi

Gloria Bonilla-
    Santiago

Andrés Chávez

D. D. Entreassi

Sally Foster

Ronie-Richele Garcia-
    Johnson

Marian C. Gonsior

Rosalva Hernandez

Jonathan J. Higuera

Carol Hopkins

Kelly King Howes

Anne Janette Johnson

Elena Kellner

Jeanne M. Lesinski

Ann Malaspina

Teresa Márquez

Diana Martínez

Yleana Martinez

Peg McNichol

Silvia Novo Peña

Tom Pendergast

Margaret Rose

Pamela L. Shelton

Diane Telgen

Michelle Vachon

Luis Vasquez-Ajmac

Carol von Hatten

Denise Wiloch

Heartfelt •

thanks to these

chroniclers

of history

ISABEL ALLENDE

*C*hilean novelist Isabel Allende has been acclaimed for her unique

writing style. Employing the "magic realism" of Nobel Prize-winning

novelist Gabriel García Márquez, Allende's works are known for their

underlying feminism and her sensitive depiction of both Latin and

American culture. A resident of the United States since 1988, Allende

brings a natural talent for storytelling to each of her novels, creating

memorable characters and vivid scenery. Prompted to write her first

book after working as a journalist in her native Chile for several years,

Allende has surmounted great personal tragedy on her way to gaining

critical praise as one of the most noted Latin American novelists at work

today. Her books have consistently been bestsellers with English- and

1942- •

Novelist, •

journalist

Spanish-speaking readers, both in the United States and abroad, making Allende the first internationally acclaimed Latin American woman writer.

Allende was born August 2, 1942, in Lima, Peru, the daughter of Chilean diplomat Tomás and Francisca Llona Baros Allende. After her parents divorced when Isabel was only two years old, she and her mother moved in with Francisca's parents. Her grandmother, a wonderful teller of tales, greatly influenced the budding writer. Allende remained in her grandparent's care until Francisca married for the second time, again to a diplomat who brought his new family to live with him in a variety of locations, including Bolivia, the Middle East, and several European nations.

In 1957 Allende moved back to Chile to finish her high school education; after graduating two years later she went to work as a secretary for the United Nations's Food and Agricultural Organization, staying there until 1965. In 1962 she married Miguel Frías, with whom Allende had two children before the couple separated in 1978. Meanwhile, she became interested in writing and began to plan her career as a journalist.

In 1967 Allende took a job with *Paula,* a feminist women's magazine that had a national circulation. While at *Paula* she worked as a reporter, editor, and as an advice columnist, whose "Impertinences" made interesting reading for many Chilean women. Allende supplemented her work there with editorship of the popular children's magazine *Mampato,* beginning in 1969. She also appeared on Chilean television's Canal 13/Canal 7, where she interviewed numerous guests on a weekly program. Unfortunately, her efforts toward building a career as a successful journalist came to an abrupt end under tragic circumstances.

The September 11, 1973, assassination of President Salvador Allende as part of a military coup against Chile's socialist government, hit twenty-nine-year-old Isabel harder than it did many of her countrymen: the president had been her uncle. "I think I have divided my life [into] before that day and after that day," she told *Publishers Weekly* of that day of bloodshed when General Augusto Pinochet Ugarte took power in Chile. "In that moment, I realized that everything was possible—that violence was a dimension that was always around you." After eighteen months of political repression and military violence, during which she helped others to find food and shelter and sometimes escape government persecution—Allende herself helped transport several people to safety—Isabel and the other members of her family were warned that it was no longer safe for them to remain in Chile. Together with several other

Military Coup •

Changes

Writer's Life

members of her family, she fled to Caracas, Venezuela in 1975. There, despite her considerable experience as a journalist, Allende found it difficult to get a job in her field; she put thoughts of writing aside and worked as a teacher for several years. Word that her aged grandfather, who had remained behind in Chile, was dying prompted her to begin writing again. "My grandfather thought people died only when you forgot them," she later told *People*. "I wanted to prove to him that I had forgotten nothing, that his spirit was going to live with us forever." She took paper and pencil and began to write the old man a letter recounting her memories.

Those memories of family and home ultimately became Allende's first novel, 1982s *La casa de los espíritus; The House of the Spirits*. Following three generations of the Trueba family through both domestic and political upheavals, *The House of the Spirits* "is a novel of peace and reconciliation, in spite of the fact that it tells of bloody, tragic events," according to the *New York Times Book Review*. The author's use of fantasy and an ambitious structure caused some critics to compare the work to Márquez's *One Hundred Years of Solitude*. Although *The House of the Spirits* includes political approaches similar to other Latin American works, it also contains "an original feminist argument that suggests women's monopoly on powers that oppose the violent 'paternalism' from which countries like Chile continue to suffer," according to the *Chicago Tribune*. Family patriarch Esteban Trueba is a strict conservative who exploits his employees and lets his rigid beliefs distance him from both his wife and his children—even in the face of catastrophic events.

● **Of Love and**

Survival

At the start of Allende's 1984 novel, *De amor y de sombra; Of Love and Shadows,* two babies with identical names are switched shortly after birth; one of them grows to womanhood only to become the focus of a woman journalist's investigation; after the reporter and her photographer expose the political murder of the girl, they are forced to flee the country. "Love and struggle a la 'Casablanca'—it's all there," states the *New York Times Book Review*. "Ms. Allende skillfully evokes both the terrors of daily life under military rule and the subtler form of resistance in the hidden corners and 'shadows' of her title." While political action comprises a large part of the story, *Of Love and Shadows* is also a love story about two people, brought together in the tide of historic circumstance, witnessing a battle between good and evil.

The illegitimate, orphaned protagonist of Allende's third novel works as a scriptwriter and storyteller. In 1987's *Eva Luna*, Eva becomes involved with a Austrian-born filmmaker who is haunted by memories of his Nazi father. In *The Stories of Eva Luna*, a companion work published in 1991, Allende recounts the tales that Eva spins to her filmmaker boyfriend to help him excape both the pressure of his job and the memories that continue to haunt him. While several of the book's stories center on the political upheavals common in Latin America, *Cuentos de Eva Luna; The Stories of Eva Luna* ultimately depicts women who are capable of survival, even in the midst of violence and turmoil.

Survival is again the focus of Allende's fifth novel, 1991's *El plan infinito; The Infinite Plan,* published in English in 1993. Taking place in California, this novel covers a forty-year span in the lives of its three main characters: Gregory Reeves, Carmen Moralez, and Gregory's sister, Judy. When Reeves, the son of an itinerant preacher, falls ill during a stop on the touring circuit, his father decides to put down roots: the Reeves family moves to the barrio of East Los Angeles. For the Reeves children, their new Hispanic neighborhood becomes almost a family. During the novel, Gregory, Judy, and Moralez—an energetic Latina with a lust for life—move in and out of the lives of others: neighbors, lovers, friends, and family. Their individual witness to life and death, moments of anger and times of joy, and their personal passions, intertwine throughout the work.

The author's encounter with yet another personal tragedy is the subject of 1995's *Paula*. Written while at the bedside of her twenty-eight-year-old daughter Paula, who, fatally afflicted with a hereditary metabolic disorder called porphyria, was lying comatose in a Madrid hospital, Allende's book is a collage of memories. The personal—memories of time spent with her mother, grandparents, and brother, and recollections of her first marriage—and the political—the legislative reforms that caused the death of her uncle in 1973 and the staunch feminist beliefs that prompted her to gain success in a patriarchal culture—fall as layers within Allende's painful account of the days leading up to her daughter's death.

Allende now makes her home in San Francisco, where she lives with her second husband, lawyer William Gordon. In addition to writing, the issue of women's rights—both in Chile and within the United States—are a major concern to this former journalist, who was finally allowed to revisit her homeland in 1988. "For women in the United States, the issues are equality through political and economic power," she told the *Chicago Tribune.* "For Latin American women, the issues are still food and shelter for their children." She views her chosen profession from a feminist perspective as well: "Women think in terms of process," she told *Hispanic.* "For them the journey is more important than the place you get to. I think men are motivated by their goals.... Thinking in terms of process makes good mothers. Being a mother is an

Profile by
Pamela L. Shelton

eternal process. My children taught me that. I have tried to apply that to all aspects of my life."

MARIA CONCHITA ALONSO

S ince her first introduction to the stage as a beauty pageant

contestant at the age of fourteen, entertainer Maria Conchita Alonso has

accomplished the formidable task of balancing a thriving career as a

Actress, •

Hollywood film actress with success in Spanish pop music. In addition to

singer

making records and movies, she has worked as a model and television

actress, starred in a Broadway musical, and created her own film

production company. For her contributions to both the entertainment

industry and to the Hispanic community, Alonso was named Hispanic

Woman of the Year by the Mexican American Opportunity Foundation

in 1990; two years later she was again honored as Hispanic Entertainer

of the Year in the Cinco de Mayo celebration.

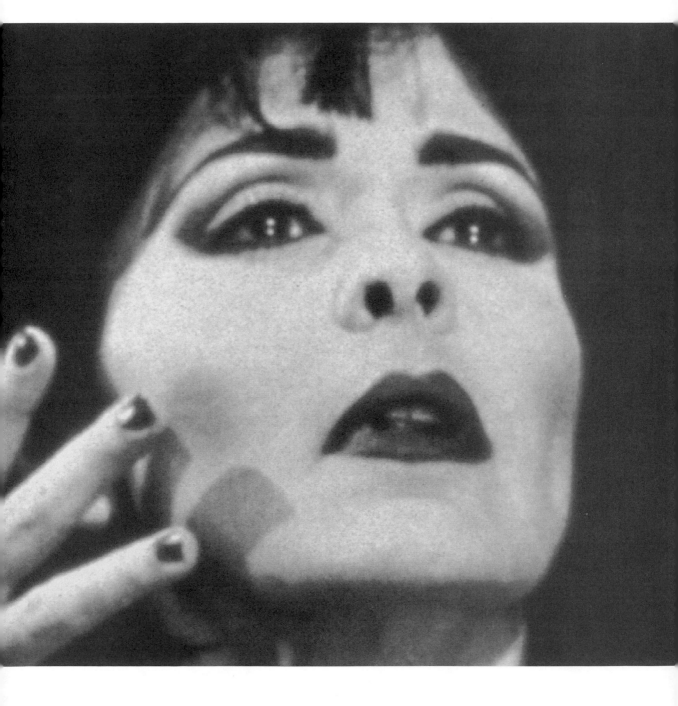

Alonso was born in Cuba to Jose and Conchita Alonso. The Alonso family, which includes older brothers Ricardo and Roberto (whom Alonso refers to as her "biggest fans"), immigrated to Caracas, Venezuela, when the actress was still a child. While she was growing up, Alonso was sent to schools in France and Switzerland. Although she loved the time she spent in Europe, she remains proud of both her Cuban blood and her Venezuelan upbringing.

Alonso's artistic calling came early. By age fourteen, she was modeling and performing in television commercials. In 1971 Alonso was named "Miss Teenager of the World" and in 1975 she represented Venezuela in the "Miss World" Pageant. In an interview with the *Los Angeles Times,* she recalled her stay in London for the Miss World Pageant: "I love food. I love to eat. Because I was nervous about the contest, I ate and ate. So much so that when it came to the night of the contest, I couldn't even get into the dress I'd bought." She still walked away from the pageant as sixth runner-up. With such stress put on her looks as a beauty contestant, Alonso's parents were wise enough to instill in her a balanced perspective that helped her in later endeavors. "They kept my feet firmly on the ground," she recalled in an interview, explaining that they helped her realize that "it's not looks, it's what is inside you, it's what you do with your life that's important."

When Alonso settled permanently in Venezuela, she pursued her acting, starring in ten Spanish-language "novelas"—television soap operas shown throughout Latin America and the United States—while also carving a niche for herself as one of the hottest singers in Spanish pop-rock music. Although she quickly became a favorite with Hispanic audiences, she opted to expand her career and try her luck in the United States. In 1982 Alonso moved from Caracas to Los Angeles. Her motto: "Dare to try new things." Her goal: The movies.

The gamble paid off when Alonso was cast as Robin Williams's Italian immigrant girlfriend in the film *Moscow on the Hudson.* Her "simpatica" effervescence caught the eye of Hollywood filmmakers and landed her roles in nine more films, including *Colors,* starring Robert Duvall and Sean Penn, and *Running Man,* in which Alonso played opposite Arnold Schwarzenegger. Other movies featuring Alonso are *Extreme Prejudice, Touch and Go, Blood Ties, A Fine Mess, Vampire's Kiss, Predator II, McBain,* and *The House of the Spirits,* a film based on the novel by Chilean novelist Isabel Allende. Though none of these films has been a box-office blockbuster, together they have established Alonso as a capable actress able to hold her own against Hollywood's top leading men.

Move to •

Hollywood

Pays Off

After proving her staying power in Hollywood, Alonso moved her sights eastward to the stage lights of Broadway. In March 1995 she took over the title role in the long-running musical *Kiss of the Spider Woman,* a role that had previously been performed by both Chita Rivera and Vanessa Williams. Critics were accepting of the Broadway newcomer: "Alonso has an updated vamp quality, by way of MTV, that could freshen up the Rivera-Williams-Alonso kick line," quipped the *New Yorker* in anticipation of her performance.

In addition to her stage and film appearances, Alonso has worked as a television actress as well. In 1989 she starred in the short-lived NBC-TV series *One of the Boys,* featuring Alonso as a young Hispanic girl newly arrived in the United States and trying to make it on her own. 1992 found her in a supporting role in the Home Box Office film *Teamster Boss: The Jackie Presser Story;* by 1994 she was all grown up and on her own, playing the Latin spitfire to Kenny Rogers's detective in the NBC-TV movie *McShayne: Final Roll of the Dice.*

The entertainer's sparkling personality and witty comebacks make her a favorite guest on the television talk-show circuit, where she is frequently asked about the difficulty of working in Hollywood as a Hispanic. Alonso explained to *Hispanic* that when television host David Letterman once inquired if she minded playing Hispanic roles, she replied, "Why not? That's what I am. The important thing is that they be good parts." Later asked by an interviewer if it was difficult for foreigners to find work in Hollywood, she pointed out, "It's difficult for any foreigner, but it's also difficult for someone from here. My best friend is an American actress and she works less than I. It's hard for anybody, but even more so for a foreigner." Alonso does not believe being a Hispanic makes the challenge more difficult: "I always try not to say 'for a Hispanic' because I don't believe being Hispanic has anything to do with the fact we don't get much work. It has to do with being a foreigner, to speak with a different accent, to have a different 'look.'" Reflecting on the obstacles particular to a woman trying to make a living in acting, Alonso stated, "There are fewer roles for women than for men. And there are two or three actresses who usually corner the female role in movies."

As a singer and live performer, Alonso's musical career has kept pace with her film work. In 1988 she was nominated for Best Latin Pop Performance at the Grammy awards for the single *Otra Mentira Mas.* This was her second Grammy nomination. In 1985 she was short-listed for Best Latin Artist for her self-titled album *Maria Conchita.* The record was certified platinum internationally and her previous four albums, including *O Ella o Yo,* went gold. Another album, *Hazme Sentir,*

- *Musical Talent*

Reaps Grammy

Nominations

coproduced by Alonso and K. C. Porter, garnered gold records in several countries after the release of only two of its singles. While expressing interest in recording in English, Alonso has turned down offers from two separate labels because the companies were interested in a type of music different from what she likes to perform. "I believe it is preferable to start off doing what one likes," she explained: "It's more difficult to change to what you want later. So I haven't yet signed a contract. I'm waiting to do what I want and to be in a position in which the contract be a good one instead of simply being 'just a contract.' I'll keep at it until it does happen."

In 1991 Alonso signed a fifty-two-show contract with Channel 13, the Mexican government's commercial TV channel, to star in *Picante!* (which means "spicy"), a weekly prime time variety program. The show, coproduced by Alonso, was conceived and shaped to showcase her many talents—singing, dancing, acting, comedy, and interviewing guest stars. Because it coincided with the series' debut, and because she "felt like it," she appeared in the December 1991 issue of *Playboy, Mexico* which, according to Alonso, ran a set of "sexy but not nude" photos. Alonso had rejected prior offers from the US *Playboy* because "they show more." In addition to her television work, she found time to create her first video in 1992. The dance and fitness program featuring the talented singer and actress has been released in Spanish as *Bailalo Caliente!* and in English as *Dance It Up!* She is currently working on an autobiographical video entitled *Asi Soy Yo.*

Reflecting on the unique challenges of maintaining two careers, Alonso admitted, "I'm very dispersed. My dedication is placed in many things." She also feels she's sacrificed some of her Hispanic career by doing American movies: "Yes, I've lost some ground. My name in the Hispanic market has maintained itself, but I've lost in the sense that other artists in the Latin market, for instance singers, that's all they do. And they spend 24 hours a day, 12 months a year doing that—their record, their concert tour, their promotions. They dedicate their mind, their energy, everything exclusively towards that goal. Same thing with Hispanic soap opera actors. They do one soap here, another there. That's the only thing they do. Instead I do too many things.... So, of course, I've probably lost some following.... In my movies, in my television program, in records, in modeling, in other side businesses I have." Managing careers on two continents and in two fields requires a discipline that Alonso explains as "patience and perseverance, and believing in yourself." And she offers this insight: "It important not to have a big ego. No Hispanic artist is likely to be valued or respected in the American market as they are valued and respected in the Hispanic market. That's why the majority of Latin stars don't do anything in the

U.S. Because they can be a big star elsewhere, but be a nobody here. An artist's ego is very big and they can't take the rejection. I think you need a very tranquil ego, very controlled. You also have to be a hard worker."

Alonso, who is single, will admit that she has sacrificed much of her private life in order to maintain multiple careers, "because if you're not working on one thing, you're working on another." She does find time to spend on hobbies: An animal lover, Alonso has two pet Yorkshire terriers that travel with her whenever possible. She favors legislation protecting the rights of animals and several years ago changed her eating habits to become a semi-vegetarian. She also spends time at her homes in Los Angeles, Caracas, Miami, and Mexico City.

Speaking Out

Brings Risks

and Rewards

Both the Hispanic entertainment community and Hollywood insiders have labeled the multi-faceted artist a true fighter. Frank and outspoken, her effervescent free-spirited image tends to belie the intensity of her mission. Asked if she ever fears that being vocal could bring negative repercussions to her career, Alonso replied: "I'd probably be very unhappy were I to shut my mouth. I never think of what could happen. If I considered the consequences, I maybe wouldn't do many things. But instead, I prefer simply to behave as I feel at that moment and forget about what could happen. And then, when things do happen, I think 'I blew it!'"

Alonso concedes that her maverick spirit has lost her some movie roles, explaining in an interview: "I find that my personality—because I am a bit rebellious, very spontaneous, very open—many producers don't see beyond that. I've had problems in getting certain roles because they don't realize that my personality can be the way it is, but as soon as I begin to act I can become whatever I want to be. It doesn't matter how I am in my daily life; what I can do as an artist is something else. When I act, I can become whatever my role requires."

Apart from her acting ability, Alonso's spunk and ingenuity have also won her roles. Auditioning for the part of a Chilean wife of a gangster in the comedy movie *A Fine Mess,* her natural temperament caught producer Blake Edwards's attention. The actress drove up to the audition in a classic Jaguar convertible and, just as it rolled to a stop, the car burst into plumes of steam and smoke. Alonso leaped out, looked under the hood and, enveloped in clouds of smoke and steam, flung her arms up in frustration. Edwards found this so funny that he gave her the role on the spot. Explaining this apparently boundless bravado, Alonso told *Time* that "we Latins have this fire inside us, in our hearts, in our skin, the flesh. You just go for it." She doesn't worry that her Spanish-flavored English may limit her roles. "Who cares? I know plenty of actresses who speak without accents. They're not working. I am."

Alonso's professional choices are not based on money but on personal instinct, as one path is often pitted against another. But, she insists, "that's the way it is and I don't want to change." Constantly involving herself in new projects—even the business end of "show-business"—she has proved to be a savvy entrepreneur. Alonso has formed a production company to develop film and television properties, in English and Spanish.

Alonso acknowledged that an important part of her success is that "I've always been 'Latina,' but with a very European mentality. My mother was an adventurer, very daring. She did not become a performer because her family wouldn't let her. My father had also been quite an adventurer and he told me to launch myself; that while one has health, energy and strength, one can conquer the world. The family's support is the most important."

And when Alonso accomplishes all her goals? "Then I'll semi-retire.... I want to work in this business because I adore my career. But I also suffer a lot. There are many lonely and sad moments. So, even though I don't think I'll completely give up my career, I will slow down in order to have a life with my man, or for whatever other reasons." Meanwhile, Alonso—beauty queen, pop-rock singer, television star, film actress, business executive—prefers to be known "as an all-around entertainer. As someone who can do it all. An artist."

**Profile by
Elena Kellner**

LINDA ALVARADO

Linda Alvarado doesn't believe in following any traditional paths.

As the only girl in a family of six children, she was accustomed to

"hanging out with the guys" from an early age. Years later, she is still

doing so, as president of the Denver-based general contracting firm

Alvarado Construction, Inc. In construction, a field usually dominated

by white males, Alvarado is one of only a handful of female executives.

And her part ownership of the Colorado Rockies baseball team franchise

makes her the first Hispanic—man or woman—to own a piece of major

league baseball.

1951- •

Business •

owner

Born Linda B. Martinez, Alvarado grew up in Albuquerque, New Mexico, where her father worked for the Atomic Energy Commission and her mother was a homemaker. "It was a very positive environment," she told Carol Hopkins in a telephone interview. "Even though I was the only girl, the expectation for me was no different." She credits her parents with giving her "huge doses" of confidence and self-esteem and encouraging her to excel both in the classroom and in athletics. Active in both high school and college sports, Alvarado lettered in girls' basketball, volleyball, and softball, and also ran track.

Alvarado says she entered the construction industry "by default." After graduating from California's Pomona College, she briefly remained on campus, employed as a lab assistant in the botany department, where she "overwatered and drowned all the plants." She then accepted a job as a contract administrator with a Southern California development company, where she learned all phases of the construction business, from preparing bids to assembling a contract. When interest rates skyrocketed, her employer decided to form a construction management group to speed up the process of getting new projects under way. Alvarado was transferred to the management group, and to her surprise, she liked it. She then went back to school and took classes in estimating, blueprint, and critical-path method scheduling to expand her knowledge of the business.

In 1974 she and a partner established the Martinez Alvarado Construction Management Corporation. Within two years Avarado had bought out her partner and was on her way to becoming a general contractor. Now known as Alvarado Construction, Inc., the company—which she now co-owns with her husband—boasts a list of accomplishments that includes dozens of projects such as commercial buildings, bus facilities, a convention center, and airport hangars. "I love what I do," enthuses Alvarado. She especially enjoys following a project from concept to construction. "There is enormous satisfaction knowing that one started from ground zero and has a terrific final project, something of great permanence and beauty."

• Joins Ranks of

Major League

Baseball Team

Owners

Outside the world of construction, Alvarado has become a partner in the Colorado Rockies, a major league baseball team that moved out onto the field during the 1993 season. When asked why she chose to become involved in baseball, Alvarado explained that she wanted to show that women can get involved in nontraditional fields. "I am entering it with money that I earned," she notes. "That is important, that we [women] participate in big business." Alvarado was also drawn to baseball because she views it as one sport where Hispanics have enjoyed tremendous success. "There are so many role models in [baseball]. I think [having a Hispanic team owner] brings the sport full circle."

As Alvarado reflects on her career, she believes her greatest challenge has been changing people's attitudes. "There is a perception that you had to be 6'2", burly, and have muscles like Popeye's to be a contractor," she notes. "These are myths. [It has sometimes been a problem] finding men who would forget the myths, men who know that this is a business that requires brains, not just brawn." She admits there are still "pockets of resistance," but they are gradually disappearing.

In the future, Alvarado envisions becoming more involved with development. "Our core business will always be construction. We're just finding new applications like design/build projects or turnkey projects. We're positioning ourselves so that if the construction industry changes and financing shrinks, we're not going to be inflexible."

Alvarado is a member of several Fortune 500 corporate boards. When increasing demands on her time have, on occasion, forced her to resign from a directorship, she has been quick to recommend another Hispanic or a woman to replace her. "I'm not there because I'm good," she explains. "I'm there because someone ahead of me was great." However, the public's perception of her within her hometown community of Denver ranks her high on the "good" scale; in fact, it has been so positive that in 1994 Alvarado was encouraged to make a bid for mayor of that city, a challenge that she might not be adverse to considering at some future juncture.

**Profile by
Carol Hopkins**

JULIA ALVAREZ

*T*hrough the mediums of poetry and prose, Julia Alvarez recreates

1950- •

the feelings of loss she experienced after her immigration to the United

States when she was ten years old. Although born in New York City, she

Novelist, •

spent her early years in the Dominican Republic until political insurrec-

poet

tion forced the Alvarez family to flee the country. After their arrival in

New York City, she and her sisters struggled to find their place in a new

world, an experience that the writer now uses as a starting point for her

exploration of culture. Her most notable work, the critically acclaimed

How the Garcia Girls Lost Their Accents, *fictionally discusses being torn*

between two cultures and the hardships faced by her immigrant family.

The culmination of many years of effort, the fifteen stories that make up the novel feature numerous memorable characters and offer entertaining insights. Hispanic women particularly find that *How the Garcia Girls Lost Their Accents* voices many of their own concerns.

"Although I was raised in the Dominican Republic by Dominican parents in an extended Dominican family, mine was an American childhood," Alvarez noted in *American Scholar*. According to the writer, her father's once-wealthy family had supported the wrong political faction during the revolution; because her mother's parents, on the other hand, benefitted from their support of the political victors, Alvarez and her parents lived on her mother's family compound. Life among so many relatives was somewhat communal; the writer and her sisters were raised alongside their cousins by her mother, maids, and many aunts. While seemingly an ideal arrangement, Alvarez's grandmother made life difficult for her daughter and son-in-law, a doctor who ran the nearby hospital and whom the revolution had now reduced to poverty.

Although not as well off as her relatives, Alvarez did not feel inferior. After all, she had been born in America, something that none of her cousins was allowed to forget. While extravagances like shopping trips to America were beyond their financial means, her family was highly influenced by American attitudes and goods. If her mother could not buy her daughters American clothing, she made sure that Alvarez and her sisters were as fashionable as their cousins. The children ate American food, attended an American school, and, for a special treat, ate ice cream from an American ice cream parlor. American cars were bought, shopping was done at American-owned stores, and American appliances were flaunted in the compound. The entire extended family was obsessed with America; to the children, it was a fantasy land.

Actually, her family's association with the United States may have saved her father's life. The members of her mother's family were respected because of their ties with America. Alvarez's uncles had all attended Ivy League colleges and her grandfather was a cultural attaché to the United Nations. The brutal dictator of the Dominican Republic, Rafael Leonidas Trujillo Molina, would not dare victimize a family with such strong American ties: he made no move against their wealth and hesitated to struggle with them for political reasons. But when Alvarez's father secretly joined the insurrectionists attempting to oust Trujillo, the police began surveillance of the compound. In 1960, just as they were preparing to apprehend him, an American agent warned the doctor in time for him to usher his family into an airplane headed out of the country. "All my childhood I had dressed like an American, eaten American foods, and befriended American children," Alvarez wrote in

American Scholar, describing the scene as their plane finally landed in her fantasy land. "I had gone to an American school and spent most of the day speaking and reading English. At night, my prayers were full of blond hair and blue eyes and snow.... All my childhood I had longed for this moment of arrival. And here I was, an American girl, coming home at last."

Alvarez's "homecoming" was not what she had expected it to be. Although she was thrilled to be in the United States, she soon faced homesickness, feelings of alienation, and prejudice. She missed her cousins, her family's large home in the compound, and the respect accorded her family name in the Dominican Republic. Alvarez, her parents, and her sisters squeezed themselves and their possessions into a tiny apartment. As she related to *Brújula Compass,* the experience was emotionally crushing: "The feeling of loss caused a radical change in me. It made me an introverted little girl." She became an avid reader, immersing herself in books and, eventually, writing.

Alvarez went on to college, earning undergraduate and graduate degrees in literature and writing. By 1987 she was hard at work on a collection of stories; the 290-page *How the Garcia Girls Lost Their Accents* was published in 1991, to considerable critical attention. The previous decade had seen a surge of ethnic novels, of which *Garcia Girls* came to be known as an exemplary example of this new literary genre.

How the Garcia Girls Lost Their Accents is a reverse-chronology of fifteen interwoven stories chronicling the lives of four sisters—Yolanda, Sonia, Carla, and Sandi—and their parents. The stories are semi-autobiographical; like their creator's family, the fictional Garcia family is Dominican and force to flee to America, where they feel like outsiders. Like Alvarez and her sisters, the Garcia girls struggle to adapt to their new environment and assimilate themselves into American culture.

The first section of the book is dated "1989-1972"; the novel's beginning seems to be the story's ending. Entitled "Antojos," which is Spanish for "cravings," the first story is the recollection of one sister's return to the Dominican Republic as an adult. Yolanda—who also ends the novel and who serves as Alvarez's alter ego—has secretly decided to return to her homeland, having found life in the United States unfulfilling. Ignoring warnings from her wealthy relatives, she drives into the country in search of the guava fruit she has been craving, only to find disappointment. Among the native Dominicans she encounters, Yolanda is regarded as an American, an outsider in her own culture. Like many of the stories in *Garcia Girls,* "Antojos" ends ambiguously. The attempts of

---

American •

Homecoming

Proves

Disheartening

---

the sisters to lead successful lives in the United States are presented more as fragments of recollections than linear stories with definite beginnings and endings.

The second section of the novel recalls the years from 1960 to 1970. The girls are younger and are experiencing their first years as immigrants. The sisters' efforts to reconcile themselves to their new culture are challenged by parents who want the girls to "mix with the 'right kind' of Americans." In this section, one sister is saved from a macho cousin's imposition, a pervert exposes himself to Carla, and Yolanda sees snow for the first time and thinks it is fall-out from a nuclear bomb. The story "Floor Show" focuses on Sandi's perception of events as the family spends a scandalous evening with an American doctor and his drunkenly indiscreet wife in a Spanish restaurant. Sandi is shocked and upset when this woman kisses her father and later dances with the flamenco dancers that the young girl so admires. Cautioned by her mother to behave at the important dinner, Sandi does as she is told and stays quiet until she is offered a flamenco doll by the American woman, who seems to understand her desire for it. "Sandi was not going to miss her chance. This woman had kissed her father. This woman had ruined the act of the beautiful dancers. The way Sandi saw it, this woman owed her something." The woman gave Sandi something more than the doll; her smile "intimated the things Sandi was just beginning to learn, things that the dancers knew all about, which was why they danced with such vehemence, such passion."

In the third and final section, "1960-1956," America is still a dream—the family has not yet left the island. The first story, divided into two parts, recalls their traumatic encounter with the Dominican *guardia,* or secret police, and their subsequent flight from home. From that moment on, the tales regress to the girls' early memories of life in the huge de la Torre compound. Yolanda tells of gifts her grandmother brought from America and an ensuing encounter with her cousin; Sandi recalls art lessons and the fright she had at the instructor's home; and Carla remembers the mechanical bank her father brought her from F.A.O. Schwarz in New York and the maid who desperately wanted it. Yolanda concludes the novel with one of her earliest memories—stealing a kitten from its mother and then abandoning it, despite the warning of a stranger: "To take it away would be a violation of its natural right to live." The mother cat haunted the girl until she left the island; as Yolanda confides in her narration, "There are still times I wake up at three o'clock in the morning and peer into the darkness. At that hour and in that loneliness, I hear her, a black furred thing lurking in the corners of my life, her magenta mouth opening, wailing over some violation that lies at the center of my art."

The *New York Times Book Review* found that Alvarez "beautifully captured the threshold experience of the new immigrant, where the past is not yet a memory and the future remains an anxious dream." "Well-crafted, *Hispanic* wrote, "although at times overly sentimental, these stories provide a glimpse into the making of another American family with a Hispanic surname." And *Library Journal* called Alvarez "a gifted, evocative storyteller of promise."

In 1994 Alvarez released her second novel, *In the Time of the Butterflies,* which recounts an actual event in Dominican history. One night in 1960, the three Mirabal sisters were returning from a visit with their husbands, who had been incarcerated as political prisoners, when they were brutally murdered on orders of Trujillo. A fourth sister, who had decided not to make this particular trip, is left to cope with the guilt and sadness caused by this tragedy, the anniversary of which is now observed as International Day Against Violence Toward Women in some sections of Latin America. Organized in a manner similar to her first novel, Alvarez layers reminiscences of the four sisters, from their childhood in a middle-class family up through the time of the murder. While some reviewers found the book too melodramatic, *In the Time of the Butterflies* was highly praised for its ability to express the sisters' "courage and their desperation, and the full import of their tragedy," according to *Publishers Weekly*.

In addition to novels, Alvarez has published several books of poetry, including 1984's *Homecoming*. In 1995 she released another collection of poems as *The Other Side: El Otro Lado*. Grouped into five separate sections, the verses depict the life and concerns of an immigrant in the United States: self-identity, class consciousness, childhood memories of the "old country," and the power of language. The book ends with the title poem, a twenty-one cannon narrative that relates the poet's experience upon returning to the mountains of her native Dominican Republic to spend a term at an artist's colony. Seeking "something that would require all of me," Alvarez retreats to a fishing village where, amid the stories of those around her, she accepts her transformation into the rhythms of American life.

Married and the mother of two children, Alvarez is currently professor of English at Middlebury College in Vermont. She has received grants from the National Endowment for the Arts and the Ingram Merrill Foundation, in addition to serving as Robert Frost Fellow in Poetry at the 1986 Bread Loaf Writers Conference. The winner of several other awards, she was the recipient of the General Electric Foundation award for young writers in 1986, and 1991's PEN Oakland/Josephine Miles Award for excellence in multicultural literature. Her novel *In the Time of the Butterflies* was nominated for Best Book of 1994 by the National Book Critics Circle.

"That is the most passionate part of the process of writing," Alvarez once confided of her craft to *Brújula Compass* "It is only possible to discover it as it is done; upon writing the ideas . . . a direction is found. A voice is discovered: the rhythm, the characters, but one cannot know before-hand." Her work continues to be praised for its significance to Hispanic culture and to Hispanic women in particular. In the words of a critic for *Más*, Alvarez, along with other celebrated Latina writers such as Sandra Cisneros, brings "a bilingual and bicultural vision" that highlights women's experiences.

Profile by Ronie-Richele Garcia-Johnson

JUDITH F. BACA

J udith Francisca Baca has risen from the role of premiere muralist of

the streets of Los Angeles to that of an international chronicler of the path

to global peace. In more than two decades of painting large-scale

projects, Baca has sought to display the history and culture of a variety of

races in her artwork. In addition to her work as a muralist and

community organizer, Baca helped found the Social and Public Art

Resource Center (SPARC) in Venice, California, an organization dedi-

cated to the promotion and cultivation of Latino artists. Her stature in

the art world rose in 1976 with her Great Wall of Los Angeles, *the*

largest outdoor mural in the world. Her next large-scale public art

project, *the* World Wall, *which envisions a world without fear,*

1946- •

Artist, •

muralist,

professor

includes participation by international artists and has been displayed in locations as diverse as Moscow's Gorky Park and the Smithsonian Institution in Washington, D.C. Calling her a "pivotal figure since the early 1970s," Paul Von Blum noted in *Z Magazine* that "Her combined efforts as a muralist and artistic director of SPARC have brought her national acclaim," and added that "initial projects established Baca as a major public artist whose work encompassed a communal process culminating in vivid, socially conscious imagery."

Baca, a second-generation Chicana, was born September 20, 1946, in south central Los Angeles. Growing up in the Huntington Park neighborhood, she was raised in a strong female household that included her mother, grandmother, and two aunts, one of whom was mentally retarded. While her mother, Ortensia Baca ("She dropped the 'H' because she didn't like the Anglos calling her 'Hortense,'" Baca once explained in a telephone interview), worked at a tire factory, Baca was raised primarily by her grandmother. Although she did not know her father, a musician named Valentino Marcel, Baca was very happy. "It was a very strong, wonderful, matriarchal household," she recalled. "I was everybody's child. I had a wonderful playmate in my grown-up aunt who wasn't grown up in her head. It was like she was five, my age, only she was big."

When Baca was six her mother married Clarence Ferrari and moved to Pacoima, where Baca spent her formative years. She spoke English poorly in elementary school and felt like an outsider in her new community. She missed living in a Spanish-speaking household with her grandmother, who stayed behind in south central Los Angeles. Out of this alienation, however, came her first opportunity to practice art, when her teacher allowed her to sit in a corner and paint while the rest of the class carried on with their studies.

Baca graduated in 1964 from Bishop Alemany High School, a Catholic school in Mission Hills, California, run by the Sisters of St. Joseph Carondelet. A year later, at the age of nineteen, she married. After a divorce six years later, she returned to her alma mater to teach after receiving a bachelor's degree in art in 1969 from California State University. That same year Baca embarked on her first cooperative art venture when she rounded up a number of ethnically diverse students to paint a mural at the school. It was, according to her, "a method to force the group into cooperation," a method she employed time and again in future projects.

Baca's days as a high school teacher were numbered after she became involved with the peace movement against the war in Vietnam and participated in marches alongside many of the nuns who also taught with her at school. A change in Alemany High School's administration resulted in the purge of the "Alemany Eighteen." Ten nuns, Baca, and seven other lay teachers were fired for their anti-war activities. Shortly thereafter the rest of the nuns withdrew from the school in protest of the action.

Baca recalled being "quite traumatized" by the event, for she believed her teaching career was over. However, she soon found employment in a special program of the City of Los Angeles Cultural Affairs Division, traveling from schools to parks, teaching art, and eventually forming her own group, "Las Vistas Nuevas." The group, made up of twenty kids from four different gangs and neighborhood groups, painted her first mural for her, in Hollenbeck Park. "The city was amazed at the work I was doing," she recalled, "putting up murals with kids who'd run directors out of neighborhood centers. The city let me do my own thing."

• *Inspired by*

"Los Tres

Grandes"

Shortly after the completion of the Hollenbeck Park mural, someone handed Baca a book on "Los Tres Grandes"—Mexican muralists Diego Rivera, David Alfaro Siqueiros, and José Clemente Orozco—and Baca began to study the traditions of Mexican mural painting. In the mid-1970s she went to Siqueiros's studio in Mexico to take classes in mural materials and techniques, and also traveled around the country looking at the murals. "The precedence of all mural painting in America lies with 'Los Tres Grandes'," she told interviewer Ann Malaspina. And Baca is firmly fixed in that tradition. "I believe taking art to the people is a political act," she said, echoing her forebears. "I am a Mexican mural painter in the true sense, but I took it to the next level. To keep an art form living, it has to grow and change."

Back in Los Angeles, with the support of the city firmly behind her, Baca expanded her program into the Citywide Mural Project. At least 250 murals were painted under her supervision. She can rightfully claim to be the first in Los Angeles to work with multicultural youth to produce murals. "Walls were already used as community billboards in L.A., so the extension of graffiti to images was not that big a leap to make," she explained.

Baca's most ambitious project during the 1970s was the *Great Wall*, a half-mile-long narrative mural painted on the Tujunga Wash drainage canal in San Fernando Valley. Its subject is Los Angeles' multi-ethnic history from neolithic times up to the 1950s, encompassing such events as the freedom bus rides, Japanese-American internment during World War II, the great Dust Bowl migration, and the infamous Zoot Suit riots of 1942. The *Great Wall* was painted during five summers over the course of nine years. Baca developed the concept, hired people, and helped raise money for the project, which she likened in an interview to "developing a military encampment."

Baca began to see the value in working with diverse groups to create public art. "It still is the only example of interracial work that focuses on working on racial differences in Los Angeles. It was not only a mural program, but it addressed ethnicity and acknowledged the differences between cultural groups," she said. Using the *Great Wall* project as a model, Baca went on to found the Social and Public Art Resource Center (SPARC), in Venice, California, in 1976. This non-profit, multicultural art center continues a program that involves artists, community groups and youth in presenting and preserving murals and other public art. The internationally recognized alternative art center also houses an archive of more than 16,000 slides of public art from around the world.

In 1987 Baca embarked on an even grander project, *World Wall: A Vision of the Future without Fear.* Its themes of global interdependence, peace, and the end of racism and sex discrimination grew out of brainstorming sessions with people selected for their diverse cultural backgrounds and their ability to provide expertise in particular areas. The portable mural is made of seven 10-by-30-foot panels painted by Baca that are arranged in a one hundred-foot semicircle. With four panels completed, the piece premiered in Finland in June 1990. It then traveled to the Soviet Union, where it was displayed in Gorky Park. The mural includes seven panels to be painted by artists from the countries in which it will be displayed. These additional panels will be hung on the outer circle.

World Wall •

Mural

Establishes

Reputation

For Baca the jump from producing murals with neighborhood groups to working with artists from around the world was a natural transition. "My idea was that what we had learned with the interracial work in Los Angeles could be applied to an international scope, from the neighborhood to the global," she said. "The *World Wall* is an attempt to push the state of arts in muralism so that the mural creates its own architecture. It makes its own space and can be assembled by any people anywhere." Second, she asked the participating artists to act as visionaries: to envision the future without fear. The panels painted by Baca—entitled *Triumph of the Heart, Nonviolent Resistance, New World Systems, Balance, Human Based Technology, Missiles to Starships, and Triumph of the Hands*—will use striking imagery to present specific allegories.

In her artist's statement for the *World Wall*, Baca wrote: "Many of us read Jonathan Schell's *Fate of the Earth,* in which he said that we must imagine the eventuality of nuclear war before we can change our destiny. It occurred to me later that it was not imagining destruction that was so hard to us but rather imagining peace. One of the students on the *World Wall* team said, 'Is peace everyone sitting around watching TV?' If we cannot imagine peace as an active concept, how can we ever hope for it to happen?"

Creating the *World Wall*—especially working with young people— was a labor of love. In *Artweek*, Baca recounted an exercise she often did with her young assistants. She asked them to gather in a large circle and hold out their hands. "And then you'd see all these wonderful little hands, these little brown fingers, stubby Asian hands, slim-fingered white hands, all these various hands," Baca recalled. Then she told the teenagers: "We need every hand here. We have nine weeks and we have 350 feet of wall. It's these hands that will make that."

Despite her success on numerous levels, Baca has constantly struggled to raise funds for her work. She told the *Los Angeles Times* that it was "ironic" that she had received more support for the "World Wall" from abroad than on a local level. Other countries have sponsored visits for her and her assistants, providing free accommodations and other arrangements. However, she had been turned down by several influential US foundations and art councils. However, she did secure funding from groups like the Rockefeller Foundation, the Women's Foundation, and Arco. "The intention is to create a dialogue of a vision of the future where there will be a world without fear," Baca told the *Los Angeles Times*. "As artists, we have the power of spreading ideas, and this is a way in which the power of ideas can move around the world."

In addition to her artistic endeavors, Baca holds a master's degree from California State University at Northridge and is a full professor at the University of California at Irvine. Her art continues to reflect her commitment to addressing social ills. This interest, she claims, is inspired by her grandmother, whom she described as being a very religious person and the neighborhood's resident healer. The artist remembers her grandmother using herbs and prayer to make her well as a child, and she imbues her artwork with that same conscientiousness. "[My work] focuses on social struggles, issues, and ills that come about from racism," she said.

**Profile by
Yleana Martinez**

MAXINE BACA ZINN

*I*n the mid-1960s, while an undergraduate at California State

College (now California State University) at Long Beach, Maxine Baca

Zinn attended sociology classes and listened as her professors discussed

minorities. A Chicana raised in Santa Fe, New Mexico, she could not

identify with what her teachers were saying. "They didn't describe social

life as I experienced it," she recalled to an interviewer. "So I decided to

set the record straight." Baca Zinn, credited with being one of the first to

conduct sociological work on Latino families and Mexican American

women, has been affectionately referred to by her colleagues as one of

"the foremothers of Chicana feminism."

1942- •

Sociologist, •

educator

Baca Zinn's studies in family sociology have indeed earned her a

reputation as a pioneer in the field of family, race, and ethnic relations. She has published widely in scholarly journals on the topic of Mexican American families, edited several books on revisionist sociology, and has presented her findings at numerous professional conferences and association meetings. In addition, Baca Zinn has received several awards honoring her for her research, including the 1990 Outstanding Alumnus Award from the College of Social and Behavioral Sciences of her alma mater, California State University, Long Beach, and the 1989 Cheryl Miller Lecturer Award on Women and Social Change, cosponsored by Sociologists for Women in Society and Loyola University of Chicago. In 1988 she received special recognition for her contributions to the Western Social Science Association, where she served as president from 1985 to 1986.

Maxine Baca was born June 11, 1942, in Santa Fe, New Mexico, to Presente and Louise Duran Baca. After graduating from high school, she entered California State College at Long Beach, earning a bachelor of arts degree in sociology in 1966. Two years later she returned to her home state to begin graduate studies at the University of New Mexico, where she also worked as a graduate teaching assistant. She received her master's degree in sociology in 1970, and was inducted to the Phi Kappa Phi Honor Society the following year. She entered the doctoral program in sociology at the University of Oregon, where she held a graduate teaching fellowship from 1971–73. Also in 1973, she was awarded a dissertation fellowship from the Ford Foundation. Baca Zinn received her Ph.D. from the University of Oregon in 1978.

Meanwhile, she moved to Michigan in 1975 to begin teaching at the University of Michigan at Flint, where she has been honored several times for her ability to inspire her students. In 1975 she received a Faculty Special Merit Award and in 1982 the Faculty Achievement Award for Scholarly or Creative Achievement. One year later she was given the Distinguished Faculty Award from the Michigan Association of Governing Boards. In the summer of 1984 Baca Zinn served as visiting scholar at the Center for Research on Women at Tennessee's Memphis State University; she returned there in spring 1987 as a research professor in residence.

While on leave from the University of Michigan at Flint, Baca Zinn worked as a visiting professor of sociology at the University of California at Berkeley, a guest professor of sociology at the University of Connecticut, and a distinguished visiting professor in Women's Studies at the University of Delaware. She was named a senior research associate at the Julian Samora Research Institute at Michigan State University in 1990.

A member of the American Sociological Society, she was elected to that organization's governing council in 1992. She said her election to the ten-member council came as a surprise because all 13,000 members of the society vote to select the council. She sees this victory as an indication of how the studies she has conducted have "pushed the margin" but does not claim this accomplishment as stemming from her unique insight into the field of race and family studies. Rather, she regards it as testimony to the importance of the work: "Society is becoming so diverse that the old ways of thinking do not work any more," she explained.

Baca Zinn's dedication to the area of ethnic families was formed in the late 1960s and early 1970s. Her early work revolved around changing myths about minority people. "I wanted to move away from the 'blaming the victim' stance," she recalled. "I then found, as I did more and more scholarship, that when you change models and explanations of minorities, you have to change the whole explanation of how society works—and change explanations of white people as well." This led to her increasing interest in "the whole global picture"; the connection between the circumstances of different classes and races. "Economically privileged people are where they are largely because of where minorities are now."

As a beginning sociologist, Baca Zinn began conducting what she termed "oppositional scholarship," questioning the mainstream view that minorities are their own worst enemy. But as her studies took her more deeply into the world of women, especially that of Mexican American women, she found that her "oppositional scholarship" approach could not apply: "When you add women and minorities (to the research), you have to change the explanations of social relations." She compares her discovery to a recipe that cannot be adapted. "The metaphor is that you can't just add women and stir. Like when you have a recipe, and then go on with it as usual. When you add women and minorities . . . you have to explain and rethink the position and explanation of European Americans."

In one of her earliest articles, "Chicanas: Power and Control in the Domestic Sphere," published in 1975 in *De Colores: Journal of Emerging Raza Philosophies,* Baca Zinn sought to examine the traditional depiction of Chicanas in sociological literature. She writes that the "passive, submissive, Mexican woman is a creation of social scientists and journalists who have taken for granted the idea that women are dependent and unproductive creatures." She backed her contention up with several examples that went against the prevailing notion that Chicanas are dependent, concluding that sufficient sociological evidence exists suggesting that women control family activities, despite the patriarchal orientation of Chicano life. Baca Zinn notes that Chicano families are indeed mother-centered, and that Chicanas develop alignments with other women—alignments that nurture a collective sense of their own worth. She calls upon her sisters to replace the stereotype of the passive Chicana "with concepts of diverse women whose responsibility for the physical and cultural survival of Chicanos is acknowledged and seriously examined."

Baca Zinn's studies on Mexican American women have brought her closer to her goal of making sociology more "minority inclusive." She believes there are more and more scholars "revising the past," offering new interpretations of the sociological framework of minorities and their families. However, her mission has been an arduous one. As a self-proclaimed "marginal intellectual," she works within the system by publishing scholarly articles, by having her views publicly aired at association gatherings, and through mentoring students—particularly Latinas and women of color.

Baca Zinn has refocussed her interest in recent years to analyzing what it means to be a Chicana feminist. She maintains that the ideals of feminine liberation necessarily differ between racial groups. "I think that Chicana and Latina feminism is very much overlooked," she declared. "We are looking at how Chicanas and Latinas are claiming their own feminism, but how? That's one of the difficult issues. The question is, what is Chicana-Latina feminism, and how does it differ from Black feminism?" That question is explored in *Women of Color in U.S. Society*, a book Baca Zinn edited with Bonnie Thornton Dill in 1993. An examination of how minority women deal with oppression and the limited opportunities that result, the book was praised by *Publishers Weekly* for its ability to "[broaden] the white, middle class perspective of earlier feminist scholars."

Since 1990 Baca Zinn has combined her studies with teaching sociology at Michigan State University in East Lansing, where she lives with her husband, Alan Zinn, and their son, Prentice. As she and other like-minded sociologists continue to break down stereotypes, her work, she believes, has become more theoretical. She cherishes her tight social network of sociologist friends, which includes men, white women, and women of color. "We really have invented a new 'women of color' feminism. It doesn't take white women's experiences as the starting point for theorizing and analyzing women's lives. It takes the lives and experiences of women of color and uses them as a standpoint. We all think of ourselves as marginal intellectuals, like outsiders," she noted, adding: "We're really challenging the boundary of mainstream scholarship."

Analyzes •

Chicana and

Latina

Feminism

**Profile by
Yleana Martinez**

JOAN BAEZ

As a prominent folksinger, Joan Baez has become part of the

American cultural fabric of the decade of the 1960s. She appeared on

the cover of Time, *sang before the 350,000 people gathered at the Lincoln*

Memorial for Martin Luther King Jr.'s "I Have a Dream" speech, toured

with legendary entertainer Bob Dylan, campaigned against the Viet-

nam War, and performed at Woodstock. But despite her connection

with so many pivotal events and personalities, Baez refuses to see herself

as a symbol of that era, telling a Rolling Stone *interviewer that she would*

rather be seen as an example of "following through on your beliefs,

using your talents to do so."

The beliefs and talents that brought Baez such fame over her long

1941- •

Singer, •

songwriter,

activist

career had their start in her childhood. She was born Joan Chandos Baez on January 9, 1941, in Staten Island, New York. Her mother, Joan Bridge Baez, was a Scottish immigrant; her father, the physicist Albert Baez, came to the United States from Mexico. From her parents the singer inherited both a rich multicultural background and nonviolent Quaker beliefs that inspired her own active crusade for peace and justice. Her father, guided by moral concerns, turned down lucrative defense work to devote his life to academic research. Commenting on the consequences of his choice in her 1987 autobiography *And a Voice to Sing With*, Baez notes: "We would never have all the fine and useless things little girls want when they are growing up. Instead we would have a father with a clear conscience. Decency would be his legacy to us."

Because of her Hispanic roots, Baez was introduced to racial inequality at a young age. In her autobiography she recalls being taunted as a child because of the color of her skin and relates her experiences in junior high school where she felt isolated from both the Mexican and Anglo children. "Few Mexicans were interested in school and they were ostracized by the whites," she writes. "So there I was, with a Mexican name, skin, and hair: the Anglos couldn't accept me because of all three, and the Mexicans couldn't accept me because I didn't speak Spanish." She was also considered strange because of her pacifist beliefs. While other students spoke with fear of the Soviet Union and echoed the anticommunist feelings of their parents, Baez adopted the antimilitary stance that she learned from family discussions and Quaker activities.

The singer admits that loneliness was an important factor in choosing her future path. Seeing music as a means of becoming popular, she spent a summer developing her voice and learning to play the ukulele. She soon gained a reputation as an entertainer and made her stage debut in a school talent show. Baez also became known among her peers for her sketches of Disney characters and her ability to paint school election posters with ease. At age fourteen she wrote a short, self-illustrated essay titled "What I Believe" in which she related her beliefs on many topics. The essay expresses many of the moral truths that guided the singer's actions throughout her life. "I think of myself as hardly a speck," she wrote as a teen. "Then I see there is no use for this tiny dot to spend its small life doing things for itself. It might as well spend its tiny amount of time making the less fortunate specks in the world enjoy themselves."

A family move from California to the Boston area after her high school graduation created the circumstances that soon allowed young Baez to act on her beliefs; to help "the less fortunate specks." Although she enrolled at Boston University, intellectual pursuits were quickly superseded by her growing interest in folk music. Bolstered by the popularity of such folk musicians as Pete Seeger and the Kingston Trio, the folk music genre had experienced a revival during the late 1950s, and coffee houses featuring local singers were popular gathering spots for college students such as Baez. At first she and a roommate sang duets ("Fair and Tender Maidens" was their specialty) at coffee houses in the Boston area, but Baez soon went solo. She accepted an invitation to perform two nights a week at Club Mt. Auburn 47, a Harvard Square jazz club that was hoping to add folk enthusiasts to its clientele.

Discovers Folk •

Scene in Boston

By 1959 Baez had acquired enough of a following to record her first album, *Folksingers 'round Harvard Square*, which she recorded with two friends. That same year she sang for a couple of weeks at The Gate of Horn, a Chicago nightclub. While there she met popular folk singer Bob Gibson, who invited her to appear with him at the first Newport Jazz Festival that August. Her three-octave soprano voice captivated the festival crowd of 13,000 and made her an instant celebrity. Although she returned to her coffee house engagements after the festival, Baez sensed the increasingly important role that music would play in her life. In *And a Voice to Sing With* she writes that, following Newport, "in the book of my destiny the first page had been turned, and that this book could no longer be exchanged for any other."

Turning down more lucrative deals with larger record companies, Baez chose to sign her first contract with Vanguard, a small label known for its quality classical music recordings. Her first solo album, simply titled *Joan Baez*, was released near the end of 1960. The album was made up entirely of traditional folk songs, including "All My Trials" (an often requested favorite among Baez fans) and "The House of the Rising Sun," a song previously popularized by the black blues singer Leadbelly. A song in Spanish, as well as the popular Scottish ballad "Mary Hamilton," were also included. The album was a success, reaching the number-three spot on the sales charts. Near the time of the record's release, Baez moved back to the California coast.

From her new home, Baez often commuted to the East Coast, joining other folksingers to play college crowds in auditoriums that seated two to five hundred people. In November 1960 she played her first solo concert to an audience of 800 in New York City. By 1963 her third album had been released; she was playing at venues like the Forest Hills Music Festival and Hollywood Bowl, with 10,000 to 20,000 in attendance. With her career poised to take over her life, she recalled the essay she had written as a teenager. "I was in a position now to do something more with my life than just sing," she writes in her autobiography. "I had the capacity to make lots and lots of money. I could reach lots and lots of people. It would be a while before this sentiment would take root and grow into something tangible, but the intent was now evident and becoming stronger by the day."

• **Becomes Active**

in Vietnam War

Protest

The Vietnam War protest movement was the cause to which Baez devoted an increasingly larger amount of energy as the Sixties progressed. In 1964 she announced that she would stop paying the sixty percent of her federal income tax that she calculated went to financing the U.S. Defense Department. The following year she founded the Institute for the Study of Nonviolence—now called the Resource Center for Nonviolence—in Palo Alto, California. Her forthright political beliefs at times affected her career: In 1967, citing the singer's strong antiwar stance, the Daughters of the American Revolution (DAR) refused Baez permission to play at their Constitution Hall in Washington, D.C. When news of their actions received sympathetic coverage in the press, Secretary of the Interior Mo Udall gave Baez permission to play an outdoor concert at the base of the Washington Monument, where an estimated 30,000 people came to hear her sing. Several months later she was arrested and jailed for her active opposition to the Vietnam War draft. The following year she married David Harris, a leader in the draft resistance movement.

Baez's highly visible social activism during the Sixties sometimes overshadows the reason for her rise to fame: her voice. From the beginning of her career, reviewers had struggled to describe its quality. In early reviews *The New York Times* referred to Baez's voice first as "a soprano voice, surprisingly never trained, that has a purity, penetrating clarity and control that not a few art singers would envy," later adding that it was "as lustrous and rich as old gold." *Time*, in a cover story on Baez, discovered in her voice "distant reminders of black women wailing in the night, of detached madrigal singers performing calmly at court, and of saddened gypsies trying to charm death into leaving their Spanish caves." In *And a Voice to Sing With* Baez refers to her voice as her "greatest gift" closely followed by a "second greatest gift," that of "a desire to share that voice, and the bounties it has heaped upon me, with others."

Despite her increasing involvement in politics, Baez shared her voice in concert appearances and on numerous albums during the 1960s. Reluctant to completely abandon the traditional melodies she loved, the singer nonetheless slowly added more contemporary music to her repertoire. Her fourth album, *Joan Baez in Concert: Part Two*, released in 1963, included a Bob Dylan song, "Don't Think Twice, It's All Right." That same year she helped Dylan's career by inviting him to appear with her during her concert tour. The two singers eventually toured together with equal billing and Baez recorded *Any Day Now*, an entire double album of Dylan tunes, and participated in the 1992 collection *I Shall Be Unreleased: The Songs of Bob Dylan*. She further expanded the scope of her musical offerings during the decade with *Baptism*, an album of spoken and sung selections from the poetry of Arthur Rimbaud, Federico García Lorca, James Joyce, and others, as well as *David's Album*, a collection of country and western music. As one of the highlights of her career, Baez appeared at what many consider to be the pinnacle of 1960s culture, the Woodstock Music Festival. The five-day event, held in 1969, brought some of the most important and influential musicians of the decade to a farm in upstate New York. The concert drew more than 500,000 people with its theme of "five days of peace, love, and music."

The 1970s saw Baez emerge as a songwriter on her album *Blessed Are . . .*, which featured several songs based on her experiences as a wife and mother, including "A Song for David" and the lullaby "Gabriel and Me." In 1971 she and Harris were divorced; in the same year she decided to end her association with Vanguard. "The Night They Drove Old Dixie Down," a cut off her last Vanguard album, *Blessed Are . . .*, became one of the most popular songs of 1972 and Baez's biggest commercial success. Continuing her political activism, that same year she and a small group of friends toured what was then North Vietnam to witness the effects of the continuing war on the Vietnamese people. During eleven of the thirteen days, Baez stayed in the capital city of Hanoi, where the United States carried out the heaviest raids of the war. On her return home, she edited the fifteen hours of tapes recorded during her trip into her 1973 album, *Where Are You Now, My Son?*, a very personal plea for an end to the war.

Baez remained engaged in political and social activism in the United States as well. During the same year as her Vietnam visit, she led a gathering of women and children in joining hands around the Congressional building in Washington, D.C., to protest continued U.S. involvement in Vietnam. 2,500 marchers, braving the flood waters left in the recent wake of Hurricane Agnes, linked arms around Congress while simultaneous demonstrations took place in San Francisco, Palo Alto, Minneapolis, and Boise. Since the end of the war, Baez has served on the national advisory board of Amnesty International, a worldwide organization that works for the release of people imprisoned for their religious or political beliefs; she was also instrumental in founding Amnesty West Coast, the group's California branch. And in 1979 she founded Humanitas International, for which she still serves as president. Based in Menlo Park, California, Humanitas promotes human rights, disarmament, and nonviolence through seminars and other educational opportunities.

In her autobiography, Baez reveals that sometime during the late 1970s she "began the painful and humiliating process of discovering, ever so slowly, that though I might be timeless in the world of music, at least in the United States I was no longer *timely*." Her waning popularity received a boost in 1985 when she was asked to open the U.S. portion of Live-Aid, a multi-act rock concert designed to raise funds to help famine victims in Africa. In 1986 she took part, along with fellow musicians Sting, U2, and Peter Gabriel, in the "Conspiracy of Hope" concert tour celebrating Amnesty International's twenty-fifth anniversary. In 1987 she released *Recently*, her first album to appear in the United States in eight years. The album included such diverse offerings as the traditional "Let Us Break Bread Together," a South African chant called "Asimbonanga," and a cover of Peter Gabriel's "Biko," which tells the story of slain South African activist Steven Biko.

In 1987 the publication of *And a Voice to Sing With* met with critical praise in the mainstream press, once again bringing Baez to the attention of the nation. In the book, and during numerous interviews in the wake of its publication, Baez spoke of the materialism she saw pervading society. *Christian Science Monitor* reviewer Amy Duncan referred to the fact that "Baez writes a bit dispiritedly about the '80s, and decries particularly the 'me generation' mentality and what she sees as a lack of ethical and humanitarian values." In an interview for *U.S. News & World Report*, Baez contrasted the politically concerned music of her early career to contemporary music: "The prevailing ethos is: No negative thoughts, and everything is beautiful! You just jog, eat enough of the right yogurt, and everything is going to be all right."

Social historian Barbara Goldsmith has characterized Baez's life as the story of not just one person but of an entire society. "Baez's 20-year metamorphosis from popular folk singer to 80's survivor provides an instructional tale from which one could extrapolate the changes in values in our society in the past two decades," Goldsmith wrote in the *New York Times Book Review*. Although Goldsmith may have detected a change in Baez's value system, the singer herself believes she has remained consistent. As Cathleen McGuigan pointed out in *Newsweek*, "Baez's music may have gone out of style, but according to her book, she never altered her art or her politics to suit fashion." In the preface to *And a Voice to Sing With* Baez is proud of the fact that, despite what she has been through, her "social and political views have remained astoundingly steadfast." "I have been true to the principles of nonviolence," she continues, "developing a stronger and stronger aversion to the ideologies of both the far right and the far left and a deeper sense of rage and sorrow over the suffering they continue to produce all over the world."

Although she now lives a relatively quiet life in a house near San Francisco that she shares with goats, a rooster, and half-a-dozen chickens, Baez continues to attract public attention with both her voice and her activism. A 1989 concert performance prompted New York Times reviewer Stephen Holden to write: "Her voice, though quite different in texture from the ethereal folk soprano of her first albums, remains a powerful instrument." 1993 marked the release of *Play Me Backwards*, followed a year later by *Rare, Live, and Classic*, a three-volume Baez retrospective. "She remains a compelling live performer," noted *Rolling Stone*, of the singer's musical evolution over three and a half decades, ". . . and almost embarrassingly honest in her songwriting."

In addition to her music, Baez continues to dedicate her time to causes in which she believes; on the thirtieth anniversary of her first album of folksongs, *Joan Baez*, the singer released an album of social commentary titled *Speaking of Dreams*. In the late 1980s she toured Israel and the occupied territories of the Middle East in search of the means for a peaceful end to the conflict there. In 1991 she announced plans to develop low-income housing on 140 acres of land in northern California. And 1993 found her in Bosnia, during a low point in the Balkan war, attempting to lift the morale of a people numbed by violence. She has survived what she refers to in her autobiography as "the ashes and silence of the 1980s," and appears to be firm in her dedication to do what she can to make life easier for "the less fortunate specks in the world."

**Profile by
Marian C. Gonsior**

LOURDES G. BAIRD

*A*lthough Lourdes G. Baird had what she described to the Los

1935- •

Angeles Times *as a "rather Spanish colonial upbringing," it did not*

incline her to perform as the traditional "colonial" wife and mother.

U.S. District •

Instead, after bearing three children, the homemaker decided to go back

judge

to school; her initiative and hard work has made Baird one of only a few

women in the United States to serve as an attorney general. While her

late mother was "very surprised" of the prestigious position her daughter

acquired on her way to becoming a U.S. District judge, Baird's col-

leagues are not; her work as both an attorney and a judge has been

repeatedly applauded.

The *Los Angeles Times* wrote of her reputation: "Baird is widely praised in legal circles for her judgment, fairness, administrative skills, her sense of humor and her ability to relate to a wide variety of individuals and groups." Baird was so well suited to a position of high authority that in 1989, two Republicans—a U.S. senator and the current president of the United States—nominated the Democrat for the office of U.S. attorney general for the Central District of California. She was, in fact, nominated ahead of three highly qualified Republican male candidates. Considering that this Hispanic woman began her career late in life, it is a testament to her abilities that she has presided, in a variety of capacities, over the largest federal judicial district in the nation. With her determination and consequent success, Baird provides an inspirational example for both Hispanics and women.

Baird was born the seventh child of James C. Gillespie and Josefina Delgado on May 12, 1935, in Quito, Ecuador. Gillespie's career required a move to Los Angeles, were the family relocated when Baird was just one year old. Because her mother was a devout Catholic, Baird was educated in Catholic, all-girl schools. She told the *Los Angeles Times,* "There's something in retrospect that was great about going to an all-girls high school." Because the nuns who ran the schools provided positive role models and encouragement to their female students, the Catholic schools instilled independence in Baird's character and led her to enjoy sports. The impact the schools had on Baird is evident in how she works and plays; one of the most powerful women in the United States still hikes, runs, and skis, despite being in her fifties.

Baird married businessman William T. Baird in December 1956, after graduating from Immaculate Heart High School and spending time in secretarial college. Together the couple had three children, William Jr., Maria, and John. Baird stayed home to take care of the children for eleven years. By the time John, their youngest child, entered elementary school, Baird decided that it was time for her to return to school as well.

• Education and

Early Judicial

Career

Baird became a part-time student at Los Angeles City College. Admitting one of her fears about going back to school, she told the *Los Angeles Times* that she was afraid that her "Blue Chip stamps would fall out of my purse and I'd be discovered for what I was." Five years later, the homemaker had earned her associate of arts degree. With her confidence renewed, she transferred to the University of California at Los Angeles. By 1973 Baird had received her B.A. in sociology, and was headed for law school at the same university. Although her marriage faltered—she and her husband divorced in 1975—Baird did well in law school. After graduation, she passed the California Bar exam the first time she took it. In that same year, she celebrated her forty-first birthday.

Baird began her career in law in 1977, working for William D. Keller as an assistant prosecutor in the U.S. Attorney's Office. In 1983 she became a private attorney as a partner in the firm Baird, Munger & Myers. By 1986 she had become a judge in the East Los Angeles Municipal Court, maintaining that position until 1987. After an appointment by Governor George Deukmejian in 1987, Baird served as a Los Angeles Municipal Court judge. With Deukmejian's next appointment, Baird became the Los Angeles Superior Court judge in 1988. She held that office, working in the Juvenile Court on abuse and custody cases, until 1990.

Courtroom experience was not the only qualification Baird would bring to her post as attorney general; her activity in social and civic organizations complimented her career. She has been involved with the California Women Lawyers Association since 1980, and served as the UCLA School of Law Alumni Association president from 1981 to 1984. From 1983 to 1986 Baird worked on the Ninth Circuit Court of Appeals advisory committee and specialized as a Ninth Circuit Judicial conference lawyer representative. In 1986, she became a member of the Mexican-American Bar Association, the Latino Judges Association, and the National Association of Women Judges, organizations of which she remains a member.

When a opening appeared for the post of U.S. attorney general within California's Central District, Baird's long resume was closely scrutinized; special qualifications would be needed for the person serving as attorney general for the largest federal district in the nation. With its seven counties and fourteen million people, the district was rife with drug trafficking, money laundering, savings and loans scams, and even cases of defense industry fraud. In addition, the new attorney general would also oversee more than 150 lawyers. When Republican U.S. Senator Pete Wilson nominated the Democratic Baird for the position in November 1989, observers were pleasantly surprised. It was not that Baird was unqualified for the position—she was clearly an excellent judge—it was that a Republican had nominated her, and that, if she were confirmed, she would be the first U.S. attorney in many years who was a member of the party opposing the president. While Senator Wilson was praised for his decision, some remarked that the choice reflected his political savvy; the nomination would garner Hispanic, Democratic, and female supporters for the Senator, who was a gubernatorial candidate at the time. The *Los Angeles Times* endorsed Baird's nomination in an editorial in early December with the headline, "Baird for US Attorney? Of Course."

Nominated for •

Attorney

General Post

Then-President George Bush, as well as the senators who were to ensure Baird's appointment to the office of U.S. attorney general, had to consider her opinions as well as her reputation. A former Republican-turned-Democrat, Baird believes the death penalty to be justifiable in certain cases. She is in favor of equal rights for women and increasing child care options for families. Baird was unwilling to reveal her personal stand on the abortion issue; as she told the *Los Angeles Times,* "My duty is to enforce federal law and it's not up to me to judge what I like and don't like."

After a formal background check by the FBI, it took President Bush six months to nominate Baird for the position. When she heard the news of her nomination, she was thrilled. "I'm delighted," she told the *Los Angeles Times.* "I know there are incredible challenges out there [in the district]."

The *Times* believed that Baird was ready for those challenges, and used its influence to urge voters to support her in her bid for reelection to the Superior Court. In both articles and editorials, the paper reviewed Baird's career and provided the opinions of several of her peers regarding her possible performance as attorney general. She was lauded by Judge Paul Boland, who had watched Baird handle more than a year's worth of child abuse cases, and by Robert Brosio, the interim U.S. attorney general. Assistant U.S. attorney William F. Fahey, head of the government fraud unit and one of Baird's coworkers during the early 1980s, remarked in the *Los Angeles Times,* "I think she'll be a great leader." Baird herself felt good about the cases she had worked on as a prosecutor, and later as a judge, for the government.

One person who did not favor Baird's nomination was Lew Gutwitz, who reminded the media of a case which exemplified Baird's tough stance towards criminals. Gutwitz, a lawyer who had defended American Indian activist Leonard Peltier in 1979, thought that Baird had been "meanspirited" during the proceedings. Peltier, who had been imprisoned for consecutive life sentences for killing two FBI agents, later escaped from a federal prison in Lompoc, California, insisting that his escape had been necessary to avoid being killed by government agents. When U.S. District Judge Lawrence T. Lydick refused to allow Peltier's attorneys to defend the convict on the basis of this alleged government conspiracy, the attorneys attempted to circumvent his decision. Baird and her cocounsel, Robert Biniaz, objected to these activities, and their objections were sustained by the district judge. Peltier was finally convicted despite Gutwitz's objections, and Baird was proud of her contribution to that outcome. The entire Peltier case was brought to new light in the early 1990s with the release of filmmaker Michael Apted's documentary *Incident at Ogalala*.

One-and-a-half months after Bush's action, Baird's nomination for the position of U.S. attorney general of California's Central District was confirmed by the U.S. Senate. When the silver-haired woman was sworn into office by U.S. District Judge Manuel L. Real in mid-July 1990, she was fifty-five years old. Her proud children were grown—William Jr. was working in television in Los Angeles, Maria was a mother herself and living in Berkeley, California, and John was a student at the University of California at Santa Cruz. While Baird had proven that it is possible to achieve success as a woman, a mother, and a Hispanic, she also demonstrated the benefits of returning to school to find a rewarding career after raising a family.

After her confirmation, Baird was eager to begin work on the many problems that awaited her in a district notorious for its criminal activity. Of particular concern was the drug abuse that was a constant source of illegal activities in an area that ranged from San Luis Obispo to San Bernardino. As she told the *Los Angeles Times,* "Crime is rampant. My experience on the bench has indicated to me the horror of drugs—the main problem in the United States." Discussing the relationship of drug abuse to alcohol abuse, she added: "Drugs pervade the society. I'm not a prophet of doom, but I can't tell you how it's going to be overcome." While Baird continues to fight drug abuse with tough sentencing, she also states that more treatment facilities are needed to rehabilitate drug users.

Observers hoped that Baird would deal with other thorny issues, such as bringing charges against then-mayor Tom Bradley, and the Los Angeles Sheriff's Department's alleged misused of jailhouse informants. Dealing with such issues meant that Baird would have to restructure the attorney general's office itself. Not only was the office dealing with a higher percentage of cases than when Baird worked there as an assistant attorney, but these cases were becoming more and more complex. Additional attorneys would have to be hired to handle the savings and loan fraud cases. Finally, the new attorneys, along with the veteran attorneys, would have to be organized to work efficiently.

In April of 1992 Baird became involved in one of the most controversial legal proceedings of the 1990s. In March of 1991 an African American motorist named Rodney King was stopped by several white police officers. What ensued remains controversial and hotly debated, but a videotape emerged that showed the police officers savagely beating King. The officers were brought to trial and eventually acquitted; the black community in Los Angeles erupted in a rage, sparking one of the worst riots in U.S. history. When the smoke cleared, more than fifty people were dead and more than $800 million in damage had been wrought. Much of the legal community expressed dissatisfaction with the verdict, citing a clear violation of King's civil rights. In the wake of the acquittal and riot, Baird headed up a new prosecution of the officers. Civil rights infraction charges were leveled not only at the officers who beat King but at those officers who had looked on but failed to interfere with his beating. Baird's prosecution and administrative skills would figure prominently in the new case.

By the close of 1992, Baird had decided to seek another post, this time as a judge in the U.S. District Court located within her home base of California's Central District. Not surprising in a district as large and as densely populated as hers, Baird's schedule remains busy. Although she herself is middle-aged, her career is still young. In citing her past achievements, observers predict future successes—whether Baird serves both justice and her community as a U.S. District Court judge or moves on to a position of even greater influence and authority.

**Profile by
Ronie-Richele
Garcia-Johnson**

MARIAH CAREY

In 1990, nueva pop diva Mariah Carey, with her sensational five-

octave vocal range, became the third songstress in the long history of the

Grammy Awards to receive nominations for best new artist, best song,

and best album, all in the same year. The album, Mariah Carey, *held on*

to the Number One spot in the Billboard *charts for an astonishing*

twenty-two weeks in a row, selling more than seven million copies in its

first year alone. In yet another first, with the release of her Daydreams

album five years later, Carey became the first female vocalist to have two

consecutive singles debut at the coveted Number-One position on

Billboard's *Hot 100 chart. Citing singers Aretha Franklin, Michael*

Jackson, and Stevie Wonder as her main influences, Carey's strong

1970- •

Pop singer, •

songwriter

gospel- and blues-inspired vocal stylings continue to draw legions of fans—who express their admiration for the singer by purchasing over 55 million of her albums.

Carey was born in New York City in 1970, the daughter of Patricia and Alfred Roy Carey. From her Irish mother, a former solo performer with the New York City Opera company, she inherited her vocal talent, as well as an early determination to become a singer. "I remember always wanting to be next to the radio and singing," she recalled to Steve Morse in the *Boston Globe*. "I had to be dragged away from the radio to be put to sleep. And whenever I was down, I would sing to feel better. It seems I've always known this is what I wanted to do. There was like no choice." In 1973 her parents divorced; Carey had little contact with her father, a Venezuelan-born aeronautical engineer of African heritage. She, her older brother and sister, and her mother remained in the New York City vicinity, where young Mariah listened to jazz, rhythm and blues, and gospel, as well as the opera her mother loved so well. Financially, things were hard for the family; they moved more than a dozen times prior to Carey's graduation from high school in 1987. While Carey's mother eventually remarried, Carey's relationship with her stepfather was not close; in fact, he eventually filed a lawsuit, claiming the existence of a contractual right to a share of his stepdaughter's earnings due to his early support of her career.

Despite the struggles she faced while growing up, Carey's meteoric rise to fame reads like a fast-paced fantasy tale. In 1988, while attending a fashionable New York party at the invitation of friend and fellow musician Brenda Kay Starr, eighteen-year-old Carey managed an introduction with Sony Music Entertainment president Tony Mottola. Like so many other aspiring singers before her, she handed him a copy of her demo tape. Later that night, to pass the time while on his way home, Mottola gave the tape a listen—and immediately ordered his driver to return to the party. Unfortunately, Carey had already gone, leaving Mottola, not a glass slipper, but her address. He contacted her within the next few days and immediately signed her with Sony subsidiary Columbia Records. "When I heard and saw Mariah, there was absolutely no doubt she was in every way destined for stardom," Mottola later told Fred Goldman in the *New York Times*.

With the vast resources of Sony Music behind her, Carey's self-titled debut album was released in 1990 after an intensive advance-publicity campaign. Its first popular single, "Vision of Love," shot to the top of the *Billboard* music charts shortly after its release; *Mariah Carey* won its artist Grammy Awards for both best female pop vocal performance and best new artist of 1990. Carey's vocal abilities—which were not witnessed by a live audience for another three years—were hailed by critics; as Dennis Hunt commented in the *Los Angeles Times,* she is a singer "blessed with both a remarkable command of her upper register and the ability to invest a song with gut-wrenching passion." The danceable tunes and ballads that filled the album also showcased Carey's writing abilities; may of the tracks were cowritten by Carey and longtime writing partner, composer Ben Margulies.

Emotions, released the following year on the heels of Carey's debut album's success, had its first single—the title track—hit the charts at Number Four. Again featuring songs cowritten by the vocalist—collaborators included Carole King, C & C Music Factory's David Cole, and Walter Afanasief—Carey's sophomore effort received mixed critical reviews, many reviewers maintaining that the level of vocal intensity was overdone. Others, however, hailed *Emotions* as an even better recording than its predecessor, echoing Carey's own opinion. "I was like 16 years old when I wrote some of the songs on the first album," the vocalist revealed to Steve Morse of the *Boston Globe*. "So I have a different outlook on things now.... And I've learned to let go a little bit more with my singing.... There's more character when you just sing and let it go. If something's not perfect, it's OK." In addition to several Grammy nominations, Carey walked away with her arms full after 1991's 5th Annual Soul Train Music Awards; she won the best single-female award, as well as honors for album of the year and best rhythm and blues/urban contemporary new artist.

In 1992 Carey released *MTV Unplugged,* a recording made during a rare live performance on the popular televised acoustic showcase. A self-proclaimed introvert, she described the disadvantages to not working the club/performance circuit to Edna Gunderson in *USA Today:* "I never thought of myself as a performer. I wasn't into the whole glam aspect of music." While comfortable with her performance on the MTV soundstage, Carey admitted that *MTV Unplugged* "was the first time I did that many songs in front of an audience. I had to learn in the public eye, and I'm still learning." The reclusive star's vocal performance was lauded on a national level; *Unplugged* earned Carey a Grammy nomination for best female pop vocal, as well as a nomination for best rhythm and blues vocal duet for her cover of the Jackson Five-hit "I'll Be There," performed with fellow artist Trey Lorenz.

In 1993 Carey married Mottola, the same man who, three years previous, had recognized her incredibly talent and worked to help shape her successful career. At the same time, she was putting the finishing touches on music *Music Box;* upon its release later the same year it made a steady climb up the charts to its eventual Number-One spot. The album received the usual high praise from critics; it also served as the subject of serious analysis for Michael Eric Dyson, who commented in the *New York Times* that Carey's significance has more to do with "the confusion and discomfort that her multiracial identity provokes" than her vocal abilities "in an American culture obsessed with race. Though she has made no secret that she is biracial . . . Carey's candor evokes clashing response from fans and critics. Some see her statement of mixed heritage as a refusal to bow to public pressure to choose whether she is black or white."

Despite any ongoing debates over Carey's "right" to sing black music—and with sales of her albums crestin the ten million mark—she crowned 1993 by appearing in a December concert at New York City's Madison Square Garden. The performance was part of a long-awaited world tour that took Carey to stages in every major city, from Miami to Los Angeles and beyond. While reviews were mixed when her show opened in Miami in early November, by the time Carey walked offstage in Boston a few weeks later, the audience barometer was reading a resounding A-plus.

1995 marked the release of Carey's sixth album, *Daydream*. Successful for the back-to-back, chart-topping success of "Fantasy" and "One Sweet Day," which each debuted at Number One, the album is also interesting because of the video of *Daydream's* first single, which marked Carey's debut as a film director.

Carey has shared the results of her many successes with others, appearing at numerous benefit concerts and other fundraising events. In addition, she has been both an organization director and a continuing sponsor of the Fresh Air Fund, donating upwards of $1 million in 1994 to help 10,000 children from urban neighborhoods visit a camp in upstate New York, where they can explore both the out-of-doors and a possible career in the performing arts; the camp now bears the name Camp Mariah. And she finds ways to leave the worries and responsibilities of her fast-track career behind; Carey keeps horses on a farm in upper New York State, and also indulges in a tropical vacation now and again. Has wealth and fame changed the young vocalist? "I don't sit around and think about it," Carey told Alan W. Petrucelli of the *New York Times,* adding: "When I have a minute to reflect, I realize that my life has been pretty amazing. But I consider myself a normal person who wants to have a normal life. It's exciting to do what I do, but I also like to stay real and grounded."

**Profile by
Pamela L. Shelton**

ROSEMARY CASALS

*W*inner of over one hundred tennis tournaments—including five **1948-** •

Wimbledon doubles titles with partner Billie Jean King—athlete Rose-

mary Casals has earned a reputation as a rebel ever since she first **Professional** •

entered organized competition in the early 1960s. She has been one of **tennis**

the game's more outspoken critics, a player whose all-consuming cause **player**

has been the betterment of tennis, especially women's tennis, for more

than two decades. Casals was a motivating force behind many of the

controversial changes that shook the tennis world and led to the tennis

boom of the 1960s and 1970s. Commenting on her influence on the

game of tennis in Rosemary Casals: The Rebel Rosebud, *author Linda*

Jacobs wrote: "Along the way, there have been lots of breakthroughs—

lots of 'firsts.' Rosemary Casals has been in on all of them."

Born September 16, 1948, in San Francisco, California, to poor immigrants from the Central American country of El Salvador, Casals has always considered her great-uncle and great-aunt, Manuel and Maria Casals, as her parents. After her parents found themselves unable to provide for their young daughters, Manuel—a Salvadoran immigrant and former member of that country's national soccer team—accepted one-year-old Casals and her older sister, Victoria, into his home. The owner of a small stamp machine business, Manuel introduced his new charges to the public tennis courts of San Francisco; he was the only coach Casals would ever have.

Casals's first rebellion regarding the game of tennis occurred when she was just a teenager. She hated the established tennis tradition of having younger players compete against each other on the junior circuit. Gutsy and determined from the start, Casals saw junior tennis as a barrier rather than a stepping-stone to her participation in women's tennis. Wanting more challenge than she received from her contemporaries, she often entered tournaments for girls two to three years older than herself, knowing that playing against them would make her work as hard as possible to better her game. "[I]n spite of all her trophies," Jacobs noted, "Rosie didn't like junior competition. It made her feel like a little girl playing polite little girl games."

Junior tennis was just the first of several obstacles Casals faced during her tennis career. At five feet two inches in height, she was one of the shortest tennis players, a fact that left her at a decided disadvantage on the court. However, Casals soon realized that height was not to be her only handicap when it came to the game. She became quickly acquaint-ed with the class distinction prevalent in tennis circles at the time. Traditionally, tennis was a sport practiced by members of the white upper classes in posh country-club surroundings; Casals's ethnic heritage and disadvantaged background immediately set her apart from most of the other players. Recalling these early years of her career, Casals told *People*: "The other kids had nice tennis clothes, nice rackets, nice white shoes and came in Cadillacs. I felt stigmatized because we were poor."

An unfamiliarity with country club etiquette also made Casals feel different from the majority of other players. But traditions such as polite applause from the crowd instead of noisy cheering, or wearing only white on the courts, were concepts that were nonsensical to the future tennis star anyway. She believed in working hard to perfect her game and looked to the crowd to show its appreciation for her extra efforts. As for wearing white, in one of her first appearances at the tradition-laden courts at Wimbledon, England—site of the prestigious British tennis championships—she was nearly excluded from competition when she showed up in a dress that was not white. Later in her career, the "wearing white" tradition was one more convention she regularly ignored, becoming known for her brightly colored outfits.

The frustrations Casals had to endure on and off the court due to her size and background had a significant impact on her playing style. Despite her delicate-sounding nicknames "Rosie" and "Rosebud," she built a reputation as a player who would do anything—even attempt a between-the-legs shot—in order to win a match. "I wanted to *be* someone," she is quoted as saying in Alida M. Thacher's *Raising a Racket: Rosie Casals*. "I knew I was good, and winning tournaments— it's a kind of way of being accepted." Through a combination of this dogged determination and natural talent, by age sixteen Casals was the top junior and women's level player in northern California. The follow- ing year she was ranked eleventh in the country and appeared in the semi-finals at Forest Hills, New York, home of the U.S. tennis champion- ships, against the then top-ranked women's player in the world, Brazil's Maria Bueno. Although Casals lost the match, the crowd loved her aggressive playing style and gave her a standing ovation.

More experience on the national and international levels of play helped Casals continue to improve her game. In 1966 she and Billie Jean King, her doubles partner, won the U.S. hard-court and indoor tourna- ments to reach the quarter-finals in the Wimbledon women's doubles. The two also dominated women's doubles play in the years to follow with fifty-six titles won, becoming one of the most successful duos in tennis history. Casals also teamed with Ian Crookenden in 1966 to win the U.S. hard-court mixed doubles. She met success as an individual player that same year, being ranked third among U.S. women players. She emerged victorious twice over King (then sharing first ranking among U.S. women players with Nancy Richey) in singles play and even beat Bueno, who had continued to be regarded as the world's top women's player.

In February 1967 Casals started out another successful year by winning the women's singles title at the Wills Invitational tournament in Auckland, New Zealand. In June she and King won the Federation Cup in Berlin for the United States. In other tournament play, she beat King in the semi-finals of the national clay-court matches in Milwaukee, Wisconsin, and defeated Margaret Court, one of the top women tennis players of all time, in the quarter-finals of the Victoria championships in Melbourne, Australia. Although Casals was disappointed to lose at

Wimbledon in the semi-finals of the women's singles tournament that year, she and King took the doubles crown there as well as at the U.S. and South African championships.

• **Fights to Make**

Tennis a

Professional

Sport

The next year a battle between tennis traditionalists and the new breed of players like Casals culminated. For decades the philosophy of the tennis establishment had been to advocate amateur tennis in the belief that professional play was somewhat tainted because players accepted money. Critics argued that the country club set could afford to remain playing as unpaid amateurs. Many of the less wealthy players, however, were forced to take under-the-table payments for their efforts in order to be financially able to stay on the tennis circuit. Many of these athletes believed they should be able to derive a living from their sport, just like professional football or baseball players. Nonetheless, the tennis players who admitted their professional status suffered when major tournaments such as Wimbledon and Forest Hills refused to admit them into competition. All this changed, however, in December 1967, when the British Lawn Tennis Association, the governing body of British tennis, voted to allow amateurs and professionals to compete against each other in the same tournaments. The measure was quickly seconded the following March by the International Lawn Tennis Federation (ILTF).

Fed up with the amateur status that she and her fellow players had been forced into for so many years, Casals was eager to become publicly what she truly had been all along—a professional tennis player. Almost as soon as the ILTF voiced its decision, Casals, along with King, French tennis star Francoise Durr, and British player Ann Jones became the first women in the history of tennis to become touring professionals. But as Casals and her fellow women players soon discovered, as women they had even more to contend with than their male counterparts. "Some people called Rosie a rebel," Jacobs observed, "because she dared to go on tour, to play tennis for money. Women didn't do such things. They played in amateur tournaments for pretty trophies and left the money to the men."

Money was the reason that Casals became one of the ringleaders in the next rebellion to rock the tennis establishment. She left the National Tennis League after little more than a year, happy to be able to compete as a professional in nearly any tournament she wanted to enter. The differentiation between amateurs and professionals had faded; the distinction between women and men tennis players presented a new hurdle. And the vast difference in prize monies awarded to male and female tennis players in the same tournament was yet another inequity that angered women players. Such practices seemed to indicate that female athletes were somehow inferior to their male counterparts.

In 1970, despite the limited financial opportunities available to women tennis players at the time, Casals earned close to $25,000, the sixth-highest amount among women players at the time. But her level of success was shared by relatively few women in the sport. That same year, female players were outraged to learn that in the season's last major tournament, the Pacific Southwest Open, the men's first-place winner alone would receive $12,500, while total prize money allotted for women was $7,500 . . . to be split among each of the quarter-finalists. Casals and other women players warned the United States Lawn Tennis Association (USLTA; now known as the United States Tennis Association) that they planned to boycott future tournaments if three demands were not met: 1) Prize money for women be at least one third as high as that slated for men; 2) More media attention be focused on women's matches; 3) Women receive equal access to center-court play.

When USLTA ignored the women's threat, the players took their grievances to the promoter of the Pacific Southwest Open. When he also disregarded their protests, they looked for and found a strong supporter in Gladys Heldman, editor of *World Tennis* magazine. Heldman managed to organize a women's tournament that would be held in Houston, Texas, at the same time as the Pacific Southwest Open. The tournament—dubbed the Virginia Slims Invitational after the Philip Morris cigarette company became its corporate sponsor—occurred despite strong disapproval from the USLTA. Casals, in turn, became the first winner of a women's professional tennis tournament when she took home the $1,600 top prize. Although the seven U.S. players who participated in the Virginia Slims event were suspended by USLTA, they were successful in bringing the inequity of their situation to light and gained a lot of attention.

The success of the Virginia Slims invitational led to Casals's involvement with the newly formed Virginia Slims eight-tournament women's professional tennis circuit—and an end to any financial problems she had experienced earlier in her career. The first year she was one of the top money winners among the sixteen women participating. In 1972 her winnings totaled $70,000; the attention that was now focused on women's tennis helped Casals nearly triple her income in the space of two years. In 1973 she collected the largest prize ever awarded in women's tennis to that time, defeating Nancy Richey Gunter in the finals of the Family Circle tournament and winning $30,000.

That same year women's tennis and Casals also received much publicity thanks to Bobby Riggs, a 55-year-old former tennis star of the 1930s, who challenged Billie Jean King to a match to be held in late September in the Houston Astrodome. The event was a prime-time media spectacular—billed as the "Battle of the Sexes"—that drew a crowd of more than 30,000 to the arena and commanded a viewing audience of fifty-nine million. Casals was seen and heard during the match as the women's color commentator for the American Broadcasting Company, Inc. (ABC-TV). A number of people found Casals's observations, however, a little too colorful. King won the match, but the next day newspapers and newscasts were filled with public debate about Casals's performance. She explained her somewhat acrid remarks about Riggs in *Raising a Racket*: "Actually, all I was doing was being honest. I said he walked like a duck because he does. I didn't say anything just to be controversial. I just said it the way I meant it."

The enthusiasm for tennis generated by the Riggs-King battle helped launch another innovation in the sport in which Casals was involved—World Team Tennis (WTT). WTT included tennis teams from cities throughout the United States, each made up of two women and four men. A meeting between two teams included men's and women's singles and doubles games, as well as a mixed doubles match. Scoring for each event was on a point system, with the win going to the first team to earn five points. In another change from traditional tennis, the WTT coach could take a struggling player out of a game and send in a substitute. During her years with the WTT Casals played with the Detroit Loves and the Oakland Breakers and coached the Los Angeles Strings.

While involved in team tennis, Casals continued to enter regular tennis tournaments. However, the strain of playing almost seven hundred tournaments took a toll on her body and she had to undergo knee surgery in 1978. The operation forced a change of direction in Casals's fast-track career, but she meet those new challenges with the persistence that had always marked her tennis court appearances. On the court, she again teamed with Billie Jean King, winning the U.S. Open Seniors' women's doubles championship in 1990. And off-court, Casals serves as president of Sportswomen, Inc., a Sausalito, California-based company she formed in 1981 to act as an agency for new tennis players, as well as to promote both herself and a Women's Classic tour she has organized for female tennis players over the age of thirty. She also began Midnight Productions television company and has broadened her sporting activities to include golf. Although younger women now appear at Wimbledon and other tournaments, Casals continues to work in her chosen sport, finding new opportunities to improve the game to which she has been a major contributor.

**Profile by
Marian C. Gonsior**

ANA CASTILLO

1953- •

Poet, •

novelist

*W*idely known for elegantly written poetry inspired by her unique

feminist philosophy, Ana Castillo is one of a group of distinguished

Chicana writers from the Chicago area that includes fellow poet and

novelist Sandra Cisneros. Over the years, Castillo has broadened her

artistic contributions to include musical performance and prose. With

several well-received novels to her credit, Castillo's Chicana-feminist—

Xicanisma— message can also be found in such diverse media as high

school texts and musical theater pieces.

Castillo was born in Chicago, Illinois, on June 15, 1953, to Mexican American parents who had migrated from the Southwest. Her interest in a variety of creative experiences prompted her to major in art at Northeastern Illinois University, where she received her B.A. in art education in 1975. The heady artistic and intellectual climate of the 1970s encouraged activism and fostered Castillo's interest in writing and performing her poetry. She was an early contributor to *Revista Chicano-*

Riqueña (now *The Americas Review*), a literary magazine edited by Nicolás Kanellos that captured the artistic ferment of Midwest Hispanics. Her first collection of poems, *Otro Canto*, was published as a chapbook in 1977 with a grant from the Illinois Art Council. Two years later, coinciding with her graduation from the University of Chicago with an M.A. in social sciences, Castillo published a second chapbook of poems, *The Invitation*, this time with a grant from the Playboy Foundation.

In the early 1980s Castillo's work took on musical overtones. Her interest in flamenco dancing led her to create and manage the Al-Andalus flamenco performance group from 1981 to 1982. She also adapted the poems from *The Invitation* for music and saw them performed at the 1982 Soho Art Festival in New York City. Castillo also wrote the play *Clark Street Counts*, performed by the Chicano Raza Group in June 1983.

Castillo's elegant style and feminist thematic created a great deal of interest in her poems. Her work appeared in a variety of anthologies, including 1979's *The Third Women: Minority Women Writers of the U.S.*, 1982's *Women Poets of the World*, and the high school text *Zero Makes Me Hungry* published in 1975. Her next two poetry collections were *Pajaros enganosos*, published in 1983, and 1984's *Women Are Not Roses*. *My Father Was a Toltec*, which Castillo published in 1988, explores an urban existence born of poverty as the poet focuses her verse on welfare, violence, and lives torn apart.

In later years, Castillo has developed consistently as a writer of prose fiction. In 1984 one of her short stories was included in the anthology *Cuentos Chicanos*. In 1986 she published her first novel, *The Mixquihuala Letters*. Written in epistolary form, *The Mixquihuala Letters* was widely acclaimed for its treatment of women, receiving the Before Columbus Foundation Book award in 1987 and an award from the Women's Foundation of San Francisco in 1988. *So Far from God,* a novel about environmental racism that was published in 1993, features a Hispanic family living in Tome, New Mexico, struggling to improve their life while beset by a host of modern—and legendary—ills. Sofi and her four daughters are the protagonists in what a reviewer for *Booklist* called "a riotous and rascally novel infused with mysterious forces both malevolent and divine." Death and reincarnation, madness, ghostly visitations, and evil each make their mark upon this family of women, brought on by maladies as modern as getting dumped by a brutish boyfriend and becoming a press corps casualty of the Persian Gulf Crisis.

Castillo's feminism is nowhere more strongly stated than in the ten essays collected in 1994's *Massacre of the Dreamers: Essays on Xicanisma*. Reflecting on the importance of a strong Chicana-feminist activism,

Castillo examines the role of Mexican American women during the women's movement of the 1960s and 1970s. Other essays put *machismo* under the microscope to discover its roots and set forth a well-constructed analysis of the role of Catholicism in the sexual and social duality that subtly manifests itself in the lives of many modern Mexican American women. Drawing from the deep well of legend and myth, spirituality, and woman-centered tradition that make up her cultural heritage, Castillo continues to write, perform readings of her work, and lecture throughout the United States, providing Mexican American women with a passionate, sensitive voice for solidarity and strength.

**Profile by
Silvia Novo Peña**

LORNA DEE CERVANTES

L orna Dee Cervantes has the distinction of being one of the few

1954- •

Mexican American poets to have had her verses published by a major

publishing company. Her work, according to Marta Ester Sánchez in

Poet •

Contemporary Chicana Poetry: A Critical Approach to an Emerging

Literature, *is characterized by "two conflicting but central positions." In*

Cervantes's poetry, Sánchez finds both a "desire for an idealized,

utopian world" and "a realistic perspective that sees a world fraught

with social problems." The tension created between these two contrast-

ing perspectives is one of the central elements underlying Cervantes's

work.

Cervantes was born on August 6, 1954, in San Francisco, California,

but grew up in San Jose. She began writing poetry when she was eight years old and published some of her earliest poems in her high school's newspaper. In 1974, at the age of twenty, she gave her first poetry reading at the Quinto Festival de los Teatros Chicanos in Mexico City, Mexico. The poem she read that day, "Barco de refugiados" ("Refugee Ship"), was published in *El Heraldo*, a Mexico City newspaper. The following year, after several of her poems appeared in *Revista Chicano-Riqueña*, Cervantes was encouraged to begin contributing verse to other periodicals as well.

By the end of the 1970s, Cervantes had gained a reputation both as a poet and as editor and publisher of *Mango*, a small literary review. In addition to her work on *Mango*, she edited chapbooks containing works by other Chicanos that were published through the Centro Cultural de la Gente of San Jose and by Mango Publications. Cervantes's efforts soon garnered critical attention, and in 1978 she received a National Endowment for the Arts grant. While on the Hudson D. Walker poetry fellowship at the Fine Arts Work Center in Provincetown, Massachusetts, in 1979, she completed the group of poems that make up her 1981 collection, *Emplumada*.

The poems in *Emplumada* are divided into three sections. While the poetry of the first two sections deals with social conflicts, the verse in the remaining third is perceived by critics as being more lyrical. Some commentators note that the alienation Cervantes feels as a Chicana in an Anglo society is evident in pieces such as "Poem for the Young White Man Who Asked Me How I, An Intelligent Well-Read Person, Could Believe in the War Between Races" and "Visions of Mexico While at a Writing Symposium in Port Townsend, Washington." Sánchez notes that in the first poem, Cervantes explains her feelings at having a "subordinate place in society as Chicana, as woman, and as poet." In the second, which deals with the theme of migration and opposing societal values, Roberta Fernández concludes in *Dictionary of Literary Biography* that Cervantes "comes to terms with herself, finding resolution for the many conflicts in her life and in her role as poet."

Emplumada also contains "Beneath the Shadow of the Freeway," which Fernández describes as "Cervantes's most celebrated poem." The work depicts a young Chicana who must formulate her own world view after learning about male-female relationships and life in general from an idealistic grandmother and a cynical mother. Sánchez maintains that the poem "not only confronts the question of Cervantes' existential voice as a woman and as a Chicana, but it also brings out the conflict between her two literary voices: a discursive one and a lyrical one. By juxtaposing these two poetic voices, 'Beneath the Shadow of the

Freeway' combines the principal elements of Cervantes' style, thus suggesting that it also confronts the question of her literary voice."

Three years after publication of *Emplumada,* Cervantes obtained a bachelor of arts degree from San Jose State University; since then she has also taken graduate courses at the University of California, Santa Cruz. In 1989 she was honored by her alma mater as an outstanding alumnus of the year. Her second published work of poetry, *From the Cables of Genocide: Poems on Love and Hunger,* was published in 1991. She has also been honored with several awards for her work, including the Pushcart Prize. In addition to her writing, Cervantes gives poetry readings around the country.

Profile by
Marian C. Gonsior

DENISE CHÁVEZ

*Y*ou don't have to go anywhere. Not down the street. Not even out of

this house. There's stories, plenty of them all around." With these words

the mother of a character in the title story of Denise Chávez's short story

collection, The Last of the Menu Girls, gives advice on writing to her

daughter. Chávez might have been penning these words to herself, for

her short and novel-length fiction and plays are characterized by their

focus on working-class characters and scenes from everyday life.

Chávez explains that the presence of the ordinary in her work springs

from her belief that, as a Chicana writer, she must speak for those who

have no one to vocalize for them. "My work as a playwright is to capture

as best as I can the small gestures of the forgotten people, the old men

1948- •

Playwright, •

novelist, short

story writer

sitting on park benches, the lonely spinsters inside their corner store," she once explained to an interviewer.

The future author and dramatist, daughter of attorney Ernesto E. Chávez and Delfina Rede Favor Chávez, a teacher, was born on August 15, 1948, in Las Cruces, New Mexico. She earned her bachelor of arts degree in drama from New Mexico State University in 1971 and three years later received a master of fine arts degree from Trinity University in San Antonio, Texas. In 1984 Chávez obtained a second master's degree, this time in creative writing, from the University of New Mexico. While she has considered herself a full-time playwright since 1977, Chávez has also spent much time teaching, including two years as an instructor of English at Northern New Mexico Community College in Espanola. She has also taught at the American School in Paris, and has served as an assistant professor of drama at the University of Houston in Texas since 1989.

In 1970, when Chávez was only twenty-two, her writing talent was already receiving recognition. That year she won New Mexico State University's Best Play Award for her work, *The Wait*. During the remainder of the 1970s, she wrote nearly a dozen more plays and saw most of them produced in Taos, Santa Fe, or Albuquerque, New Mexico. Since 1980, she has broadened her writing to include other genres: her body of work has grown to include the poetry anthology *Life Is a Two-Way Street*, a collection of short stories entitled *The Last of the Menu Girls*, a book for children called *The Woman Who Knew the Language of Animals*, and *Face of an Angel*, a novel published in 1994. But Chávez has continued to write for the theater, including *Novena narrativas*, a one-woman show that toured New Mexico in 1987, a one-act adaptation of *The Last of the Menu Girls*, and *Women the State of Grace*, another one-woman show that showcases the author's acting talents as she continues to perform it on tour throughout the United States. Her work has been selected in several collections, including *An Anthology of Southwestern Literature*, *An Anthology: The Indian Río Grande*, and *Voces: An Anthology of Nuevo Mexicano Writers*.

Characters have always been more important to Chávez than plot, and in her first novel, *Face of an Angel*, she has created one of her most memorable characters in the book's narrator, Soveida Dosamantes. Seven-and-a-half years in the writing, *Face of an Angel* is a saga of three generations of a Mexican American family, as young Soveida grows up under the strong influence of her mother and grandmother who believe strongly that women should live to serve their husbands and God. After she leaves her home in a small New Mexico town and goes to college, has several love affairs, and gets a job as a waitress, Soveida broadens her view of her role in the world and learns to welcome her independence, understand her strength as a survivor, and take pride in her heritage.

While several of the characters in *Face of an Angel* are martyrs to bad relationships, alcoholism, widowhood, divorce, and adultery, Chávez explained that including negative aspects of Chicano culture was a way to demonstrate to other women that empowerment can come from speaking the truth. "I think I show the good aspects of our culture too," she told *Los Angeles Times* writer Julio Moran. "That we are passionate, loyal and long-suffering. We are a people of survivors. These are secrets of the human heart. To empower people to become the faces that we are without these masks. To be able to speak the truth of our families without shame, without whispers."

Chávez's work has continued to draw critical recognition. She has received grants from the New Mexico Arts Division, the National Endowment for the Arts, and the Rockefeller Foundation. In 1982 she received a creative writing fellowship from the University of New Mexico and, in 1990, a creative artist fellowship from the Cultural Arts Council of Houston, Texas. In 1986, her short story, "The Last of the Menu Girls"—from the collection of the same title—received the New Mexico State University's Steele Jones Fiction Award. The accompanying stories in the published collection revolve around the life of Rocío Esquibel, a seventeen-year-old whose job is delivering menus to hospital patients. Writing in *New York Times Book Review,* Beverly Lyon Clark notes that many of the stories revealed "Chávez's strengths in dialogue and in juxtaposing evocative scenes."

Married to photographer and sculptor Daniel Zolinsky, Chávez currently resides in New Mexico. Throughout her career, she has demonstrated a social conscience that has prompted her to serve as a teacher to inmates at Radium Springs Center for Women, a medium-security prison, and as co-director of a senior citizen workshop in creative writing and puppetry at Las Cruces, New Mexico's Community Action Agency. This social conscience is also represented in her written work as a continuing theme of love, a theme that Chávez sees embodied in the landscape of the American Southwest. "I write about the neighborhood handymen, the waitresses, the bag ladies, the elevator operators," she explained to an interviewer. "They all have something in common: they know what it is to love and to be merciful.... My work is rooted in the Southwest, in heat and dust, and reflects a world where love is as real as the land. In this dry and seemingly harsh and empty world there is much beauty to be found. That hope of the heart is what feeds me, my characters."

**Profile by
Marian C. Gonsior**

LINDA CHAVEZ

*F*ormerly the highest-ranking woman in the Reagan administra-

tion and a Republican candidate for U.S. Senator from Maryland,

Linda Chavez has made a career out of defying expectations and

refusing to be classified. Although she is proud of her Hispanic heritage,

Chavez has insisted on making her own way in politics and is opposed to

many "traditional" policies relating to minorities, such as racial hiring

quotas, comparable worth and pay equity, and bilingual education

programs. Although a conservative Republican, Chavez did not hesitate

to speak out against problems in the Reagan administration, once

noting of the covert activities of Lieutenant Colonel Oliver North in the

Christian Science Monitor *that "zealots have no place in democratic*

1947- •

Political •

analyst,

writer

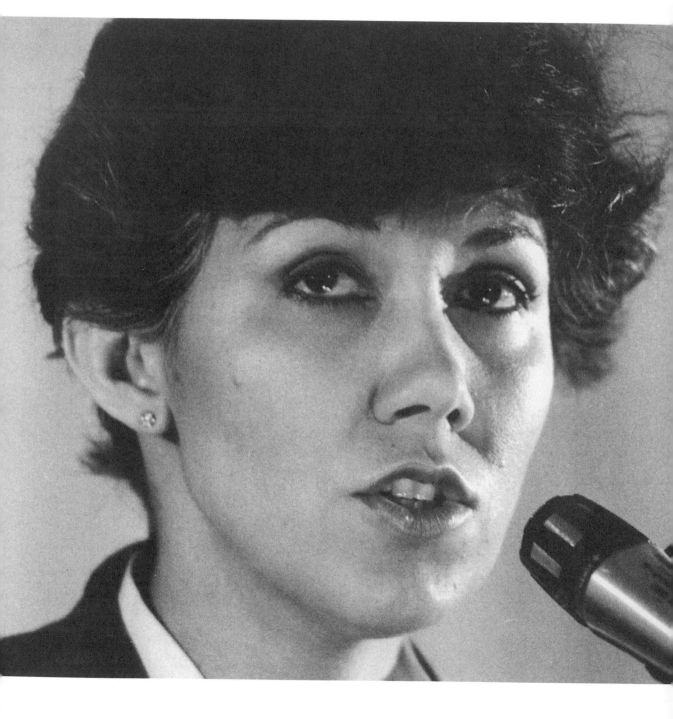

governments." "It would be easier for me to be a liberal Democrat, I guess," she explained in the *Washington Post.* "People would expect that. But I guess I'm just stubborn. I do go against the grain. I do things that are not always popular. There's a tenacity there. I guess I've always thought of myself as different and sometimes I've gotten more attention for myself than I wanted."

While Chavez has been accused of abandoning her Hispanic community, she contends that her ethnic background has actually contributed to her conservativism. Chavez was born in Albuquerque, New Mexico, in 1947, the daughter of Velma, an Anglo, and Rudy Chavez, a conservative Spanish-American whose family had roots in the Southwest extending back over three hundred years. When she was nine the family moved to Denver, Colorado, where Chavez first began to notice racial discrimination. As a teenager she marched against segregation and recalls that in school she was never encouraged to excel or further her education. Motivated by her father, a World War II veteran who taught her to value her Spanish heritage without using it as an excuse, Chavez finished high school and entered college. As her mother told the *Washington Post,* Linda's "dad would tell her screaming and yelling doesn't accomplish anything. You have to think about things, decide what's wrong and do something about it and that's it."

It was in college during the late 1960s that Chavez first showed indications of the conservative views she later espoused as a public official. At the University of Colorado, where she told *Washington Monthly,* "I made it on hard work," Chavez began tutoring Mexican American students in a remedial program; she became disenchanted, however, when she found the students were lobbying the administration to lower their minimum grade requirements. After receiving a B.A. in 1970, Chavez went on to graduate study in English literature at the University of California, Los Angeles. Because of her background, Chavez found herself pressured into teaching a course on Chicano writing, despite her assertions that there was not enough material by Hispanic Americans to develop an entire course. Instead of intending to learn, Chavez relates, her students "sort of expected that this was the course they could take to come and 'rap,' in the jargon of the day," as she told *Washington Monthly.* She recalls that her students wanted to discuss their own experiences instead of doing class work: "They *lived* Chicano literature," she recalls, so "they didn't [want to] have to read books about it." Things took a turn for the worse when, as she states in *Hispanic,* "some of the students stood up and turned their backs to me. I had to lecture with a class of kids facing their backs to me—it was a disaster." When she failed students for not completing the reading list, they retaliated by vandalizing her home and threatening her family.

Believes in •

Hard Work, Not

Quotas

Discouraged by this experience and her treatment as a "token" Hispanic, Chavez left the university in 1972 and traveled to Washington, D.C., to join her husband, Christopher Gersten, whom she married in 1967.

In the mid-seventies, Chavez began working for Democratic and liberal causes in the capitol, holding a series of jobs with the Democratic National Committee and the National Education Association. While wanting to learn more about specific issues, she felt these organizations failed to treat her as an individual with opinions and instead saw her only as an ethnic representative. "They were specifically looking for an Hispanic woman," she told *Washington Monthly*. "It was very clear to me they expected me to be the Hispanic lobbyist, to be their link to the Chicano caucus inside the NEA. I balked at that." After serving with the Department of Health, Education, and Welfare as a consultant on education, Chavez joined the staff of the American Federation of Teachers (AFT), where she was allowed to express her views. While editor of the AFT quarterly, *American Educator*, Chavez wrote a series of articles urging a return to "traditional values" in American schools. These writings soon brought her to the attention of conservatives in Washington; in 1981 she began working as a consultant for President Ronald Reagan's administration.

In 1983 Chavez was asked to become a member of the U.S. Commission on Civil Rights, a non-partisan agency designed to monitor the government's progress in enforcing civil rights laws. Dissatisfied with the offer, however, Chavez held out for a position of greater power and influence and was eventually appointed staff director of the agency. She immediately stirred up controversy by issuing a memo counseling the reversal of many traditional civil rights measures, such as racial hiring quotas, a practice she believes demeans people by reducing them to an ethnic category. She also authorized a study to explore the negative effects of affirmative action on minorities, which she had experienced first hand. "I find it offensive that some people think those of us with darker skins need to be taken care of," the forthright Chavez told *USA Today*. "This idea that we can't compete is something liberals simply don't want to talk about. They're saying to us, 'We feel sorry for you. You don't have to come up to our standards.'"

In addition, Chavez hired many temporary employees and consultants "to promote work that would reflect her and the commission majority's views," as noted in the *Washington Post*. Many civil rights activists criticized Chavez for what they perceived as a transformation of the traditionally impartial agency into an instrument of the Reagan administration; Chavez claimed she was only remedying the liberal bias of past years. As the *Washington Post* summarized, "Chavez counter[ed] that she helped redirect the agency toward its traditional goal of a colorblind society.... She maintain[ed] that her critics have been unable to separate their ideological differences from their assessments of her character and performance."

It was her performance as the commission's director, however, that helped Chavez become the director of the White House Office of Public Liaison in 1985, a position that made her the highest-ranking woman in the administration. Appointed because of her strong conservative background—despite her Democratic affiliation—Chavez nevertheless changed parties, becoming a Republican, and began working to promote administration policy within Congress and public groups. Chavez lasted only ten months in the position, however, for as she noted in *Policy Review,* "I learned while in the administration . . . how little policy actually emanates from the White House, whether by design or accident. My chief reason for wanting to leave the Civil Rights Commission to join the White House staff was to be able to have a greater role in influencing administration policy on a broad array of issues. What I discovered was that the White House was more involved in process than policy." Upon leaving the Office of Public Liaison in early 1986, Chavez was encouraged to seek a political office of her own.

Highest- •

Ranking

Woman in

Reagan

Administration

Chavez began campaigning for the Maryland Republican nomination for senator in 1986, and she gained attention during the primaries when she gave more correct answers than any other candidate during a television quiz on current affairs. A victor in the primaries, Chavez began to prepare for a tough race against Democratic Representative Barbara Mikulski. The contest brought the national spotlight upon Maryland, for it was only the second U.S. Senate race ever contested by two women.

Despite her success in the primaries, Chavez was at a disadvantage in a state whose voters consisted of two-thirds registered Democrats. In addition, she was drawing criticism for her conversion to the Republican party and her short term as a Maryland resident. When Chavez, married and the mother of three children, called the unmarried Mikulski a "San Francisco-style Democrat" and accused her of being "anti-male," she drew fire for her campaign tactics and was accused of mud-slinging. Her strategy backfired; despite a successful fund-raising effort that included appearances by then-President Reagan, Chavez lost the election by over twenty percent of the vote.

After the long campaign, Chavez retired from public office but remained in the public eye, frequently appeared as a political commentator on both television and radio. In addition, she became president of U.S. English, a private non-profit organization lobbying to make English the official national language. Some controversy ensued from this position when, in late 1988, she resigned from U.S. English. Chavez's reasoning was that she could not work with its founder, John Tanton, who, in her estimation, had demonstrated an "anti-Hispanic" and "anti-Catholic" bias. An "embarrassing question," according to Anna Maria Arias in *Hispanic,* "is how Chavez could have allowed herself to be duped by what many believe is a racist organization."

• Joins

Conservative

Think Tank

After leaving U.S. English, Chavez went on to become a senior fellow at the Manhattan Institute for Policy Research, a conservative think tank based in Washington, D.C. Recent duties have included serving as director of the Center for the New American Community, which, according to Arias, "will study a common heritage that is threatened by multiculturalism."

One of the fruits of Chavez's work for the Institute has been *Out of the Barrio: Toward a New Politics of Hispanic Assimilation,* a 1991 book that discusses such topics as affirmative action and Hispanic involvement in all levels of politics. One of the motivations for writing the work arose out of a debate she had with Arnold Torres, former executive director of the League of United Latin American Citizens. While Torres felt that Hispanics were largely poor and disadvantaged, Chavez had a different view. "I saw lots of opportunity," she told Arias. "I saw Hispanics rapidly moving into the middle class. I saw my generation, and particularly the generation after me, making huge strides, and yet I didn't see that reflected in the rhetoric." While some have attacked the book for using oversimplifications and generalizations, Chavez defended her work, telling Arias, "I think that to the organized Hispanic movement, what I say is not in their best interest. If you were an organization out there trying to get support from the private and public sector to help Hispanics who are poor and disadvantaged . . ., my coming along and saying, 'Wait a second, we are really doing okay, we're moving into the middle class and discrimination has not been nearly as severe as it has been for blacks'—that isn't a view you want out there."

While continuing to be been criticized for her conservative views, Chavez maintains that her liberal detractors are guilty of stereotyping her; they assume that because she is Hispanic, she must hold the political views that a minority is "supposed" to espouse. Countering criticisms that she has changed her views to further her career, Chavez explained to *Washington Monthly* that her opinions have changed, in part, "from watching [the Reagan] administration. I look around, and I see things sort of working and the country working and inflation having been brought down.... So I moved on those kinds of issues .... relatively recently." She also notes that many different groups are included within the "Hispanic" designation, and that her own Spanish-American background, as opposed to that of Mexican Americans or Puerto Ricans, is traditionally conservative. "I'm very proud of my heritage," she told the *Washington Post*. "I see myself as what I am. I've never run away from being Hispanic. It doesn't mean I have to endorse the whole agenda."

Profile by Diane Telgen

SANDRA CISNEROS

S andra Cisneros has become a fresh, new voice in mainstream

American literature. In her poetry and fiction, she presents vivid and

compelling vignettes of the lives and loves of Chicanas and Latinas from

a distinctly woman-oriented perspective. In a review of her 1991

collection of short fiction, Woman Hollering Creek and Other Stories,

Newsweek wrote that "her feminist, Mexican American voice is not only

playful and vigorous, it's original—we haven't heard anything like it

before.... Noisily, wittily, always compassionately, Cisneros surveys wom-

an's condition—a condition that is both precisely Latina and general to

women everywhere." The Washington Post Book World deemed Cisneros

"a writer of power and eloquence and great lyrical beauty," while

1954- •

Poet, •

author

Mirabella announced her as "the foremost Mexican American woman writer."

The first Chicana to receive a major publishing contract, Cisneros is one of the leading writers in the growing field of Latino literature. The author, who sees herself as something of a pioneer, asserted to Jim Sagel of *Publishers Weekly*: "I'm trying to write the stories that haven't been written. I feel like a cartographer. I'm determined to fill a literary void." Cisneros further explained in *Woman Hollering Creek and Other Stories* her attempt "to populate [the] book with as many different kinds of Latinos as possible so that mainstream America could see how diverse we are."

Cisneros was born in Chicago, Illinois, in 1954, to a Mexican father and a Chicana mother. The only girl in seven children, Cisneros grew up in poverty. During her childhood she developed a fear of mice—an anxiety that was "not as a female thing, but a class thing," she told the *Los Angeles Times*. "To me mice are all my poverty, the whole neighborhood I grew up in, embodied in a little skittering creature that might come to get me at any moment." Many of her early years were spent moving from place to place, with regular trips to Mexico City, Mexico, so her paternal grandmother could see her favorite son.

These frequent relocations were unsettling, she recalled in *Publishers Weekly*. "The moving back and forth, the new school, were very upsetting to me as a child. They caused me to be very introverted and shy. I do not remember making friends easily.... Because we moved so much and always in neighborhoods that appeared like France after World War II—empty lots and burned out buildings—I retreated inside myself." Being the only girl in her family also contributed to her shyness. "I spent a lot of time by myself by just the fact that I was the only daughter, and my brothers—once they became socialized—pretty much hung out with their own gender. They all kind of teamed up and excluded me from their games." Cisneros acknowledges, however, that one positive aspect of her shyness was that she became an astute observer of the people and things around her, a trait that would stand her in good stead in her later literary career.

Cisneros attended Catholic schools in Chicago, but found her basic education to be inadequate. "If I had lived up to my teachers' expectations, I'd still be working in a factory, because my report card was pretty lousy. That's because I wasn't very much interested, or I was too terrified to venture or volunteer." She avoided displaying her creative talents because she felt the nuns would dismiss the importance of the minority experience; instead, she wrote secretly at home. Fortunately, her parents stressed education. Her mother, who was self-taught, saw to it that all her children had library cards; her father encouraged his offspring to study hard. As Cisneros recalled in *Glamour,* "My father's hands are thick and yellow, stubbed by a history of hammer and nails and twine and coils and springs. 'Use this' my father said, tapping his head, 'not this' showing us those hands."

It was in high school that Cisneros first began to express her creativity publicly by reading her poems in class. During her sophomore year she "had a teacher who was . . . a would-be writer," the poet explained. "I started writing for her. I became more public through that class and she encouraged me to work on a literary magazine . . . which I did—and I became the editor eventually." After high school, Cisneros attended Loyola University, with the support of her father, who believed that college would be a good place for her to find a husband. "In retrospect, I'm lucky my father believed daughters were meant for husbands," Cisneros commented in *Glamour.* "It meant it didn't matter if I majored in something silly like English. After all, I'd find a nice professional eventually, right?"

Unleashes •

Creative Voice

Instead of a professional, what Cisneros found was a profession: Writing. In the late 1970s, one of her teachers helped her enroll in the poetry section of the Iowa Writers' Workshop, a program leading to a master's degree. However, as a Chicana, Cisneros found herself alienated from her surroundings and her classmates. "It didn't take me long to learn—after a few days being there—that nobody cared to hear what I had to say and no one listened to me even when I did speak. I became very frightened and terrified that first year." When these feelings finally surfaced, they led the young author to a great insight.

During a seminar on archetypal memories in Gaston Bachelard's "Poetics of Space," her classmates spoke about the "house of the imagination," using their childhood homes as examples. They described houses with attics, stairways, and cellars—dwellings that were a far cry from the miserable bungalow of Cisneros's childhood. Focusing on her early poverty made her doubt her own worth. What was a young Chicana named Sandra Cisneros, when compared to these children of privilege from the finest schools in the country? "They had been bred as fine hothouse flowers. I was a yellow weed among the city's cracks," she recalled. Describing the cultural epiphany that changed her, she added: "It was not until this moment when I separated myself, when I considered myself truly distinct that my writing acquired a voice. I knew I was a Mexican woman, but I didn't think it had anything to do with why I felt so much imbalance in my life, whereas it had everything to do with it! My race, my gender, my class! That's when I decided I would write about something my classmates couldn't write about."

This revelation enabled Cisneros to write her first book, *The House on Mango Street*, in which she described her house of imagination. "It's small and red with tight steps in front and windows so small you'd think they were holding their breath. Bricks are crumbling in places, and the front door is so swollen you have to push hard to get in. There is no front yard, only four little elms the city planted by the curb. Out back is a small garage for the car we don't own yet." Published in 1983, *Mango Street* features a series of interlocking vignettes told by Esperanza Cordero, a young Chicana growing up in a Chicago barrio. Through Esperanza's eyes the reader obtains a glimpse of the lives of the people around her. She wants a better life for herself and, by the novel's end, Esperanza has gained a measure of the power and determination to achieve it. "I have decided not to grow tame like the others who lay their necks on the threshold waiting for the ball and chain." However, Esperanza is reminded by one of the characters that leaving the barrio does not mean leaving one's identity: "When you leave you must remember to come back for the others. A circle, understand? You will always be Esperanza. You will always be Mango Street. You can't erase what you know. You can't forget who you are."

Students from junior high school through graduate school have used *The House on Mango Street* in classes ranging from Chicano studies to psychology: Stanford University adopted the work as part of a new curriculum during the late 1980s. And in 1994, portions of the book were republished as *Hairs/Pelitos,* a bilingual picture book with illustrations by artist Terry Ybáñez. "Everybody in our family has different hair / Todos en nuestra familia tenemos pelo diferente," announces the book's young Latina narrator, drawing young readers into her house on Mango Street and its diverse inhabitants.

In addition to gaining her entry into "Las Girlfriends," the inner circle of Chicana writers, the book brought Cisneros to the attention of literary agent Susan Bergholz, who began a four-year search for the author. Meanwhile, Cisneros received her master's degree from Iowa, after which she worked part-time as a teacher of literacy skills to Latinos and held various positions within several universities. In 1986 she received a Dobie-Paisano fellowship and moved to Texas. During this time she finished *My Wicked, Wicked Ways*. A book of poetry, the book introduces readers to an independent woman, a wife and mother to none, who says, "I've learned two things./ To let go/ clean as a kite string./ And to never wash a man's clothes./ These are my rules." She adds, "What does a woman owe a man/ and isn't freedom what you believe in?/ Even the freedom to say no?" Although Cisneros received critical acclaim following the book's publication in 1987, that year proved to be a low period in her personal life.

Wishing to remain in Texas after her fellowship had ended, she found herself unable to make a living. Reduced to passing out fliers in supermarkets and laundromats in a vain attempt to organize a private writing workshop, her confidence was soon shattered. In a deep depression, she left Texas to accept a guest lectureship at California State University in Chico. Cisneros described this period in her life to *Publishers Weekly*: "I found myself becoming suicidal.... I was drowning, beyond help.... It was frightening because it was such a calm depression." Help arrived in the form of an National Endowment of the Arts fellowship in fiction, which revitalized the author both financially and spiritually. Her enthusiasm building, she finally contacted Bergholz, whose Manhattan phone number she had carried in her pocket for months. That call led to a contract with Random House and the publication of *Woman Hollering Creek*.

With Random House behind her, Cisneros was thrust into the national limelight, and *Woman Hollering Creek* received wide distribution. A series of short stories about the lives and loves of Chicanas on both sides of the Texas-Mexico border, the tales feature strong female characters. For her work Cisneros received glowing reviews from critics and was lauded as a new star on the literary horizon. The *Los Angeles Times* called the collection "stunning," while the *New York Times Book Review* deemed the work's protagonists "as unforgettable as a first kiss." And the *Washington Post Book World* added a positive note of their own, calling the stories "a kind of choral work in which the harmonic voices emphasize the commonality of experience."

The success of 1991's *Woman Hollering Creek* was followed three years later by *Loose Woman,* a collection of poems that reiterate the voice of what *Publishers Weekly* calls Cisneros's "street-smart, fearlessly liberated persona who raves, sometimes haphazardly, always with abandon, about the real thing." "You bring out the Mexican in me./ The hunkering thick dark spiral./ The core of a heart howl./ The bitter bile./ The tequila lágrimas on Saturday all / through next weekend Sunday," Cisneros writes in an exploration of the sensual, carnal nature that her Mexican American speaker is heir to. Praised by critics for its passion, *Loose Woman* successfully expresses "being the tough, independent free-spirited 'loose woman' of [its] title," according to *Library Journal*.

Although some successful Latinos have felt uncomfortable about becoming a "representative" of their ethnic group, Cisneros welcomes being so labelled. "I don't feel any sense of self-consciousness about my role as a spokesperson in the writing, because I've taken that responsibility on from the very beginning," she explained. "That isn't something I'm nervous about or begrudging about. Actually, the fact that I *can* write

Publication in •

Mainstream

Press

Profile by Andrés Chávez

about the things I write about.... I feel very honored to be able to give them a form in my writings and to be able to have this material to write about is a blessing."

JUDITH ORTIZ COFER

1952- •

"We lived in Puerto Rico until my brother was born in 1954,"

Educator, •

poet,

novelist

wrote award-winning poet, essayist, and fiction writer Judith Ortiz Cofer. "Soon after, because of economic pressures on our growing family, my father joined the United States Navy. He was assigned to duty on a ship in Brooklyn Yard . . . that was to be his home base in the States until his retirement more than twenty years later." In these brief sentences from an essay published in Georgia Review and included as part of her Silent Dancing: A Partial Remembrance of a Puerto Rican Childhood, Cofer introduces the dual reality that makes up her literary universe: the effect on Puerto Rican Americans of living in a world split between the island culture of their homeland and the teeming tenement

life of the United States.

Although Cofer was born on February 24, 1952, in Hormigueros, Puerto Rico, she was soon brought to the United States by her parents, J. M. and Fanny Morot Cofer. The family's official residence was in Paterson, New Jersey, but whenever her father's Navy job took him to sea, Cofer and her mother and brother went back to Puerto Rico to stay with her maternal family. As a child Cofer spoke only Spanish; when she was finally introduced to the English language, she found it difficult but rewarding.

Cofer earned a bachelor of arts degree in English from Augusta College in 1973 and a master of arts in English from Florida Atlantic University in 1977. Since receiving her advanced degree, she has served as an English instructor at several institutions, including the University of Miami, the University of Georgia, and the Georgia Center for Continuing Education. Since 1992 Cofer has been assistant professor of English at the University of Georgia. "It was a challenge, not only to learn English," she notes in *Contemporary Authors*, "but to master it enough to teach it and—the ultimate goal—to write poetry in it."

Begins Career •

as English

Teacher

Cofer's first books of poetry were three chapbooks published in the early 1980s: *Latin Women Pray, The Native Dancer,* and *Among the Ancestors.* Three more volumes of poetry followed in the same decade: *Peregrina* in 1986 and *Terms of Survival* and *Reaching for the Mainland,* both in 1987. Branching out from verse by the end of the decade, Cofer saw the release of her novel, *The Line of the Sun,* in 1989. Two collections of poetry and prose followed: 1991's *Silent Dancing* and *The Latin Deli,* released in 1993. *An Island like You: Stories of the Barrio* was released the following year, to critical praise. Among the honors she has received for her work are a 1989 National Endowment for the Arts fellowship in poetry, the 1990 Pushcart Prize for Nonfiction, and the 1994 O. Henry Award for short fiction.

Cofer's first novel, *The Line of the Sun,* was lauded by various critics for its poetic qualities. In the *New York Times Book Review,* Roberto Márquez described the book's author as "a prose writer of evocatively lyrical authority." In the *Los Angeles Times Book Review* Sonja Bolle also referred to the beauty of many of the novel's passages. The book is narrated by Marisol Santa Luz Vivente, who tells the story of three generations of her family. The first part of the book describes the origins of the Vivente clan in the Puerto Rican village of Salud and introduces the reader to the culture and landscape of the island. The second part of the novel is set in Paterson, New Jersey, where Marisol strives to find an equilibrium between the clashing values of her Puerto Rican ancestors and those of her new American homeland.

The conflict of cultural duality appears again in the autobiographical essays and poems that make up Cofer's *Silent Dancing*. The title is derived from the author's memories of a silent home movie filmed at a New Year's Eve party when her parents were young, which ends with a silent conga line of revelers. As each of the dancers comes into view she comments, in essays that include "The Looking-Glass Shame," and "Los Nueva Yores," on how each has responded to the cultural differences in their lives. In the collection's title essay, Cofer writes of her fascination with the short film clip: "The five-minute movie ends with people dancing in a circle—the creative filmmaker must have set it up, so that all of them could file past him. It is both comical and sad to watch silent dancing." In her writing, Cofer "recovers the warp and weft of her experience in stellar stories," according to *Publishers Weekly*.

The *Latin Deli* continues in the same manner: "a delicious smorgasbord of the sights, smells, tastes, and sounds recalled from a cross-cultural girlhood," according to *Booklist*. Featuring autobiographical short stories, essays, and verse, this 1993 collection depicts the coming of age of a Puerto Rican American confused by racial prejudice, integrating the dogma of the church into a personal faith, falling in love for the first times, and seeking to find acceptance in a new culture while retaining her Puerto Rican identity. In *An Island Like You*, Cofer gives voice to adolescents trying to break free of Puerto Rican traditions of their parents and join mainstream American culture. Each focusing on a different young person, taken together, the stories draw the reader into the vibrant, musical, familial world of the barrio.

Cofer explains her use of autobiographical elements in her poetry, an explanation that seems equally applicable to *The Latin Deli* and *Silent Dancing*. "My family is one of the main topics of my poetry," she notes of the characters she fills her book with. "In tracing their lives, I discover more about mine. The place of birth itself becomes a metaphor for the things we all must leave behind; the assimilation of a new culture is the coming into maturity by accepting the terms necessary for survival. My poetry is a study of this process of change, cultural assimilation, and transformation."

**Profile by
Marian C. Gonsior**

MIRIAM COLÓN

A *pioneer of the Hispanic theater movement in New York City,*

1945- •

Miriam Colón founded the Puerto Rican Traveling Theater in 1966 and

still serves as its artistic director. In addition, she co-founded the Nuevo

Actress, •

Círculo Dramatico, the first Spanish-language theater in New York. A

director,

critically praised performer on stage, as well as in both film and

playwright

television roles, Colón has been described in the New York Times *as "the*

most famous Puerto Rican actress in America."

Colón, born in 1945 to working-class parents in the Puerto Rican city of Ponce, emphasizes the importance of her mother's influence. "My mother has been the major force in my life," she commented in an interview with Gloria Bonilla-Santiago. "To this day, I am very, very attached to her. She is my role model . . . [and] a wonderful, warm woman. I am totally sure of her love—the only thing I'm sure of in my life." Her mother's encouragement allowed Colón to pursue her career in the arts. "'If you want to, be an actor,' she said, as long as I didn't come home too late," Colón related. "She never pushed me away from the direction I wanted to go."

A scholarship to the Erwin Piscator Dramatic Workshop and Technical Institute in New York City paved the way for Colón's entry into the theater world. After earning her degree, Colón embarked on a career that has grown to include work both behind the scenes and in the spotlight, in play, movie, and television productions. She made her Broadway debut in 1953 with *In the Summer House,* and also appeared in *The Innkeepers* in 1956, 1980's *The Wrong Way Light Bulb,* and a well-received Los Angeles production of Eduardo Machado's *Floating Islands* in 1994. Her film appearances include 1961's *One-Eyed Jacks* and *The Appaloosa,* filmed in 1966, both starring Marlon Brando; 1972's *The Possession of Joe Delaney* starring Shirley MacLaine; *Back Roads,* filmed in 1961 with star Sally Field; and 1983's critically acclaimed remake of *Scarface,* starring Al Pacino. In addition, Colón has appeared in more than 250 television shows.

An acknowledged trailblazer in the realm of theatre, Colón has encountered struggles in her personal life as well. She described her second husband as "a sophisticated man, a very strong man" who supported her work; when he died, Colón related, "I was emotionally devastated." She turned to her work for comfort, "trying to turn the energy out instead of in." When she met her current husband, actor George P. Edgar, in a play she was directing, "I really was not looking for romance. But I found I was developing an interest in him.... I was amazed that I still had the capacity to love and trust and to give of myself." The couple married in 1966.

Throughout her career Colón has worked towards increasing both recognition and opportunities for Hispanics in the performing arts. She was the first Puerto Rican accepted as a member of the famed Actors Studio, and was appointed by then-Governor Nelson Rockefeller to New York's Council on the Arts, a position she held for over ten years. Colón also served on the Expansion Arts Panel of the National Endowment for the Arts, and has acted as a cultural adviser to a variety of state and national organizations. Her Puerto Rican Traveling Theater, housed in a former fire station on West 94th Street in New York City, has provided a stage for perhaps her most important contribution: the premieres of more than fifty plays by dramatists from Chile, Puerto Rico, Spain, Venezuela, Columbia, Brazil, and Mexico since its curtain first rose in 1966.

Colón has been awarded for her achievements by the National Council of Christians and Jews, the Puerto Rican Legal Defense and Education Fund, the University of the State of New York, and the Asociación de Cronistas de Espectáculos de Nueva York. She received the New York City Mayor's Award of Honor for the Arts and Culture in

Works to •

Provide

Opportunities

for Hispanics

1982 from then-Mayor Edward Koch, and was presented with the Athena Award from the New York Commission on the Status of Women in 1985. In addition, Colón received an honorary degree in letters from Montclair State College in 1989.

The active playwright and actress told Bonilla-Santiago that her overriding goal in life has been "to leave the Puerto Rican Traveling Theater very stable, artistically and financially. I have not achieved that—maybe on the artistic side, because we have national respect and recognition, [but] I am unhappy about the financial side. I would be happy if I could say that the theater has a reserve of half a million dollars in the bank with all expenses paid, [but] we are not in that position." With her numerous contributions to the promotion of Hispanics in the arts, as well as the monument of the Puerto Rican Traveling Theater, Colón's wish to be remembered as an artist who never forgot her people should be easily fulfilled.

**Profile by
Gloria
Bonilla-Santiago**

GRACÍELA DANIELE

A talented dancer and choreographer, as well as an ambitious

director, Gracíela Daniele has both entertained and challenged her

theatre audiences. Her choreography for the Broadway productions of

The Mystery of Edwin Drood *and* The Pirates of Penzance *won her*

fame; for the latter musical she was nominated for a Tony award in

1981. Daniele's work has also drawn critical controversy, particularly

Tango Apasionado *and* Dangerous Games, *bold dance theater events*

that she both conceived and directed.

1939- •

Choreographer, •

director

Born December 8, 1939, in Buenos Aires to Raul and Rosa (Almoina) Daniele, Graciela Daniele has attributed many of her themes to the culture of her native Argentina. She graduated from a program at the Theatre Colon in Buenos Aires with a degree in Bellas Artes. It was while performing as a ballet soloist for the Nice Opera in France that she saw a Paris production of the popular American musical *West Side Story*. "That's what brought me to New York," Daniele told the *New York*

Times. I didn't even speak English." Despite this obstacle, she danced well enough to earn roles in several Broadway musicals. After studying with choreographer Matt Mattox and dancing in his *What Makes Sammy Run*, Daniele found her way into *Coco, Follies, Chicago,* and *Promises, Promises*.

It was not long before Daniele began to design her own musical numbers, gaining her first job as choreographer at a Milliken industrial show at New York City's Waldorf Astoria Hotel. She then went on to choreograph *The Most Happy Fella* and *A History of the American Film*, both produced on Broadway. Later jobs included the New York City Opera production of *Naughty Marrietta, Joseph and the Amazing Technicolor Dreamcoat* for the Brooklyn Academy, and *Die Fledermaus* for the Boston Opera Company. In 1981 Daniele choreographed *Alice in Concert,* a musical that starred Meryl Streep and opened at New York's Public Theater.

Her choreography for another show, 1981's *The Pirates of Penzance*, brought Daniele a great deal of attention. As a critic for the *New York Times* remarked, "Graciela Daniele can take credit for making an ensemble of actors and singers, most of whom have never taken a dance class in their life, as satisfying to watch as a highly trained dance company." The critic continued, "Miss Daniele's choreography, described by Frank Rich as 'intricately batty,' is a consistently strong element in a show that has a cast of widely differing bodies and voices." The success of *The Pirates of Penzance,* which was later made into a film, was very much due to Daniele's work. Accordingly, respect for Daniele in the world of show business increased: she received an Antoinette Perry (Tony) Award nomination and won a Los Angeles Critics Award. Her next effort, the choreography for 1983's *The Rink*, garnered her yet another Tony nomination.

Daniele's choreography of *The Mystery of Edwin Drood* was rewarded with favorable reviews in late 1985. While commenting that her choreography "has often been too minimalist or derivative for my taste," a critic for *New York* magazine praised her work in *Edwin Drood,* commenting that Daniele "here comes up with decorative curlicues of dance that seamlessly blend into the calligraphy of the staging, so that we are at a loss to say where direction leaves off and choreography begins, and vice versa."

The Pirates of Penzance and *The Mystery of Edwin Drood* was followed by work that drew sharp criticism for its controversial content. *Tango Apasionado*, which Daniele conceived and directed, as well as choreographed, appeared in December of 1987, a little more than two years after *Edwin Drood*. INTAR, the Hispanic American Arts Center,

Recognized for •

Work in

Pirates of

Penzance

had then invited the choreographer to develop a show and had given her the freedom to do what she wanted. The result, a "cross between a musical and a dance piece," as a reviewer for *New York* called it, was based on three short stories and a prose poem written by the great Argentinian writer Jorge Luis Borges. But, as a critic for the *New Yorker* commented, "Under the onslaught of [Daniele's] misery tangos and knife duels (every other scene seems to end with a slashing), Borges gets lost and reason takes flight."

While some viewers could not see through the violence and the abuse of the female characters in *Tango Apasionado,* including such elements was crucial to Daniele; she recalled such a culture from her childhood and wanted to reflect upon it from an adult perspective. "I'm a very nonviolent person," she told the *New York Times,* "but the first opportunity I had to do something of my own, this power and passion and violence that was inside me came out....I don't want to make any judgements about violence or the treatment of women in that culture, but in presenting it maybe I'm making a statement. I realize I'm screaming against it, but I'm not doing it verbally, I'm doing it visually. It's not about intellect, this piece, it's about raw human emotions."

Daniele's next project, which appeared in late 1989, was similarly violent; similarly, also, it was not understood and it was not well received. *Dangerous Games*, which was conceived, co-written, directed, and choreographed by Daniele, consists of two interrelated acts, "Tango" and "Orfeo." According to a *New York* critic, "Many people are offended by the show's brutality, and indeed, it is mostly crude sex, fighting with knives, fighting with whips, fighting with boleadoras, fighting with poles, torture, and still more and cruder sex." Although this same critic acknowledged that "There is solid dancing here," he concluded that "dancers, like children, should be seen, not heard." A critic for the *New Republic* was equally unimpressed: "One needs a new term to describe this evening—choreopathology. I don't recall ever leaving a show with such queasy feelings about the gangrenous possibilities of dance." The *New York Times* added to the general critical assessment of *Dangerous Games,* asserting that "Ms. Daniele exposes the limits of her own talent by stretching it over too much time and space."

In late 1990 Daniele directed and choreographed *Once on This Island,* a Broadway musical about a doomed love affair between a beautiful peasant girl and an aristocratic boy that takes place in the French Antilles. Her work for this musical received mixed reviews, with some residual criticism from *Dangerous Games* undoubtedly influencing critical reception of the new musical. A critic for *The Nation* wrote, "earlier this season, in *Dangerous Games,* [Daniele] did for the dance traditions of Argentina what she now does for those of the Caribbean—turns them into shticks." A *New York* reviewer decided that, considering the "fiasco" of *Dangerous Games, Once on This Island* "proves—conclusively, I think—that Miss Daniele has shot what was, at most, a slender wad." Despite these pans, a critic for the *New Yorker* found no fault with the choreographer, commenting, "All goes well under Graciela Daniele's direction."

In 1992 Daniele took on the classic *Captains Courageous,* a production that was based on the 1937 film adaptation of a book by Rudyard Kipling. Serving as both director and choreographer of the musical, she attempted to capture on stage the majesty of the seabound tale of a young boy's life aboard ship. However, the production was limited by its ability to recreate the technical drama of the film; as a critic for the *New York Times* noted of the production, "a few more Saturday afternoon movie thrills wouldn't hurt the show." More resounding successes for Daniele followed, including well-received productions of both *Falsettos* and the Edwin Sánchez-penned *Clean* at Connecticut's Hartford Stage Company as well as *El Nuevo Mundo,* Ballet Hispanico's celebration of the 500th anniversary of the landing of Christopher Columbus that was punctuated by the excitement of Daniele's flamenco-inspired choreography.

1993's *The Goodbye Girl* also showcased Daniele's choreography to good effect, and as director and choreographer for *Hello Again* on Broadway in 1994, her "streamlined and sexy stage pictures make the music seem better than it is," according to a *New Yorker* critic. In the following years' *Chronicle of a Death Foretold,* she choreographed and directed an adaptation of the novella by Gabriel García Márquez; "a colorful show, with its percussive Latin rhythms, could be a tonic for Broadway," noted *Time* of the production. Vincent Canby agreed in the *New York Times,* calling *Chronicle* "a frequently stunning show that is less a conventional musical adaptation than a performance piece....performed with verve." However, as with many of Daniele's productions, critical reception remained mixed: "This clumsy, kitschy spectacle drains all the vitality and strangeness from the book," concluded a *Wall Street Journal* critic, "and inserts in their place every foot-stomping, flounce swirling, fan-snapping Latino musical cliché imaginable."

It is to Daniele's credit that she has attempted to convey to audiences her personal impressions of the Argentinian culture of recent history through her chosen medium, the dance. If critics have sometimes neither understood nor appreciated some of her more original works, it is because she has not yet been able to present the horror of such violence without horrifying her audiences at the same time. However, theatre-goers will continue to be intrigued by her efforts towards

**Profile by
Ronie-Richele
Garcia-Johnson**

finding that combination of dance and aggression that artfully, as well as accurately, represents the Argentinian culture that loomed so large in her childhood.

DOLORES DEL RIO

*T*he type of role offered to Hispanic actresses in Hollywood during

the twenties and thirties—the most important years of Dolores Del Rio's

career—is evident in the following excerpt from George Hadley-Garcia's

Hispanic Hollywood: *"In the early '30s, producer David O. Selznick*

informed his staff, 'I want Dolores Del Rio in a South Seas romance. . . I

don't care what story you use so long as we call it Bird of Paradise *and*

Del Rio jumps into a flaming volcano to finish.'" According to Hadley-

Garcia, Hispanic actresses like Del Rio often had to endure changing

their names, being cast as a member of another ethnic group, or

pretending to be of European descent if they wanted to work. Del Rio did

not change her name, but did appear in a variety of ethnic roles and was

billed as a "Spanish" actress at the beginning of her career. Although often typecast in exotic parts—such as the one suggested by Selznick—Del Rio became one of the first Mexican film personalities to achieve international stardom.

Del Rio was born Lolita Dolores Asúnsolo y López Negrete in Durango, Mexico, on August 3, 1905, to Jesus and Antonia (López Negrete) Asúnsolo. The family was split apart a few years later, when Del Rio's father, who was director of the Bank of Durango, was forced to flee to the United States during the Mexican Revolution of 1910. Left behind in the comparative safety of Mexico City, Del Rio attended a French private school, the Convent of St. Joseph, where among other subjects she studied Spanish dancing. In 1921 she married Jaime Martínez Del Rio, a lawyer eighteen years her senior, and left Mexico for a two-year European honeymoon. It was while traveling in Spain that Del Rio had her first taste of stardom, as she used her dancing skills to entertain wounded Spanish soldiers returning from that country's war with Morocco.

In the early twenties Del Rio was invited to Hollywood by the American film director Edwin Carewe, who had met her through a mutual friend. By 1925 she had begun her film career with a small part in United Artists's *Joanne,* the first of fifteen silent films the actress made between 1925 and 1929. Three of Del Rio's most important films of the period include *What Price Glory?, Resurrection,* and *Ramona.* In the first, directed by Raoul Walsh and released in 1926, Del Rio played a French peasant girl named Charmaine. *What Price Glory?* became the second best-selling film of the year, earning $2 million at the box-office. 1927's *Resurrection,* an adaptation of Count Leo Tolstoy's work of the same title, featured Del Rio in her first starring role, as a Russian peasant. Del Rio's performance in the title role of *Ramona,* released in 1928 through United Artists, was praised by Mordaunt Hall in the *New York Times,* who then noted: "Del Rio's interpretation of Ramona is an achievement. Not once does she overact, and yet she is perceived weeping and almost hysterical. She is most careful in all the moods of the character."

Because she had yet to learn English, the silent film era was especially helpful to Del Rio's career, and she was one of Hollywood's top ten money-makers during the 1920s. Her voice was first heard in the 1929 release *Evangeline* which, although silent, included three songs sung by Del Rio in French, which had been edited into the movie before its release. The year 1930 marked the release of the now-widowed actress's first talkie, and of her second marriage to Metro-Goldwyn-Mayer art director Cedric Gibbons. Gibbons was the designer of the

Silent Films •

Bring Fame

Academy Award "Oscar" statuette; he eventually earned twelve of the awards himself. The couple settled into a Gibbons-designed house in Santa Monica, California, and pursued an extravagant lifestyle. While Gibbons produced the sets for films such as *The Thin Man, Mutiny on the Bounty,* and *A Tale of Two Cities,* Del Rio signed a contract with United Artists which paid $9000 a week. The marriage lasted eleven years.

A serious illness caused Del Rio to lose her contract with United Artists, but once she recovered she signed with RKO Studios. In 1932 she starred in *The Girl of the Rio* which, although very popular, angered the Mexican government due to a plot line implying that Mexican justice could be bought; the film was banned in Mexico, Panama, and Nicaragua. That same year Del Rio also appeared in *Bird of Paradise*—the film imagined by Selznick—in which she played a Polynesian girl who throws herself into a volcano to appease the "God in the Mountain of Fire." In 1933 Del Rio starred in a movie with one of Hollywood's most famous dance teams: Fred Astaire and Ginger Rogers. The film, *Flying Down to Rio,* which featured a scene in which Astaire and Del Rio take the dance floor together, also served as a vehicle for Del Rio's introduction of the two-piece swimsuit to U.S. audiences.

• **Works to Build**

Fledgling

Mexican Film

Industry

In 1942, after starring in twenty-three U.S. films, Del Rio left the country for her native Mexico. "By 1940 I knew I couldn't build a satisfying career on glamour, so I came home," she told Chris O'Connor in a *Modern Maturity* interview. "My father had died, and I felt a need for my country, my people. Also I wanted to pioneer with our beginning Mexican film industry." The famous actress made good on her plans and appeared in two important films of the early Mexican cinema, *Flor silvestre* ("Wild Flower") and *María Candelaria* (released in English as *Portrait of Maria*). Both titles were released in 1943, the product of influential Mexican director Emilio "El Indio" Fernández. *Portrait of Maria* won the best picture award—the Palma d'Or—at the first post-World War II Cannes Film Festival in France in 1946; it was also be a prize winner at the international film festival held the following year in Locarno, Switzerland. The film, which tells the story of a Mexican beauty who is stoned to death after being falsely accused of posing for a nude portrait, introduced the fledgling Mexican cinema to international audiences and established Del Rio as an important international screen personality.

During the 1940s and 1950s Del Rio continued on as the most important Mexican actress of her day, but she continued to stay away from Hollywood. According to Hadley-Garcia, her absence from U.S. screens was due in part to the suspicious attitude that surrounded the movie industry during the height of the Cold-War era. "During the 1950s she was barred from the U.S. for having aided anti-Franco refugees from the Spanish Civil War," Hadley-Garcia wrote. In 1947 Del Rio played what would be her last role in an American film until the 1960s, appearing in John Ford's *The Fugitive*, a film based on Graham Greene's novel *The Power and the Glory*. Made almost entirely in Mexico, the movie starred Del Rio as an unwed Indian mother and Henry Fonda as an alcoholic Mexican priest. Although it received a limited distribution in the United States, the presence of Fonda in its cast and Ford as its director assured continued interest in *The Fugitive* from movie buffs. In fact, Del Rio's role in the movie has remained one for which she is best remembered.

In the 1950s the actress combined film engagements with stage productions, including a tour through New England in a 1956 performance of *Anastasia*. During the same period she starred in two Mexican films based on classics of Spanish literature: *La Malquerida*, based on leading Spanish playwright Jacinto Benavente's play of the same title, and *Doña Perfecta,* based on the novel by Spanish novelist Benito Pérez Galdós. An American theater producer and director, Lewis Riley, encouraged Del Rio to make her debut on the Mexican stage in his production of *Lady Windmere's Fan*, a comedy of manners by Oscar Wilde, in the late 1950s. She also appeared in Henrik Ibsen's *Ghosts* and other stage productions. On November 24, 1960, Del Rio and Riley were married; they made their home in an affluent suburb of Mexico City.

During the sixties the pace of Del Rio's film career slowed considerably; she made only five films in Mexico from 1960 to 1978. She returned to Hollywood in 1961 in *Flaming Star,* where, cast in the role of Elvis Presley's Native American mother, the seemingly ageless beauty seemed far to young for the part. In 1964 Del Rio starred in what was to be director John Ford's last Western, *Cheyenne Autumn,* which featured she and Ricardo Montalban as the parents of a character played in the film by teen idol Sal Mineo. In 1966 she appeared in a Spanish film, *La Dama del Alba,* and in a made-for-television travelogue, *Dolores Del Rio's Mexico,* shown on U.S. television screens in 1968. At age 63 she appeared as the leading role in a Mexico City stage production of *The Lady of the Camellias.* As the decade drew to a close, Del Rio took a small part in Italian film director Carlo Ponti's film, *C'era una Volta* (released in English as *More Than a Miracle*), as the mother of the character played in the film by Omar Sharif. The film also starred Sophia Loren.

In 1970 Del Rio announced her retirement and began to devote herself to the charitable work to which she dedicated much of her time in her later years. In 1971, with government sponsorship and the support of the Mexican Actors' Association, she founded the Estancia Infantil, a day-care center for children of Mexican performers. As chairperson of the board of the center, Del Rio spent many hours at the nursery with her young charges. She explained the concept behind the center in *Modern Maturity*. "Babies are special in Mexico, you know, and their first six years are the most important. We play Brahms and Bach to them, teach them English, folklorico dancing—all the arts." Del Rio interrupted her retirement briefly in 1978 to make *The Children of Sanchez*, a U.S.-Mexican production co-starring Anthony Quinn, which Hadley-Garcia referred to as a "minor (and little seen in the U.S.) masterpiece."

Del Rio's role in *The Children of Sanchez* was to be her last. The actress died on April 11, 1983, at her home in Newport Beach, California, of chronic hepatitis. In *Mexican Cinema: Reflections of a Society, 1896-1988,* Carl J. Mota quotes from a *Hispanoamericano* article written upon the actress's death in which Jorge Carrasco evaluated Del Rio's contribution to Mexican cinema. In his comments, Carrasco maintained that Del Rio's impact on the Mexican film industry was "very great and much time would pass before another star of her magnitude would arise. Her death [deprived] Mexican cinema of one of the great figures that gave it an international reputation during its golden age."

**Profile by
Marian C. Gonsior**

GLORIA ESTEFAN

F rom their Hispanic roots to their current position in the pop music

mainstream, the award-winning Gloria Estefan and the Miami Sound

Machine are the embodiment of the American dream come true.

Originally a Cuban American quartet that performed popular music

with decidedly Latin influences, the Miami Sound Machine grew from

being a sensation in Spanish-speaking countries to international best-

seller status, due to the talent and hard work of Estefan and the sound

business sense of her husband, Emilio, onetime bandmember and later

its manager. Estefan has received the distinction of being named

Billboard's *Best New Pop Artist* in 1986, and won an American Music

Award in 1989 and a lifetime achievement award from 1992's Premio

1958- •

Pop singer, •

songwriter

109 •

lo Nuestro a la Musica Latina; in 1993 she was honored with a star on the Hollywood Walk of Fame.

Estefan was born Gloria Fajardo in Cuba in 1958; as a toddler she and her family fled the country when Communist dictator Fidel Castro rose to power. Her father, José Manuel Fajardo, who had been a Cuban soldier and bodyguard of deposed Cuban President Fulgencio Batista, was recruited into the 2506 Brigade, a Central Intelligence Agency-funded band of Cuban refugees that was captured during the unsuccessful 1961 Bay of Pigs invasion. After President John F. Kennedy negotiated the release of the brigade, Fajardo rejoined his family, eventually joining the U.S. Army and serving for two years in Vietnam.

As a child Estefan liked to write poetry, and though she took classical guitar lessons, she found them tedious. Although she had no inkling that she would some day become a popular music star, music played a very important role for her as a teenager. After her father's return from Vietnam, he was diagnosed as having multiple sclerosis, possibly as a result of having been exposed to the herbicide Agent Orange while serving in the army. Estefan's mother, who had been a teacher in Cuba, worked to support the family during the day and attended school at night. Young Gloria was left to take care of her father and younger sister. She had little social life and, because she felt the weight of such responsibilities, she turned to music as a release. "When my father was ill, music was my escape," Estefan told *Washington Post* reporter Richard Harrington. "I would lock myself up in my room for hours and just sing. I wouldn't cry—I refused to cry.... Music was the only way I had to just let go, so I sang for fun and for emotional catharsis."

In 1975 Gloria met keyboardist Emilio Estefan, a sales manager for the rum dealer Bacardi and the leader of a band called the Miami Latin Boys. The band played popular Latin music, but because there was no lead singer, the quartet members took turns singing. A mutual friend asked Emilio to advise Gloria and some friends about organizing a band for a special event. Emilio heard Gloria sing and was impressed; when he met her again at a wedding at which the Miami Latin Boys were entertaining, he asked her to sit in with the band. A few weeks later Emilio asked Gloria to perform as lead singer with the band, and she accepted. At first she sang only on weekends, because she was still attending the University of Miami, from which she graduated with a degree in psychology in 1978. A year and a half after she joined the group—by then renamed the Miami Sound Machine—the band recorded its first album for a local label. *Renacer* was a collection of disco pop and original ballads sung in Spanish.

Joins Future •

Husband's

Band

Although Estefan was somewhat plump and very shy when she joined the band, she slimmed down with a rigorous exercise program and worked to overcome her natural reticence. After several months, Emilio and Gloria's professional relationship turned personal; September 1, 1978, they were married and their son Nayib was born two years later. At about the same time, Emilio left Bacardi's to work full-time with the band, then made up of bassist Marcos Avila, drummer Kiki Garcia, keyboardist, arranger, and saxophonist Raul Murciano, keyboardist Emilio, and soprano Gloria.

By 1980 the group had signed a contract with Discos CBS International, the Miami-based Hispanic division of CBS Records. Between 1981 and 1983 the Miami Sound Machine recorded four Spanish-language albums made up of ballads, disco, pop, and sambas, which met with success in Spanish-speaking countries. The group had dozens of hit songs around the world—particularly in Venezuela, Peru, Panama, and Honduras—but enjoyed little recognition in the United States.

• Enters North

American

Market

The Miami Sound Machine's first North American hit was from the band's first English album, *Eyes of Innocence*. The disco single "Dr. Beat" went to the top of the European dance charts; the song's popularity prompted CBS to move the group to Epic, a parent label, and inspired group members to write songs in English. Several of these songs first appeared on the otherwise Spanish-language record *Conga*. The rousing dance number "Conga" itself became the first single to crack *Billboard's* pop, dance, black, and Latin charts simultaneously. Estefan reminisced to Jesse Nash of the *New York Tribune,* "I'll never forget when we first did 'Conga.' A producer told us that the song was too Latin for the Americans and too American for the Latins. 'Well, thank you,' I said, 'because that's exactly what we are!'" Estefan and the group, the membership of which has changed over the years, pride themselves on the combination of Latin rhythms, rhythm and blues, and mainstream pop that makes up their hybrid sound.

In 1986 the album *Primitive Love*, the band's first totally English recording, sparked a string of hit singles. "Bad Boys" and "Words Get in the Way" made their way onto Billboard's Top Ten pop chart. Behind the scenes, the album's success was, in part, due to the work of a trio known as the "Three Jerks"—producer/drummer Joe Galdo and his partners Rafael Vigil and Lawrence Dermer—who wrote, arranged, and performed the majority of the music on both *Primitive Love* and its follow-up album, *Let It Loose*.

As a band, the Miami Sound Machine developed a split personality. In the studio the "Three Jerks" and session players made records, while, for concerts, a road band that included Garcia and Avila performed.

Estefan was the common denominator. Extensive tours, concerts in 40,000-seat stadiums, and music videos on MTV and VH-1 made the Miami Sound Machine a leading American band. Estefan gradually became the star attraction, and the act came to be billed as "Gloria Estefan and the Miami Sound Machine"; sometimes simply "Gloria Estefan." Some commentators on the popular music scene called Estefan a demure, Hispanic version of Madonna.

After the *Let It Loose* album, Galdo and friends quit working with the Miami Sound Machine, so the band was on its own creatively. Although early in its evolution the band's biggest hits had been rousing dance numbers, by the end of the 1980s it was Estefan's ballads that engendered its success. "Ballads are basically what I'm about," Estefan confessed to Dean Johnson of the *Boston Herald*. "I just feel you can express yourself more completely and eloquently in a ballad. It's easier to identify with someone else and form a closer bond with the audience." From the *Let It Loose* album the singles "Rhythm Is Gonna Get You," "Betcha Say That," and "1-2-3" made it to *Billboard's* Top 10 list, but it was the ballad "Anything For You" that topped the charts.

Despite the group's popularity with English-speaking listeners, the Estefans have not forgotten their roots. There are always Spanish language projects in the works, and the title of their 1989 album *Cuts Both Ways* attests to their intention to live up to their international reputation. Estefan contributed to *Cuts Both Ways* in more capacities than as just the lead singer. She was involved in its planning and production, composed some of the music, and wrote lyrics to most of the songs. The rollicking salsa finale "Oye Mi Canto" ("Hear My Song") rivaled "Conga" for its appeal.

Emilio Estefan relinquished his position as keyboardist with the Miami Sound Machine after the birth of son Nayib. He then devoted his considerable energy and managerial talent to promoting the band and the other enterprises that were to eventually make the Estefans producers of their own and others' records. While Estefan continued to tour with the band, her husband ensured that Nayib would have at least one parent at home. A close family, the Estefans arranged to meet as often as possible during tours. Tragically, while traveling together on March 20, 1990, after one such meeting, the band's bus was involved in an accident with a tractor-trailer truck on snowy Interstate 380 near Pennsylvania's Pocono Mountains. While Nayib suffered a fractured shoulder and Emilio received minor head and hand injuries, Gloria suffered a broken vertebra in her back. During a four-hour operation several days later, surgeons realigned Estefan's spine and implanted steel rods to buttress the fracture. With a prognosis for complete recovery doubtful, Estefan

Fractures Spine •

in Traffic

Accident

retired to her home on Star Island, near Miami, to begin her long recovery.

Thanks to extensive physical therapy, intense determination, and the support of her family and fans, Gloria Estefan made what many consider a miraculous comeback. She marked her return to performing with an appearance on television's American Music Awards in January of 1991 and, shortly thereafter, launched a year-long tour to tout her comeback album *Into the Light*. When Hurricane Andrew struck her hometown of Miami in 1992, Gloria and Emilio were quick to focus the momentum of their successful tour on organizing a concert to aid in the relief effort.

Gloria Estefan's Greatest Hits was released two years later to good reviews, accompanied by the Spanish-language *Mi Tierra*. "The songs the Estefans and a number of collaborators have written for *Mi Tierra* qualify as instant classics," *Hispanic* stated of her 1993 album; guest performances by such stellar talents as drummer Tito Puente, Cubans Cachao on bass and Arturo Sandoval on trumpet, and Miami-based flautist Nestor Torres made Estefan's return to her musical roots a musical gift to her fans as well. "*Mi Tierra* includes unknown songs and even new songs that were made to reflect the spirit of [the 1930s and 1940s]," Estefan told Enrique Lopetegui in the *Los Angeles Times*. "We were even very careful when choosing the instruments we wanted to play with, because it had to be as close as possible to that old style. It's a work of love." In the wake of *Mi Tierra*, which reached number one on the Latin charts and number twenty-seven on the pop charts, was 1994's *Hold Me, Thrill Me, Kiss Me,* a collection of pop-rock covers from the likes of Blood, Sweat & Tears, Carole King, and Vicki Sue Robinson, whose "Turn the Beat Around" was a disco classic. Estefan also recorded portions of the soundtrack for the movies *Heroes* and *Made in America*.

According to *People,* Estefan's "long, sometimes uncertain recovery" gave the singer-songwriter "a renewed feeling about life," as she told writer Steve Dougherty. "It's very hard to stress me out now. It's hard to get me in an uproar about anything because most things have little significance compared with what I almost lost." She added that "so many people got behind me and gave me a reason to want to come back fast and made me feel strong. Knowing how caring people can be, how much they gave me—that has changed me forever."

**Profile by
Jeanne M. Lesinski**

CLARISSA PINKOLA ESTÉS

I n Women Who Run with the Wolves: Myths and Stories of the Wild

Woman Archetype, *Jungian psychoanalyst, award-winning poet, and*

cantadora, *Dr. Clarissa Pinkola Estés tells old stories from her ethnic*

families with the warmth and compassion of a mother sharing a quiet

moment with her child. And like that mother, Estés spins her stories in the

hope that lessons will be learned. The message in her first book is clear:

Women must learn to trust their natural, powerful—and often neglected—

instincts. The public's response to Estés's message has been equally clear:

Women Who Run with the Wolves *was awarded critical acclaim and*

appeared on the New York Times *best-seller list only five weeks after its*

publication in the summer of 1992. Hispanic *hailed it as "feminine*

1946- •

Writer, •

Jungian

psychoanalyst

manifesto for all women, regardless of age, race, creed, or religion, to return to their wild roots. . . she is a *cantadora, curandera*, midwife, mentor."

Estés was born in January of 1946 to Cepción and Emilio Maria, both mestizos—Mexicans of Spanish and Indian descent. She was adopted by Maruska and Joszef, immigrant Hungarians who raised young Estés in Michiana. She grew up, surrounded by woodlands, orchards, farmland, and the natural beauty of the Great Lakes region. Her community was filled with field workers, the working class and "lower economic" class, and with people of different Eastern European cultures, as well as Mexicans, Puerto Ricans, African Americans, and families from the backwoods of Tennessee and Kentucky. Within such cultural diversity, Estés "carried in her blood" the mestizo stories of her heritage, according to the *San Francisco Chronicle*. After World War II, her adoptive father brought his four widowed sisters from Eastern Europe to America. These women, Estés recalled to the *Chronicle,* treated her as though she "was the future," into which "they tried to pour everything they knew." This newfound wealth—the Hungarian folklore of these women—along with a love of nature, became an integral part of her life.

"People who are 'twice born' as adoptees, especially if they are adopted into another culture, have the special ability to bridge those groups," she told the *Chronicle.* Estés is fond of saying she is *una Mexicana* by nature, and a Magyar by nurture.

In the 1960s Estés moved west to Colorado and lived among Jewish, Irish, Greek, Italian, African American, and Alsatian "strangers who became kindred spirits and friends," as she later described these new neighbors in *Women Who Run with the Wolves*. Struggling to raise a family as a divorced, single mother, in 1976 she earned a bachelor of arts degree in psychotherapeutics from Loretto Heights College in Denver; five years later she earned her doctorate in philosophy in ethno-clinical (inter-cultural) psychology from Cincinnati, Ohio's Union Institute. Ethno-clinical psychology is the study of both clinical psychology and ethnology, the latter emphasizing the study of the psychology of groups, particularly tribes. In 1984 Estés was awarded her post-doctoral diploma in analytical psychology from the Inter-Regional Society of Jungian Analysts in Zurich, Switzerland, thereby certifying her as a Jungian analyst.

In the early 1900s, noted German psychoanalyst Carl Jung utilized storytelling as a means of studying the archetypal patterns revealed by the human unconscious. Estés, married and the mother of three daughters, uses her Jungian training as a springboard to develop new insights into the psychology of the creative and gifted person. In addition to helping her analysands—many of whom are members of the artistic community or people coping with the tragedy of AIDS—she served as the executive director of the C. G. Jung Psychoanalytic Institute in Denver from 1987-1990. Now a senior Jungian analyst, Estés has become a specialist in inter-cultural mythology and her work is touted internationally as seminal and ground breaking work on the psychology of women.

In 1971, "in response to seeing that so little of psychology seemed to apply to actual women and to all kinds of women in the real world—middle class, working class, educated, uneducated, Latinas, African Americans, Japanese Americans, Italian Americans and so on, recent immigrants, lesbians, women from religious orders, widows, artists, intellectuals, women in prison, women activists and on and on—" she began writing the 100 fairy tales, myths and psychological commentary that comprise her work. "In essence, it is a work that de-pathologizes the innate and instinctual nature, and that asserts that all women are born gifted."

"I have this feeling that sometimes comes over me—I call it 'the wind of Santa Ana'—and it fills up my blouse and my skirt and causes my hair to fly back. I was filled with the wind of Santa Ana, and that is what, back then, made me stand up at my desk and say, 'By God, I'm going to write about gifted and talented women, and the creative center of the psyche.'"

Women Who Run with the Wolves contains original stories, folktales, myths, and legends by Estés, along with psychoanalytic commentary based on women's lives. In the first few pages of the book, Estés explains her inspiration for the work: "Traditional psychology is often spare or entirely silent about deeper issues important to women; the archetypal, the intuitive, the sexual and cyclical, the ages of women, a woman's way, a woman's knowing, her creative fire. This is what has motivated my work on the Wild Woman archetype for the better part of two decades." *Library Journal* observed that the book, written in a "clear, richly evocative style," was a "perceptive study of women's deep nature."

In *Women Who Run with the Wolves* Estés recalls feeling close to wolves while growing up in the northern woodlands. "Healthy wolves and healthy women share certain psychic characteristics," she asserts:

"keen sensing, playful spirit, and a heightened capacity for devotion. Wolves and women are relational by nature, inquiring, possessed of great endurance and strength. They are deeply intuitive, intensely concerned with their young, their mate, and their pack. They are experienced at adapting to constantly changing circumstances, they are fiercely stalwart and very brave. So that is where the concept of the wild woman archetype crystallized for me, in the study of wolves." *Publishers Weekly* noted that this comparison "defines the archetype of the wild woman, a female in touch with her primitive side and able to rely on gut feelings to make change."

Each of the stories in *Women Who Run with the Wolves* are designed as illustrations of how women should trust their instincts. For example, "La loba" teaches the transformative function of the psyche, "Bluebird" talks about wounds that will not heal, and "Skeleton Woman" gives the reader a glimpse of the mystical power of relationship and how dead feelings can be revived. At the end of the book, the author has written a lighthearted "Wolf Rules for Life: eat, rest, rove in between; render loyalty; love the children; cavil in moonlight; tune your ears; attend to the bones; make love; howl often."

Estés tells her readers that the wild woman "passed through" her spirit twice: once by her birth into a "passionate Mexican-Spanish bloodline," and later through "adoption by a family of fiery Hungarians." As a *cantadora* (keeper of the old stories in the Latina tradition), "I've spent many hours seated at the feet of old Hungarian and Latina women who storytell in plain voices. For them, story is a medicine which strengthens and arights the individual and community. From them I learned that story greases and hoists the pulleys, shows us the way out, down, in and around, cuts for us fine, wide doors in previously blank walls–doors that lead us to our own knowing as wildish women."

Estés's work delves into the healing power of the female psyche. Unlike some feminist writers, she avoids denigrating men, noting in *USA Today* that she is "tired of divisiveness." However, in *Women Who Run with the Wolves,* she reveals how the "wild woman archetype" is damaged when a stifling culture discounts what is feminine. By using her own stories and myths from Asia, Europe, Mexico, and Greece, given to her by elderly people she grew up with, Estés shows readers how they can reclaim their soul lives. Women who study the meanings of the stories can find an inner power that strengthens self-determination and creativity, thus leading to greater personal power and freedom. Estés's stories explore the female power in sex, love, money, marriage, birthing, death, and transformation.

The second book in the series, *The Dangerous Old Woman: Myths and Stories of the Wise Old Woman Archetype* will be published by Knopf in October 1996. Estés is also the author of *The Gift of Story: A Wise Tale about What Is Enough*, a tale told through the eyes of one of her beloved refugee aunts from the old country, and *The Faithful Gardener: A Wise Tale About That Which Can Never Die*. Estés has also recorded several audio volumes including *Warming the Stone Child: Myths and Stories about Abandonment and the Unmothered Child* and *The Red Shoes: On Torment and Recovery of the Soul-Life*. Her poetry has been published in *Exquisite Corpse, Los mochis, The International Signal, Fennel Stalk, Icon, Palabras,* and *Muse*. Her forty years of poetry writing will be published by Knopf in 1997.

A lifetime activist, Estés founded and directs the C.P. Estés Guadalupe Foundation, which has as one of its nascent missions the broadcasting of strengthening stories, via shortwave radio, to trouble spots around the world. In 1971, Estés helped to open one of the first shelters for battered women in the Southwest. For her lifelong social activism and writing, she is the recipient of the *Las Primeras* Award from MANA, The National Latina Foundation in Washington, D.C.; the 1994 recipient of The President's Medal for social justice from The Union Institute; the first recipient of the annual Joseph Campbell festival "Keeper of the Lore" Award; a winner of the Associated Catholic Church Press Award for Writing; and the recipient of The Gradiva Award 1995 from the National Association for the Advancement of Psychoanalysis, New York. She is co-director of the Colorado Authors for Gay and Lesbian Equal Rights. Heavily involved in the arts, she is a former long term artist-in-residence in her home state.

An enthusiastic author, speaker, and performance poet, Estés continues to dedicate herself to helping men and women engage in a dialogue with their inner selves. As she ended *Women Who Run with the Wolves*: "I hope you will go out and let stories happen to you, and that you will work them, water them with your blood and tears and your laughter till they bloom, till you yourself burst into bloom. Then you will see what medicine they make, and where and when to apply them. That is the work. The only work."

**Profile by
D. D. Entreassi**

SANDRA MARÍA ESTEVES

S *andra María Esteves is a poet affiliated with the Nuyorican group*

of writers—those of Puerto Rican heritage living and working in New

York City. As such, her work reflects the conflicts of living between two

languages and two cultures, as well as the problems of surviving as an

Hispanic woman in a world dominated by Anglo males. Esteves has

been compared by critics to the late Julia de Burgos, a poet from a

previous generation of émigrés whose double burden as a woman and

as a Puerto Rican living in New York led to her untimely death in 1953

at the age of thirty-nine.

1948- •

Poet, •

artistic

consultant

The child of immigrants, Esteves was born in the Bronx, New York, on May 10, 1948. Her mother, a garment factory worker from the Dominican Republic, and her father, a sailor from Puerto Rico, separated when Esteves was very young; at age six the child was sent to a Catholic

boarding school. The seven years Esteves spent at Holy Rosary Academy would leave an indelible mark on her poet's psyche. Subjected to the strictures of Irish-based American Catholicism, she was not permitted to speak Spanish at the Academy, where she remained during the week. On weekends she reentered the Puerto Rican world of her family, staying at the home of her paternal aunt, who cared for young Esteves while her mother was working to support the family. Such early experiences formed an awareness of living in two cultures, themes that would later be manifested both in the subjects and in the bilingualism of her early poetry.

After graduating from high school in 1966 and beginning the study of art by enrolling at the highly competitive Pratt Institute, Esteves grew discouraged and went to Puerto Rico, where she intended to remain. She returned to New York after a few months, however, with a renewed sense of her ethnicity and proud of her Puerto Rican heritage. Esteves was soon participating in various protest movements of the 1970s and expressing her growing social awareness through poetry. After Nuyorican poet Jesus Papoleto Melendez introduced her to the world of young Hispanic artists, Esteves joined this group, which included Tato Laviera and Miguel Algarin. She also became part of "El Grupo," a collective of Nuyorican socialist poets, performers, and musicians committed to taking the message of protest throughout the eastern United States. Her work as a painter followed a similar course through her contact with the Taller Boricua art collective.

In 1978 Esteves received her bachelor's degree in fine art from the Pratt Institute. Two years later her first collection of poetry, *Yerba buena*, was published by Greenfield Review Press and selected as the Best Small Press Publication for 1981. At this time Esteves began to write almost exclusively in English, desiring to express her experiences as an urban Hispanic woman living in the United States to an Anglo audience. Two other collections of Esteves's poetry have since been published, *Tropical Rains: A Bilingual Downpour* in 1984, and *Bluestown Mockingbird Mambo* in 1990.

The following decades were full of intense creativity and cultural involvement for the creative and energetic Esteves. Among her many accomplishments have been participation in the Cultural Council Foundation of the CETA Artistic Project from 1978-80, and her appointment as executive artistic director of the African Caribbean Poetry Theater in 1983. Esteves also serves as art consultant to the Bronx Council on the Arts, a position she has held since 1983. In 1990 Esteves, who resides in New York City with her husband and four children, was appointed residential theatre director of the Family Repertory Company.

**Profile by
Silvia Novo Peña**

ANITA PEREZ FERGUSON

T *he time she spent serving as aide to a United States senator helped*

fuel Anita Perez Ferguson's interest in politics. After several years of

involvement within the Santa Barbara, California, political community

and a three year apprenticeship in the office of California Senator Gary

Hart, she decided to have a run at office herself. A Mexican American,

Perez Ferguson has been the two-time recipient of the Democratic

nomination for her state congressional district, in both the 1990 and

1992 elections.

1949- •

Consultant, •

trainer

Born in 1949, Perez Ferguson attended Westmont College, where she obtained her bachelor's degree in communications studies in 1971. After completing a master's degree in counseling psychology at the University of Santa Clara four years later, she began working as a counselor and instructor for the California Community College System, moving to her alma mater, Westmont College, to head their admissions department in 1977. Perez Ferguson served as Westmont's director of admissions for four years, spending her evening hours at the University of Redlands, accumulating academic credit towards a second master's degree—this time in business administration—which she obtained in 1982.

In 1981 Perez Ferguson left Westmont College; in fact, she left the continent and spent the following year in Kenya as volunteer registrar and director of curriculum development for Daystar International Institute's Nairobi campus. Back in the United States by 1983, she joined the staff of Gordon College, where she worked as a development officer for two years.

In 1986 Perez Ferguson made a jump from the hallowed halls of academe onto the fast-moving political bandwagon, joining both the National Women's Political Caucus and the staff of California's Senator Gary Hart as a field representative based out of Santa Barbara. Two years later she joined Hart and other fellow democrats as a delegate to the 1988 National Democratic Convention. While the excitement of the convention was contagious, Perez Ferguson decided to leave Hart's camp a year later to pursue her involvement in politics a little closer to home: at the community level. Active in Santa Barbara's Chamber of Commerce Hispanic Business Committee and Earth Day Committee, she had already been appointed commissioner of Santa Barbara County's Department of Affirmative Action in 1986, and served on the Labor Council for Latin American Advancement; she left both those positions in 1989 in order to focus her energies and talent in other political arenas.

In 1990 Perez Fergusen took on the high-profile position of Community consultant for Citizen 2000, a forward-looking organization dedicated to improving life in the Santa Barbara community for all its citizens during the coming years. Her soon-to-be-announced nomination as a candidate for state house of representatives drew the optimistic and energetic Latina even further into the political limelight.

In 1990 Perez Ferguson campaigned as the Democratic candidate for Santa Barbara's 19th Congressional district. Running on a platform that included a plan to re-distribute monies allocated for defense into health care, housing, education, and research and development, she also campaigned on her promise to battle the legislation that allowed the number of oil rigs dotting the Santa Barbara coastline to proliferate over the previous two decades. And she ran pro-choice: "I believe that choice is every woman's, every family's right," Perez Ferguson later told the *Los Angeles Times*. "I talked about choice at every meeting and in every interview. Our analysis shows, and intuitively I know, that Republicans came over to vote for me on that issue alone." With a swelling of volunteer support—Los Angeles City councilwoman Gloria

Molina and state representatives Ed Roybal and Esteban Torres each added their efforts to her bid for office—and $200,000 in campaign funds, she was able to make a strong showing against eight-term Republican incumbent Bob Lagomarsino, despite the fact that the district contains only 60,000 registered Hispanic voters—enough to be a deciding factor but, at twenty percent of the electorate, not enough to carry an election.

While Perez Ferguson lost both bids for office, she has not been discouraged by the experience. "We had 500 volunteers in a congressional race. That's fantastic," she told the *Los Angeles Times* in 1990. "We had more Hispanics involved than ever had been before in Santa Barbara or Ventura. We came from nowhere and closed to within eight percentage points of the incumbent winner. We didn't run as an Hispanic candidate, or a woman candidate; we ran as a candidate who cared about human issues, family issues."

Until another political opportunity comes her way, Perez Ferguson continues to serve her community. In 1991, in addition to teaching at the Ventura campus of California State University—Northridge, she was a member of the Santa Barbara planning commission. Since pursuing the second leg of her failed bid for state office, Perez Ferguson had been director of education and training for the Democratic National Committee. Her efforts on behalf of others have been rewarded by numerous organizations: She was awarded special recognition for her efforts on behalf of United Way in 1984, and in 1991 received both the Woman of Distinction award from the Soroptomist Club and the Santa Barbara County Commission for Women's Outstanding Woman Award.

**Profile by
Pamela L. Shelton**

GIGI FERNÁNDEZ

B *orn in 1964 in San Juan, Puerto Rico, Gigi Fernández was first*

introduced to tennis on her eighth birthday, when she received lessons

as a gift from her wealthy parents, physician Tuto Fernández and his

wife Beatriz. That present has led to a stellar career in tennis that

already includes accomplishments such as an Olympic gold medal, a

world doubles championship, a doubles crown at Wimbledon, and a

championship at the French Open. A strong server and volleyer, Fernández

reached the number-one ranking in the world in doubles in 1991. By

1995 she was setting courts afire with Russian player Natasha Zvereva,

her doubles partner of four years; together, the two have been hailed as

the best doubles team in the world and compared to the top-ranked

1964- •

Professional •

tennis

player

Martina Navratilova—Pam Shriver duo in their playing ability.

Almost immediately upon picking up a tennis racquet, Fernández found that the game came naturally to her. She was ranked number one in Puerto Rico as a junior player, despite the fact that she didn't practice a lot; her wins, as well as her racquet-breaking bouts of temper on court and extravagant tastes off-court kept her in the news. It wasn't until she arrived at South Carolina's Clemson University as a scholarship student that she began to dedicate herself to mastering the game of tennis. During her freshman year, Fernández made the finals in the NCAA singles championship, which fueled her decision to turn professional in 1985. That same year, Fernández was recognized by *Tennis* magazine as a "player to watch" for achieving a singles ranking of twenty-third in the world. Six years later, with a singles victory in Albuquerque, a semifinal finish in Eastbourne, and a quarterfinal finish at the U.S. Open—her best finish at a Grand Slam event—Fernández was ranked seventeenth in the world, her highest singles ranking to date.

Despite her success as a singles player, many observe that Fernández's strong serve-and-volley game is actually better suited to doubles playing. She has garnered six Grand Slam Women's doubles titles to date, including the U.S. Open in 1988, 1990, and 1992, the French Open in 1991 and 1992, and the Wimbledon Championships in 1992. In 1991, she and her partner captured the top spot in doubles tennis and at Barcelona in 1992, Fernández and partner Mary Joe Fernández (who is no relation) captured the doubles title, making Gigi the first Puerto Rican ever to win an Olympic gold medal.

• *Chance Meeting*

with Martina

Navratilova

Fernández credits an encounter with tennis great Martina Navratilova as giving her focus as a professional tennis player. The two first met at a players' party at Wimbledon when Navratilova approached Fernández, then an unknown on the tour, and asked if she had received a note Navratilova had sent in which she praised the young woman's performance, comparing it to her own doubles partner, Pam Shriver. Fernández had not yet seen the note but was shocked that the best player in the world had taken the time to write to her. When she later read what Navratilova had written, she was even more surprised: Navratilova went on to state that if Fernández worked hard and was disciplined, she had the potential to be among the game's best players.

"It was thrilling to me," Fernández later recalled in the *New York Times*. "I was ranked about 150 in the world and I weighed about 170 pounds. I had lost about 14 matches in a row in the first round and I was eating in frustration, porking out on ice cream and chocolate chip cookies—anything I could get my hands on. But when I read the note, I decided to change my diet and habits. I went home for a week and thought about what kind of tennis player I wanted to be."

Although Fernández said she took Navratilova's words to heart— the two even played doubles together for a time—she still intends to have as well-rounded a life as possible while maintaining her competitive edge. Her interests outside tennis include skiing, board-sailing, and modeling. She is also a promotional spokesperson for Avia clothing and footwear and Yonex racquets, and she frequently endorses products native to Puerto Rico. Even at work, Fernández is determined to enjoy herself: as she told the *Los Angeles Times*: "That's very important to me— to be able to have fun on the court because I play most relaxed when I'm having fun."

While tennis is not considered a major sport in Puerto Rico, Fernández has nevertheless captured her country's admiration with her winning ways, nominated as one of the five most influential women in her country's history in 1991. She has come under some criticism, however, for her decision to compete under the flag of the United States rather than Puerto Rico in the Federation Cup and Olympic tournaments. This choice, which she said in *Más* was "the most difficult of her life," was based solely on professional reasons. "Representing Puerto Rico I would have lost in the first round," she explained. The comments of her detractors are "like criticizing Raúl Julia for going to work in Hollywood or Justino Díaz for singing at the Metropolitan Opera of New York."

Her success thus far—numerous doubles titles, two individual titles, and over $1.8 million in lifetime prizewinnings—has nevertheless made Fernández an object of pride on her home island. Her success as a doubles player since pairing up with Zvereva—"We're having a great time" Fernández says of their 60-4 match record for the 1994 season. And as the first female Puerto Rican athlete to turn professional, she has paved the way for a new generation of female athletes on her island home. "In a way, it's kind of neat," Fernández remarked in *Hispanic,* "because it's opening a door for female athletes in Puerto Rico. Before, it was taboo for a female to make a living out of a sport. Girls are supposed to get married and have kids, so now maybe this opens the door."

Profile by Rosalva Hernandez

GISELLE FERNANDEZ

G iselle Fernandez's abilities as a top-ranking journalist and news **1961-** •

correspondent have fueled her rapid rise through the ranks of radio and

television news to become correspondent for the CBS Evening News. ***Journalist,*** •

Beginning her career at local stations in California, Illinois, and **network**

Florida, Fernandez worked as a news anchor on CBS This Morning **correspondent**

before gaining the slot on the major network's national evening news

program in 1992. But the climb upward has shown no signs of slowing

for the reporter: by 1994 she had been lured to CBS-rival NBC, where

late the following year it was announced that Fernadez would be

making the shift from hard news to entertainment as coanchor of that

network's syndicated Access Hollywood.

Fernandez was born on May 15, 1961, in Mexico City, Mexico. At the age of four, her family relocated to East Los Angeles, where her father worked as a flamenco dancer and her mother was a folklorist and professor at the University of California, Los Angeles (UCLA). In a telephone interview with Sally Foster, Fernandez recalled spending summers with her mother doing research in isolated Mexican villages. In her studies of mysticism, mythology, and Mexican traditions, Fernandez's mother interviewed hundreds of villagers; the reporter attributes her ambition to "get the story from the people" to those early experiences with her mother in Mexico.

At the age of fifteen, Fernandez moved to West Lake Village, California, where she attended and graduated from the public schools. When selecting a college, she was attracted to Goucher College in Baltimore, Maryland, because of both its reputation as a women's college and the recommendation of a number of friends. However, an internship in Washington, D.C., and the absence of family drew Fernandez back to California and the strong journalism program at the University of Southern California, Sacramento, where she participated in many internships in radio news. In 1983 she was awarded her bachelor of arts degree.

After graduation, Fernandez's first job in television was as a reporter at ABC affiliate KRDO in Colorado Springs. Offered advancement at Santa Barbara's KEYT, she was promoted to reporter and weekend anchor. In 1986 Fernandez had the opportunity to move to a larger media market in Los Angeles, when KTLA, the largest independent broadcaster in Los Angeles, hired her as a reporter and weekend anchor.

Wishing to expand her experience, Fernandez moved to Chicago in 1988 to work as a weekend anchor and reporter at a CBS affiliate. Her next major step was to take the position of weeknight anchor with a Miami station in 1989. In October 1991 Fernandez came to national attention as one of the anchors of *CBS This Morning*. Her talent was quickly recognized by corporate decision-makers, and she was promoted to correspondent on the *CBS Evening News* within only six months.

Fernandez revealed to Foster that she felt that all of the stories she had covered had importance. Several, however, have brought the talented journalist a special satisfaction. While serving as local news anchor in Miami, her coverage of the role of Israel in the Gulf War was of particular importance to the large Jewish community in the Miami area. The ability to furnish timely coverage on a major world event with a significant local perspective was very rewarding to both Fernandez—who is herself half Jewish on her mother's side—and the viewing audience. More recently, Fernandez was able to make use of her special knowledge of the Miami area in the CBS coverage of the devastation caused by 1992's Hurricane Andrew, a storm classified as one of the most destructive in history. During her ten days on site in Miami, Fernandez significantly contributed to the CBS news team's outstanding coverage—a reporting excellence recognized even by network competitors.

When asked about future trends in journalism, Fernandez predicts that "technology is heading to regionalize the news business, using special segments from networks. Culture and changing family patterns will change the way news will be delivered." She sees the news as a service industry providing the down-to-earth information people need in their daily lives. In spite of the trend toward cutbacks in network news departments, Fernandez believes that there has already been a return to thorough and aggressive reporting on important issues and a movement away from the "star" industry.

And of her own life? Because of the hard work and crazy hours demanded of people in her profession, Fernandez has little free time; when she does manage to find some, she likes to dance, run, and read books on topics as diverse as science fiction and philosophy. "I've been all over," the television journalist told *Hispanic,* describing her erratic schedule. But for Fernandez it has definitely been worth it: "I get to see history unfold. It's a tremendous privilege."

**Profile by
Sally Foster**

MARY JOE FERNÁNDEZ

A well-known name on the women's professional tennis circuit,

1971- •

Mary Joe Fernández has been playing professionally since the age of 14.

It has only been since 1990, when she started playing full time on the

Professional •

women's circuit, that Fernández has begun to make a serious bid to

tennis

become the world's top-ranked female player. Probably her brightest

player

moment in tennis thus far was when she and doubles partner Gigi

Fernández of Puerto Rico captured the gold medal for the United States

at the 1992 Olympics in Barcelona, defeating Spain's own Arantxa

Sánchez Vicario and Conchita Martínez with King Juan Carlos looking

on.

Born in 1971 in the Dominican Republic to José and Sylvia Fernández,

Mary Joe moved with her family to Miami when she was six months old. At age three she began to play tennis. Her sister Sylvia recounted to the *New York Times* that when her father took her to play tennis, Mary Joe often tagged along. To keep his younger daughter occupied, José bought her a racquet so she could bounce tennis balls off of a wall. Two years later, Fernández started taking lessons from a professional tennis player.

Fernández showed talent for the game very early on. At age ten she won the United States Tennis Association Nationals for players aged twelve and under. At eleven she won the Orange Bowl singles title for players twelve and under and proceeded to win the title again at age fourteen for sixteen-and-under and at age fourteen for eighteen-and-under players. Fernández also won the United States Tennis Association championship for sixteen-and-under players and the U.S. Clay Court Championship for her age in 1984. She played in her first professional tournament when she was thirteen, participating as an amateur, and beat her first-round opponent, thirty-three-year-old Pam Teeguarden, but lost the following match. That same year, she defeated the world's eleventh-ranked player, Bonnie Gadusek.

As a fourteen-year-old freshman at Carrollton School of the Sacred Heart, Mary Joe began to feel pressure to turn pro and play the professional circuit full time. Despite financial considerations, she resisted and became a straight-A student at Carrollton. "I just decided that if I was going to go to school, I was going to do it right," she told *Sports Illustrated* in 1991. "And I wasn't ready to sacrifice being with my friends." Fernández did, however, enter four Grand Slam tournaments and various other tournaments over the next three-and-a-half years, working them in around her high school classes. "If Mary Joe doesn't want to study, we make her study," her father José told *Sports Illustrated*. "If she doesn't want to play tennis, we don't make Mary Joe play."

Many credit such a balanced approach with preventing Fernánez from burning out on the game too soon or pushing her body too early, as some of her contemporaries such as Tracy Austin and Andrea Jaeger have done. But she did gain valuable experience in the few Grand Slam events in which she competed. In her very first Wimbledon match as a fourteen-year-old, she faced her idol, Chris Evert Lloyd, losing in straight sets. She also missed her high school graduation because she was competing in the French Open.

1990, Fernández's first year as a full-time participant on the pro tour, proved both encouraging and discouraging. She won forty of sixty singles matches and two tournaments, including her first-ever professional tournament championship in the Tokyo Indoors. With endorsements, her earnings topped $1 million that year. However, Fernández also received several injuries during the year. In March of 1990 she tore a hamstring in a Virginia Slims match against rival Gabriela Sabatini; two months later her back went out during a third-round match in the German Open; prior to Wimbledon, a severe knee sprain prevented her from competing in that tournament; finally, after losing in the final of the Australian Open to Steffi Graf, she returned home with tendinitis in her right shoulder. Many speculated—and Fernández herself acknowledged—that some of the injuries may have resulted from her lack of a consistent conditioning program; she had sometimes ignored her coaches' suggestions that she build her upper body strength. Since her injuries, she has begun a conditioning regimen using a strength coach.

The conditioning has paid off: Fernández, consistently ranked among the top seven women players in the world, reached as high as fourth in late 1990 through early 1991. However, Fernández's approach to her sport has made her stand out from her top-ranking comrades. "I play from a different place," she told Peter Bodo in *Tennis*. "I don't think my ego gets as involved in things as some other players'.... the real joy I get out of tennis is being able to put into play what I've practiced, to work out a strategy for winning a match or for dealing with an opponent's weapons. Some people might think that I just play because I like tennis, but it does go deeper than that. I love the competition."

Even with her love of competition, one of the roadblocks Fernández has had to overcome to maintain her competitiveness with the top women has been mental toughness. "[Steffi] Graf and [Monica] Seles go into tournaments expecting to win," former coach Tom Gullickson told *Sports Illustrated*. "Mary Joe hopes she'll win . . . when she does, I think she's still a little bit surprised." Fernández herself feels that it is not whether or not she is tough. As she told Bodo, "It's a question of being able to develop a game that can win Grand Slam titles, and then execute it in a big final."

In 1992 she reached the semifinals in the singles at the U.S. Open before losing to eventual champion Seles. The following year, however, her name was absent from the U.S. Open roster after Fernández was hospitalized due to endometriosis. But as the fifth-seeded player, she recovered her strength and came back to triumph against Sabatini and Arantxa Sanches Vicario, making the finals in the French Open but ultimately losing to Graf.

With an Olympic gold medal under her belt, Fernández is still moving toward her goal: becoming the top female player in the world. Observers say she has had more success in doubles, winning eight tournaments with various partners, including the 1991 Australian Open with Patti Fendwick, Lipton with Zina Garrison, and Toyko Nichirei with Pam Shriver. In 1991, at age seventeen, she became the thirty-third woman to earn more than $1 million; her career earnings top $2.2 million. Even at her young age, she has been as successful off the court as on; in 1992 she helped organize a benefit tennis match in Miami to aid in the relief effort for the victims of Hurricane Andrew, which devastated parts of her home state.

**Profile by
Jonathan J. Higuera**

MARÍA IRENE FORNÉS

A *lthough not well known by casual theatergoers, María Irene*

1930- •

Fornés is often ranked among the most original contemporary writers

and producers of plays. Dubbed the "Picasso of theatre" by Hispanic, *she*

Playwright •

has earned six Obie Awards, a coveted prize given to shows representing

the best that Off-Broadway has to offer. Her list of achievements—

Fornés has written over thirty plays and has produced and directed

numerous stage productions of both her own works and those of other

playwrights—is all the more impressive when one considers that she

wrote her first play at age thirty.

Fornés was born in Havana, Cuba, on May 14, 1930, to Carlos Luis and Carmen Hismenia (Collado) Fornés. Although he had worked for the government at one time, Carlos Fornés was what *Hispanic* described as an "intellectual rebel." Descended from a family of educators,

Fornés's father read a great deal; to make sure that his daughters could do so as well, he taught them at home. During the years that María attended Escuela Publica No. 12 in Havana, her intellectual growth could be credited, in part, to her father's caring direction.

After the death of her husband, Carmen Fornés packed up her family of six daughters and left Cuba for New York. María was just fifteen and the fact that she could not speak English limited her opportunities. Fortunately, she found work in a ribbon factory, where she kept military decorations in their proper positions on an assembly line. However, after two weeks she was determined to improve things for herself; Fornés learned to speak English and found work as a translator. Even this job, however, did not suit the independent Fornés. She began her own business, working as a doll maker to support herself, while also beginning to paint seriously. Fornés also became a naturalized citizen of the United States in 1951. Three years later, her painting took her to Europe, but by 1957 Fornés had returned to New York. She worked in the city as a textile designer until 1960. Although Fornés's paintings went unacclaimed, the ten years she practiced her art were well spent—her painting contributed to the structures of the award-winning plays she later wrote.

Fornés explained how her concept of dramatic structure was linked to her experience as a painter: "Hans Hofmann always talked about push and pull . . . the dynamics created between colors when you place one color very close to another or anywhere else in the canvas.... The color and shape of the form would create this tension . . . that had a very strong impact on my play writing, because I compose my plays guided not by story line but more by energies that take place within each scene, and also the energies that take place between one scene and the scene that follows." While she was painting, however, Fornés had no idea that one type of art would lead to another. She only knew that she had difficulty disciplining herself to paint. "I thought that it was normal for a young person to prefer being in coffee houses to working at home," she recalled.

In retrospect, Fornés understood her trouble. "I think the reason I was having a hard time painting was that it wasn't the form of art that was best suited for me." She discovered her calling in 1960 when, in an effort to help her roommate, the philosopher and critic Susan Sontag, break her writer's block she began to write a play, borrowing her words from a cookbook. The urge to write consumed her; she spent nineteen days working on her first play. As she explained in *Interviews with Contemporary Women Playwrights,* "I loved [writing] it, it was such a thrill. I started writing late; I was around thirty. I had never thought I would write; as I said, I was an aspiring painter. But once I started writing it was so pleasurable that I couldn't stop." Fornés's first published play, *La Viuda,* or *The Widow,* appeared in 1961 in *Cuatro Autores Cubanos;* she subsequently received a John Hay Whitney Foundation fellowship in 1961, and a Centro Mexicano de Escritores fellowship in 1962. Fornés's inspiration and enthusiasm soared. She had seen Zero Mostel perform in *Ulysses,* and she unconsciously imagined him as a character in what became her first produced play, *There! You Died.* She had intended to write about a power struggle between a man and a computer, but she realized that the computer would be better replaced by a person, a Zero Mostel-like character. In the play, two male lovers battle as father and son, teacher and pupil, in a seemingly endless tango, until one murders the other in a bullfight. *There! You Died* (or *Tango Palace*) finally appeared in 1963 and was a success; Fornés's career as a serious playwright had begun.

During the mid- to late 1960s, Fornés was very active in the New York theatre world. *The Successful Life of 3,* won Fornés acclaim when it appeared with *Tango Palace* in 1965. In *The Successful Life of 3,* He, She, and 3 become entrenched in a love triangle which is presented in ten short vignettes over a sixteen-year period. Time and space are distorted and parodies abound; "freeze" shots contribute to the destruction of traditional theatrical molds. According to *American Playwrights,* this "beautifully orchestrated" play "represents Fornés at her comic best." The 1965 Off-Off Broadway musical, *Promenade,* followed, a comedy about two escaped prisoners who return to prison after spending time in the outside world. Fornés won an Obie award for distinguished play writing in 1965 for *The Successful Life of 3* and *Promenade.* She followed that success with *The Office,* which previewed on Broadway in 1965 but which never officially opened.

In 1967 *The Annunciation* was paired up Off-Off Broadway with *The Successful Life of 3.* Meanwhile, Fornés wrote and produced 1967's *A Vietnamese Wedding* to protest U.S. involvement in the Vietnam War; the following year's anti-war *The Red Burning Light: or Mission XQ,* was produced in Zurich, Switzerland and at La Mama Experimental Theatre Off-Off Broadway. In 1968, *Dr. Kheal* appeared, moving to London in 1969. One of Fornés's most frequently produced plays is this portrayal of the eccentric Dr. Kheal, as he gives lectures on ancient intellectual questions. Many of Fornés's plays were published in 1971's *Promenade and Other Plays.*

In 1972, while serving for a year as a teacher at Theatre for the New City in New York City, Fornés cofounded the New York Theatre Strategy. Serving as the group's president from 1973 to 1978, Fornés hoped to help make opportunities available for playwrights whose works would not otherwise be produced. The efforts of the now-defunct New York Theatre Strategy have contributed to the production of countless experimental productions.

Meanwhile her *The Curse of the Langston House* was produced in Cincinnati in late 1972, followed by *Aurora,* which appeared Off-Off-Broadway in 1974. The Spanish-language *Cap-a-Pie,* with music by José Raúl Bernardo, was produced in 1975 at INTAR (International Arts Relations), the native Spanish theatre of New York; *Lolita in the Garden,* also written in Spanish, was shown at INTAR in 1977. In that same year, *Fefu and Her Friends,* one of Fornés's most successful plays and the winner of an Obie award, was produced Off-Off-Broadway at New York Theatre Strategy.

According to *Performing Arts Journal,* "one could say that *Fefu* and the plays that followed it . . . have paved the way for a new language of dramatic realism, and a way of directing it.... Fornés brings a much needed intimacy to drama, and her economy of approach suggests another vision of theatricality, more stylized for its lack of exhibition-ism." Many critics recognized these traits in *Fefu and Her Friends.* Taking place in 1935, as eight friends gather in Fefu's New England home, this play symbolically discusses feminism and a host of other interrelated issues. *Fefu and Her Friends* is noted for its originality; for the second act, the audience is asked to travel to four different rooms to view four different scenes. This enables the audience to share an intimate, personal space with the characters and get to know them up close as they ponder alone in bed or review a lost lesbian love affair.

Fornés went on to write and produce *In Service* at the Claremont, California, Padua Hills Festival in 1978. *Eyes on the Harem* was her next project. Produced in 1979 at INTAR, this play exploits feminist themes in legends from the Turkish Ottoman empire. The *New York Times* wrote that while it was "farfetched" at times, the play was "hardly ever ponderous." Critics enjoyed the "Meet Me in St. Louis" scene which, according to a reviewer for the *New Yorker,* was "indelible." For this play, Fornés won another Obie Award for distinguished direction.

During the early 1980s, Fornés continued her rapid pace; she wrote or adapted and produced plays prolifically. In 1980 she produced *Evelyn Brown (A Diary)* Off-Off-Broadway. Her adaptations of Spanish poet and playwright Federico García Lorca's *Blood Wedding* and the surreal *Life Is Dream* by Pedro Calderon de la Barca, in 1980 and 1981 respectively, were both produced at INTAR. *A Visit* and *The Danube,* both original works, were produced for the Padua Hills Festival and later

Off-Off-Broadway. The former, which appeared in 1981, was a musical comedy about a young girl who flits about the home of a family in Lansing, Michigan, in 1910, and allows herself to be seduced by various men and women. The latter play, *The Danube*, was produced in 1982, 1983, and 1984; in it, Paul and Eve fail to communicate with each other and thus destroy their relationship. Frequent backdrop changes and foreign language tapes contribute to the idea that men and women speak different languages.

Mud, which concerns a more violent love triangle, was produced in 1983 for the Padua Hills Festival. As with every play Fornés wrote for this festival, *Mud* was designed for its set. It was performed outdoors, and it ended near sunset—freezes were used to end scenes instead of blackouts, and the fading light made the costumed characters look drab. Fornés liked these effects and adopted them for the work's New York production. *Sarita,* produced at INTAR, and *No Time,* a Padua Hills Festival production, contributed to Fornés's Obie Award for 1984.

Fornés's *The Conduct of Life,* a story about a Latin American man who is forced to perform violent acts as a government torturer and who acts just as violently within his own home, was produced Off-Off-Broadway, receiving an Obie for best new play in 1985. Her adaptation and translation of Virgilio Pinera's *Cold Air* won the playwright a Playwrights U.S.A. Award. *Mud, The Danube, Sarita,* and *The Conduct of Life* were collected in *María Irene Fornés: Plays* in 1986; the book's preface was written by Fornés's former roommate, Susan Sontag.

In March of 1986 *A Matter of Faith* appeared Off-Off-Broadway, and *Lovers and Keepers,* composed of three one-act musicals, was produced that same year at INTAR. *Lovers* featured music by the famous Latin jazz musicians Tito Puente and Fernando Rivas. Fornés's next project was *Drowning,* a one-act adaptation of a story by Anton Chekhov, produced with six other one-act plays as *Orchards.* Productions of *Art* and *The Mothers* rounded out 1986. *Abingdon Square,* a shocking drama about a fifteen-year-old girl who, married to an older man, seeks a real love, was produced by Fornés Off-Broadway in 1987; it won her yet another Obie. Also in 1987, she adapted Chekhov's *Uncle Vanya* and produced it Off-Broadway. In 1989, the playwright wrote *Hunger,* which explores an imaginary future of socio-economic collapse and its human consequences; it was first produced Off-Off-Broadway by En Garde Productions. *And What of the Night,* a show that included *Hunger, Springtime, Lust,* and *Charlie* (previously entitled *The Mothers*), was produced in Milwaukee, Wisconsin, in 1989.

The decade of the 1990s was one of continued success for Fornés. Her one-act play *Oscar and Bertha* was staged in San Francisco in 1992, in a production that was praised for its slapstick visual humor. "The author's directoral approach to her own material is rambunctious, often cartoonishly lewd," noted *Variety*. In 1994 Fornés directed a production of Cuban playwright Manuel Pereiras Garcia's *It Is It is Not* at Theatre for the New City. Later that same year, *Terra Incognito* emerged during the Padua Hills Festival, the story of three American tourists stop while on a vacation in Spain to argue about subjects as diverse as the Gulf War and a play by Edward Albee.

According to Fornés, although there is "a rich Spanish tradition of classic theater . . . there hasn't been a strong modern Hispanic theater" since the turn of the century. The "Hispanic American doesn't have a model yet"; she believes that it is "very important to try to work with Hispanic playwrights at a level where they are just beginning to write, so that they don't dismiss possibilities of ways of writing that would be very original to them but ways they would not see models for in the active American or English or German theater." She does more than advocate such instruction; Fornés has continually instructed young Hispanic writers both at the Padua Hills Festival and at INTAR; in 1988, she led a workshop at Manhattanville College in Purchase, New York.

A leader as well as a playwright, Fornés has made an invaluable contribution to the arts. Her plays are remarkable for their exciting and unusual forms, their striking contents, and their memorable characters. She has also received numerous awards, including fellowships from the Cintas Foundation, Yale University, Boston University-Tanglewood, and the Guggenheim Foundation, and grants from the National Endowment for the Arts, the New York State Council on the Arts, the Rockefeller Foundation, and two Creative Arts Public Service grants. In addition to numerous Obie awards, including one in 1982, for sustained achievement, Fornés received the prestigious American Academy and Institute of Arts and Letters Award in Literature in 1985.

But such awards are secondary to the aims of the playwright who, in addition to writing and producing plays, has assisted countless authors struggling to find their own voices. Fornés is considered by many to be a champion of Hispanics and women; she writes to inspire and acknowledge both groups, and serves as an extraordinary role model for each. As a critic for the *Chicago Tribune* wrote, Fornés is "one of the art form's most cherished secrets. Ask playgoers about her, and they are apt to answer with a blank look. Mention Fornés to those who work in the theater, and their faces light up." Whether or not the public appreciates her work, however, Fornés enjoys the process of creation. "I find more pleasure in the creating part of [my work], and I think that's the

Profile by
Ronie-Richele
Garcia-Johnson

reason why I am always willing to keep experimenting and inventing things."

DAISY FUENTES

*C*haucito, baby." That's the way MTV-host Daisy Fuentes signs off

on each segment of her popular "MTV Internacional" show, interna-

tionally syndicated via Telemundo. From the time she first stepped in

front of the camera in her first job as a Manhattan TV weather-girl,

Fuentes has successfully marketed her Latina good looks, effervescent

personality, and excellent speaking skills before an ever-increasing

Latin American audience. She has become, in the process, a woman

who the New York Times calls "one of the most visible American pop

culture exports, and one of the few who speak the language."

1966- •

MTV-VJ, •

model,

actress

Fuentes was born November 17, 1966, in Havana, Cuba. One of two daughters of Maria and Amado Fuentes, she and her family left Cuba in 1969 and lived in Madrid, Spain, for several years before immigrating to the United States in 1973. The family—Daisy's mother is a painter and

her father a grocer and real estate investor—eventually made their home in Harrison, New Jersey, where Fuentes and her younger sister, Rosanna, learned to adapt to living in a primarily Anglo community. After some initial shyness, Fuentes became increasingly popular with her schoolmates, and was elected as her high school's first Latina homecoming queen. With career aspirations that included, as Fuentes told *Vogue,* "open[ing] up my own beauty shop because I was always doing my friends' hair and makeup," she graduated from high school in 1984.

It was while working as a runway model assignments for an Italian couturier named Dimitri to put herself through college that Fuentes was encouraged to pursue a career in communications. An encounter with the Ecuadorian wife of an executive at a Spanish-language television station in New York led to her first job in journalism; after graduating from Bergen Community College in 1986, Fuentes applied and was hired by WXTV, where she served as a news reporter and weather anchorperson. In 1987 she moved to WNJU, Telemundo's New York base, where she kept Spanish-speaking New Yorkers informed of changes in the city climate until 1990.

Meanwhile, Fuentes, who found working the weather beat unexciting, decided to investigate other avenues in her chosen field of journalism and sent an audition tape to MTV in 1987. By the following year, Fuentes had become a VJ—short for video jock—on MTV's Latin programs. As the host of the Spanish-language "MTV Internacional" since 1988, Fuentes has travelled to many of the seventeen Latin American countries in which the popular music show is syndicated, including Costa Rica, Ecuador, Mexico, Paraguay, and Venezuela. And 1993 found Fuentes busy, both soaking up the sun while hosting the U.S.-televised summertime show "Beach MTV," and using her bilingual skills on "MTV Latino," a 24-hour-a-day Spanish-language show that premiered on the popular cable music-video network the following October. In the winter of 1995, a new show called "Mt. MTV" kept Fuentes busy during the winter months as well, as she hosted music video-based entertainment from an Aspen, Colorado, ski resort.

But chatting between music video segments wasn't the only thing to occupy Fuentes's time. In 1991 the versatile Latina was cast in a recurring role as the character "Tess" on ABC Television's popular daytime drama *Loving.* And in 1993, she also appeared in the pilot for PBS's *Ghostwriter* series. In addition to her work in front of a motion picture camera, her face graced the cover of *Spanish Bazaar* and *Cosmopolitan* in 1990; the following year found her on the cover of both *Vanity Fair* and *Vanidades,* as well as *People* magazine's best-dressed list. By 1995 Fuentes's hosting duties had extended to the Miss USA and

Life beyond •

MTV

Miss Universe pageants, and she was reportedly sounding out ABC on a possible television sitcom role.

With Fuentes' repeated appearances before the camera it was inevitable that she attracted the attention of the modeling world. In 1993 the photogenic Latina signed a multiyear contract with cosmetics giant Revlon to appear in an international ad campaign entitled "Unforgettable Women." Along with such supermodels as Claudia Schiffer and fellow-MTV host Cindy Crawford, Fuentes has appeared in both magazine and television ads around the world, extolling the virtues of Revlon products. But such success hasn't made her forget her Latina roots. "I'm well known in the Spanish market and that's something I don't want to leave," Fuentes stated in the *New York Times*. I don't want all of a sudden to become this Anglo superstar and forget where I started." However, Fuentes also maintained that her varied cultural allegiances were precisely the reason she was so ideal for Revlon. "It's very difficult to find a young person in the country who doesn't sound like where they're from, which is not really great when you're aiming to all of Latin America," she explained. "I pull off a very neutral Spanish accent. People come up to me and ask me all the time where I'm from."

In addition to her many hours spent on the road and in front of the camera, Fuentes has also managed to find the time to indulge in a few hobbies—including romance. In 1990, she married her high school sweetheart, model, actor, and fitness trainer Timothy Adams; in between his acting assignments and her many on-location film spots, the couple makes their home in Secaucus, New Jersey. It's an area that Fuentes still conciders home, even though her parents left New Jersey for Miami in the early 1990s. But neither distance nor fame has changed the actress's close relationship with her parents. "Latin families never let go of their kids," Fuentes explained to interviewer Susan Wloszczyna in *USA Today*. "I have a lot of American friends, and for them, it's like, when you turn 18, you're on your own, kid. I think I could be 50 and [my parents] would still be telling me what to do, what to eat and drink your milk."

In addition to her career as a journalist, model, and budding actress, Fuentes has also tried her hand at business as coowner of a small, trendy restaurant called Dish, located on New York City's Upper East Side and patronized by many of her friends. Even with such varied successes, Fuentes continues to expand her opportunities and her influence: she has studied acting at the American Academy of Dramatic Arts with the goal of one day starring in a television comedy sitcom. "Do you know any Hispanics who are on sitcoms, in the movies, on soaps?," she asked an interviewer for *Hispanic*. "Maybe a tiny handful. That's not enough."

• *Broadening the*

Exposure of All

Hispanics

Fuentes was honored as an outstanding woman in media by the Latin Coalition for Fair Media in 1992. Accepting that honor was one of the many things that has made Fuentes fully aware of the responsibilities that go along with being an Hispanic celebrity. "At first I thought, I don't need this," she told the *New York Times*. "I don't want to be good for the rest of my life, but I'm trying to do the right thing, and if I screw up, I hope people will realize I'm human." And her role as a media figure has made her keenly aware of the strides still ahead for Latinas. As she told *Hispanic:* "[Revlon's] openness to me was groundbreaking. Their openmindedness toward me as a Latina gave me hope to get out there into the mainstream and break barriers. I wish more companies would hire us. It would mean so much to us as Hispanics."

Profile by Pamela L. Shelton

NELY GALÁN

1964- •

N ely Galán has transcended the usually tedious process of achiev-

ing success in the television industry; in fact, many have described her

rise through the ranks in the television industry as meteoric. By 1991,

President of •

when she was only twenty-seven years old, Galán was the host of her

gaLÁn

own syndicated talk show, Bravo, produced in both Spanish- and

entertainment

English-language versions, which aired throughout the United States.

Only a few years later she was at the helm of her own production

company, gaLÁn entertainment. Galán has appeared on news

programs around the country, managed a New Jersey television station,

and has developed numerous programs for network clients that include

Home Box Office (HBO). Talented as well as persistent, Galán is determined to help shape the future of television produced for U.S.-born Hispanics. "We're a lost generation with no role models," she said of twenty-something Latino viewers in an interview with *USA Today*. "You damage a whole group of people because they're not seen anywhere, and that reflects badly on their self-esteem."

Born in Cuba in 1964, Galán came with her family to New Jersey when she was still an infant. She was raised in a traditional family—her father worked as a salesman for Goya Foods—and attended the all-girl Academy of the Holy Angels in Demarest, New Jersey. While she set her sights on becoming a writer, Galán's family thought she should follow tradition and focus on getting married. As Galán told *Hispanic*, "My mother wanted me to be a wife and a concert pianist—but only play the piano at home." Not surprisingly, considering Galán's professional ambitions, she protested when her family attempted to steer her down such traditional paths. One such protest, an article bemoaning the pain of being sent to a strict Catholic school, which she wrote at the age of fifteen, found its way to the desk of the editors of *Seventeen* magazine. "It was the best thing that ever happened to me," Galán recalled to the *New York Times Magazine*. "It was total revenge on the nuns." Impressed, the popular magazine published the young woman's article and offered her a guest editorship, which she promptly accepted. "I accelerated my class schedule and got to graduate early. And that's when I realized that being a wimp doesn't pay off."

However, Galán became more interested in television work than writing. When her editorship with *Seventeen* ended, the newly married Galán got a job as an anchor on *Checking It Out,* a PBS news show for teenagers that was produced in Boston. Working for *Checking It Out* gave Galán the opportunity to travel throughout the United States interviewing guests and filming stories. During these two years she began to understand the power of television, and those in the business began to recognize her talent. Galán decided to become a producer.

One of her first jobs was to assist with the production of the special *Since JFK: The Last 20 Years*; her contributions helped that special win an Emmy award. Her next position gave her much more authority, if not a luxurious work setting. As she recalled in *Hispanic,* she worked in a "one-room shack" as the station manager for WNJU-TV in Teterboro, New Jersey. In addition to being responsible for the Spanish-language station's $15 million budget and a staff of some one hundred people, the twenty-two-year-old producer had to cope with "asbestos falling from the ceiling." She also had to deal with some fall-out in her personal life, which resulted in a divorce. Despite the dilapidated condition of the station, Galán stayed at WNJU-TV for three years; she was then the youngest television station manager in the United States.

The ambitious young woman's dreams soon turned to buying her own television station, but she realized that, even if she could come up with the required funds, she did not have the authority needed to own a station herself. While CBS had made her a very tempting offer to anchor a show aired from WCAU-TV in Philadelphia, Galán had, at first, scorned the offer. As she explained in *Hispanic,* "I didn't want to be anchor-woman. Puhleassse. I had a chip on my shoulder.... I thought, 'Oh, these people just want a token Hispanic.'" However, she reconsidered, realizing it would gain her stature in the communications field. Galán took CBS up on their offer—but on her own terms: she also arranged to host a television talk show and contractually retained the syndication rights to her English and Spanish shows, called *Bravo.*

Finally, Galán began to earn the authority she sought, becoming a respected businesswoman in the television industry. Audiences loved both Galán and her show, which dealt with serious and intriguing topics. By 1988 *Bravo* was airing on thirty-one different television stations, including those in Miami, San Antonio, and other U.S. cities with large Hispanic populations. The twenty-six-year-old Galán found herself with the ability to enter into a joint venture with Cable-TV giant HBO and run her own television production company, which she named Tropix. By the end of the decade, Galán had another talk-show, *Nely,* which aired on WBBM-TV. She also became the co-anchor of NBC-TV's *House Party.* And in the early 1990s, E! Entertainment Television hired Galán as host of their new *The Gossip Show,* which Galán planned to spin off into a Spanish-language version.

During the early 1990s Galán became more and more concerned about the future of television shows produced for Hispanic audiences. It was apparent to her that, while some Hispanic viewers appreciated Spanish shows, other, younger Hispanics preferred English-speaking shows. As she told *Hispanic,* "I asked 30 kids, when you think of Spanish TV what do you think of? And they said things like, 'Ugh, it's embarrassing. I would never watch it.' It embarrasses them! I was heartbroken!" Recognizing the need for two kinds of television aimed at Hispanic audiences, she wrote to one of the networks to explain her concerns. "There is a tremendous gap between the Hispanic market that watches Spanish-language television and the untapped market that knows who [Nobel Prize-winning Columbian novelist] Gabriel García Márquez is. You need one for survival; you need the other for our future. The gap must be bridged."

Buys Television •

Production

Company

By creating a supply of both types of television shows, Galán is beginning to build that bridge herself. In June of 1994, her first program, a four-segment comedy special called *Loco Slam!*, premiered on HBO as part of that network's late-night lineup. "The unifying theme is that we're all second-generation Latinos," Galán told the *Los Angeles Times* of the new show. "(We're) children of immigrants, and the comedy comes from that." Since then, involvement opportunities in several sitcoms for ABC, a Latin dance show, and several dramas for Fox Television, as well as numerous hosting situations, have continued to come her way. And in 1994, Galán, along with friend and associate Concepción Lara, received the Broadcast Designers Association Gold Award for their creation of the Fox Latin American Channel logo graphics. As she continues to build the bridge between U.S. and Latin American television audiences, Galán retains a strong focus: "I want to create a company that will become a cultural institution for Latinos," she told *USA Today,* "the same way Motown was for blacks."

**Profile by
Ronie-Richele
Garcia-Johnson**

CRISTINA GARCIA

1958- •

Journalist, •

novelist

*C*ristina Garcia successfully climbed the journalistic ranks at Time

magazine before deciding to change career paths and write her first

novel, Dreaming in Cuban, *which was nominated for a National Book*

Award in 1992. Recalling the history of her own family, the characters

in Garcia's novel delve into the issues faced by her parents and so many

of their friends and neighbors during the Cuban Revolution of the

1950s. Dreaming in Cuban, *which tells the story of three strong Cuban*

women with very different perspectives on the revolution, was praised by

critics. A reviewer for Time *lauded the work, noting of Garcia, "Her*

special feat is to tell it in a style as warm and gentle as the 'sustaining

aromas of vanilla and almond,' as rhythmic as the music of Beny

More."

Garcia was born July 4, 1958, in Havana, Cuba, the daughter of Frank M. Garcia and Hope Lois Garcia. She fled with her parents to the United States when she was two years old, and was raised among American friends, with English as her primary language. As a youth, Garcia wanted to join the foreign service; she earned a bachelor of arts degree in political science from Barnard College in 1979, and went on to major in Latin American studies at Johns Hopkins University's School of Advanced International Studies, graduating in 1981.

Contrary to her early dreams, Garcia's life soon took a different path when she chose to pursue a career in journalism. Her first career move was to land a job at *Time* magazine in 1983. Beginning as a reporter and researcher, Garcia held various positions at *Time* over the next seven years, including bureau chief from 1987-88 and as a correspondent, a position she held from 1985-90. During her tenure at the noted news magazine, she focussed on subjects of interest to Hispanics, interviewing several Latin American celebrities, such as Peruvian author and politician Mario Vargas Llosa.

By 1990 Garcia realized that it was time to change directions again; instead of reporting factual information in structured journalistic prose, she wanted to use her writing to bring the pictures in her imagination to life. As she told the *Ann Arbor News,* as a journalist she found herself growing tired of "telling the truth." One day she wrote a poem about three crazy women who kill themselves; the feeling of being liberated by her words prompted Garcia to take a leave of absence from *Time* to explore her options. Although she returned to the magazine three months later, she soon quit for good, "frustrated with the constraints of journalism and the journalism of *Time*." Her surroundings were also a factor to her decision to make a break from journalism; living in Miami, immersed in Cuban culture and meeting Cubans, "all the issues of my childhood came bubbling up," the soon-to-be novelist explained.

Garcia worked towards her goal of bringing to life the stories of her imagination for two years, with *Dreaming in Cuban* the end result. Exploring the issues of her childhood and her culture was a means for Garcia to understand her ancestors and their special struggles. Like many of those who abandoned their homeland, Garcia's parents were vilified by the country's new president, the communist Fidel Castro. They were officially exiled. "First generation Americans, they live cut-off from a homeland their parents cannot forgive and their new country forbids them to visit," a *Time* reporter explained in reviewing Garcia's book. "In her impressive first novel, *Dreaming in Cuban*, Garcia takes back her island."

Explores Cuban •

Revolution in

Novel

Garcia's story concerns three generations of Cuban women and their different reactions to the revolution. The book takes the reader back to the year 1972, on to a beach in Cuba, and introduces Celia del Pino, a staunch believer in communism, who volunteers for stints in the sugarcane fields and serves as the local civilian judge. Meanwhile, Celia's daughter Lourdes Puente lives in Brooklyn, New York, where she owns a bakery and is dependent on capitalism to make her business survive. Celia's other daughter, the delusional Felicia, spouts the political dogma of santeria, a religion that uses voodoo and Christian symbolism.

Garcia's novel sheds new light on Latin Americans for her readers. As a reviewer in *Publishers Weekly* wrote, "Embracing fantasy and reality with equal fervor, Garcia's vivid, indelible characters offer an entirely new view of a particular Latin American sensibility." In addition, as Garcia told the *Ann Arbor News,* the book shed a new light on her own upbringing. As a child she had heard many anti-Castro sentiments. "When I was growing up, I was in a virulently anti-Castro home," she recalled, "so Cuba was painted for me as a very monstrous place, an island prison.... Writing this helped me to understand my parents and their generation a little better." Married to Scott Brown since 1990, Garcia now has a daughter, Pilar, in whom she hopes to instill a balanced understanding of her Cuban heritage. Since publication of *Dreaming in Cuban,* Garcia has received several honors, including a Cintas fellowship and the Hodder fellowship from Princeton University.

Profile by
D. D. Andreassi

CARMEN LOMAS GARZA

*P*aintings, etchings and lithographs are Carmen Lomas Garza's

1948- •

way of sharing her personal vision of the traditions and customs of her

rural Chicano community in Texas. Mining the vibrant images of her

Visual artist •

strong, expressive culture, the nationally honored artist creates colourful

and richly detailed renditions of her own unique history. Sharing her

creative vision with new generations, Garza has also gathered together

many of her works in Family Pictures: Cuadros de familia, *a children's*

book that reflects the strong traditional ties among Hispanic family

members.

Garza was born in 1948 in Kingsville, Texas, a small town located southwest of Corpus Christi. Her parents, Mucio B. Sr. and Maria Lomas Garza, were themselves artistic—her mother was a self-taught artist and her father was an artisan who worked in both sheet metal and wood—

and they passed their creativity on to their impressionable daughter. In an interview with Jose Adan Moreno in *Caminos,* Garza described her childhood ambitions: "I remember doing a lot of drawing in elementary school, but the turning point came when I made the decision to concentrate on being a professional artist when I was about 13 years old."

Garza began her college education at Texas Arts and Industry University. While still an undergraduate, some of her prints were featured in the journal *El grito* in 1971. By the time she received her bachelor of science degree in 1972, Garza had developed a highly individualistic style. After graduation, she she went on to study at Antioch Graduate School and was granted her Master of Education degree in 1973. Relocating to California, Garza entered the master's program at San Francisco State University, where she received her master of arts degree in 1980. She also worked as a curator administrative assistant at the Galeria/Studio 24 in San Francisco until 1981.

Since her college days, Garza has largely concentrated on weaving a pictorial depiction of the traditions of Chicano culture. Drawing on her childhood memories, she captures the magic of daily life found such activities as the gathering of cactus during Lent, children playing, family and neighborhood activities, and the maintaining of home altars using a stylized depiction of figures called *monitos*. Rather than distancing herself through commentaries, Garza shares her private visions with her audience. Prints from her earliest period are dominated by the use of stark black and white, modified only by the limited use of aquatints. Strong contrast is evident, both in the monochromatic color scheme and in the use of tightly executed patterns. Increasingly, Garza began to add more color to her work, employing water colors to enhance skin tone and to accentuate special objects in her prints.

Relates Chicano •

Culture in Art

Although Garza worked hard to establish herself in the California arts community, she also continued to exhibit work in her native Texas, especially in San Antonio, Mission, and Houston. At one of her earlier shows, "Tejano artists," Mimi Crossley of the *Houston Post* cited Garza as "one of the true 'finds' of the exhibit." The Chicana artist also participated in the group exhibitions of "Los quenandos" (1975), "Dale Gas: Give It Gas" (1979) and "Fire! An Exhibition of 100 Texas Artists" (1979). Always interested in the Mexican Museum, Garza was commissioned to create the cover for the "Los Primeros Cinco Anos," a celebration of the museum's fifth anniversary exhibition in 1980. In 1984 the Mexican Museum named her as its artist-in-residence, a position she retained until 1987.

Garza continued to display her work at public museums and private galleries throughout California and the West Coast. She participated in a two-woman show with Margo Humphrey at the San Francisco Museum of Modern Art, displaying her skills in both gouache paintings and printmaking. Her regional and national reputation was enhanced when she received a National Endowment for the Arts fellowship in printmaking, or *intaglio,* in 1981. She also continued to exhibit, alongside increasingly established artists, in shows such as the "Califas Exhibition" and the "Saved Stuff" Exhibit at the Helen Euphrat Gallery.

• *Introduces Full-*

Color Works

Between 1982 and 1984 Garza began to expand her media by adopting the use of full-spectrum color in her paintings. During this period she was commissioned by the City of San Francisco to do a series of paintings based on the theme of the development of the daily use of water throughout history. The style of her paintings was described by noted art critic Tomas Ybarra-Frausto in *Imagine* as "small and full of luminous details and keen perceptions. . .they are charged with rich reservoirs of meaning and expressive power."

On the strength of her paintings for the City of San Francisco, Garza was awarded a second National Foundation for the Arts fellowship in 1987; a fellowship from the California Art Council followed in 1990. She was also the only Chicana artist to be represented in "Hispanic Art in the United States," a highly lauded exhibition of the works of thirty painters and sculptors that toured museums in 1987. Recent installations have included a two-room Day of the Dead exhibit at Northhampton, Massachusetts' Smith College, as well as her inclusion in "Chicano Art: Resistance and Affirmation," which toured major museums in 1995.

Through the creative beauty of her art, Garza records her own history as a young Chicana and extends her hand to all those who wish to experience it. Throughout her career as an artist, as well as a cultural educator and recorder, her work has reached an ever-widening audience. In 1990 her bilingual children's book *Family Pictures* was published; in it the artist both describes and illustrates childhood daily activities. As a *Publishers Weekly* reviewer noted, "The vibrant, canvaslike illustrations, accentuated with papel Picado-images on the text pages, evoke Garza's love for family and community despite the hardships she encountered while growing up. Readers of various ethnic origins should use this exemplary bilingual book as a litmus test for exploring diversities of multicultural lifestyles."

Two years after the publication of *Family Pictures,* Garza was honored by her first retrospective show, which included forty-seven paintings, etchings, altar designs, and *papel picados* or paper cut-outs. The show, called "Pedacito de mi corazon/ A Little Piece of My Heart," travelled through seven cities in 1992. In addition to show and gallery displays, Garza's work is now included in several permanent collections, including the McAllen International Museum, Texas Women's University, and the University of Texas Library at Austin. While still very active in artistic creation, Garza has also shouldered the responsibility for helping other Chicana artists gain entry to more visible museums and galleries. But her greatest joy comes from her ability to react with her audience. "I do [my artwork] primarily for the Chicanos to see their culture and that there's something to be proud of," she told the *Los Angeles Times*. "But I also do it for people of other cultures . . . to see and learn and realize that there are a lot of similarities and that the differences are not so threatening." Garza hopes that her efforts towards building bridges between cultures will extend beyond museum and gallery walls: "I have no qualms about using artwork as a tool to enlighten, educate and inform. Because if you see my heart through my art, then you cannot discriminate against me and be disrespectful."

**Profile by
Sally Foster**

RITA HAYWORTH

1918-1987 •

Whether illuminating the screen with a song and dance or beaming from a magazine photo, Rita Hayworth was an unforgettable

Actress •

sight. Capitalizing on both her beauty and talent to become a legendary motion picture star, Hayworth captured the hearts of countless American servicemen during the war years of the 1940s. At her peak, she epitomized American beauty, and her career produced several memorable moments: dance routines with Fred Astaire in 1941's You'll Never Get Rich; the glamorous photo spreads in Life magazine; her scandalous striptease in 1946's Gilda; and the mature sophistication of The Lady from Shanghai in 1949. While Hayworth's death in 1987 saddened America, it also served, through the efforts of Hayworth's daughter, to alert the nation to the plight of those inflicted by Alzheimer's disease, the illness that slowly killed her.

Born Margarita Carmen Cansino to Eduardo and Volga Haworth Cansino on October 17, 1918, in New York City, Hayworth was no stranger to show business. Her father, a headliner on vaudeville, was descended from a line of famous Spanish dancers; her mother, a Ziegfeld showgirl, came from a family of English actors. When Hayworth was nine years old the family moved to Los Angeles, where the motion picture industry was rapidly growing. There, Eduardo taught dancing and directed the filming of dance scenes for various studios. His daughter began her education at the Carthay School and later spent her first and only year of high school at Hamilton High. Throughout her school years, Hayworth continued the family tradition by taking acting and dancing lessons.

At eleven, Hayworth had her first acting role in a school play; three years later, in 1932, she made her professional debut, appearing in a stage prologue for the movie *Back Street* at Carthay Circle Theater. At this point, Eduardo Cansino decided that his attractive twelve-year-old daughter was ready for work. The perfect dance partner, he introduced her as his wife when they danced together at the Foreign Club in Tijuana, Mexico. The "Dancing Cansinos," as they were called, worked the club for a year and a half, followed by twenty performances a week on a gambling boat off California's coast.

• *Makes Film*

Debut in

Dante's

Inferno

Rita Cansino, as she was called, received her first big break when she was noticed dancing with her father in Agua Caliente, Mexico. Winfield R. Sheehan of the Fox Film Corporation hired the young woman, then sixteen, for a role in a 1935 movie starring Spencer Tracy entitled *Dante's Inferno*. Though the film was not successful, Rita Cansino was given a year-long contract with Fox. During this year she held minor, ethnic roles in the 1935 films *Charlie Chan in Egypt, Under the Pampas Moon*, and *Paddy O'Day*, followed the following year by *Human Cargo*: she played Egyptian, Argentinean, Irish, and Russian dancers respectively. When her contract expired and was not renewed, the actress spent a year playing Mexican and Indian girls; she earned $100 for each role.

When Hayworth was eighteen she married Edward C. Judson, a car salesman, oil man, and businessman. Judson became her manager; according to the *New York Times*, he "transformed" the actress "from a raven-haired Latin to an auburn-haired cosmopolitan" by altering his wife's hairline and eyebrows with electrolysis and changing her professional name. Rita Cansino took her mother's maiden name, added a "y" to ensure its proper pronunciation, and became Rita Hayworth. Magazines and newspapers captured the image of the new Rita, who won the favor of Harry Cohn and a seven-year contract with his Columbia Pictures.

After fourteen low-budget movies, Hayworth was finally given a leading role. She was hired by director Howard Hawks to portray an unfaithful wife in his 1939 drama *Only Angels Have Wings*, which starred Cary Grant. Good reviews of her performance attracted attention: she went on loan from Columbia to Warner Brothers Pictures for the 1941 film *Strawberry Blonde* with James Cagney. That year, as she made *Blood and Sand* with Fox, Hayworth began to shine. According to *Time,* "something magical happened when the cameras began to roll"; the woman who was "shy" and "unassuming" offstage "warmed the set." The *New York Times* wrote that Hayworth "rapidly developed into one of Hollywood's most glamorous stars."

Hayworth achieved celebrity status when she starred as Fred Astaire's dance partner in Columbia's 1941 musical *You'll Never Get Rich*. She appeared on the cover of *Time* and was dubbed "The Great American Love Goddess" by Winthrop Sargent in *Life*. In 1942 she made three hit movies: *My Gal Sal, Tales of Manhattan* and *You Were Never Lovelier,* the latter pairing her again with Astaire. As her career skyrocketed, however, Hayworth's marriage failed; she divorced Judson that same year.

During the early forties, as the country geared up for World War II, Hayworth's personal life improved and she established her professional allure. She married noted actor, director, and screenwriter Orson Welles in 1943; they had a daughter, Rebecca, two years later. Hayworth was earning more than $6,000 a week as Columbia's leading actress. After she starred in 1944's *Cover Girl* alongside dancer Gene Kelly, *Life* presented a seductive photograph of the actress wearing black lace which, according to the *New York Times,* "became famous around the world as an American serviceman's pinup." The *Times* also noted that, in what was "intended . . . as the ultimate compliment, the picture was even pasted to a test atomic bomb that was dropped on Bikini atoll in 1946." Hayworth's fame continued to grow after she made *Tonight and Every Night* in 1945 and was cast in a memorable role in 1946's *Gilda*. A scene in the latter film—in which Hayworth sang "Put the Blame on Mame" and stripped off her long, black gloves—scandalized conservative viewers. It was a testimony to her popularity that her 1947 film, *Down to Earth,* was included in a twentieth-century time capsule, despite the fact that the film itself received some bad reviews.

Hayworth certainly had no objection to attracting attention as a star. "I like having my picture taken and being a glamorous person," she was

Marries Orson •

Welles

quoted as saying in the *New York Times*. "Sometimes when I find myself getting impatient, I just remember the times I cried my eyes out because nobody wanted to take my picture at the Trocadero." Hayworth's daughter, Princess Yasmin Khan later confirmed this in *People:* "Mother was very good with her fans, very giving and patient."

While Hayworth starred as a sophisticated short-haired blonde in 1948's *The Lady from Shanghai* along with husband Orson Welles—who also directed the movie—she was also in the process of divorcing him. "I just can't take his genius anymore," she was later quoted in *People* as saying, adding in *Time:* "I'm tired of being a 25-percent wife." After making *The Loves of Carmen* in 1948, Hayworth married Prince Aly Kahn, with whom she had been having an affair. This was an off-screen scandal, for Hayworth was already pregnant with their daughter, the Princess Yasmin Aga Kahn. Although she was quoted in *Time* as saying, "The world was magical when you were with him," this marriage lasted no longer than her second; the couple divorced in 1953.

During the 1950s Hayworth's career began to wane. After making the movies *Affair in Trinidad, Salome,* and *Miss Sadie Thompson* between 1952-53, she once again entered a marriage that proved to be unsuccessful as well as destructive. Her fourth husband, the singer Dick Haymes, "beat her and tried to capitalize on her fame in an attempt to revive his own failing career," contended Hayworth biographer Barbara Leaming in *People*. While Hayworth came out of temporary retirement after her divorce from Haymes in 1955 to make the 1957 film *Fire Down Below,* she was cast in only a supporting role in the same year's *Pal Joey*. Failing to maintain her box-office pull as a glamorous actress, *Pal Joey* was Hayworth's final appearance as a contracted actress.

At this point, Hayworth's personal life seemed to parallel her professional career. She married producer James Hill in 1958 and divorced him in 1961. *People* reported that Hill had wanted Rita to continue to make movies instead of "play golf, paint, tell jokes and have a home." After the failure of this fifth and final marriage, it was apparent that Hayworth's luck in love was not of the best. While she was quoted in *People* as saying, "Most men fell in love with *Gilda* but they woke up with me." Leaming speculated that these "doomed" relationships were a result of abuse that had been visited on Hayworth as a child: "[Her father] Eduardo raped her in the afternoons and danced with her at night." In her biography of Hayworth, *If This Was Happiness,* Leaming elaborates on this revelation, for which she claims Orson Welles as the source.

While critics agreed that Hayworth gave one of her best perform-ances after her retirement, playing a traitorous American in the 1959 drama *They Came to Cordura,* they also noted that her trademark beauty was fading. As a freelance actress, Hayworth found fewer roles: 1960's *The Story on Page One,* 1967's *The Poppy Is Also a Flower,* and 1972's *The Wrath of God* were some of her last films. Hayworth's 1971 attempt to perform on stage was aborted; the actress could not remember her lines.

Biographers, relatives, and friends now believe that the first stages of Alzheimer's disease were responsible for Hayworth's memory lapses, alcoholism, lack of coordination, and poor eyesight during the last three decades of her life. Although Alzheimer's—a disease still relatively unknown at the time—was not diagnosed as the source of her problems, it was obvious that Hayworth was ill. In 1981 she was legally declared unable to care for herself. Her daughter, Princess Yasmin Kahn provided shelter, care, and love for her mother, and sought to enlighten the public to the symptoms of the obscure neurological disease by helping to organize Alzheimer's Disease International and serving as its president.

Hayworth's mind slowly began to deteriorate. When she died in her New York apartment on May 14, 1987, she did not even know her own family. Nevertheless, the "All-American Love Goddess," as *Time* called her, was not forgotten by her fans. The *New York Times* reported at the time of her death that President Ronald Reagan, a former actor, stated: "Rita Hayworth was one of our country's most beloved stars. Glamorous and talented, she gave us many wonderful moments . . . and delighted audiences from the time she was a young girl. [First Lady] Nancy and I are saddened by Rita's death. She was a friend whom we will miss."

**Profile by
Ronie-Richele
Garcia-Johnson**

ANTONIA HERNÁNDEZ

A s president and general counsel for the Mexican American Legal

Defense Fund (MALDEF), a Hispanic civil rights organization, Antonia

Hernández has become a highly visible advocate for the nation's

growing Hispanic community. Her opinions and advice on how a given

issue will affect U.S. Hispanics have often been featured in newspaper

editorial pages, national magazines, television talk shows, and numer-

ous other media outlets. Immigrant rights, employment discrimination,

educational inequities, U.S. census figures, redistricting, voting, and

language rights, are among her regular topics of concern.

1948- •

Civil rights •

lawyer

Hernández began working for MALDEF in 1981, serving as a staff attorney in its Washington, D.C. office; two years later found her as its employment litigation director, working out of Los Angeles. It also found her hard at work seeking greater opportunities for Hispanics in private and public sector jobs. During the 1980s MALDEF initiated several lawsuits to get employers to compensate bilingual workers whose second-language capabilities were part of their job, an effort that demanded the legal skills of Hernández. In 1985 she became president and general counsel of the organization, succeeding former president Joaquin Avila. "Every person who heads [MALDEF] gives it his or her flavor," Hernández told *Hispanic*. "My flavor has been taking the helm of an organization and helping it into institutional maturity."

Born on May 30, 1948, in the Mexican state of Coahuila in the town of Torreón, Hernández came to the United States with her family when she was eight years old. They settled in East Los Angeles, where her father, Manuel, was a gardener and laborer and her mother, Nicolasa, a homemaker who raised six children while taking on odd jobs whenever possible. As the oldest child, Antonia was often called upon to help care for her younger siblings and to do unconventional tasks for young women of that time period, such as car maintenance. "In my time," Nicolasa Hernández told *Parents,* "women didn't have the freedom that women have today, but I wanted my daughters to have that, to learn, to travel, to work, to do whatever they wanted to do." While the Hernández family was not rich in material possessions, they provided a nurturing environment, says the younger Hernández. "I grew up in a very happy environment but a very poor environment," she told *Parents*.

Hernández credits her early upbringing in Mexico as instilling pride in her Mexican roots. "When I came to the United States, I was very proud of who I was. I was a Mexican. I had an identity. I had been taught a history, a culture of centuries of rich civilization so I had none of the psychoses of people who don't know who they are," she told the *Los Angeles Daily Journal*. Her belief in the extended family can still be seen in her daily life. Married to Michael Stern, an attorney she met while a law clerk for California Legal Rural Assistance in 1973, the two were wed in 1977, though not before receiving her father's permission. Hernández, Stern, and their three children now live in Pasadena, near her mother and her sisters.

All of Hernández's brothers and sisters have earned college degrees and several are teachers. "My parents instilled in us the belief that serving the public interest was a very noble thing to do," she told *Parents*. She was also on her way toward earning a postgraduate degree in education when she decided she could be more useful to her community with a law degree. Already in receipt of her B.A. and a teaching certificate from UCLA in 1973, Hernández was working in a counseling program, she told *Parents,* when she "realized that we couldn't help the kids as teachers unless we did something about the laws that were holding them back."

Although her professors encouraged her to attend Harvard or Stanford, Hernández chose UCLA so she could remain near her family. "I was the oldest in our family, and my parents were sacrificing everything they could to help me with school," she explained to *Parents*. "They were looking forward to me graduating and working as a teacher so I could help them with the rest of the kids. So my feeling was that if I were to ask them to sacrifice three more years, moving away would be too drastic."

Although Hernández was not a straight-A student in law school, her teachers remember her as bright and articulate. "She had the ability to get her point across without alienating other people and people respected her for that," recalled one professor in the *Los Angeles Daily Journal*. Hernández acknowledges her priority wasn't top grades; rather, it was in organizations and issues she cared about. During law school she served on the admissions committee and several Chicano student organizations. "I wasn't out there to make the law firm roster," she told the *Daily Journal*. "I knew I was going to be [in] public interest [law]…. To me, to be a really good lawyer, you have to be a well-rounded person."

After receiving her juris doctorate from the University of California at Los Angeles (UCLA) Law School in 1974, Hernández became an attorney for the East Los Angeles Center for Law and Justice, where she handled criminal and civil cases, often involving police brutality. After a year there, she became directing attorney of the Lincoln Heights office for the Legal Aid Foundation, where she directed a staff of six attorneys and took part in case litigation and fought for bills in the state legislature. In 1978 she was offered a job as staff counsel to the United States Senate Judiciary Committee, which was chaired by Massachusetts Senator Edward Kennedy. After initially declining the offer, Hernández reconsidered and took the position, with a little prodding from her husband. "I was very happy doing poverty law and being near my family," she told *Parents*. "They called me back because they thought it was the salary, and so they raised it. I didn't want to explain what the problem was so I said yes. As a professional woman you just don't say 'My mother said I shouldn't do this.'" Her husband took a more pragmatic view, telling *Parents*, "We didn't have children; we had very little furniture and few responsibilities. I figured I'd get a [new] job."

Overcoming her reluctance to leave her hometown, Hernández gained valuable experience in the nation's capital. At the Senate Judiciary Committee she drafted bills and briefed committee members, spe-

A Lawyer on •

Her Own Terms

cializing in immigration and human-rights work. She also took a brief leave of absence to coordinate Kennedy's Southwest campaign during his unsuccessful bid for the Democratic presidential nomination. "In that degree I played the Hispanic role," she told the *Los Angeles Daily News*. "But on other issues, I was just another staff member who had to do the work that had to be done."

After the Democrats lost control of the Senate in 1980, Hernández found herself out of work. Within days MALDEF had invited her to join their Washington, D.C., staff. Her progress there was steady, working as associate counsel, director of the employment litigation programs, executive vice-president, and deputy general counsel before moving into the top slot. One ofher brightest moments was her role in defeating the Simpson-Mazzoli immigration bill, which would have required Latinos to carry identification cards. Indeed, immigrant rights has been one area that Hernández has been especially effective in pushing the federal government to recognize. Throughout her tenure at MALDEF, the organization has created historic changes through court litigation for the U.S. Hispanic community, including the creation of single-member election districts and favorable public school equity court decisions in the state of Texas and successful challenges to district boundaries in Los Angeles County.

Hernández's tenure with MALDEF has also been marked by controversy. In 1987 an executive committee of the MALDEF Board of Directors abruptly terminated her, citing questionable administrative and leadership abilities. Hours later they appointed former New Mexico governor Toney Anaya to the post and gave him a $100,000 salary— $40,000 more than Hernández had been making. But Hernández refused to be dismissed, maintaining that only the full board had the power to fire her. A state judge from Texas agreed, requiring that the full board determine her status. They voted 18 to 14 to retain her.

Since then, she has gone on to become an organizational mainstay and MALDEF's most visible spokesperson, her advocacy informed by her personal experiences of growing up as an immigrant in East Los Angeles. For example, Hernández's experiences as a child learning English by the "sink or swim" method has made her an effective advocate of bilingual education. "I made it, But just because I made it cannot be used as an example that it works," she told the *Los Angeles Daily Journal*. "I say 'Don't look at me, look at all those who didn't make it.' Because you're not judged by whether you made it, whether the minority made it. You're judged by whether the majority makes it." Because of her work, the situation "will be much better for my children," she told *Hispanic*. "They will have the opportunities I had to fight for. As a consequence, they'll have a bigger responsibility to give to their community."

Hernández says her time in Washington, D.C., has given her a broader understanding of the diversity within the U.S. Latino community. "Living on the East Coast has helped me transcend the regional aspect of the organization by mixing with Puerto Ricans, Cubans and other groups," she told *Hispanic*. This new understanding has motivated her to increase the cooperation among civil rights organizations across racial and ethnic lines. "If we allow ourselves to be sucked into believing we should fight over crumbs, we will." Her resolve in this area was be tested in late 1990 when the Leadership Conference on Civil Rights failed to support the repeal of employer sanctions found in the 1986 Immigration Reform and Control Act. Citing the government's own General Accounting Office study showing that the provisions led to increased discrimination against Hispanic looking job applicants, Hernández threatened to pull MALDEF out of the coalition, which was gearing up for an intense lobbying campaign for what later became the 1992 Civil Rights Bill. In the end, the National Association for the Advancement of Colored People (NAACP) voted to support the repeal.

As much as her performance is measured by court decisions, Hernández also understands the human element of her work. " A court victory is important but just the beginning of the process. It must translate into empowerment. It is the people that have the power to give life to those court victories," she told *La Paloma*. However, despite her professional success, she acknowledges that the 1980s were not the best of times for the Latino community. "The 1980s was not the decade of the Hispanic," she told *Hispanic*. "Madison Avenue put up the expectation and said we failed. The 1990s is a threshold decade. We need to move. Otherwise, we'll develop into a community with a small middle class and a large poverty class."

Valuing the human element as she does, Hernández counts her family first, despite the demands of her high-powered job, and describes her children as "my greatest accomplishment." Even so, balancing the needs of her family with a career has been a continual struggle, but one she has become adept at. Often gone from home for long stretches of time to testify before Congress or address other national organizations, she tries "to balance my life and it has worked," she told *Hispanic*. " But I have little time to myself and very few good friends." She acknowledges that having a husband who is familiar with her culture through his work with farmworkers and who is able to speak Spanish has helped. Although of Jewish descent, Stern has embraced his wife's strong cultural ties. "I don't want him to feel uncomfortable

A Court Victory •

Is Only the

Beginning

because he's living our way," Hernández told *Parents*. "But he's very accommodating. I don't know if I could be as accommodating if it was the reverse."

Hernández's community involvement includes serving on the boards of California Tomorrow, the Quality Education for Minorities Network, California Leadership, the Latino Museum of History, Art, and Culture, and Los Angeles 2000. And she continues to address the issues of the entire Mexican American community within the national media. "Latinos have the highest work-participation [rate] of any community," she explained in an interview with the *Los Angeles Times*. "They will work anywhere. But they also have the hightest poverty rate. It's not that they don't work; it's that they don't earn enough. As for welfare, most Latinos live in two-parent families, so they don't qualify for programs like [Aid to Families with Dependent Children]. And this is not a homogenous community. There are great differences between the Puerto Rican and the Cuban and the Mexican and the now-emerging Latin American communities.... We do not meet the common stereotype profile. It's not that we are better, or that we are worse—we're just different."

**Profile by
Jonathan J. Higuera**

CAROLINA HERRERA

*W*hen she introduced her first collection in 1981, Venezuelan

socialite Carolina Herrera stunned high society and stirred the fashion

industry with her innovative creations. The deep necklines and exagger-

ated sleeves featured in her designs reminded audiences of traditional

beauty while promoting a contemporary elegance. The renowned de-

signer Bill Blass immediately recognized her talent. "I think she has

tremendous potential," he was quoted as saying of Herrera in People.

"She is going to be a force in the fashion world." Since that time, Herrera

has invigorated fashion design and dressed some of the world's most

famous women. A recipient of the 1987 MODA Award for Top Hispanic

Designer, she has secured her place among the world's most heralded

1939- •

Fashion •

designer

Carolina Herrera

fashion designers.

Herrera's success as a designer has much to do with her upbringing as a member of fashionable society. Born in Caracas, Venezuela, in 1939, to Guillermo Pacanins, an officer in the Venezuelan Air Force and, later, a governor of Caracas, Maria Carolina Josefina Pacanins y Nino was raised by people who enjoyed hosting parties in their glamorous homes and reveled in wearing the latest fashions. As a young girl, she designed garments for her dolls, and as a young woman, she designed for herself and for her friends. As *People* noted, she was "very sad" because she was not allowed to dress "like a vamp" in red as a child. Her grandmother introduced the stylish thirteen-year-old to the famous couturier Cristobal Balenciaga at a fashion show in Paris; at her first ball she wore a white gown from the House of Lavin.

When the elegant young woman married Reinaldo Herrera, her childhood friend and the eldest son of Mimi Herrera, in 1969, she found even more incentive to dress glamorously. Her mother-in-law was a wealthy art patron as well as the owner of "La Vega," an enormous house built in 1590 in Caracas. Herrera suited herself to her classically luxurious surroundings. She first made the Best Dressed List in 1971, and has been a perennial listee since, in addition to winning a spot in the Fashion Hall of Fame in 1981.

As Herrera told an interviewer with *Hispanic,* she began her professional career as a designer because her children were grown and she "wanted to try something new." She felt confident that she would be a success. When Armando de Armas, a Venezuelan publishing magnate, provided the financial backing Herrera needed for a venture into the business world of fashion, she "changed from being a mother with nothing to do but arrange flowers and parties to being a professional who works twelve hours a day at the office," she confided to *Newsweek.* While Herrera was optimistic about her chances for success, some of her societal peers and members of the fashion industry supposed that Herrera's designs would not merit a second glance.

Ellin Saltzman, fashion director for Saks Fifth Avenue, recalled in *People* that she had her own doubts about Herrera when she first heard of her 1981 collection. Saltzman assumed that Herrera was "another socialite designing a fly-by-night collection no one will ever buy or wear." Herrera, however, proved that she was not an amateur. Her work, which utilized layers, diverse fabrics, and various lengths, was received with enthusiastic praise. The skeptical fashion director from Saks Fifth Avenue found Herrera's collection to be "sensational," as she

Diversion

Becomes a

Career

remarked in *People,* and other fashion authorities agreed. Herrera was dubbed "Our Lady of the Sleeves" by *Women's Wear Daily* because of the overbroad shoulders on her fanciful evening gowns. While features such as fairy-tale sleeves and plunging necklines attracted attention, the industry respected the classic taste and superb tailoring of Herrera's work. The fashion world was buzzing—Herrera's collection promised to inspire other designers as well as incite new trends.

● *Popularity*

Spawns Success

By the end of 1982 Herrera's creations were widely acclaimed. Royal personalities, such as Princess Elizabeth of Yugoslavia, Spain's Duchess of Feria, and Countess Consuelo Crespi, were wearing Herrera's designs. Other public figures, First Lady Nancy Reagan and well-known actress Kathleen Turner among them, were donning Herrera gowns. In fact, Reagan and Turner sported the same silver-blue, one-shouldered gown of coupe de velours, which was paired with a marvelous maribou feather cape. Garments such as these, and other sleek, striped, silver and gold gowns, captured the fancies of many women and made Herrera a star designer.

It is Herrera's understanding of the socialite's lifestyle and her extraordinary talent—along with her social contacts—that attract some of the world's most famous celebrities to her clothing. As Ivana Trump, ex-wife of the wealthy Donald Trump, explained in a *Newsweek* article, Herrera's designs catch the fancies of people like herself because she "is in society, she travels and goes to the same restaurants and parties as the women who buy her clothes." Saltzman noted in the same article that Herrera contributed "dressy lunch and evening clothes that women couldn't find anywhere else" to the market. The fine quality and unique design of Herrera's works make her originals highly desirable. There is a great demand for her clothing despite exclusive prices: A luncheon suit might cost anywhere between $1,500 to $3,800. Pajamas of silk made especially for lounging at the pool were tagged at $1,200 in 1982. Herrera's exquisite gowns were priced at $2,100 to $4,000 in the same year.

During the 1980s Herrera continued to establish herself as a respected designer. As she understood the desire for slim clothing, she produced dresses and outfits that were less exaggerated than those she had previously designed; she contributed to the trends of the mid-eighties with her own adaptations of the sleek style. In 1986 Jacqueline Kennedy Onassis, a Herrera client who, as First Lady, had set the standard for American fashion in the 1960s, asked Herrera to create a wedding dress for her daughter, Caroline Kennedy. In 1994, the designer created the wedding dress for Marla Maples, the new Mrs. Donald

Trump. For such achievements, Herrera won the 1987 MODA Award as the Top Hispanic Designer, an award which had been previously won by such prestigious designers as Adolfo and Oscar de La Renta.

1988 was the year that Herrera introduced her own perfume. "Carolina Herrera," as the fragrance is called, was enthusiastically received by consumers. According to *Hispanic,* this perfume is her "most accessible and perhaps personal product." The perfume's odor of jasmine and tuberose is reminiscent of Herrera's happy childhood—a jasmine vine in the family's garden scented the girl's bedroom—and denotes her success as an adult. Herrera has been wearing this original mixture for years, and it permeates the atmosphere of her New York office.

While by late 1989 Herrera had broadened her artistry by designing leather goods, eyewear, and furs for Revillon, and had followed the designer trend of introducing a less expensive line of clothing which she named "CH," her most exclusive apparel was featured along with those of the likes of designer Bill Blass in the media's fashion reports. Her collection for the fall of 1989 exemplified the reason for her fame: her creations were fun yet functional, elegant yet bold. While Herrera was among those designers who utilized animal prints in their collections for the season, her particular adaptation of the theme was daring: she mixed the prints with crimson sequins and velvet. *Hispanic* displayed a "leopard print wool challis dress with a black persian velvet jacket lined with the same leopard spots" which could make "the switch from daytime into night," an ensemble as stunning as it was versatile.

The *New York Times* reported on Herrera's 1989 fall show at the Plaza and emphasized other aspects of the collection: shorts that were "styled with a ripply fullness that makes them almost impossible to differentiate from skirts," "graphic black-and-white cotton pique suits" with combinations of hearts and stripes, dresses and jackets in pastel shades which were "harbingers of a new suit look to come," and "trouser outfits" with pants "either wide or narrow." Especially striking was Herrera's "upwardly mobile version" of the motorcycle jacket; in pink, chartreuse, or orange satin, with rhinestones instead of nailheads, these jackets contributed to a "fun" outfit and an equally fun outlook. Her various evening gowns were characteristically beautiful, whether long and black, reminiscent of Fabergé eggs, or white with crystal beading. Herrera's diverse designs have continued to be a testimony to her ideas. She told *Hispanic,* "Nowadays, everything [in fashion] is accepted.... There's a craziness going around the world." Despite this "craziness," Herrera acknowledges that odd designs are not as market-

Collections •

Showcase

Unique Designs

able as designs that take the needs of the buyer into account. "Nobody wants to look like a costume," she quipped, adding that "The thing to do is to have a sensational simple dress."

Onto the fashion runways and city streets of the 1990s, Herrera introduced Carolina Herrera Collection III, a group of sportswear geared towards a younger audience than her previous lines. In addition, she continued to produce versatile, elegantly designed clothing. The *New York Times,* discussing her fall fashion show at the Plaza in 1991, noted that Herrera had highlighted red plaids for daytime, and lamé, wool crepe, and "bold checks" for night. She utilized opaque tights for daytime; feathers, silver sequins, and rhinestones with her evening wear. According to the *Times,* the "basic Herrera look is slick and uncomplicated, expressed in lamé jumpsuits and jersey dresses," yet her designs were not "shy and retiring." The *Times* observed that Herrera offered women the choice of a suit or a dress "in the same fabric," slim long gowns, or puffy short ones. "Clearly she is thinking about the different figures and needs of her followers."

Herrera's life continues to be a busy one. She has, however, managed to balance her roles as a designer and businesswoman, as wife, mother to four daughters, and grandmother to three grandsons, as well as homes in New York and Caracas and an active social schedule. Although she believes that it is imperative that a designer observe and involve herself in social activity, she commented in *Newsweek:* "I never go to lunch anymore. It interrupts my day and it's boring." While it is obvious that Herrera is very serious about her work, she insists that she loves it. "The more I do the more I like it," she told *Hispanic.*

Herrera has earned her place as a distinguished fashion designer, and she is prepared to continue to dress women beautifully, refresh the world of fashion, and introduce exciting new products. As she confessed in an interview in *Hispanic,* "I am never satisfied. I'm a perfectionist. When I see the show is ready and the collection is out and they're quite nice, I still say, 'I could do much better.'" She also credits a great deal of her fashion acumen to her Latina upbringing. "You just do it," Herrera told *Américas* in a discussion of women's role of being attractive and well-groomed. "It becomes second nature; you're taught that this is a way of showing respect for others and for yourself. Being well-groomed is your contribution to society and I think Latin American women are very good at this."

Profile by Ronie-Richele Garcia-Johnson

MARIA HINOJOSA

P *erhaps because she has always recognized the power of her heritage, journalist Maria Hinojosa has made a point of making it accessible to others. She celebrates Mexican, Mexican American, and Latino culture as she works, writes, and creates. Through her radio reports and shows, her writing, her artwork, and her social activities, Hinojosa continues to contribute to the cohesiveness of a booming Mexican American community, both in her adopted hometown of New York City and beyond.*

1961- •

Radio •

reporter

The fourth child of Raul and Berta (Ojeda) Hinojosa, Maria de Lourdes Hinojosa was born on July 2, 1961, in Mexico City. When she was eighteen months old, the Hinojosa family moved to the United States, where her father, a medical research doctor, studied and worked. After spending some time in New England, the family settled in Chicago. According to Hinojosa, instead of forgetting about their roots, her parents maintained strong ties with their family in Mexico; each summer

during her childhood, the reporter accompanied her family on a car trip to a different part of the country. Those trips to her native land instilled a love of Mexican culture in Hinojosa and gave her a profound sense of pride in her heritage. "I was very, very proud to be a part of this huge country," she explained during an August 1992 interview.

While the trips Hinojosa took to Mexico made her aware of her cultural roots, they also opened her eyes to socioeconomic inequity. She noticed that the poverty she had witnessed in Mexico was also present in Latino immigrant areas of Chicago, and she became increasingly more politically active. While attending private school at the University of Chicago High School, she created the organization Students for a Better Environment. It was important to Hinojosa that her fellow students realize that not everyone lived the privileged life that they enjoyed.

At that point in her life, Hinojosa had no idea that she would pursue a career as a socially responsible radio reporter. She wanted to be an actress. She applied to Barnard College, the women's undergraduate arm of Columbia University in New York City, and was accepted. Hinojosa was enthusiastic about school and New York, but she became increasingly frustrated with acting. At just five feet tall and not clearly classifiable as either "Mexican"- or "white"-looking, there didn't seem to be a niche for her in theater. While her failure as an actress was disappointing, it allowed Hinojosa to become involved in radio.

It was by chance that Hinojosa heard about an opening for a Latino show on Columbia University's 24-hour student radio station, WCKR-FM. She created the radio show *Nueva cancion y demas* (*New Song and More*). As the show's producer and host, Hinojosa spent three hours each week on the air playing Latin American music, announcing the news, and discussing Latin American issues in a talk show format. While she continued to produce *Nueva cancion y demas,* she also went on to become the program director of WCKR. While serving in this demanding position, Hinojosa maintained excellent grades, majoring in both Latin American studies and political economy.

In 1985 Hinojosa graduated magna cum laude from Barnard College, still unsure what she should do with her life. She applied for an internship with National Public Radio (NPR) and nine months later was hired as a production assistant in their Washington, D.C., office. There Hinojosa produced mini-documentaries and news stories for the *Weekend Edition–Saturday* show. Her next position, which she accepted in late 1986, was as associate producer of *Enfoque nacional (National Focus),* NPR's weekly Spanish-language national news program, at KPBS in San Diego, California. That same year she received the Silver Cindy Award for her work on the program "Immigration and Deten-

Joins National •

Public Radio

189 •

tion." Hinojosa commuted from her home in Tijuana, Mexico, for the duration of her time with KPBS.

By 1987 Hinojosa was ready for a change. She returned to New York City and became a producer for CBS News. While there, she produced the network radio broadcasts *The Osgood File, Where We Stand, with Walter Cronkite, Newsbreak, Today in Business, First Line Report,* and *Newsmark.* January 1988 found her working as a researcher/producer on live segments of *CBS This Morning.* In August of that year, Hinojosa returned to NPR as a freelance reporter/producer based in New York City. She worked as a reporter for *Latin File* and programs such as *All Things Considered, Morning Edition, Weekend Edition, Crossroads, Latino,* and a documentary series called *Horizons,* as well as *Soundprint of American Public Radio.* Hinojosa won a 1989 Corporation for Public Broadcasting Silver Award for the piece "Day of the Dead."

In January 1990, Hinojosa began to work on general assignments as a staff member of WNYC Radio. In August of that year, she began serving as a general assignment reporter for NPR's New York bureau. By September, Hinojosa was ready to take on another challenge. She began hosting her own live, call-in, public affairs, prime-time television talk show, *New York Hotline,* which aired on WNYC Television. She was the first Latino to host a prime-time public affairs television news show in New York City.

Hinojosa has accumulated a considerable amount of television experience. She hosted a national broadcast called "Beyond the Browning of America," which was produced in conjunction with the Center for Puerto Rican Studies and aired on public television stations throughout the United States. Another program, "Crosswalks," which aired on a municipal cable system, featured coverage of the Democratic National Convention. Hinojosa has also moderated and hosted the public access television show *Latinos en accion.* From 1993 to 1995, she hosted the Latino public affairs show, *Visiones* on WNBC-TV in New York. Hinojosa is also a frequent guest on New York public television's *Informed Sources* and on CNN's *CNN and Company.*

In 1990 Hinojosa won an International Radio Festival of New York Silver Award for "Drug Family," and a fellowship from the New York Foundation for the Arts for her work in radio. In 1991, for "Crews," a radio program about members of youth gangs that later inspired a book, she was awarded the Unity Award from Lincoln University, Top Story and First Place Radio Awards from the National Association of Hispanic Journalists, and a First Place award from the New York Newswomen's

Club. Also in 1991, she earned a First Place Award from the Associated Press for her coverage of South African leader Nelson Mandela's visit to New York City on WNYC. Her 1992 distinctions include a Kappa Tau Alpha Award for Excellence in Journalism from New York University, a Latino Coalition for Fair Media Award for Outstanding Service in Journalism, and a first place, radio, from the National Association of Hispanic Journalists for "Body Bags." 1993 marked her receipt of the Deadline Award from the New York Society of Professional Journalists. In 1995 Hinojosa received the Robert F. Kennedy award for radio journalism for the piece, "Jail as a Right of Passage"; the Hispanic Association for Media Arts and Sciences recognized her work with the Outstanding Body of Work for Radio award; and *Hispanic Business* magazine listed her among the 100 Influential Hispanics in America.

Hinojosa has continued working for NPR as a New York bureau staff correspondent. Her beats as a general assignment reporter have included Latino and multicultural affairs, race relations, youth issues, and labor and politics. She has also hosted the show she had begun in 1980, *Nueva cancion y demas,* for WCKR-FM. She is a member of the board of *NACLA* magazine. Hinojosa is a frequent guest lecturer at colleges, universities, and women's and Latino events nationwide.

Known in and around New York City for her artistic talent as well as for her radio personality, Hinojosa, in collaboration with her artist husband, Gérman Perez, has been creating altars in celebration of the Day of the Dead, a traditional Mexican holiday, since 1988. One of these, dedicated to undocumented immigrants, is especially moving. It features paper bags—symbols of those people who cross the border into the United States carrying such bags—as well as tiny skeletons. Hinojosa has also highlighted the plight of people with the AIDS virus in her altars. One of Hinojosa's altars has been installed in the Bronx Museum of Art. She has also exhibited artwork at the Cooper-Hewitt National Design Museum in New York and the Mexican Fine Arts Center in Chicago. In her August 1992 interview, Hinojosa explained that, in addition to enjoying the actual construction of each altar, she considers their creation and presentation as a way to establish a Mexican American cultural presence in New York City and as a method of reaching out to the city's Mexican American community. She wants New Yorkers to realize that Mexican Americans are a social and cultural force, and encourages the Mexican Americans themselves to revel in their cultural heritage. Hinojosa seems to thrive on her busy schedule. While she spends a great deal of her day working, she always manages to find time for her friends and for her husband, Gérman Perez, whom she married on July 20, 1991. In January 1996, Hinojosa and her husband celebrated the arrival of their son, Raul Ariel. Perez, who was born in the Dominican

Dedicated to •

Community

Involvement

Republic, is a painter of large-scale acrylic works and shares Hinojosa's devotion to Hispanic American culture and her love of New York City.

The influx of Mexicans and Dominicans into New York during the 1980s—and their growing cultural influence—have enriched the Pan-American community that so enthralled Hinojosa during her early years in the city. She finds the cultural transformation that is taking place in the city exciting and counts it as part of the reason she enjoys her job as a reporter, "being on the street" and allowing "those [Hispanic] voices to be heard." To Hinojosa, radio reporting is "a part of my life." She intends to continue enjoying her "dream job" in New York and is not interested in management work in radio. Meanwhile, she is working on a new book.

In 1995 Hinojosa's first book *Crews: Gang Members Talk to Maria Hinojosa* was published. The work, which is based on her 1990 "All Things Considered" interview with teen-age gang members in New York City, includes striking black-and-white photographs by her husband. *Crews*—the title refers to the street word for "gang"—was favorable reviewed in the nation's major newspapers, including the *Los Angeles Times,* which also profiled the writer and radio host. The book contains a transcript of the original "All Things Considered" broadcast as well as seven in-depth interviews Hinojosa conducted with both male and female "crew" members after she took to the streets as an NPR reporter following the brutal 1990 stabbing of an out-of-state tourist in a New York City subway. Her open, non-judgmental approach encouraged her young subjects—many of them from Latino gangs—to openly express their streetworn, casual acceptance of the poverty, crime, drug abuse, and violence they witness in their daily lives, and are sometimes party to. "I feel that young kids often don't have anyone talking to them and asking them what they think and how they feel about things," Hinojosa told Julio Moran of the *Los Angeles Times*. "As a journalist, this was a chance to spend hours and hours with a subject and establish a relationship with them."

Hinojosa's continuing contributions to Mexican American culture in New York City are becoming increasingly important as that community grows and as more people become aware of the growing Hispanic influence throughout the United States. Her determination to celebrate the culture that she loves has not only resulted in her personal success, but has helped to give voice to an entire community.

Profile by Ronie-Richele Garcia-Johnson

DOLORES HUERTA

C ofounder and first vice-president of the United Farm Workers **1930-** •

union, Dolores Huerta—referred to by some as Dolores "Huelga" or

"strike"—is the most prominent Chicana labor leader in the United **Labor leader,** •

States. For more than thirty years she has dedicated her life to the **social**

struggle for justice, dignity, and a decent standard of living for migrant **activist**

farmworkers, one of the United States' most exploited groups. The

recipient of countless community service, labor, Hispanic, and women's

awards, and the subject of many newspaper articles, corridos (ballads),

and murals, Huerta serves as a singular role model for Mexican

American women living in the post–World War II era.

Dolores Fernández Huerta, the second child and only daughter of

Juan and Alicia (Cháves) Fernández, was born on April 10, 1930, in the small northern New Mexico mining town of Dawson. On her mother's side, Huerta is a third-generation New Mexican; like his wife, Huerta's father was born in Dawson to Mexican immigrant parents. When Huerta was a toddler, her parents divorced, and Alicia Fernández moved her three children—John, Dolores, and Marshall—first to Las Vegas, New Mexico, and then to Stockton, California, where she had relatives.

As a single parent during the Depression, Alicia Fernández had a difficult time supporting her family. To make ends meet, she worked at a cannery at night and as a waitress during the day. For child care, Alicia depended on her widowed father, Herculano Chávez, who had followed her to Stockton. "My grandfather kind of raised us," Huerta recalled, adding that "He was really our father... My grandfather's influence was really the male influence in my family." The gregarious Huerta enjoyed a close relationship with her grandfather during a happy childhood spent learning respect for one's elders, Mexican *corridos*, and rosary recitations. She recalled being a dutiful but playful child: "My grandfather used to call me seven tongues . . . because I always talked so much." Such verbal skills served Huerta well in later life.

Alicia's economic fortunes improved during the war years; she ran a restaurant and then purchased a hotel in Stockton with her second husband, James Richards, with whom she had another daughter. During the summer, Huerta and her brothers helped run these establishments, which were located on the fringes of skid row and catered to the working classes. Huerta relished the experience and learned to appreciate different types of people. "The ethnic community where we lived was all mixed. It was Japanese, Chinese. The only Jewish families that lived in Stockton were there in our neighborhood.... There was the Filipino pool hall . . , the Mexican drug stores, the Mexican bakeries were there."

In contrast to this vibrant community life, relations between her mother and stepfather were strained and eventually ended in divorce. In the early 1950s, Alicia married Juan Silva, a union that produced another daughter and endured until Alicia's death from cancer in 1962. Huerta and her mother maintained a caring relationship that extended into Huerta's adult years.

Although Huerta was primarily influenced by her mother and grandfather, she never lost contact with her father, whose activities inspired her. Like most people in Dawson, Juan Fernández worked in the coal mines, but, to supplement his wages, he also joined the migrant labor force and traveled to Colorado, Nebraska, and Wyoming during the beet harvest. Indignant over poor working conditions and low

Raised by •

Mother and

Grandfather

wages, he became interested in labor issues. Leaving Dawson after his divorce from Alicia, Fernández became secretary-treasurer of a Congress of Industrial Organizations (CIO) local in Las Vegas. From there, in 1938 he won election to the New Mexico state legislature as a representative for San Miguel County. Fernández worked to promote a labor program, including New Mexico's "Little Wagner Act" and a wages–and–hours bill. However, his independent demeanor and outspokenness cost him a second term in office.

After her parents' divorce, Huerta had little contact with her father, except for one summer she spent traveling around New Mexico with him while he worked as a cookware salesman. This changed in later years, particularly after he settled in Stockton, living in a labor camp, working the asparagus fields, and holding other odd jobs that enabled him to return to school for a college degree. Proud of her father's union activism, political achievements, and educational accomplishments, Huerta revealed in an interview that "he was always supportive of my labor organizing."

As a youngster growing up in Stockton Huerta enjoyed a middle-class upbringing. After graduating from Stockton High School, the outgoing Huerta continued her education at Stockton College, unlike most Hispanic women of her generation. She interrupted her studies temporarily after her marriage to Ralph Head; when divorce quickly followed, she gained financial and emotional help from her mother and raised two daughters, as well as completing her A.A. degree.

During and after her divorce, Huerta had worked in the sheriff's office. Dissatisfaction with her job caused her to resume her education, pursue a teaching career and obtain her provisional teaching credential. An interview published in *Regeneración* in 1971 revealed Huerta's subsequent frustrations with this profession: "I realized one day that as a teacher I couldn't do anything for the kids who came to school barefoot and hungry."

• *Influenced by*

Postwar

Activism

Meanwhile the fresh wave of civic activism that was then sweeping through Mexican American communities increased Huerta's political consciousness. One manifestation of this activism was Community Service Organization (CSO), a Mexican American self-help association that eventually became a major influence in her life. However, Huerta's transformation to social and labor activism occurred gradually. Initially suspicious of the CSO and its chief organizer, Fred Ross, she explained to *Regeneración*: "I thought he was a communist, so I went to the FBI and had him checked out.... See how middle class I was." Her misgivings allayed, Huerta soon got involved, participating in the CSO's civic and educational programs, registering people to vote, organizing citizenship classes, and pressing local government for barrio improvements. As a result, she was hired to lobby in Sacramento for CSO legislative initiatives, such as the ultimately successful old-age pensions for non-citizens.

During this period she met and married her second husband, Ventura Huerta, who was also involved in community affairs. While the marriage produced five children, it eventually deteriorated."I knew I wasn't comfortable in a wife's role," Huerta confided to the *Progressive,* "but I wasn't clearly facing the issue. I hedged, I made excuses, I didn't come out and tell my husband that I cared more about helping other people than cleaning our house and doing my hair." During a trial separation that eventually ended in a bitter divorce, Huerta's mother again provided her with emotional and financial support, as well as backing her CSO career.

In the late 1950s, while struggling to balance a failing marriage, family, and work with a commitment to social concerns, Huerta became drawn to the conditions of farm workers. She joined a Northern California community interest group, the Agricultural Workers Association (AWA), which later merged with the AFL-CIO-sponsored Agricultural Workers Organizing Committee (AWOC), for which Huerta served as secretary-treasurer. During these years she met César Chávez, a fellow CSO official who shared her interest in farm labor. The two cooperated to bring rural labor issues to the attention of the more urban-oriented CSO. Frustrated by that organization's unresponsiveness, Chávez and Huerta left the group to dedicate themselves to organizing field workers. Together they took a step that changed the course of agricultural and labor history in California: In 1962 they founded the Farm Workers Association (FWA), the precursor to the United Farm Workers (UFW), in Delano.

From the very first, Huerta held decision-making posts and maintained a visible profile in the UFW. As second in command to Chávez, she continued to exert a direct influence, shaping and guiding the union's fortunes. During a 1965 strike in Delano, Huerta devised strategies and led picket lines. She was also the union's first contract negotiator, founding directing that department in the early 1960s. In these and other positions Huerta fought criticism based both on her gender and ethnicity. Reacting to her uncompromising and forceful style, a grower once exclaimed in *The Progressive,* "Dolores Huerta is crazy. She is a violent woman, where women, especially Mexican women, are usually peaceful and calm." Such attacks highlighted the extent of her challenge to the political, social, and economic power of California agribusiness, as well as to patriarchy.

Forms UFW •

with César

Chávez

197 •

Another major responsibility for Huerta was the directorship of the Manhattan table grape boycott and her assignment as East Coast boycott coordinator from 1968 to 1969. Her leadership there, at a primary grape distribution point, contributed to the success of the UFW's national effort to mobilize unions, political activists, Hispanic associations, community organizations, religious supporters, peace groups, student protestors, and concerned consumers. In New York City, Huerta also became aware of the emerging woman's rights movement through her contact with noted feminist Gloria Steinem, resulting in the emergence of a feminist critique in her personal philosophy. In 1970 the UFW's grassroots coalition finally forced grape producers to negotiate new contracts with farmers.

Huerta's organizational skills and ability to inspire others were felt again when she returned to New York to administer lettuce, grape, and Gallo wine boycotts during the 1970s. The concerted pressure of such boycotts there and in other major cities across the US resulted in the passage of the Agricultural Labor Relations Act (ALRA) in 1975, the first law to recognize the collective bargaining rights of farm workers in California.

In the midst of boycott duties and a heavy speaking schedule, Huerta began a third relationship—with Richard Chávez, César's brother, with whom she had four children, thus bringing the total number of her children to eleven. "I don't feel proud of the suffering that my kids went through," she once confessed to an interviewer, recalling her frequent absences from home. "I feel very bad and guilty about it, but by the same token I know that they learned a lot in the process."

During the late 1970s, Huerta assumed the directorship of the Citizenship Participation Day Department (CPD), the political arm of the UFW, and carried the union's battle to protect the new farm labor law into the Sacramento legislature. In the 1980s she became involved in another ambitious UFW project, the founding of Radio Campesina (KUFW), the union's radio station. Her schedule continued to include speaking engagements, fund raising, and testifying before state and congressional committees on a wide range of issues, including pesticides, health problems of field workers, Hispanic political issues, and immigration policy.

Huerta has dedicated her life to the UFW as an outspoken leader, executive board member, administrator, lobbyist, contract negotiator, picket captain, and lecturer, but at great personal cost. In addition to being arrested more than twenty times, in 1988 she suffered a life-threatening injury during a nonviolent demonstration against then-presidential candidate George Bush on his campaign swing through San

- *Severely*

Injured During

Demonstration

Francisco. Rushed to the hospital after being clubbed by police officers, Huerta underwent emergency surgery to remove her spleen and remained hospitalized while recovering from the operation and six broken ribs. The incident caused the police department to change rules regarding crowd control and police discipline; another result was a financial settlement to Huerta as a consequence of the personal assault.

In the 1990s, now recovered from her injuries, Huerta resumed work for the farm workers. It was a period when the political tide had turned conservative , diminishing public concern for the farm workers' cause, and the UFW was forced to undergo internal reassessment and restructuring. Still, Huerta has maintained that the union would continue as a strong force in the Hispanic community and beyond. "I think we brought to the world, the United States anyway, the whole idea of boycotting as a nonviolent tactic," she told an interviewer. "I think we showed the world that nonviolence can work to make social change.... I think we have laid a pattern of how farm workers are eventually going to get out of their bondage. It may not happen right now in our foreseeable future, but the pattern is there and farm workers are going to make it."

**Profile by
Margaret Rose**

MARI-LUCI JARAMILLO

M ari-Luci Jaramillo holds the position of assistant vice-president

for Educational Testing Services, one of the largest non-profit testing

corporations in the world. Her career in education spans nearly four

decades, though Jaramillo took a brief break from her educational

career from 1977-80 to serve as U.S. ambassador to Honduras under

then-President Jimmy Carter. "Being able to serve my country at that

level was a wonderful experience," she recalled during her interview

with contributor Michelle Vachon. "I knew that everything I said or did

reflected on the United States. I had the opportunity to carry the best of

my country and translate the best of my host country towards making

the two nations understand each other." Jaramillo's post at the Honduras

1928- •

Educator, •

ambassador,

businesswoman

American Embassy had come as a surprise to her. "I was not rich and had never participated in party politics, two things I thought were essential to political appointments. The only explanation I can offer is that many Chicano representatives close to President Carter were aware of my involvement in Latin American educational projects." Jaramillo handled her diplomatic duties in her usual way: "I worked like a fool. I'm a workaholic and I don't mind being labelled as such."

Jaramillo was born in Las Vegas, New Mexico, on June 19, 1928; her father was originally from Durango, Mexico, and her mother was a Las Vegas native. The second of three children, Jaramillo grew up in this small town of 14,000 inhabitants. When she was still a child, she developed the life-long habit of getting up at four or five o'clock in the morning. "We were poor and did not have enough wood to keep the house warm at night," Jaramillo recalled in her interview. "So my mother would get up and bundle me up in the chair, with only my hands sticking out to do my homework." She attended public school and won all the awards conferred by her high school. "My father demanded academic perfection. After graduation, I pursued the education track to become a teacher because it was the only career opportunity in town—I could complete the program in four years and my friends had already enrolled in it. Luckily for me, I loved teaching once I started."

However, after her first year in college, Jaramillo quit her studies to marry a school teacher. They moved to a small rural town where she held a series of odd jobs while raising her three children. Although she had earlier given up the idea of going back to college, she also resumed studying on her own, and soon began classes. "For years, I was taking care of my children, holding a job, and studying, all at the same time. During my last semester, a teacher helped me financially, which allowed me to concentrate on school." In 1955 Jaramillo obtained a baccalaureate from the New Mexico Highlands University in Las Vegas, with a major in education and a minor in Spanish and English. Shortly thereafter she secured a position with the West Las Vegas school system where she remained for a decade. She served as an elementary school teacher and, eventually, as language arts supervisor for all of the county's schools.

• Reaches Out to

the Hispanic

Community

While teaching elementary school, Jaramillo worked actively to increase the level of education in the Hispanic community. "Growing up where I did and seeing the desperate need for education among people who looked like me made me believe that we could break the poverty hold on Chicanos if we educated ourselves," she told Vachon. "I started reaching out to help and it became a way of life. I did all I could on my own, trying to teach English and reading, and trying to reach adults as well as children. When I got out of my small community, I realized that the problem was everywhere, that Hispanics were not really getting their fair share in educational and professional opportunities." In 1965 Jaramillo started lecturing at the University of New Mexico, in Albuquerque, teaching English as a second language and conducting classes in Spanish for Latin American students. Later she joined the Department of Elementary Education as assistant professor, eventually becoming its professor and chairperson.

Jaramillo greeted the emergence of the civil rights movement in the late 1960s and early 1970s with enthusiasm. "Suddenly, I had the chance to take on larger projects. Among others, I took part in the university's Cultural Awareness Center activities. We would meet with administrators, counsellors, teachers, parents and anyone else willing to listen to tell them that maybe Chicanos and Hispanics are not your average father, mother, two-point-three children and a dog and a cat and a white fence families; that they bring a beautiful language and a unique culture with them; that we shouldn't try to kill it off, but instead that we should look for these qualities and nurture them while we teach English."

Through these and other activities, Jaramillo extended her involvement nationally and internationally. In conjunction with the U.S. Agency for International Development and the university's Latin American educational programs, she travelled to Argentina, Columbia, Ecuador, Venezuela, and throughout Central America to train teachers and hold workshops on education and school development. "I saw similarities in the needs of the poor across the world. I did everything I could to call attention to it and to be part of the solution."

When Jimmy Carter became president in 1976, he asked Jaramillo to serve as ambassador to Honduras. "I could hardly believe my ears when I got the phone call," she recalled. "During the presidential election campaign, the Democrats had created a talent bank that included the names of minorities and women to be considered for appointment. A friend of mine put my curriculum vitae in it without my knowing. Since I had not revised it for a long time, I was not expecting anything out of it. But many Chicanos working on the Carter campaign knew that I spoke Spanish fluently, that I was bicultural, and that I had repeatedly visited Latin America." Between 1977 and 1980 Jaramillo and her second husband lived in Tegucigalpa, Honduras. She served as chief of mission for six government agencies and 500 Peace Corps volunteers operating in the country, and attended to the American community of about 2,000 people. "It was a fairy tale," Jaramillo remembered. "It was also hard work. The Central American region was starting to flare up. When the trouble began in Nicaragua, many Nicaraguans fled to Honduras,

Appointed U.S.

Ambassador to

Honduras

which is next door. Also, the Honduran military establishment had just abdicated power. We undertook to assist in holding the first free election in years. It was so exciting to watch a country go from military rule to a democracy. The election took place after my departure, but I am proud to say that Honduras has been choosing its president through democratic elections ever since."

Jaramillo returned to Washington, D.C., in 1980 to become deputy assistant secretary for inter-American affairs at the U.S. Department of State. Two months later, Jimmy Carter lost the presidential election. "I stayed at the Department of State until March 1981 and then left of my own accord," she explained. "I would have liked to continue representing my country abroad, but I really belonged to the Carter administration. I believed in human rights and in the work done by the administration. It would have been difficult to represent a government with which I disagreed on major issues. Besides, I was not asked to stay." Upon leaving the State Department, Jaramillo returned to the University of New Mexico—which had been awaiting her return to teaching—as special assistant to the president. In 1982, she was named associate dean for the university's College of Education and, in 1985, the university's vice-president for student affairs.

• *Enters the*

Corporate

World

Two years later, Educational Testing Services (ETS) hired Jaramillo as vice-president of its San Francisco Bay-area office, located in Emeryville, California. ETS has one of the most specialized staffs in the field of developing and administering tests. Headquartered in Princeton, New Jersey, the non-profit corporation contracts with universities, departments of education, and professional organizations worldwide. In 1992 Jaramillo secured the position of assistant vice-president for field services at ETS; she now administers the corporation's eight U.S. field offices.

Jaramillo admits that her concept of education has changed throughout the years. "I used to think that if you educate people, they will be able to make it," she explained in her interview. "I found out that it isn't so. Some highly educated people cannot get into the system for a variety of reasons. Today I counsel students to learn about the importance of economics and the political aspects of our democracy, regardless of their field of expertise. 'Know the system and make it work for you,' I tell them. You have to understand how the business world operates and what it means when our government talks about protecting American interests in a foreign country. You have to see yourself in relation to currents events in order to participate. Politically, I believe that our American system works as long as you participate in it. You must vote and make your voice heard. Otherwise you will be left out."

Jaramillo has accumulated numerous awards in the course of her career. In 1986 she was named co-recipient of the Harvard Graduate School of Education's Anne Roe Award honoring leading educators who have contributed to women's professional growth. In 1988 the Miller Brewing Company recognized her as one of the country's Outstanding Hispanic Educators, and *Hispanic Business* magazine named her one of the 100 Most Influential Hispanics in the United States. In 1990, the Mexican American Women's National Association honored her with its Primera Award as the first Hispanic woman to be appointed U.S. ambassador to Honduras, and the American Association for Higher Education granted her an award for Outstanding Leadership in Education in the Hispanic Community. Jaramillo continues to participate actively in community and professional organizations: she sits on the board of directors of both the Children's Television Workshop and the New Mexico Highlands University Foundation, as well as the board of trustees of the Tomas Rivera Center at California's Claremont University. She also serves as a minority recruiter for the U.S. Department of State.

Jaramillo—who is now divorced—makes her home in Emeryville, California. "Looking back—would I do it again?," she pondered during her interview. "I think that I have occasionally made a difference in my children's and students' lives. Many of my students call me after all these years, and I am close to my children and grandchildren. Yes, I have enjoyed every minute of it!"

**Profile by
Michelle Vachon**

TANIA LEÓN

*T*ania León is just one of a handful of women to have made a successful career as an orchestral conductor. Since she first arrived in the United States from Cuba in 1968, she has become known not only for her conducting skill, but also as an important composer for New York's Dance Theater of Harlem. Combining her work as a composer with serving as a musical director and conductor of some of the world's most notable musical productions, León has presented her interpretation of a wide variety of classical and modern musical scores to audiences during a career that has spanned close to three decades.

1943- •

Composer, •

conductor

León was born on May 14, 1943, in La Habana, Cuba, the daughter of Oscar León Mederos and Dora Ferran. After graduating from high school in Cuba, she attended Havana's National Conservatory of Music, where she obtained a degree in music education in 1965. In 1969, just one year after arriving in the United States, León became the first music director of the Dance Theater of Harlem, a position she held until 1979. She also enrolled at New York University where, after earning her baccalaureate in music education in 1973, she was awarded a Master's degree in music composition two years later.

From 1977 to 1988 León served as the director of the popular Family Concert Series for the Brooklyn Philharmonic Community. She has also served as both conductor and music director of the 1978 Broadway production of *The Wiz*; as musical director of *Maggie Magalita,* produced at the Kennedy Center for the Performing Arts in 1980; and as conductor of the Whitney Museum Contemporary Music Concert series from 1986-87. In 1985 León also joined the faculty of Brooklyn College as an associate professor, teaching both composition and conducting. Other honors have included the CINTAS Award in composition, which she received in both 1976 and 1979; 1980's National Council of Women of the United States Achievement Award; the ASCAP Composer's Award, from 1978 to 1989; 1985's Dean Dixon Achievement Award; the American Academy's 1991 Academy-Institute Award; and numerous other awards.

Skilled in the use of a baton, León has honed her skills as a conductor by studying under such teachers and coaches as Laszlo Halasz, Leonard Bernstein, and Seiji Ozawa. She continues to maintain a busy schedule as both a recording artist and a guest conductor, performing orchestral compositions on many of the important symphony stages throughout the United States and Puerto Rico, as well as to audiences in Paris, London, Spoleto, Berlin, and Munich. In addition, León has several musical works to her credit, including "Paisanos Semos" for solo guitar, and "Momentum" and "Ritual," both for solo piano.

**Profile by
Pamela L. Shelton**

NANCY LOPEZ

ince becoming a professional golfer in 1978, Nancy Lopez has

consistently ranked among the top women on the international circuit.

She is one of only five women in the sport to have earned more than $1

Professional •

million in her career. In addition to winning nearly fifty tournament

golfer

victories on tour, in 1987 Lopez became the youngest woman ever to be

named to the Ladies Professional Golf Association (LPGA) Hall of Fame.

Born January 6, 1957, in Torrance, California, Lopez first became a golf enthusiast as a child after her parents, Domingo and Marina Lopez, took up the game for her mother's health. By the age of eleven it was obvious to her father that Nancy had become a better golfer than either he or his wife; convinced that his daughter was champion material, he began to groom her for tournament play.

The Lopez family set many of its own needs aside to support Nancy's training, but even with that strong support her career had a rough start. "My dad worked so hard to do so much for me and a lot of doors were shut in our faces, because he couldn't afford to get me into the country club so I could play golf there," she recalled to *Hispanic*. "It was a shame, because I had the talent to produce, and no one was giving

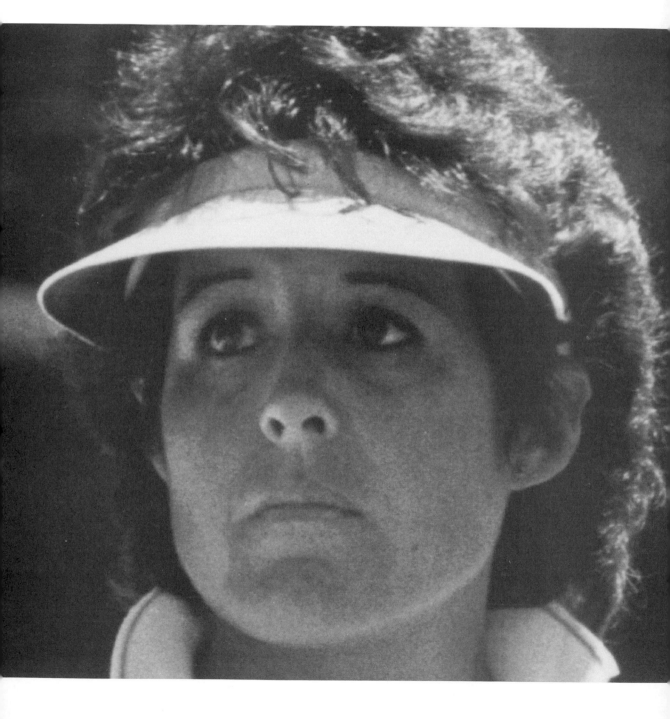

me the opportunity." However, with her family behind her, Lopez pushed onward: At the age of twelve she won the first of three state women's tournaments and, while still in high school, she finished second in the Women's Open. In 1972 and 1974, Lopez won the U.S. Golf Association Junior Girls; in 1978, while attending undergraduate classes at the University of Tulsa, she won the intercollegiate title. Her continued success spurred Lopez to the decision to make a permanent commitment to golf. In 1979 she left college and turned professional.

During her first year on the professional circuit, Lopez broke several standing records: She began the year by winning the Bent Tree Classic at Sarasota, Florida, and then went on to win a record five tournaments in succession, including the prestigious LPGA title. She has since won her second and third LPGA titles as well as a Nabisco Dinah Shore title. By August of 1978 she had surpassed the $150,000 earnings record set by fellow golfer Judy Rankin in 1976, she ended the year with total earnings of $200,000. Lopez also endorsed or made commercials for various golf products.

Record- •

Breaking First

Year

Since her initial appearance on the pro circuit, Lopez has always been ranked at the very top of her sport. In 1979 she won eight of the nineteen tournaments she entered, a feat *Sports Illustrated* called "one of the most dominating sports performances in half a century." Lopez had her best year in 1985, when she earned more money—over $400,000— than any other player on the circuit. She won five tournaments and set a record-high scoring average of 70.73 percent. Two years later marked her entry into the LPGA Hall of Fame, "which has the most difficult requirements for entry of any sports Hall of Fame in the nation," as the *New York Times* noted. Thirty tournament victories—two of them major titles—are needed for Hall of Fame inclusion. In 1987, Lopez also shared her advice on improving golf technique in *Nancy Lopez's the Complete Golfer.*

The 1990s saw Lopez's fast-track to the top change its course. A win during her 1993 tour was her last for several years. Nagging ailments, a growing family, and playing twenty-three tournaments a year were beginning to take its toll. But Lopez's dedication to the game of golf was too strong to ignore, and by 1995 she felt she was hitting a new stride. "I'm rededicating myself to the game this year," she told *USA Today* in March of that year. "I haven't done justice to myself over the past two years."

Despite the many challenges faced by a professional woman athlete, Lopez has managed to balance the demands of her game with those of being a devoted wife and mother. In fact, she admitted to the *New York Times,* "I like being a wife and mother more than I like professional golf." Lopez and her husband, former New York Met and MVP'er Ray Knight, split the domestic duty roster in caring for their three children. "We complement each other," Knight explained. "We help each other with the chores." And Knight, who now coaches for the Cincinnati Reds, occasionally caddies for his wife. Because of their respective status in golf and baseball, Lopez and Knight are "probably the most prominent married couple in sports," according to the *New York Times*. They are also among the happiest. Lopez told Jaime Diaz in *Sports Illustrated*: "I'm so happy with my life, that now when I play, there is no pressure. It's just all fun, and when it's fun, you perform better."

**Profile by
Denise Wiloch**

MÓNICA CECILIA LOZANO

A s the associate publisher and executive editor of the largest **1956-** •

Spanish-language daily newspaper in the United States, Mónica Cecilia

Lozano is determined to keep the 450,000 readers of La Opinión *both* **Newspaper** •

informed and entertained. In an interview with Ronie-Richele Garcia- **editor**

Johnson, Lozano explained that there is an overlap between "straight

journalism and journalism with a sense of commitment. And, clearly,

she is committed to the readers of La Opinión. It is important to Lozano

that Hispanics—especially politically neglected Spanish-speaking His-

panics—empower themselves. "As a group," she contends, "we can have

power if we are informed and educated.... I really believe in what I am

doing."

Lozano comes from a long line of journalists: her grandfather founded both *La Prensa* in San Antonio, Texas, in 1913, and *La Opinión* in Los Angeles, California, in 1926. It is a bloodline she is proud of, remarking that "you can't separate my success from my family." Lozano was born the third of four children, to Ignacio E. and Marta (Navarro) Lozano, on July 21, 1956, in the city of Los Angeles. While her parents were very strict, sending her to Catholic schools through high school, they did not pressure her to work for the family business.

Although Ignacio Lozano had published *La Opinión*—the newspaper founded by his father—from the time of his father's death in 1953, his own son, Jose, took over the reins of publisher at Ignacio's retirement in 1986. Although Jose's sister Mónica also worked for the paper, her father could not predict that she would become seriously involved with *La Opinión* to the point that she would make it a career. He knew that his daughter wanted to excel on her own; she did not want to dwell in the shadows of her grandfather, father, or brother.

After earning her bachelor's degree from the University of Oregon in 1977, Lozano moved to San Francisco. Although she did not know anyone in that city, she soon began to feel at home. For over five years she worked at a large printing company, first as a press operator and then as a manager of a company branch, as well as on local community newspapers. While working these full-time jobs, she also attended night classes at San Francisco City College. According to Lozano, she wanted to help her community, and she realized that she needed to use any resources, including the power of the print medium, to facilitate her goals. She also became intrigued with the workings of the newspaper business and was determined to learn every procedure involved in running a paper—including pre-press and press operations. Lozano eventually received her degree in printing technology from San Francisco City College in 1981.

Reviewing her decisions to work for a printing company and earn a degree in printing technology, Lozano wonders if she knew, subconsciously, that she wanted to join the family business. "I guess there is such a thing as [having] ink in your veins," she will laugh. In any case, by the time she returned to Los Angeles and began working for *La Opinión*, she had prepared herself to supervise—and even manually complete— every step of the paper's production. In addition, she was well equipped to provide the newspaper's Hispanic readers with the valuable information she gained through her involvement in community projects in San Francisco.

While *La Opinión* provided employment for several members of her family, Lozano inherited more than simply a career in the newspaper

Destined to Join •

La Opinión

business. Her father and grandfather imparted their sense of dedication, moral responsibility, and ethical ideals to the young woman. "I wanted to do something to help my community," she stressed. "I wanted to use whatever resources I had to help.... It became clear that .... [i]f I wanted to be useful I should come back to L.A. to work for *La Opinión*."

When Lozano became managing editor of *La Opinión* in 1985, she immediately began to focus on the needs and concerns of her readers. One of her first major projects was the publication of a special tabloid that addressed the threat of the AIDS virus within the Hispanic community. The Hispanic Coalition of AIDS honored her new publication with an advocacy award in 1988, as a life-saving, educational contribution to the community; the public-service tabloid also received the Inter-American Press Association's award. As a result of her hard work and dedication, Lozano was named associate publisher of *La Opinión* in 1989. The following year she was appointed publisher of the widely read and respected weekly Spanish newspaper, *El Eco del Valle*, becoming its publisher in 1991.

Spanish-speaking Hispanics living in Southern California have indeed benefitted from Lozano's commitment to the community and her readers. Largely because of her efforts, *La Opinión* has published public service supplements, tabloids, and other publications that discuss such important topics as drug abuse prevention, prenatal care, education, AIDS, and immigration issues. Lozano's seemingly tireless determination to keep the readers of *La Opinión* well-informed has been lauded by many community leaders.

Lozano, a member of the National Association of Hispanic Journalists, the California Chicano News Media Association, and the American Society of Newspaper Editors, has also received state-wide, national, and even international recognition for her newspaper work. In 1987 she was named one of the one hundred most influential Hispanic women by *Hispanic Business* magazine. Lozano was among the one hundred most influential Hispanics by the same publication in 1992. The March of Dimes DIME—Distinction in Media Excellence award—was presented to her for a supplement she published on prenatal care. And in 1992 Lozano was elected vice-president of the California Hispanic Publishers Association, a position she held until 1995.

Although Lozano feels a "tremendous sense of tradition" in working for *La Opinión* and is dedicated to both the paper and its readers, her children take priority over all else. Lozano believes that spending quality time with her children is better than spending great amounts of time with them. Her children, she says, understand that she loves them more than anything despite the fact that she works long hours. As an experienced

*   *Family Takes*

    Top Priority in

    Life

working mother, Lozano readily acknowledges that combining working and mothering is difficult. Her daily life necessitates a "tremendous balancing act" in order to find time to spend with her family, but she feels she has found the "rhythm that working mothers get into."

Lozano's chosen profession is a demanding one and her working hours are unpredictable. Responsible for the contents of almost the entire paper, she cannot return home at the end of the day and leave her work in the office. Her days, which are filled with deadlines, begin early in the morning and end late at night. There is no telling when an important news item will occur. A large gas explosion in Mexico, for example, sent reporters and staff members rushing. They all knew that it was important that readers, who might have families in that area, get the facts about the disaster. Such an event, explained Lozano, requires thorough yet quick work. "This is what you are here to do," Lozano stated. "You go into a different gear."

Los Angeles, Lozano pointed out in her interview, has "real deep social problems, the kind of problems that need real deep structural changes." In a personal effort to better the city, from 1991 to 1992, she was one of seven members—and the only woman, at that time—on the board of Los Angeles's Community Redevelopment Agency (CRA), an organization mandated to "eliminate blight" in needy urban neighborhoods. Since a major purpose of the CRA is to motivate and empower neighborhoods through funding, Lozano stated that the CRA has the "opportunity to do something concrete . . . for the homeless population in the city."

While Los Angeles first struck her as "big," "impersonal," and "difficult" after her move from San Francisco, Lozano now feels that the energy being expended in efforts to revitalize the city makes the place very exciting. In addition to contributing to those efforts as she works for *La Opinión*, Lozano is an active member of the Los Angeles community. She serves on the board of trustees of the University of Southern California and as the vice-chair of the Los Angeles Annenberg Metropolitan project, a multi-million dollar school reform initiative. She holds a position on the board of directors of the Venice Family Clinic, a non-profit facility that provides health care to low-income minority patients. In addition, Lozano works with the Central American Refugee Center.

Lozano has been recognized on many occasions for her community service. In 1988 the Central American Refugee Center (CARECEN) awarded her contribution to immigrant rights. Other honors Lozano has received for her work include the 1989 Outstanding Woman of the Year Award from the Mexican American Opportunities Foundation, Northern Trust of California's 1990 "Hispanic Excellence" award, an award from

Comision Femenil of Los Angeles for outstanding contribution as a woman in media in 1990, and the National Organization for Women (NOW) Legal Defense and Educational Fund award in 1992. In December of 1995, the *California Journal* named Lozano one of twenty-five Californians "with the power, influence, and ideas to shape the dreams for generations to come."

In addition to being an exemplary journalist, Lozano is well aware of the role model she has become for young Hispanic women, both in her city and beyond. As she told Garcia-Johnson, as an influential Latina she feels a "real sense of responsibility" to the next generation. While continuing to encourage young Hispanics to excel, Lozano cautions that it takes a great amount of courage and persistence to succeed. "If you are going to do it," she advises, "you should be prepared to go all the way."

**Profile by
Ronie-Richele
Garcia-Johnson**

WENDY LUCERO-SCHAYES

*I*n over ten years of competitive diving, Wendy Lucero-Schayes has

had a distinguished career that includes participation in the 1988

Olympic Games. A member of the U.S. National Diving Team for eight

consecutive years, she is the winner of nine national titles, three U.S.

Olympic Festival titles, and several medals in international competition,

including a silver at the 1991 World Championships. Her accomplish-

ments have not been limited to athletics, however; Lucero-Schayes has

also begun a career in television broadcasting, appearing on national

networks as a sports commentator and hosting a local talk show in her

hometown of Denver. Her ability to develop her athletic talents—thereby

providing herself with opportunities to travel the world and obtain an

1963- •

Olympic •

athlete,

broadcaster

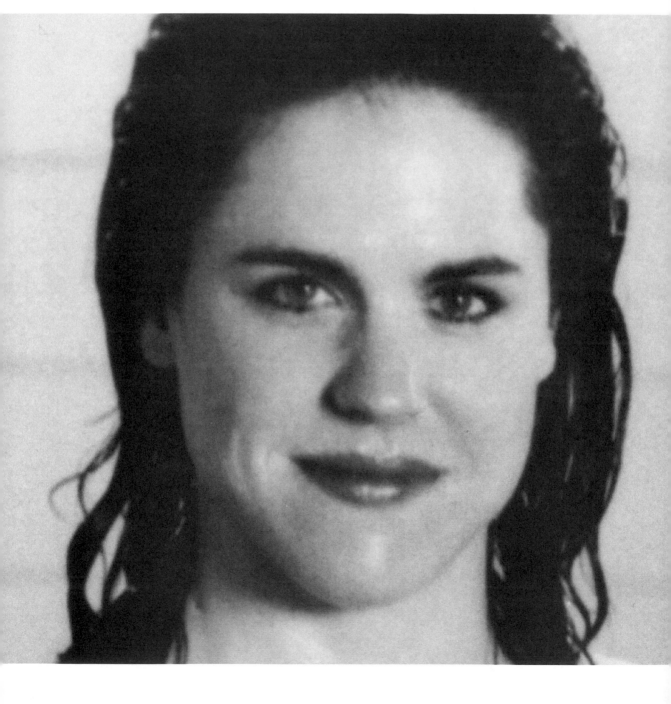

education—has made Lucero-Schayes an example of someone who has succeeded through hard work and determination.

Lucero-Schayes was born on June 26, 1963, in Denver, Colorado, to Shirley and Don Lucero. The son of Spanish immigrants, Don Lucero worked as an electrician; he was able to work steadily because employers thought he was Italian, not Hispanic. Her mother, of Irish extraction, maintained the household, raising Lucero-Schayes and her sister and brother. The family was active and athletic; Lucero-Schayes began swimming and dancing at an early age, and she picked up gymnastics, tennis, and diving while tagging along to her older sister's lessons. She became competitive in each of her endeavors; sports provided an opportunity for a tomboy to excel, in contrast to school, where she felt teachers frowned upon her because of her energetic nature.

Her sister provided an additional motivation to excel, for the two often ended up competing in the same age group at meets. Their two-year age difference doomed the younger sister to being second best, Lucero-Schayes revealed in a personal interview. "For me to compete with my sister—well, she's my older sister, she's always going to win because she's two years older." Always being the runner-up "kept me in a 'trying to achieve' mode," she explained. "I would always strive to be the best I could be because I wanted to grasp what my sister was attaining—but I wanted it now, even though I was two years younger." When Lucero-Schayes began to close the gap between them, her sister moved on to other activities; but the young athlete still felt driven to excel.

Part of Lucero-Schayes's ambition was to fulfill a dream she had harbored since the age of nine: to compete in the Olympic Games. While she first thought she would compete in gymnastics, she soon realized her late start in the sport would limit how far she could go. But her enthusiasm for sports soon found a new focus. "I fell in love with ice skating," she told an interviewer. "After I saw Dorothy Hamill in 1976 win the Olympic gold, that really inspired me. I knew I wasn't going to be an Olympic gymnast; so I thought 'Well, I'll make it in ice skating.'" Besides providing an athletic outlet, figure skating gave Lucero-Schayes a chance to express herself artistically. "I did enjoy it because of the aesthetic ability required," she explained. "Being able to dance to the music and perform, and be creative that way—I just fell in love with that aspect."

After competing for four years, however, she came to the conclusion that she would not attain her Olympic dream through ice skating. Not only did she come late to the sport, which left her at a disadvantage

Skating Star •

Inspires

Olympic Dream

221 •

in the exacting school figures portion of skating competitions, but her family lacked the financial resources necessary for her to be successful in national competition. "As far as getting into the Ice Capades, I probably could have done that," Lucero-Schayes recalled, "but I wanted to get a college education, and ice skating wouldn't have done that." In the early 1980s, while she was contemplating ways to continue her education, a series of federal laws and court decisions finally mandated that universities give women equal access to athletic scholarships. By competing in a varsity sport, Lucero-Schayes would be able to take advantage of the full-ride scholarships increasingly being made available to female athletes.

While still in high school Lucero-Schayes returned to diving, which she had tried for a time as a preteen. Her gymnastics training served her well, and she quickly became very competitive on the springboard events. She placed fourth in her state's championships as a sophomore, and came in second as a senior. By the time she finished high school, she was competing in the Junior Olympic Championships, where she placed sixth in the three-meter event, and the Phillips 66 National Diving Championships, where in both indoor and outdoor competitions she finished in the top twenty on the one-meter springboard. Her success led her to be named 1981's Hispanic Athlete of the Year, cited as an Academic All-American, and also resulted in a scholarship offer from the University of Nebraska.

Lucero-Schayes was looking forward to the challenges of college; although she had encountered problems with teachers as a child, her competitive nature had since emerged; she was earning top grades by the time she entered high school. In addition, her parents had instilled in her the value of an education; because neither of them had been to college, they wanted their children to have the advantages higher education could give them. "My parents were great role models to me, my mother was *the* highest role model that I had," Lucero-Schayes stated in her interview. "I had other role models, the sports role models like the Dorothy Hamills and the Peggy Flemings and the Olga Korbuts. But my mother was always the one I respected and that I thought of as the most wonderful; and I had a dad that was very supportive and tried to give his kids whatever he could with the limitations that he had. They were successful enough with what they had done, but they wanted me to be as self-confident as I could be, because they knew the outside world wasn't going to give that to me."

While attending the University of Nebraska Lucero-Schayes had the difficult task of balancing her classes with a demanding schedule of training and competition. She had to work particularly hard to master the three-meter springboard, a new event for her. "I was born and raised in a climate that really was for winter sports," the athlete explained. "I was really lucky they had some high school pools, but they only had the lowest springboard [one-meter] available to me and that's what you dove in high school anyway. So I really didn't learn the Olympic [three-meter] springboard event until college, which is a very late date to start out. I've been trying to play catch-up ever since." After two years she transferred to Southern Illinois University, seeking a more compatible coach and better opportunities to compete nationally. The move proved successful; she won the 1985 NCAA championship on the one-meter event and earned her first national titles, placing first at the 1984 and 1985 Phillips 66 Outdoor Championships. During these years she was also named an Academic All-American for her performance in the classroom.

Lucero-Schayes had goals outside of athletics, however, and worked hard to achieve those as well. To complement her education— she earned a B.S. in television sales and management in 1986—with hands-on experience, she sought opportunities to work in broadcasting and television production. "As I was training for the Olympic Games in 1988 and the few years before that, I would try to be a production assistant for golf tournaments, horse tournaments, Monday Night Football anything I could do." She worked as a freelance sportscaster for NBC, ABC, and ESPN—including a stint as a commentator for the 1991 World Championships—and hosted a talk show, "Focus Colorado," in her hometown of Denver. Lucero-Schayes particularly enjoyed that experience, "because then I could get involved with people that have helped shape not only the state, but eventually the U.S. and what we think."

Training and competing in preparation for the 1988 Olympic Trials was her immediate focus coming out of college, however, and Lucero-Schayes was making great progress. Although she felt she had the potential to dive well on the ten-meter platform, she relinquished the opportunity to learn that event in order to focus on what would be her best shot to make the Olympic team: the three-meter springboard. Her rigorous training for the Olympic event paid off; in 1987 she won her first three-meter diving titles at the U.S. Olympic Festival and the American Cup II; she also won the bronze in one-meter events at such international meets as the McDonald's International and at a competition between the U.S. and the Soviet Union.

During the period Lucero-Schayes was making great strides toward her Olympic goal, two separate incidents hindered her training: her mother, who had been a constant source of encouragement throughout her career, was diagnosed with an advanced form of breast cancer; meanwhile, her coach was undermining her self-confidence. Although she had won the HTH Classic early in 1988, in three subsequent competitions she placed no better than fourth—and she needed to finish second at the trials to make the Olympic team. "I had people in my life that basically didn't believe in me," Lucero-Schayes recalled; "I had a coach, a top Olympic coach who told me, 'I'm sorry, but you remind me of me and you'll never make it.' I didn't stay with that person and I ended up realizing that I wanted to prove him wrong."

The diver switched coaches and continued training for the trials; her previous coach's lack of faith only deepened her determination. Another motivating factor was her mother, who had completed chemotherapy for her cancer and would be able to attend the Olympic trials. Lucero-Schayes cites this meet as her most memorable, for the recovery of her mother and her presence at the meet allowed her to enjoy the competition. She turned in one of the best performances of her career and finished second, just eighty-one hundredths of a point ahead of the next diver. She had made the Olympic team, vindicating herself in the face of her former coach's doubt. "To try to believe in myself and surpass what other people think was a big step for me, and I ended up competing and winning, overcoming his top people that he thought *would* succeed."

Lucero-Schayes competed at the 1988 Olympics in Seoul, Korea, finishing sixth. Although she didn't win a medal, she recalls the trip fondly for other reasons: "One of my favorite incidents was with the Russian coach—her name was Tatiana—she gave me a wonderful gift. We had been creating a nice friendship throughout my couple years of seeing her in international competitions, and I really liked her. After the Olympic games were over, she ended up giving me this wonderful china bowl. And that friendship and that bond—I'll never forget that. I think that is one of the neatest things that could have ever happened, because you cross boundaries through sports that you could not do with anything else."

Since competing in the 1988 Olympics, Lucero-Schayes has continued her work in communications, increasing her involvement in public speaking. She has participated in conferences and charity events and has visited schools. Although she enjoys her work in television, the former Olympic athlete gets a special reward from speaking to people in person. "I end up being able to touch people's lives that way," she explained in her interview, "and I think it's more important because people really need to see you face-on—to talk to you and be able to touch you. The experience may be a short span of time but enough to give them one positive thought that maybe will change their lives for the better." Lucero-Schayes has served as a spokesperson for the American Cancer Society and often appears as a motivational speaker in front of audiences that include Hispanic organizations. "The success I've had in sports overcoming those people who didn't think that I could [succeed] has made me like myself better and find out, 'Yeah, I am capable and I'm not going to let them determine what I can do.' Hopefully I can share that with others."

Public appearances also introduced the diver to her husband, professional basketball player Dan Schayes. The two were appearing at a benefit for a charity promoting organ donation; he gave her a note, joking "I will share my organs with you anytime," and she gave him her number. They began dating, and two years later, in late 1991, they married. The couple often trains together; but more important is the support they provide as each undergoes the strains of competition. "I had dated athletic guys before, but not elite athletes, and it makes a big difference," Lucero-Schayes told Michelle Kaufman of the *Detroit Free Press*. "Danny understands what it feels like to be under pressure, to win and to lose."

The pressure was certainly on for Lucero-Schayes as the 1991 Olympic year approached. She had continued to improve her diving, winning Olympic Festival titles in 1989 and 1990, and capturing one-meter and three-meter championships those same years. She followed those performances with her best year ever in 1991: she took both springboard events in the indoor championships, placed first in the one-meter and second in the three meter outdoors, and garnered silver medals at the Sixth World Championship and Alamo International competitions. For her efforts Lucero-Schayes was voted U.S. Female Diving Athlete of the Year in both 1990 and 1991. Although an illness prevented her from competing in late 1991 and hampered her training time going into 1992, she was still considered a likely Olympian and a medal contender for Barcelona. These expectations were harder on her than the physical difficulties of training: "It's definitely more mental than it is physical, because as much as I have trained, my body now knows [what to do]; it's letting the mind relax and do what I have trained it to do for years. It is more of a mindset, whether or not I feel I'm capable of getting out there and performing to the best of my ability and overcoming the stress and the pressure. But I think this is good," she explained, "because in a way if you're not learning or growing or achieving in that aspect then it's not fun to do it."

Lucero-Schayes finished third in the 1992 Olympic trials, one place short of making the team. Although competing in a second Olympics—

Tale of Success •

Motivates

Others

in Spain, the country of her ancestors—would have been "a dream come true," the athlete still finds much to be satisfied with her career. "Diving has been wonderful to me; not only did it pay for a college education, but I was able to travel around the world, nothing that my parents were ever financially capable of doing. Not only did it expand my horizons and make me understand what the world is all about," she added, it provided an opportunity to experience "camaraderie, getting to create friendships with [athletes from] other countries." At the end of the 1992 season, she was still investigating the possibility of combining competitive diving with lecturing and various opportunities in broadcasting. In the long term, Lucero-Schayes and her husband plan to return to Denver, where she will continue her career in communications. Now that she has made her mark in the world of athletics, she wants to inspire others on a broader scale. "I always felt that communications—whether radio and television, or through newspapers and journalism—it's going to shape our world, it is the up-and-coming future. I really believe that instead of being on the other side just watching it happen, I want to be involved with helping in a positive way."

**Profile by
Diane Telgen**

SONIA MANZANO

*S*onia Manzano, an actress and writer for PBS's critically acclaimed Sesame Street *children's television series, provides her young*

audiences with a positive Latina role model. While growing up in the

United States, Manzano could not remember seeing Hispanic images,

either in children's books or in the media. "I think it has a terrible impact

when you don't see yourself reflected in the society because then you get

the feeling you don't exist—like Richard Wright's Invisible Man,*" she*

explained during an interview with Luis Vasquez-Ajmac. "That's why I

love being on Sesame Street *so much. I'm happy to be in a situation*

where I'm not asked to be like anyone else."

1950- •

Actress, •

writer

Born June 12, 1950, in New York City and raised in the South Bronx,

Manzano grew up in a very close-knit, Spanish-speaking community. Of Puerto Rican descent herself, Manzano is one of four children. Her father, Bonifacio Manzano, is a roofer by trade while her mother, Isidra Rivera, is a seamstress. While growing up Manzano never thought of pursuing a career in show business—at least until she was a junior in high school. Then, with the help of a supportive teacher, she enrolled at Manhattan's prestigious High School for the Performing Arts. Subsequently, she attended Carnegie Mellon University in Pittsburgh, Pennsylvania, on a scholarship, where she majored in drama; she later obtained a master's degree in education as well. While in the middle of her undergraduate years in college Manzano was cast in the musical *Godspell* and was later part of the original cast when the production came to Broadway. During her performance in *Godspell,* an agent noted her talent and helped her obtain an audition at *Sesame Street.*

When Manzano began working at *Sesame Street,* the emphasis of the public-television-aired series was on helping black inner city children. But with the addition of the character "Maria," Manzano brought to the show a fresh new face, someone that captured the attention of young Hispanic viewers. In 1993, the year that *Sesame Street* turned its attention to Hispanic culture—it traditionally has focused on a different ethnic group each year—Manzano found her role and responsibilities to be particularly challenging. She gladly accepted the challenge of writing for and about Hispanics on the popular show.

After ten years on *Sesame Street* as "Maria," Manzano began writing scripts for the show with hopes of making her character more visible. Understanding the importance of incorporating Hispanic culture into the show's plot line, she has often written material based on her own real-life experiences, particularly in developing the relationship, marriage, and eventual parenthood of characters "Maria" and "Luis", played by fellow actor Emilio Delgado. To date, Manzano has earned seven Emmy awards as a member of the *Sesame Street* writing staff as well as an award in 1991 from the Hispanic Congressional Caucus in Washington, D.C.

Television has not served merely as a stepping stone for Manzano. She enjoys her career acting and writing for the young *Sesame Street* audience, which includes viewers in over eighty-five countries worldwide. By enriching children's lives and expressing her ideas, she believes that she can continue to have a positive influence by developing Hispanic role models that youngsters can both like and look up to. Manzano, who has been married since 1986, enjoys working with her daughter, Gabriela, on *Sesame Street.* When time allows, she also lectures on the importance of Hispanic role models.

Creates Role •

Model for

Hispanic

Children

**Profile by
Luis Vasquez-Ajmac**

MARISOL

Never content to confine herself to a single medium or limit her

creativity to one style, the artist who has gone by the single name of

Marisol since she began her career in the mid-1950s has explored

diversity in both her art and life. Early in her career she began carving

wooden figures, painting them, and adorning them with the unexpect-

ed. Today her sculptures—incorporating everything from bronze to

scorched, weatherbeaten timbers—are housed in museums and private

collections around the world. Marisol is arguably one of the most

influential artists of the latter 20th century. Known for works such as

Baby Boy, Baby Girl, The Kennedys, The Party, *and* The Last Supper,

she challenges viewers to consider both the essence of art and the

1930- •

Sculptor, •

painter

singular message she conveys in each of her creations.

Marisol Escobar was born in Paris, France, on May 22, 1930, to Gustavo and Josefina (Hernandez) Escobar, well-to-do Venezuelans. She traveled with her parents and her brother throughout Europe, Venezuela, and the United States; it was not until the death of her mother during World War II that Marisol's father decided to settle in one place. Escobar and his daughter moved to Los Angeles, where Marisol was promptly enrolled in the Westlake School for Girls.

In many ways, Marisol was an exceptional young woman: She disapproved of the life-style her parents had led; she went through a phase in which she had visions of becoming a saint; and she began studying art in earnest at a young age. Marisol wanted to be a painter and Howard Warshaw, an instructor at the Jepson School, helped her develop her talent. By age sixteen it was clear that the young woman required advanced instruction; in 1949, with the encouragement of her father, Marisol left California to study at the Académie des Beaux Arts in Paris. From there she went on to the Art Students League in New York City and from 1951 to 1954 studied at the New School for Social Research under noted impressionist Hans Hofmann. As a student, Marisol frequented New York City's Cedar Bar, where fellow artists Jackson Pollock, Willem de Kooning, Franz Kline, and Philip Guston—who all became major American painters—often congregated. She came to know de Kooning, who became a kind of mentor to the young woman. Marisol soon found herself less involved with traditional impressionism and increasingly intrigued with sculpture, pre-Columbian figures, and South American folk art.

Now focussing her talent on sculpture, the young artist made a name for herself in New York City during the mid-1950s. The figures she created of metal, carved out of wood, or molded from terra cotta were shown in a gallery on Tenth Street; by 1957 her work could be seen at the Leo Castelli Gallery. Critics were enthusiastic about Marisol's art; the freshness and humor of her work made it instantly recognizable. Marisol (who, by this time, had dropped her last name because she thought it sounded too masculine) began earning a reputation for originality. At this point in her career, however, she decided to take some time to reflect upon her success. After spending a year alone in Rome, she returned to New York City with a renewed sense of purpose and vision; she began working even more productively than ever before.

Marisol, as an artist, has been constantly engaged and inspired by her surroundings; a sack of wooden forms used by a hat-maker served as the basis for her sculpture *Tea for 3*. After that creation, Marisol began carving figures herself. As she told an interviewer in *Smithsonian*, "I first started drawing faces on wood to help me carve them. Then I noticed that drawing looked like carving, so I left it. Then, once, I couldn't get a drawing the way I wanted it, so I put a photograph up to help me. I liked it there. So I thought, 'Why not use a photograph?'" Marisol has since incorporated glass, metal, wire, old clothing, wigs, hats—anything she finds in the street—in her creations. Her artistic vision has transformed a wooded beam discovered lying in the gutter into a representation of the *Mona Lisa* and a discarded couch into a piece she calls *The Visit*. For this piece, Marisol even parted with her favorite coat and her own purse.

Early in her career, Marisol became intrigued by the possibilities inherent in the self-portrait. At first, she made casts of her body and took photos of herself; since she often worked late at night when no models were available, she became her own model out of necessity. Later, however, she realized that these reproductions of herself—whether they were hands sprouting from blocks of wood, photographed smiles tacked to a wooden image, or even full-body, miniature Marisol figures in the arms of a larger wood figure—could make statements. In *The Party,* a wall-to-wall sculpture completed in 1966, thirteen images of the artist "mingle" in a social setting. "I did a lot of self-portraits then because it was a time of searching for one's identity," she explained to Paul Gardner in *ARTNews.* "I looked at my faces, all different in wood, and asked, *Who am I?"*

By the early 1960s, Marisol's fame had grown to the point that she became an increasing presence in the New York art scene. Celebrated Pop artist Andy Warhol became a good friend and featured Marisol in several of his movies. In 1961 she was invited to exhibit her work in the Museum of Modern Art (MOMA)'s "Art of Assemblage" show. *Life* magazine carried photos of her work to readers throughout the United States. One of Marisol's carved portraits, *The Family,* a representation of a dust bowl farm family done in wood and mixed media, was purchased by MOMA after it appeared at Marisol's exhibition at the Stable Gallery (now defunct) in 1962. Buffalo, New York's Albright-Knox Art Gallery purchased another piece, *The Generals,* which featured representations of George Washington and Símon Bolívar, each astride horses with barrels for bodies. Clearly well on her way to becoming an influential artist, Marisol was given a room of her own for the MOMA show, "Americans, 1963"; viewers of the exhibit found her work as engaging as that of any of the fifteen other artists in the show.

While Marisol's artwork continued to be well reviewed, the media was more intrigued by her stunning looks and mysterious, independent lifestyle. Who was Marisol? The artist herself was not forthcoming on this point. In 1961 she arrived at a MOMA panel discussion wearing a

Japanese mask painted white. By the end of the evening, the audience demanded that she remove the mask. When she finally did, the onlookers were more surprised and amused than disappointed—Marisol had painted her face in the exact image of the mask that had covered it. What had perhaps been intended as a statement about the relationship between art and artist became, instead, an enigma. *Vogue, Glamour,* and *Cosmopolitan* magazines quickly featured Marisol, and the public wanted more.

Even *Smithsonian* magazine commented on the "Marisol myth": Marisol was thought to be "an enigmatic 'Latin Garbo,' someone who wouldn't mind being marooned on a desert island with only herself." Of course, this perception of the artist was misleading. Marisol avoided public scrutiny as a way of saving herself from the prying eyes of a relentless media; she did not intentionally wish to appear mysterious and secretive. Nevertheless, the myth of the "Latin Garbo" remained, diverting attention from the seriousness of Marisol's work.

During the Vietnam War years, America's increasingly politicized atmosphere influenced Marisol's work. The London *Telegraph Sunday Magazine* commissioned her to portray Prime Minister Harold Wilson and the British Royal Family, along with de Gaulle, Francisco Franco, and Lyndon Johnson. As *Smithsonian* recalled, this proved to be a "hit list": the resulting creations incorporated an "interplay of ridicule and menace; the good-natured spoofing of *The Kennedys* (1960) had vanished with the upheavals of the era." Perhaps the emotions that inspired Marisol to work on the political figures were strong enough to prompt her to leave the United States. Between 1969 and 1973 she abandoned her studio and traveled, exploring the Caribbean, South America, and the Far East. Camera in hand, she also took up scuba diving; the underwater photographs and fish sculptures with Marisol-like features that resulted confused critics upon her return. "I began doing these long fish pieces, like missiles," she recalled to Gardner. "I wanted to do something beautiful and dangerous. Some critics were quite angry: I had changed my style completely—or maybe they just don't like fish."

When Marisol exhibited "Artists and Artistes" at Manhattan's Sidney Janis Gallery in 1981, her style, as *Smithsonian* noted, had indeed changed. "Instead of offering sly generalized criticism of the rituals of American social and political life as she had before, Marisol focused on more pointedly personal ruminations in delineating beings she views as mentors and beacons." There were portraits, in aged, chipped wood, of Georgia O'Keeffe, Louise Nevelson, Pablo Picasso, Marcel Duchamp, and other artists. Finally, there was Marisol's interpretation of Leonardo da Vinci's *The Virgin and Child,* which had taken her five years to complete.

Fascinated with the work of da Vinci, Marisol was next inspired to create *Madonna and Child with St. Anne and St. John* in 1978. In 1984, as part of a New York show, she presented a work based on another of the Italian painter's masterpieces, *The Last Supper.* Marisol's interpretation was well-received, a critic for *New York* magazine writing that "[Marisol] is a commanding craftsman who can endow relief sculpture with more elegant pathos than is currently fashionable. Her effortless brilliance at joining seemingly unjoinable forms and materials puts to shame the relative awkwardness of Louise Nevelson's endless wood collages."

In May 1989, as part of her first show in five years, Marisol featured sculptures of the Archbishop Desmond Tutu and Japanese Emperor Hirohito at the Sidney Janis Gallery. The Tutu sculpture includes a panel, a portrait bust, and a scepter, while the Hirohito work has bulbs for eyes and a carved and painted wooden body. Another piece, *John, Washington and Emily Roebling Crossing the Brooklyn Bridge for the First Time,* depicts a famous family of pioneers. The exhibit also included portraits of impoverished families. *Working Woman,* completed in 1987 was deemed by the *New York Times* as Marisol's "most amusing" sculpture, "a rendition of a working woman who is the embodiment of grim determination. Dressed in a business suit, she grips in one hand a briefcase while holding in the other a baby who appears destined to make millions selling junk bonds."

In 1991 Marisol was honored by an invitation to exhibit her sculptures at the National Portrait Gallery in Washington, D.C. October 1995 saw the first New York City exhibit of Marisol's artwork in six years. The show, at Manhattan's Marlborough Gallery, included wooden collage sculptures with an Old West theme, proving that, even in her mid-sixties, Marisol continues to be a vital presence in the art world. H. H. Aranson, in his *History of Modern Art,* describes her as one of the most important figures in Pop sculpture. Few argued with Aranson's further assessment that Marisol "has created a world of her own. . . from wood, plaster, paint, and unpredictable objects." It is a world that draws deeply of her Venezuelan roots and of her constant willingness to explore change. "I've always wanted to be free in my life and art," she told Gardner. "It's as important to me as truth."

**Profile by
Ronie-Richele
Garcia-Johnson**

ELIZABETH MARTINEZ

*B*oth as former chief librarian for the city of Los Angeles, California,

and the reigning head of the American Library Association (ALA) since

1994, Elizabeth Martinez has administered operating budgets of more

than $37 million, and has supervised staffs of up to 1,200 employees.

Reaching the top of her profession has been a long climb for Martinez,

who started her career as a children's librarian. And as the only

Hispanic woman to head either one of the nation's largest library

systems or the ALA, she admits that her ascent to the top was especially

arduous. "Being a woman, and a Mexican American woman at that, I

had to be the best at all times in order to gain professional acceptance,"

she explained in an interview with Michelle Vachon. "I was perceived as

1943- •

Library •

association

executive

representing all Hispanics, and strongly felt the responsibility of showing what the entire Hispanic population could accomplish."

Martinez was born April 14, 1943, in Pomona, California, where she grew up in the poorest part of town. "I was a library kid," she recalled in an interview for the Orange County Register. "Books were a kind of escape. I visited places I'd never seen." Her local children's librarian supported Martinez's interests and encouraged her to read and learn about the world; Martinez ended up going to the library as much for the librarian as for the books. After graduating from high school with excellent grades, "I was turned down at the local private college because of my ethnic background," she told Vachon. But she tried again, entered the University of California at Los Angeles in 1961, and received her bachelor of arts in Latin American studies in 1965. The following year, Martinez secured her master's degree in library and information science from the University of Southern California (USC) in Los Angeles. She obtained a certificate in management from USC in 1978, and an executive management program certificate from the University of California at Irvine in 1986.

• **Making a**

Difference

"I more or less chose this career by accident, because I did not want to be a teacher," Martinez admitted to Vachon. However, she was determined to make a difference in people's lives, and realized that she could accomplish that by being a librarian. In 1966, the year Martinez graduated, there were only five Mexican American librarians in the country and "we all knew each other." There are now almost 450 Hispanic librarians working in academic and public libraries. "One of my efforts since I became a librarian has been to recruit more Hispanics into the profession," Martinez told the *Los Angeles Times*. "There are very few Hispanics who go into the library profession, and one of the reasons is that they don't have a tradition of library services in their community." But things are changing: In 1966, shortly after Martinez had joined the Los Angeles County Public Library as children's librarian, a young Hispanic girl brought her mother to the library to meet Martinez. "'See mom, she looks just like me,'" the child said. "You never understand how much a role model you are until something like this happens," remarked Martinez.

In 1972 the Los Angeles County Public Library promoted Martinez to the position of regional administrative librarian for the west and central county regions. During the following seven years she administered between twelve to fifteen libraries with a personnel budget of more than $1 million. Among other accomplishments, Martinez established a Chicano resource center in East Los Angeles and an Asian cultural center in Montebello; she also developed a multilingual telephone information center. From 1974 until 1976 Martinez lectured at the California State University's School of Library Science at Fullerton, served on its advisory committee, and contributed to the school's success in obtaining a federal grant for the creation of a Mexican American librarians' institute.

After serving for a short period of time as the Los Angeles County Public Library's chief of public services, Martinez accepted the position of county librarian for the Orange County Public Library in 1979. She handled the system's $24-million budget and oversaw its 600 employees. During her tenure, Martinez also supervised the construction of eight new community libraries, including the San Juan Capistrano regional library, the concept of which earned architect Michael Graves national and international acclaim; implemented one of the largest computerized circulation control systems; established multicultural services and a books-by-mail loan service; created the Friends of the Library Foundation; and set an annual recognition day for the library's friends and volunteers. In June of 1990 Martinez returned to the Los Angeles Public Library as city librarian. In addition to revitalizing the library's sixty-three existing branches, Martinez supervised the construction of twenty-six new branches, including the central library built at an estimated cost of $214 million.

In June of 1994 Martinez was honored with an appointment to the position of executive director of the American Library Association (ALA). At the helm of the ALA, the world's oldest and biggest library association and the ship that will carry U.S. libraries into the future, she heads a staff of over 270, and manages both financial operations and all ALA programs. Among the key issues she has identified are addressing new technologies and finding and serving both disadvantaged young people and the thirty-three percent of Americans identified as library "non-users." Through her five-year plan, called ALA Goal 2000, Martinez plans to expand the role of the public library, providing a forum for sampling the vast array of ever-increasing technological information and developing computer literacy among all users. "The American Library Association must quickly transform itself into a force capable of fully engaging in the age of information, embracing new technological forms but within the traditional values of freedom of expression, quality of access, and respect for multiplicity of points of view," she wrote in summarizing her ALA Goal 2000.

In addition to articles on library management and book reviews, Martinez has also written extensively on racism. In a 1988 article published in *Library Journal,* she stressed that "Racism is an epidemic, like AIDS. It . . . permeates every aspect of our society." Mentioning

Appointed to •

Head National

Association

incidents from her personal life—"I didn't look 'American'"—she concluded: "I continue to be an optimist—a cautious, sometimes suspicious, but still vigilant optimist. And my message is this: Now that we know what was, and what is, think about what if? What if we worked together to overcome racial bias?. . . What if we dialogued and learned about each other so as to lessen sensitivity and hostility? What if we gave each other the benefit of the doubt?. . . What if we begin today?"

Martinez's achievements have earned her numerous awards throughout her career. She received the George I. Sanchez Award from the National Association of Spanish Speaking Librarians in 1976, the Edmund D. Edelman Certificate of Commendation from the Los Angeles County Board of Supervisors in 1977, the Hispanic Women's Recognition Award from Orange County's League of United Latin American Citizens in 1982, Orange County's Women of Achievement award in 1988, and Orange County's Women's Alert Award in 1990. The Hispanic Book Distributors named Martinez Hispanic Librarian of the year in 1990, and since 1987, by governor's appointment, she sits on the board of trustees of the California State Summer School for the Arts. Martinez was also honored with the PEN West USA Freedom to Write award in 1993.

Building on the success of her past accomplishments as a librarian, Martinez is eminently qualified to lead the American library system into the future, and is committed to making libraries institutions responsive to the changing needs of their communities. But the certain evolution of libraries into the next century has not altered her appraisal of the personal requisites for pursuing a librarian's career. "You must enter the profession with a sense of responsibility as well as a love of literature and knowledge," Martinez told Vachon. "You must yearn to share a vision, a quest for knowledge with people, and long to impart information that will enable them to improve their lives."

**Profile by
Michelle Vachon**

VILMA MARTINEZ

1943- •

ilma Socorro Martinez is a nationally known and respected

attorney and lecturer who has dedicate herself to furthering the cause of

Attorney, •

civil rights throughout her entire life. "I didn't think my parents were

public

treated fairly and I don't think I was treated fairly," stated the resolute

speaker

Martinez during a telephone interview with Carol von Hatten.

Martinez was born in San Antonio, Texas, the daughter of Salvador and Maria Piña Martinez. During high school she served as an officer in the National Honor Society and looked forward to continuing her education. Her guidance counselor thought otherwise, however, and tried to dissuade the young Mexican American from going to college, advising her that vocational school would be more "appropriate." That was not the first time the young student had encountered such prejudicial thinking; she recalled to the *Los Angeles Daily Journal* that some well-meaning teachers referred to her as Spanish, presuming that calling her Mexican might hurt her feelings. Undaunted, Martinez went on to attend the University of Texas in Austin. To help finance her education, she worked at the university, where one of her jobs took her to the biochemistry lab. There, a professor took an interest in he, advising the young undergrad to leave Texas and attend graduate school at a more liberal Eastern university. She follow that advice: after

obtaining her degree in Austin, Martinez enrolled in law school at Columbia University in New York City.

Recalling her encounters with prejudice against Mexican Americans while growing up, Martinez acknowledged in her interview: "I was bitter. I remember ranting to my mother, who told me, 'If you're going to let them destroy you like that you will be the only one hurt and no one will listen to what you have to say.'" Determined to make people listen to what she had to say, Martinez, fresh from law school in 1967, took a position with the Legal Defense and Education Fund of the National Association for the Advancement of Colored People (NAACP). Her clients were minorities and poor people living in New York City and the South. One of her most noted cases during her years with the NAACP was Griggs vs. Duke Power. In this case, Martinez won a ruling establishing as a violation of Title VII of the U.S. Civil Rights Act a company's requirement for a high school diploma and intelligence tests from job applicants, because of the disproportionate impact it would have on minorities.

In 1970, Martinez joined the New York State Division of Human Rights as an equal employment opportunity counselor. She helped draft and implement new regulations and administrative procedures on employment rights. The following year she joined the prestigious New York law firm of Cahill, Gordon & Reindel and worked as a labor lawyer. While at Cahill, Gordon & Reindel, Martinez and Notre Dame Law School-graduate Grace Olivarez became the first women to join the board of the Mexican American Legal Defense and Education Fund (MALDEF). In 1973, at the age of twenty-nine, Martinez was appointed general counsel and president of MALDEF. During her presidency she advocated diversification of the organization. "You can accomplish only so much if you join hands only with those from your own background," Martinez stated in her interview.

One of Martinez's major accomplishments during her years with MALDEF was her tireless efforts towards expanding the U.S. Voting Rights Act to include protection of Mexican Americans. The original act, passed in 1965, applied only to blacks and Puerto Ricans. Typical violations of the U.S. Voting Rights Act had included polling places that suddenly ran out of ballots when Mexican Americans tried to vote, and ads that ran on Spanish language stations warning Mexican Americans that they would be fined or arrested if they voted. Her endeavor met some opposition from Clarence Mitchell, head of the NAACP Washington office, who argued that expanding the U.S. Voting Rights Act would dilute voting rights enforcement for blacks. However, Martinez skillfully

Becomes •

President of

MALDEF

enlisted the help of a coalition of groups to aid this important case. Supporting her effort to expand voter protection were organized labor, the Congressional Black Caucus, and Japanese Americans. Congress responded to her efforts and in 1975 extended voting protection to Mexican Americans. That victory came on the heels of a ruling the previous year in which MALDEF secured a guarantee of bilingual education for non-English speaking children attending public schools.

Another one of Martinez's important MALDEF achievements was her ground-breaking work on the Plyler vs. Doe case, which challenged a Texas law denying free public school education to undocumented children—children of illegal aliens. Before this 1982 legal decision, a public school tuition of $1,000 was required for each undocumented child. As Martinez declared in her interview: "This put school out of reach for many of these children, basically our children—American children who had lived here for years but who weren't citizens. Without that educational opportunity those kids wouldn't have a chance." Plyler vs. Doe set a precedent in extending rights to undocumented aliens.

However, Martinez believes her greatest executive accomplishment at MALDEF was to institutionalize the organization. "I was able to create a mechanism for MALDEF to exist through fund-raising, recruiting, and learning to juggle resources so it could continue to grow year in and year out," she explained. When she arrived at MALDEF in 1973 the organization had no endowments and Martinez spent many restless nights worrying about how to meet the payroll. But she was determined to build MALDEF into an organization that would continue to be capable of furthering the cause of Mexican Americans. When she left in 1982 the organization had been transformed into a force that operated with a $4.9 million annual budget and a staff of twenty-three attorneys working nationwide.

• *Joins Los*

Angeles Law

Firm

"Personally and professionally it was time to move on," Martinez explained to von Hatten. But she was uncertain what to do next. She considered running for elective office or teaching at the college level. Eventually she decided to join the Los Angeles law firm of Munger, Tolles & Olson. Becoming a partner in such a large law firm would give her real independence in her career, she concluded. However, it was a move that required some thought for Martinez. During her years at MALDEF she frequently had been questioned during lectures at law schools by students worried about "selling out" to corporate institutions. That was not an issue in her move from MALDEF, Martinez decided. "People should be free to grow up and be whatever type of lawyer they want to be." At Munger, Tolles & Olson, she still litigates labor disputes, including wrongful termination, employment discrimination and insurance bad-faith cases.

As a result of her extensive and successful work on behalf of civil rights, Martinez is sought after as a speaker and has addressed groups at the University of California (All-University Faculty Conference), Yale University, Rice University, University of Notre Dame, and her alma mater, the University of Texas. She has also lectured at a number of law schools, including those affiliated with Harvard University, Yale University, Stanford University, and the University of Michigan. In addition to being a guest speaker at the Ditchley Foundation in Oxfordshire, England, she has addressed the National Association of Hispanic Journalists and the California Newspaper Publishers Association.

Throughout her career, Martinez has been extraordinarily active in community, legal, educational, and public service projects. Many of those positions have enabled her to continue her lifelong efforts to expand opportunities for minorities. Martinez has generously given her time and expertise to serve as a board member or officer for a wide array of institutions and corporations. She is chair of the UCLA Board of Visitors and is a co-founder of its Achievement Council. The council, formed after she discovered low eligibility rates of Mexican Americans in the University of California system, seeks to increase the number of minority students attending college. Continuing her seventeen-year campaign in the voter rights area, Martinez serves as vice-chair of the Southwest Voter Registration and Education Program. She has been a member of the board of Anheuser-Busch since 1983, and in 1984 she became vice-chairman of the board of the Edward W. Hazen Foundation in Los Angeles, a post she held until 1994. In 1990 she joined the board of the Sanwa Bank of California and is a member of its Community Reinvestment Committee and has served on the board of People for the American Way since 1991. Martinez is a member of the advisory board of the Asian Pacific Women's Network, the Loyola Law School's Institute for Latin American Legal Studies, and the Asian Pacific American Legal Center of Southern California and is also a member of the Council of Foreign Relations and Columbia University's Law School Board of Visitors.

From 1975 to 1981 Martinez served as an unpaid consultant to the U.S. Census Bureau, chairing a panel that persuaded the bureau to add a question on the census form asking if a person is of Hispanic origin. As a result the heritage of Hispanics now is included in the official count of the American population: states include such information in their demographics studies and the information has led in part to the redrawing of some electoral districts. During the Carter Administration, Martinez served as a member of the advisory board on ambassadorial appointments and in 1976 she was appointed by Governor Jerry Brown to the California Board of Regents, serving fourteen years, including a two-year term as chairman.

Martinez's service and achievement have not gone unnoticed or unappreciated. She has earned a number of awards, including the Jefferson Award in 1976 for public service from the American Institute, a medal of excellence from Columbia University's Law School in both 1978 and 1992 as a major figure in civil rights, the Valerie Kantor Award for Extraordinary Achievement in 1982 for her work with MALDEF, and a 1988 University of Texas distinguished alumnus award. In the early 1990s Martinez returned to MALDEF, this time as a member of its board of directors.

**Profile by
Carol von Hatten**

Despite her busy schedule and continued dedication to attaining civil rights for Hispanics and all people, Martinez finds time outside her career and life of public service to raising her two sons, Carlos and Ricardo, with her husband of more than two decades, fellow attorney Stuart Singer. The family makes its home in the Los Angeles area.

NICHOLASA MOHR

*A*s an impoverished young girl, Nicholasa Mohr used her imagina-

tion to temporarily escape her often shocking surroundings. As an adult,

she channels this same creativity into relating her feelings as both a

woman and a Puerto Rican American. Once an aspiring painter and

printmaker, Mohr has become an acclaimed writer and illustrator of her

own books. While her award-winning novels and stories have captured

a growing following among readers, Mohr has found personal satisfac-

tion in using her many talents to assist those she cares about. "As a

writer I have used my abilities as a creative artist to strengthen my skills,"

Mohr explained, "and at the same time in small measure have ventured

to establish a voice for my ethnic American community and our

1938- •

Writer, •

visual artist

children."

Mohr was born on November 1, 1938, to Pedro and Nicolasa (Rivera) Golpe. During the Great Depression, her mother migrated with her four children from Puerto Rico to a barrio in Manhattan; Nicholasa was the last of three children born to the couple in New York City—and their only daughter. When she was eight years old—after her family had moved again, this time to the Bronx—Mohr's father died. Despite her own frequent illnesses, Mohr's mother struggled to keep her family together, constantly encouraging her children to develop their talents and work hard. It was her mother who gave Mohr paper, a pencil, and some crayons, providing Mohr the awareness that "by making pictures and writing letters I could create my own world . . . like 'magic.'" Mohr remembered her mother telling her, "*Mi hijita* [My little daughter], you are special with these God-given talents. Someday you must study so that you can become an important artist . . . make an important contribution to the world and really be somebody."

Although her mother died before Mohr began high school, her positive influences did not. "My mother's strength and independence served as a strong role model for me," said Mohr. "As I look back, she was the first feminist I knew." Of strong character herself, Mohr continued to excel in school despite a lack of emotional support from her guardian aunt. Mohr credits her school artwork with allowing her to partially escape the bigotry many Puerto Rican children had to endure. As a "gifted" child she would be respected; her abilities gave her confidence and the belief that she would overcome poverty and prejudice. "I used my imagination and was able to create something interesting and pleasing where previously there had been a sense of despair," she said. As Mohr developed her writing, drawing, and painting skills, she also gained the ability to portray the situations and characters that would later appear in her books.

Mohr was determined to become an artist. When it was time for her to attend high school, she was frustrated by her guidance counselor's insistence that, as a Puerto Rican girl, she did not need a solid academic education and would be well served by attending a school where she could to learn to sew. Mohr managed to find a school with a department in fashion illustration, where she was able to continue drawing. After high school graduation, she attended New York City's Arts Students' League from 1953 to 1956, supporting herself by working as a waitress, a clerk and a factory worker.

Although she had saved enough money to study art in Europe, Mohr decided to travel to Mexico City instead. There, at the Taller de Gráfica Popular, she studied the works of Jose Clemente Orozco, the

Imagination

Provides

Escape from

Reality

murals of Diego Rivera, and the paintings of Rivera's wife, Frida Kahlo. The colors, figures, and methods that these artists used to express their feelings about their cultures greatly influenced the young artist: "In a profound way their work spoke to me and my experiences as a Puerto Rican woman born in New York," she wrote. "The impact was to shape and form the direction of all my future work."

Mohr returned to the United States, and began studying at the New School for Social Research in New York City. It was there that she met Irwin Mohr, who was working on his doctorate in clinical psychology. The couple was married on October 5, 1957, and they soon had a son, David. Mohr continued studying fine art at the Brooklyn Museum Art School from 1964 to 1966; from 1966 to 1969 she studied printmaking and silkscreening at the Pratt Center for Contemporary Printmaking. She worked as an art instructor at the Art Center of Northern New Jersey from 1971 to 1973. From 1969 to 1972, Mohr also served as artist-in-residence with the New York City public schools.

A second son, Jason, was born to the Mohrs in 1970. The growing family moved to a home in the suburb of Teaneck, New Jersey. With the help of a grant for the artist's work, Mohr set up a huge art studio. According to the artist, her works of that period were not "just . . . literal scenes of social injustices . . . or aesthetically abstract . . . [they were] filled with bold figures, faces, and various symbols of the city . . . numbers, letters, words, and phrases . . . a kind of graffiti." Such bold innovations brought Mohr some measure of fame in the New York art scene.

As a successful artist, with both her own one-woman exhibitions and an art agent, Mohr never considered writing until she was asked by a publisher to write about her life as a Puerto Rican American. Mohr wrote fifty pages of vignettes and, although the publisher liked the work, she did not want to publish it. As Mohr recalled it in an interview: "I think what she expected was something much more sensational, the sort of stereotypical ghetto person. So I told her that much to my embarrassment I had never stolen anything, taken hard drugs, been raped or mugged. So I guess she thought my life was uneventful."

Mohr put away her pen and continued to work as an artist until Harper & Row Publishers asked her to do a cover for one of their books. Instead, Mohr brought them her vignettes. Harper editor Ellen Rudin was enthusiastic; she encouraged Mohr to develop what she had written and gave the artist a contract. Withdrawing to the MacDowell Colony in New Hampshire, Mohr finished her first book, *Nilda*, in 1973. She recalled in an interview with Paul Janeczko in *From Writers to Students*, that she "fell very much in love with writing" although she was "a little bit nervous." While it was difficult to make the transition from artist to writer, she found that she could "do certain things in writing and there was a crying need for what [she] had to say as a Puerto Rican, as someone living here, and as a woman." Mohr "could draw a picture with words, and it was extremely stimulating and eye-opening to realize what one could do with words."

While Mohr found herself intrigued with writing, readers were equally fascinated by *Nilda*, the autobiographical story of a poor Puerto Rican girl living in New York's Spanish Harlem. While the story is set during World War II, the book focuses on the situation at home. Puerto Ricans, already American citizens, were called "spics" and "animals" by the very people who were supposed to guide, uphold, and assist them. In *Nilda*, teachers, social workers, nurses, and even policemen refer to Puerto Ricans as "you people," and the young girl's peers behave just as cruelly. Two scenes are particularly effective: in one a very poor girl is taunted for her lack of a real suitcase at camp, and in another a girl who has just given birth to a baby is denied entrance to her home by her own embarrassed mother. *Nilda* is powerful in other ways too; according to Mohr, it illustrates how to escape reality through imagination. "Once there [in her imagination], she [Nilda], would also find relief from an environment she, in fact, is powerless to change in any other way," the author explained.

Nilda was a great success. Critics praised the story's fresh characters, content, and style, as well as the cover art and the eight illustrations Mohr had provided. *Children's Literature* lauded the work, noting that "There is no pity here, for the author is too much aware of the humanity of her characters and of the other implications of pity to be in any way condescending." *Nilda* earned the New York Times Outstanding Book Award in juvenile fiction in 1973. Mohr also received the Jane Addams Children's Book Award from the Jane Addams Peace Association in 1974. And the Society of Illustrators presented Mohr with a citation of merit for the book's book jacket design. *Nilda* eventually made *School Library Journal*'s "Best of the Best 1966-1978" list in 1979.

After her experience with *Nilda,* Mohr felt she had to write more. Her next book, complete with a book jacket of her own creation, was published in 1975. The twelve stories and the novella in *El Bronx Remembered* are set in post-war New York, and deal frankly with once-delicate subjects. One story, for example, centers on a doomed marriage between a pregnant teenager and an aging homosexual. Another story is about a lonely, dying old Jewish man who is befriended by a Puerto Rican family. Other tales deal with racism, religion, as well as sexuality and death. All the stories, spiced with Spanish words, are realistic. "If there is any message at all in these stories, any underlying theme," wrote the *New York Times Book Review,* "it is that life goes on."

For *El Bronx Remembered,* Mohr was awarded the New York Times Outstanding Book Award in teenage fiction in 1975 and received the Best Book Award from *School Library Journal* that same year. *El Bronx Remembered* also was a National Book Award finalist for the "most distinguished book in children's literature" in 1976. Mohr realized by writing books—combining her love of art with her talent for writing—she could reach more people. She made the decision to continue writing, and became a writer-in-residence at the MacDowell Colony.

• *Continues to*

Write for Adults

and Children

Her next book, *In Nueva York,* is similar to *El Bronx Remembered.* First published in 1977, *In Nueva York's* related short stories featured mature subjects. In one story, a woman who searches for her son finds that he is a dwarf. In another, a homosexual woman marries a homosexual man. Both "The Robbery" and "Coming to Terms" deal with the violent shooting death of a teenage thief by a store owner, and the incident's consequences. "Mohr creates a remarkably vivid tapestry of community life as well as of individual characters," wrote one critic in the *Bulletin of the Center for Children's Books.* "Tough, candid, and perceptive, the book has memorable characters, resilient and responsive, in a sharply-eyed milieu." Mohr received School Library Journal Best Book Award, as well as the Best Book Award in young adult literature from the American Library Association. *In Nueva York* also earned the distinction of being named a Notable Trade Book in the Field of Social Studies by the joint committee of the National Council for the Social Studies and the Children's Book Council.

Mohr's fourth book, *Felita,* was published in 1979. A novel for younger children, *Felita* related the story of a Puerto Rican girl whose parents decide to move to a better part of town. Felita misses her old friends, and the neighbors won't let their children befriend her. Discouraged by discrimination and harassment, Felita's family returns to their old neighborhood, and Felita is forced to readjust. Well-received by critics, the book won an American Book Award from the Before Columbus Foundation in 1981.

From 1977 to 1980, Mohr contributed to her community as an educator. She was a lecturer in Puerto Rican studies at the State University of New York at Stony Brook, and a visiting lecturer in creative writing for various groups, including the University of Illinois Educational Alliance Program in Chicago, the Cedar Rapids, Iowa, community schools, a writers-in-residence seminar at the University of Wisconsin at Oshkosh, and the Bridgeport, Connecticut, public schools from 1977 to 1978. She also served as the head creative writer and co-producer of the television series, *Aquí y Ahora* (Here and Now), and as a member of the New Jersey State Council on the Arts. She was a member of the board of trustees as well as a consultant, both for the Young Filmmakers Foundation and on bilingual media training for Young Filmmakers Video Arts.

After the death of her husband and the departure of her sons for college, Mohr moved to a townhouse in Brooklyn in 1980. The following year, her brother Vincent, with whom she was very close, also died; Mohr did not publish another book until 1985. In that year, *Rituals of Survival: A Woman's Portfolio*, a collection of short stories and a novella written for adults, was published by Arte Público Press. For this work, Mohr was presented a Legislative Resolution from the State of New York, commending her for her "valuable contributions to the world of literature."

Mohr has written another children's book, including 1986's *Going Home*, a sequel to *Felita*. In *Going Home*, Felita takes a trip to Puerto Rico with her family, and is sad to leave by the end of the summer, despite adjustment problems at the beginning of her vacation. *Going Home* garnered a warm reception: A critic for *School Library Journal* commented, "Felita is a vivid, memorable character, well realized and well developed. It is a pleasure to welcome her back." She followed the success of *Going Home* with 1994's *All for the Better: A Story of El Barrio*, a biography of social activist Evelina Lopez Antonetty. She published *The Magic Shell*, and *The Song of El Coquí and Other Tales of Puerto Rico*, in 1995. In the latter volume, Mohr relates three stories that represent the races—the Taínos (indigenous people), African Slaves, and escaped Spanish slaves—that make up the population of her native island. Her original fairy tale, *Old Letivia and the Mountain of Sorrows*, will be published by Viking in June 1996.

Mohr published *Growing Up inside the Sanctuary of My Imagination* in 1994. An autobiographical account of her life until age fourteen, the work is geared for a young audience and is written in a clear and straightforward style. "Young adults of similar heritage will find truth and comfort in the account," wrote *Booklist* of Mohr's work; "others will find it enlightening." Her story has been adapted for inclusion in the ABC television documentary, *The Dignity of Children*, and scheduled for viewing in the spring of 1996.

Mohr continues to involve herself in writing and teaching projects. Her work has been published in *Family in Harmony and Conflict*, edited by Peter Reinke; her short stories have appeared in *Children's Digest*, *Scholastic Magazine*, and *Nuestro*. Mohr is a member of the board of contributing editors of *Americas Review*, and is a member of both the Authors Guild and the Authors League of America. She is the author, with Ray Blanco, of the screenplay, *The Artist*, and she has contributed to textbooks and anthologies such as *The Ethnic American Woman: Problems, Protests, Lifestyles*, edited by Edith Blicksilver. In addition, she is the author of the radio script *Inside the Monster,* written for the Latino Writers Symposium. From 1988 to 1990, Mohr served as distinguished visiting professor at Queens College in New York City. Mohr was writer-in-residence at Richmond College, The American International University in London, England, from 1994 to 1995.

Mohr, who has been awarded an honorary doctorate from the State University of New York at Albany, is currently working on another novel and a collection of stories. In all her writing, she continues to challenge readers of all ages to view the world with open eyes, to encourage them to alter their perception, and to entertain them. As a child, she escaped reality through her imagination; today she uses her creative talents to cast a positive light on her readers' reality—as well as on their view of the future.

Profile by Ronie-Richele Garcia-Johnson

PAT MORA

1942-) •

W hile Pat Mora has earned distinction as both a poet and an

educator, she is best known for the cause that has required each of her

many talents: improving cultural appreciation and conservation. Mora

Poet, •

has been an essential part of the movement to understand and uphold

educator

Mexican American culture: as an poet she has explored her personal

ethnicity and, as an educator, she has promoted the cultural explora-

tions of others. In leading many to ponder their own cultural back-

grounds, Mora has worked variously as an instructor, an assistant to

administrators, and a museum director, given poetry readings and

presentations, served on various committees, written, and been both

wife and mother simultaneously. Her success at these many accom-

plishments serves as an excellent example for young Hispanics attempting to understand their past as they embark upon promising futures.

Mora was born January 19, 1942, to Raul Antonio and Estella (Delgado) Mora. She grew up in the town of her birth, El Paso, Texas, where her father was a practicing optician and Mora's mother stayed home to care for her children. As is typical of adolescents of any culture, Mora eschewed her Hispanic family customs. Realizing that mainstream American culture looked down on being Mexican American fed her preference to look and feel "American." While the young Mora spoke Spanish at home to her grandmother and her aunt, she ignored her ethnicity in school and cringed when her father played Mexican music on the radio. She did not realize until years later that such assimilation meant a loss of cultural identity.

Shortly after receiving a bachelor's degree from Texas Western College in 1963, Mora married William H. Burnside; the couple had three children, William, Elizabeth, and Cecilia. She began to teach at a school in the El Paso Independent School District, where she stayed until 1966. By 1967 Mora had earned her master's degree from the University of Texas at El Paso, and from 1971 to 1978 she taught English and Communications part-time at El Paso Community College. In 1979 she became a part-time lecturer, remaining in this position until 1981, the same year that she and Burnside divorced. It was also during 1981 that she became the assistant to the vice-president of academic affairs.

Living near the Mexican border, continually surrounded by Mexican American relatives and friends, Mora could no longer ignore the influence of Mexican culture. She finally began to appreciate her birthright for the gift that it was and became devoted to preserving it. "I revel in a certain Mexican passion not for life or about life, but *in* life," she explained to the *Christian Science Monitor*, "a certain intensity in the daily living of it, a certain abandon in such music, in the hugs, sometimes in the anger."

Mora's intense concern for her culture needed an outlet; she began to express her feelings in writing. "For a variety of complex reasons, anthologized American literature does not reflect the ethnic diversity of the United States," she explained. "I write, in part, because Hispanic perspectives need to be part of our literary heritage; I want to be part of that validation process. I also write because I am fascinated by the pleasure and power of words." Mora believes that Hispanic writers need to work together to make their mark on American literature, that Hispanic culture can be preserved through words.

Discovers Value •

of Mexican

Heritage

257 •

Despite the stress that inevitably accompanies a divorce and a change in career, Mora managed to establish a reputation in literary circles during the early 1980s. She contributed to *Revista Chicano-Riqueña: Kikiriki/Children's Literature Anthology,* which was published by Houston's Arte Público Press in 1981, under the editorship of Sylvia Cavazos Peña. Then Mora's career as a writer and advocate of cultural appreciation began to really take off. From 1983 to 1984 she hosted the radio show, *Voices: The Mexican-American in Perspective,* on National Public Radio-affiliate KTEP, and received her first important literary award in 1983, when she was recognized by the National Association for Chicano Studies.

• *Gains Fame as*

Writer

Mora's next award came from the magazine *New America: Women Artists and Writers of the Southwest,* which honored her poetry in 1984. That year was one of professional and personal triumph for Mora: In addition to the New America award, she was honored with the Harvey L. Johnson Book Award from the Southwest Council of Latin American Studies. In addition, her first poetry collection, *Chants,* was published by Arte Público Press. And finally, she married Vernon Lee Scarborough, an archaeologist who studies the Maya of Central America.

For Mora the latter half of the 1980s proved to be just as fruitful as the first half. Two years after *Chants* was published, Arte Público released *Borders,* her second collection of poetry; both *Chants* and *Borders* won Southwest Book Awards from the Border Regional Library Association. In 1986 Mora contributed to another children's literature anthology edited by Peña, *Tun-Ta-Ca-Tun.* That same year, she also received a Kellogg fellowship, which aided her in her study of international and national issues of cultural conservation. Mora's research made her an invaluable source of information, and she was invited to become a consultant to the W. K. Kellogg Foundation on U.S.-Mexican youth exchanges, and to serve on the advisory committee for the Kellogg National Fellowship program. Mora also served as a member of the Texas Commission on the Arts's Literary Advisory Panel from 1987 to 1988, and as a poetry judge for the Texas Institute of Letters in 1988. That same year she was named to the *El Paso Herald-Post* Writer's Hall of Fame.

While Mora was gaining fame as a writer, she continued to distinguish herself as an educator at the University of Texas at El Paso. She won a Leader in Education Award from El Paso Women's Employment and Education, Inc., in 1987. Later that year she was honored for her outstanding contribution to the advancement of Hispanics at the University of Texas at El Paso with the Chicano/Hispanic Faculty and Professional Staff Association Award. Finally, in 1988 she became the director of the University Museum, as well as the assistant to the University's president.

In September 1989 Mora moved to Ohio. While missing the food and company she was used to, Mora also began to crave the sound of the Spanish language. "When I hear a phrase in Spanish in a Cincinnati restaurant, my head turns quickly," she wrote in a *Christian Science Monitor* article. "I listen, silently wishing to be part of that other conversation—if only for a few moments, to feel Spanish in my mouth."

Eventually, Mora began to appreciate her new Midwestern environment. She enjoyed the lush greenery and the cold snow in the winter. She also began to recognize the differences between her new home in the Midwest and her old home in the desert. As she wrote in the *Monitor,* "No forest conceals the shacks on the other side of the Rio Grande.... I miss that clear view of the difference between my comfortable life as a U.S. citizen and the lives of my fellow human beings who also speak Spanish." Instead of losing her affiliation for, and loyalty to her culture, Mora was able to view it from a fresh perspective.

The decade of the 1990s have presented many more opportunities for Mora to continue her contributions to cultural conservation. Her third collection of poetry, *Communion,* was published by Arte Público Press in 1991. By the following year her work had been included in many anthologies and textbooks, including *Woman of Her Word: Hispanic Women Write, The Norton Introduction to Literature, Sisters of the Earth,* and *Hispanics in the United States.* Mora, who is a member of the Poetry Society of America, the Academy of American Poets, and the Texas Institute of Letters, also contributed articles and stories to periodicals, including *Calyx, Hispanics in the United States: An Anthology of Creative Literature, Horn Book, New America: Women Artists and Writers of the Southwest,* and *Kalliope: A Journal of Women's Art.* Her poems and stories have been translated into Spanish, Italian, and Bengali.

The children's book *A Birthday Basket for Tia,* a celebration of the relationship between children and the elderly, was published in 1992 and followed by two other books for young readers, *Pablo's Tree,* and *Tomas and the Library Lady,* published the following year. And 1994's *Oye al desierto/Listen to the Desert* is a bilingual tale about the sounds of desert life, told with a poet's skillful use of simple words to bring to life nature's grand design. In *Nepantla: Essays from the Land in the Middle,* a collection for adults that appeared in 1993, lectures, essays, poems, and vignettes from memory expand upon Mora's contention that mainstream U.S. society devalues diversity in the face of materialism. Other efforts include her fourth collection of poetry, which has tentatively been titled, *The Narrow Rim,* as well as more books for children.

As a successful writer able to capture in words the intimate thoughts and unique moments that make up the lives of her fellow Hispanics, Mora is an exemplary role model for future generations of an increasingly multi-cultural America. And she is well aware of the influence she has on minority youths. While noting in *Horn Book* that some young minorities are "proud of their cultural roots," Mora acknowledges that a constant barrage of advertisements "convince us that our cars, clothes, and even our families aren't good enough," that "being beautiful is being thin, blond, and rich, rich, rich." She hopes, through her writing, to counter the influence of a post-literate, consumption-oriented and often prejudiced society. "I write to try to correct these images of worth," Mora wrote in *Horn Book*. "I take pride in being a Hispanic writer. I will continue to write and to struggle to say what no other writer can say in quite the same way."

**Profile by
Ronie-Richele
Garcia-Johnson**

RITA MORENO

1931- •

A remarkably versatile performer, Rita Moreno has received all four

of show business's top awards. For her acting in West Side Story, *Moreno*

won an Oscar in 1962. A Grammy followed her vocal performance on

Actress, •

the Electric Company Album *for children in 1972. Her role as Googie*

singer,

Gómez in The Ritz *(1975) on Broadway won her a Tony. And finally,*

dancer

Moreno has been awarded two Emmys: one for guest appearances on

The Muppet Show *in 1977, and another for an episode of* The Rockford

Files *in 1978. Although impressive, this long list of prestigious awards*

merely hints at the variety of Moreno's excellent performances; it cannot

convey the spirit of determination with which she has pursued her goal

of becoming a respected actress.

Moreno, a woman who has appeared on both screen and stage since she was a teenager, had to fight to win roles that merited talent. Too often, the need to earn a living as an actress forced her to take parts which were stereotypical and sometimes even debasing; for quite some time she was cast as either a "Latin Spitfire" or an "Indian Princess." She struggled to exorcise these images, especially after the media began to refer to her as "Rita the Cheetah." Finally, after receiving an Oscar for her portrayal of Anita in *West Side Story*, Moreno became one of the few Hispanics to "cross over" into stardom and become internationally famous and respected. "I have crossed over, but never, not for one minute, have I forgotten where I came from, or who I am," she commented in *Hispanic* magazine. "I have always been very proud to carry the badge of honor as a Hispanic." While using her Hispanic identity to portray characters such as that of Anita, Moreno has also used her wit and talent to poke fun at stereotypes, as in her portrayal of the role of Googie Gómez in *The Ritz*.

Moreno was born Rosa Dolores Alverio, to Paco and Rosa María (Marcano) Alverio in the small town of Humacao, Puerto Rico, on December 11, 1931. Moreno's parents divorced soon after her birth, and her mother left her with relatives while she went to New York to work as a seamstress. When Moreno was five years old, she and other members of the family joined her mother in her Manhattan tenement apartment. It was in New York that she began to take dancing lessons; Paco Cansino, uncle of the legendary actress and dancer Rita Hayworth, was a very effective dance teacher and the young Moreno found herself performing on stage at the age of six and a half.

While still in school, Moreno performed at Macy's Department Store's children's theater and entertaining at weddings and bar mitzvahs. By the time she was thirteen, she had exchanged the life of a schoolgirl for that of an actress. "Rita Cosio" was her stage name for her first role on Broadway as Angelina in Harry Kleiner's *Skydrift*. Nightclub performances in Boston, Las Vegas, and New York followed, as well as jobs dubbing in the Spanish for Elizabeth Taylor, Margaret O'Brien, and Peggy Ann Garner in their movies. Moreno's first film, *So Young, So Bad* (1950), led to a meeting with Louis B. Mayer, who contracted the young Latina with Metro-Goldwyn-Mayer (MGM).

Under the name Rosita Moreno (her stepfather's surname)—later shortened to Rita Moreno—the actress garnered minor roles in some twenty-five movies, including *The Toast of New Orleans* (1950) and *Pagan Love Song* (1950), with Esther Williams. Freelancing after her contract with MGM expired, Moreno found only stereotypical, ethnic roles. With the exception of her part as Zelda Zanders in *Singin' in the*

Gains •

Recognition

with

Stereotypical

Roles

Rain (1952), Moreno portrayed a series of Latin vamps in movies like *The Fabulous Senorita* (1952), *Cattle Town* (1952), and *Latin Lovers* (1953). For variety, she was hired to play an Arab in *El Alamein* (1953), and an American Indian in *Fort Vengeance* (1953) and *The Yellow Tomahawk* (1954).

Although Moreno was now a recognizable actress, these "Latin Spitfire" roles created a troublesome image. She became known as "Rita the Cheetah"; her highly publicized relationships with actor Marlon Brando, and Geordie Hormel of the Hormel meat company only strengthened her vamp image. Disheartened with roles which, she later told the *New York Times,* she "played . . . the same way, barefoot, with my nostrils flaring," the physically petite actress attempted to return to the stage, without success. She lost a part in *Camino Real* because the playwright, the renowned Tennessee Williams, did not think her voice was suitable.

Moreno's career seemed to take a turn for the better when she was featured on the cover of *Life* magazine. She immediately signed a contract with Twentieth Century-Fox, singing in *Garden of Evil* (1954), and doing a Marilyn Monroe takeoff in *The Lieutenant Wore Skirts* (1955). Once again, however, she was cast in stereotypical roles that frustrated her ambitions as a serious actress. And Moreno was not the only one who was disappointed with her acting opportunities. After her performance in *Untamed* (1955), a writer for the *New York Post* voiced the frustration of Moreno and her fans: "Will the powers in Twentieth Century-Fox wait patiently until Miss Moreno loses half of her youth, vitality and beauty before they get around to giving her a romantic break?"

It wasn't until she was given a part as a Burmese slave girl in the hit musical *The King and I* (1956) that Moreno found a truly satisfying role. As Tuptim in the Rogers and Hammerstein film adaptation, she sang "We Kiss in a Shadow" and "I Have Dreamed" with Carlos Rivas. She also narrated "The Small House of Uncle Thomas," which was choreographed by Jerome Robbins, for the film.

Despite these professional successes, Moreno found the latter half of the 1950s to be unrewarding; she won a role in *The Vagabond King,* followed by *The Deerslayer* in 1957, and after her contract with Twentieth Century-Fox expired she appeared in *This Rebel Breed* (1960). Once again, Moreno sought to return to the stage; she performed in a summer theater tour of Arthur Miller's *A View from the Bridge.* Although her stage performances were well received, Moreno could no longer cope with the frustration she had been experiencing. A failed suicide attempt with sleeping pills landed her in the hospital; when she woke, however, she realized that she wanted to live. She recovered and went on to star in the movie for which she is most famous, *West Side Story* (1961).

Moreno had been asked by Jerome Robbins a year after her performance in *The King and I* to try out for the role as Maria in the original theater production of *West Side Story*, but she had declined. However, by the time the movie version of the play was being made, Moreno's face had matured, and she was better suited to the character of Anita, the more experienced friend of Maria, who was ultimately portrayed by Natalie Wood. As Anita, Moreno illuminated the screen with her singing and dancing. *West Side Story* was an instant success, winning ten Academy Awards, including Moreno's Oscar for best supporting actress.

During the 1960s Moreno didn't rest on her laurels. Although she played Rosa Zacharias in Tennessee Williams's *Summer and Smoke* (1961), and a camp follower in *Cry of Battle* (1963), she did not find such parts rewarding. Seeking better roles, Moreno left Hollywood for London, where, in 1964, she portrayed Ilona Ritter in Hal Prince's *She Loves Me* before being forced to return to the United States because of British performance laws. Once again on Broadway, Moreno won the role of Iris Parodus Brustein in Lorraine Hansberry's *The Sign in Sidney Brustein's Window,* which ran for 101 performances. Brando, whom Moreno had dated on and off for eight years, assisted the actress as she renewed her movie career with a portrayal of a drug addict in *The Night of the Following Day* (1969). This role led to appearances in various movies, including *Marlowe* (1969), *Pop!* (1969), and *Carnal Knowledge* (1971). In 1970 she returned to the theater to portray Sharon Falconer in *Gantry* on Broadway, and replace Linda Lavin in Neil Simon's *Last of the Red Hot Lovers.*

It was during this same period that Moreno met and married Dr. Leonard Gordon, a cardiologist and internist at New York City's Mount Sinai Hospital. After being introduced in 1964, Gordon asked her to attend a New Year's party with him. When Moreno instructed Gordon to pick her up at the Henry Miller Theater before the party, Gordon "couldn't figure out the sense of it," as he later told *Hispanic*. "Why would this attractive young lady be going to the theater on New Year's Eve? Was she going on a date with some other guy and then planning to dump him and go out with me?" The doctor, still perplexed, was still waiting for Moreno to leave the theater long after the audience exited; meanwhile an angry Moreno waited inside her dressing room, thinking she had been stood up. It wasn't until Gordon checked the marquee to see if he was at the right theater and saw her name in lights that he realized his date was *the* Rita Moreno. Moreno and Gordon finally went

Wins Academy

Award for

West Side

Story

on their date; they were married in June of 1965 and celebrated their twenty-fifth anniversary in 1990.

Moreno took a break from both theater and film to perform for television in 1971. When the Children's Television Workshop, producer of the popular *Sesame Street* educational series, asked her to star in *The Electric Company*, a television series for older children, she was enthusiastic. "I jumped at the chance," she told the *New York Times*. As Pandore, a bratty blond girl, and Otto, a movie director, she encouraged children to develop reading skills. Moreno's performance was delightful and, in 1972, her participation—with Bill Cosby and others—in the show's soundtrack recording won her a Grammy award for best recording for children.

• *Laughs at*

Stereotypes in

The Ritz

Apart from *The Electric Company*, Moreno's success continued to be in stage and film. Her next role was that of the Shoplifter in the play *Detective Story*, which ran in Philadelphia in 1973. She then portrayed Staff Nurse Norton in *The National Health*, first in New Haven, Connecticut, from 1973 to 1974, and then at New York City's Circle in the Square. It was around this time that Moreno's antics at a party inspired the character that eventually won her a Tony Award. Combining a rendition of "Everything's Coming up Roses" with her mother's Spanish accent and the mannerisms she had developed during the filming of *West Side Story*, Moreno was hilarious, especially to fellow party-goer Terrence McNally. McNally, a noted playwright, later invited her to attend his new play, *The Tubs*, at the Yale Repertory Theater. She was shocked to see the character she had created singing on stage. McNally immediately asked her to take on the role of this character, which he named Googie Gómez, when the play, renamed *The Ritz*, came to Broadway in 1975. She accepted.

The Ritz was a hit, and so was Moreno; the *New York Times* noted that her performance as the Puerto Rican singer was "variously hailed as 'pure beauty,' 'wonderfully atrocious' and 'a comic earthquake.'" "*The Ritz* ran for 400 performances, and it was no surprise when Moreno received the Antoinette Perry, or "Tony," Award, for best supporting actress.

Although some worried that the performance would offend Hispanics, Moreno was not among them. She felt that the character she and McNally had created made fun of the stereotypical roles she had always been cast in. Saying that she had not received any "feedback flak from her own people," Moreno told the *New York Times*: "The Spanish people who come backstage say they love what I'm doing. Of course, some *Latins* might take offense, but I don't want to meet them. I don't want to talk to anyone who doesn't have a sense of humor about themselves.... I have had to learn to laugh at myself—otherwise there would be lines of sorrow from my forehead to my toes."

Moreno next starred in the film version of *The Ritz,* which was not as widely hailed as its Broadway predecessor. Guest appearances on *The Muppet Show* in 1977 won her an Emmy for outstanding continuing or single performance by a supporting actress in variety or music. She won another Emmy for outstanding lead actress for a single appearance in a drama or comedy series in 1978 for her appearance in *The Rockford Files.* Moreno portrayed a Jewish mother in *The Boss's Son* (1978), and developed a nightclub act, which she has since performed in Chicago, New York City, Lake Tahoe, Toronto, Atlantic City, and on various cruise ships. Her next motion picture role came in 1980 when she played an Italian American mistress in *Happy Birthday, Gemini.* And in 1981 Moreno starred with Alan Alda and Carol Burnett in the motion picture comedy *The Four Seasons.*

In 1982 Moreno found herself on television once again. She appeared as secretary Violet Newstead in the ABC situation comedy *Nine to Five* which ran from 1982 to 1983 and garnered her an Emmy nomination. Other television roles continued to come her way, including a part on Burt Reynolds's *B. L. Stryker* series and playing housekeeper Angie Corea to "detective" Bill Cosby in 1994's *Cosby Mysteries.* With James Coco and Sally Struthers, she appeared in *Wally's Cafe* on Broadway for twelve performances in June of 1981. In 1985 she worked opposite Struthers again, this time as the berumpled Olive Madison in a Broadway revision of Neil Simon's *The Odd Couple.* 1992 found her along side grand dame of the stage Carol Channing in the revue *Two Ladies of Broadway.*

Since then, Moreno has been involved in a variety of activities, serving as a member of the board of directors of Third World Cinema and the Alvin Ailey Dance Company, and included on the theater panel of the National Foundation of the Arts. Although she loves to spend time with her family at their homes in Pacific Palisades, California, and Manhattan, Moreno also finds ways to spend time with them professionally. She has appeared several times with her daughter, dancer and actress Fernanda Luisa, in productions such as *Steel Magnolias* and *The Taming of the Shrew.* And, with manager/husband Gordon, Moreno remains committed to the Hispanic community, telling *Hispanic,* "Lenny and I are very involved in trying to make the Hispanic community understand that education is everything."

While Moreno is aware of her responsibility as a role model for other Latinas, she is also, as she told *Hispanic,* an actress with career aspirations. It is to her credit that she has continued to seek opportunities to combine her love of acting with her desire to assist the Hispanic community; it remains her aspiration to play the part of a strong, socially active Hispanic woman. "And that is a woman of some sophistication, who speaks English very well, who is quite political," she explained in a 1989 *Hispanic* interview prior to being named one of that magazine's women of the year. "She is the emerging Hispanic woman, the one that nobody has gotten to see yet on television." Moreno herself is seen as such a woman; as she told another *Hispanic* interviewer, "When I was a young starlet, I wanted to be an all-American girl.... But when I grew up and developed a sense of self-esteem as a Hispanic, I learned how essential it was to cling to one's own heritage, for only in that way can we truly understand our ancestors, our culture, and ultimately understand ourselves."

Profile by Ronie-Richele Garcia-Johnson

EVELYN NIEVES

E velyn Nieves was raised in the Bronx, where going to college never

1959- •

crossed the mind of most of her schoolmates. But with determination

and the backing of supportive parents, she overcame the odds dictated

Journalist •

by her area's poor educational system to become one of the first Hispanic

journalists at the New York Times, *among the most prestigious newspa-*

pers in the world. Although she had originally wanted to be a social

worker, when Nieves became aware of her potential as a writer, she

realized that she would be able to reach more people and make a bigger

impact as a journalist. "It wasn't until I got to college that I realized I

could combine a social activism with writing, and that is the definition

of journalism that I had," she told interviewer D. D. Andreassi. "It wasn't a lifelong dream. It was very natural."

Nieves was born November 3, 1959, in the Bronx, New York; she was the last of four children born to Antonia Martinez and Angelo Nieves. Her parents, Puerto Rican immigrants, instilled in all their children a strong allegiance to their heritage. "The first trip I took to Puerto Rico was when I was nine," Nieves recalled, adding that her father wanted his children to "know where we came from and where he came from."

Angelo Nieves also made sure that his children understood where they were going. "From the time we were in kindergarten, there was no question that we would go to college," Nieves said. When her father's friends complimented him on having four children who attended college, his common response was that he was sorry he could not have given them more when they were growing up, because they would have attended Harvard University.

Nieves excelled in school; she graduated from Adlai E. Stevenson High School two months after her fifteenth birthday with sufficient credits to have received her diploma six months earlier. She attended New York State University, where she received a bachelor of arts degree in 1981 and a master's degree in English two years later. Nieves did well in college, even though the public schools in the Bronx did not provide the best preparation for higher learning. "Sometimes when I look at my education I get upset because the schools weren't better," she told Andreassi. "I think if I accomplish anything, it's in spite of where I grew up."

Her first experience as a reporter was with her high school newspaper. After college she worked at various small papers before she landed a job at the *Middle Town Times Herald Record* in Orange County, New York. Nieves remained there for three and half years before applying at the *New York Times*. "I had to do a lot of selling, because I came from a small newspaper," and the *New York Times* customarily hires reporters from large papers, she explained to Andreassi. Beating the odds, she was hired by the *Times* in July 1990.

Nieves has always felt a strong tie to the Bronx and similar neighborhoods. "I feel an empathy towards groups that are poor," she noted. The Bronx is also where she still feels most comfortable. "When I go to Union City and back to the Bronx, I feel happy. I feel I don't have to explain to these people. I feel they already know what I'm about." Her

- *Feels Affinity*

towards the

Poor

father, who owned restaurants in the Bronx, had that same type of bond. "He was the cook and the food was really good," Nieves proudly explained. "People told him that if he moved the restaurant he would make a fortune. But he didn't want to leave the neighborhood."

Sometimes when Nieves visits her parents in the Bronx she uncovers stories for the *New York Times* just by being in the neighborhood, knowing the problems people face and the emotions they feel. And having grown up in an impoverished area, she brings to her writing an understanding that reporters without that rearing would not know. Nieves also adds a Hispanic perspective to the paper that might otherwise be overlooked. She explained that Hispanic reporters naturally tend to draw on Hispanics for story information, because, like all journalists, they turn to the people and organizations with whom they are familiar. "Until you see more Hispanic journalists, you won't see Hispanic surnames and the guy at the corner store being quoted," she explained. "I don't want to use a political word, but it's empowering. I get calls from people, and they say maybe you will want to do this story—and it's strictly from my name. You don't see too many Hispanic journalists." Other times she feels helpless because the callers are reaching out, but the ideas do not lend themselves to stories. In those cases, her instincts toward social work surface and she finds herself giving advice.

In addition to covering the timely events occurring in New York City, New Jersey, and other nearby areas, Nieves is drawn to stories that reveal an injustice or in some other way influence people to make improvements for the oppressed. One such story revealed the plight of Newark, New Jersey, residents who were living in housing complexes that appeared to be abandoned. She wrote another story about a group of people in the Bronx—mostly immigrants from Central America— who took over an abandoned building and got kicked out by city officials. "I went into journalism to do those kinds of stories," the reporter noted. But there are also the stories of success, as in her 1994 account of the Vasquez family, Panamanian immigrants who rose from being undocumented aliens to gaining their "American Dream."

In addition to her newspaper work, one of Nieves's goals is to write about Latinos and Puerto Ricans "and not just as a subculture, but about Puerto Rican lawyers and other groups." Married since 1990 to Peter Olafson, she also hopes to someday find the time within her busy life to write a book about Puerto Ricans in the Bronx, as a means of illustrating some of the obstacles they face daily. "It's the poorest Hispanic group in the country," Nieves noted of the place she still considers to be her

Profile by
D. D. Andreassi

home. "When I go back there and see a train station that hasn't been fixed, it angers me, because these people don't complain."

ANTONIA NOVELLO

1944- •

*W*hen C. Everett Koop announced in late 1989 that he would retire

from the post of U.S. Surgeon General, speculation about who his

predecessor was particularly lively. During his eight-year tenure, Dr.

Former Surgeon •

General of the

United States

Koop had played an unusually prominent role in American public life,

elevating the previously soft-spoken voice of the Surgeon General to a

forceful, opinionated one that people paid attention to. Koop gained

national prominence and respect by speaking out on controversial

issues, sometimes colliding openly with the views of the presidential

administrations of Ronald Reagan and George Bush on such topics as

sex education and the use of condoms to prevent the spread of AIDS.

When Dr. Antonia Novello, deputy director of the National Institute

of Child Health and Human Development at the National Institutes of Health (NIH), was chosen to follow Koop as the fourteenth Surgeon General, many observers noted that filling her predecessor's illustrious footsteps would not be easy. But Dr. Novello brought to her three years as Surgeon General a reputation for hard work and dedication. Both the first woman and the first Hispanic to hold the position, she told the *Washington Post* several months after she was sworn in, "I'm for the people who deserve help . . . how I vote is not relevant. I think that as a woman, as a Hispanic, as a member of a minority . . . I bring a lot of sensitivity to the job."

Novello was born in Fajardo, Puerto Rico, on August 23, 1944. She and her brother were raised by their mother, school teacher Anna Delia Coello, after her father died. Novello suffered from a painful congenital colon condition until it was corrected when she was eighteen years old; she has often credited this illness as her motivation in becoming a doctor and helping ease the suffering of others. Novello received both her B.S. and M.D. degrees from the University of Puerto Rico, where she was, as Dr. Ivan Pelegrina, one of her former teachers, stated in the *Detroit Free Press,* "one of our brightest students." Her mother was a major motivating force in her daughter's life at this stage; Novello told *Glamour.* "I wasn't allowed to work until I graduated from medical school because my mother felt that once I earned money I might be sidetracked by material rewards before I got to my real work."

Novello quickly got to her "real work," beginning with an internship and residency in pediatrics from 1970 through 1973 at the University of Michigan (UM) Medical Center in Ann Arbor. She then served as a fellow in pediatric nephrology at UM through 1974, and recalled this "first job" as germinal in her eventual decision to enter government work; she "learned how many people slip through the cracks." Monitoring the progress of patients waiting for kidney transplants, Novello was dismayed at the number who could not be helped. Those cases in which she, personally, was powerless to help were especially affecting: "You become a true caring physician when you're able to share the pain."

Develops Early •

Interest in

Pediatric Care

In 1971 Novello was the first woman to receive the UM Pediatrics Department's Intern of the Year award. Classmate Dr. Samuel Sefton, now a neonatologist in Kalamazoo, Michigan, told the *Detroit Free Press,* "It was difficult for women to be accepted [in the medical field] then, and I always was impressed with the way she handled situations." Barbara Lanese, head nurse of the UM perinatal unit, concurred with Sefton: "[Antonia] was a resident when female physicians weren't as readily accepted as they are today.... She was a wonderful physician, and she was warm, friendly and well-respected. She was able to break the tension just by the kind of person she is."

In 1974 Novello joined the staff of Georgetown University Hospital in Washington, DC, as a pediatric nephrology fellow. She served as project officer at the NIH's National Institute of Arthritis, Metabolism and Digestive Diseases in 1978 and 1979, as staff physician at NIH from 1979 through 1980, and as the executive secretary of the Division of Research Grants at NIH from 1981 through 1986. She earned a master's degree in public health from Johns Hopkins University in 1982.

From 1986 until her appointment as Surgeon General in 1990, Novello served as deputy director of the National Institute of Child Health and Human Development, where she nurtured a special interest in children with AIDS. Concurrently, Novello was a clinical professor of pediatrics at Georgetown University Hospital. Her colleague there, pediatric department chairman Dr. Owen Rennert, told the *New York Times* that Novello "is tremendously concerned about the medical and social problems of children and she has a way of drawing others into that concern." In 1982 and 1983 Novello was a Congressional fellow on the staff of the Labor and Human Resources Committee chaired by Republican Senator Orrin Hatch of Utah. As reported in the *Washington Post,* Hatch later commented that she had "given good advice on several bills . . . including legislation on organ transplants and cigarette warning labels."

Novello's appointment to the post of Surgeon General came at a time of controversy over public health issues between several scientists and the Bush administration. Several candidates for top jobs at such organizations as the NIH, the Center for Disease Control, and the Health Care Financing Administration had withdrawn their names from consideration for the position, complaining that their interviews had included questions about their views on abortion and on the use of fetal tissue in research—another controversial practice opposed by the Bush White House. Some observers speculated that Novello's views against abortion, as well as her reputation for cooperative, dedicated, and essentially low-key work, made her a particularly desirable choice after the outspoken reign of Dr. Koop. Yet Novello claimed at a press conference covered in the *Washington Post* that "as long as the data can be trusted and is not just hearsay, I'll say it like it is.... I was never told I have to keep a low profile. I really intend to be like Dr. Koop when the data is there."

As head of the 5,700 commissioned officers of the Public Health Service, Novello focused her energies on AIDS-infected children, smoking—she fought the glamorous portrayal of smoking in advertisements and instituted a "We don't sell cigarettes to kids" campaign in

1991—and other women's health issues, such as breast cancer and heterosexual AIDS. Other areas of concern for Novello include teenage drinking, drinking and driving, and finding ways to diminish the social stigma of mental illness.

The Surgeon General's is an essentially public role, and Novello—who received several hundred invitations to speak per month—spent many hours on the road promoting the cause of better health. In addition to speaking with the Secretary of Health and Human Services three or four times a week, she focused much of her time on community outreach. Novello's understanding of the potential power and high visibility of her new job became more sharply defined, when she visited her birthplace, Puerto Rico, shortly after becoming Surgeon General. "When I got off the plane, kids from my mother's school lined both sides of the road handing me flowers.... I went to the VA hospital to speak. When the veterans saw my gold braid [she is a Vice-Admiral in the Public Health Service] they all stood and saluted.... I realized that for these people, for women, I have to be good as a doctor, I have to be good as a Surgeon General, I have to be everything."

After her appointment to the Surgeon General post in 1989, Novello directly addressed many of the problems that have concerned her, including teenage drinking. In late 1991 she met with some of the largest beer and wine companies in the United States and asked them to stop aiming their advertising at children and teenagers. "The ads have youth believing that instead of getting up early, exercising, going to school, playing a sport or learning to be a team player, all they have to do to fit is learn to drink the right alcohol," remarked Novello during a press conference covered in the *New York Times*.

Novello addressed, in particular, the health problems of Hispanic Americans. In 1993 she proposed a federal plan to address the needs of Hispanic/Latino citizens, the majority of whom are without health insurance, who carry a tuberculosis rate as high as four times the U.S. average, and who comprise twenty percent of all AIDS sufferers. While her proposal ultimately went the way of then-President Clinton's National Health Care plan, she continued to focus on the needs for increased health care in the Latino community prior to leaving office. On the eve of relinquishing her post, Novella published "Perspective on AIDS: A Woman-to-Woman Call to Arms" in the *Los Angeles Times,* an article wherein she challenged Latinas to "envision the future from a more realistic, assertive and proactive stance" in both protecting themselves and their families and demanding a solution to the AIDS crisis.

In addition to her attempts to aid the Hispanic population, Novello worked hard to provide better health care for all men, women, and children before she left office in 1993. Her efforts were awarded with several honors, including the Simon Bolivar National Award in 1991, and the Outstanding Achievement Award from Cuban American Women USA. Since her departure from office, she has become a special representative for UNICEF, tackling the issues childhood nutrition and woman's health on a global scale. It is a position that will allow her to continue to provide inspiration and aid to young people and families, as well as remain a role model for others to look up to.

Profile by
Kelly King Howes

ELLEN OCHOA

W hen Ellen Ochoa became the Johnson Space Center's first female

Hispanic astronaut in 1990, she was as interested in future stars on

earth as she was those that sparkled in the heavens. She made a

commitment to being a role model for young girls and Hispanics—

demonstrating to them that, by studying hard and reaching far enough,

the possibilities are, indeed, endless. As an astronaut, Ochoa is among

the selected few able to explore the mysteries of outer space. And, like

other astronauts who have ventured into that starlit realm, her work is

destined to influence the future study of astronomy. Before Ochoa

turned thirty-three, she was equally influential in other realms of

science: she held three patents for developing special techniques in

1958- •

Astronaut •

279 •

optical processing.

Immediately after the National Aeronautics Space Administration (NASA) selected Ochoa to become an astronaut, she began speaking to groups, especially young girls and Hispanics, advocating the importance of education. She emphasized her Hispanic heritage, hoping it would spark a hidden part of themselves, that "it may encourage them to do something like someone who is similar to them," she explained to D. D. Andreassi in a telephone interview. Otherwise Ochoa's gender and heritage have no influence on her work. "When I'm at work, I don't consider myself any different from any other astronaut," explained Ochoa. "I consider myself one of the astronauts in the office.

Ochoa was born in Los Angeles, California, May 10, 1958, to Rosanne (Deardorff) and Joseph Ochoa, born in California but of Mexican descent. Ochoa, whose parents were divorced when she was in junior high school, grew up with her mother, three brothers and one sister in La Mesa, California, in a close-knit family of high achievers. When her brother, Tyler Ochoa, a lawyer in Palo Alto, California, heard that his thirty-one-year-old sister was selected by NASA, he told a *Houston Post* interviewer that she had worked incredibly hard in order to be chosen from among the thousands of other applicants. "She's always been very diligent about studying and working for what she wanted to do," remarked Tyler. He described his sister as calm, rational and thoughtful, all qualities that would be useful to her as an astronaut.

Ochoa's mother instilled the value of education in her daughter at an early age. "From my mother we were all encouraged to do whatever we wanted to do," Ochoa told Andreassi. "She placed a high premium on going to college." Ochoa's mother lived according to her own advice: she took college courses for twenty-three years, finally finishing a triple major in business, biology, and journalism. Her daughter Ellen, while considering following in her mother's footsteps, later decided against studying journalism in favor of physics.

The Value of •

Education

Ochoa was just as dedicated to school work as her mother. Not only did she do exceptionally well in math and science, but she easily mastered all of her other courses as well. When Ochoa was thirteen years old she won the San Diego County spelling bee, and in junior high school she was named outstanding seventh and eighth grade female student. From then on she consistently went to the head of her class, becoming valedictorian at Grossmont High School in La Mesa, and achieving the same honor at San Diego State University where she earned a bachelor of science degree in physics. "I try to work hard for whatever I try to do," she commented in her interview with Andreassi.

"That's what I tried to do in school and that's what I'm trying to do now on my job."

Ochoa went on to Stanford University where she earned a master's degree and a doctorate in electrical engineering, and was the recipient of the Stanford engineering fellowship and IBM predoctoral fellowship. Ochoa told a *Hispanic* interviewer that she demonstrates the value of education. "If you stay in school, you have the potential to achieve what you want in the future," she maintained. "Education increases career options and gives you a chance for a wide variety of jobs." This is often a theme of her speeches to school children; Ochoa stresses the importance of children studying math and science to increase their worth in the job market.

During all of her scholastic achievements, Ochoa found the time to kept active with another love—music. In high school, she had become an accomplished flutist, capturing the top musician recognition at Grossmont High School; she was named student soloist winner at the Stanford Symphony Orchestra in 1983. While she once considered playing the flute for a career, Ochoa eventually opted for something more stable, telling Andreassi, "I like to ea.... I still play a lot whenever I can on the side," she continued, "so it's something that you can do as a hobby as well."

Ochoa took on another hobby after her older brother earned his private pilot's license. She decided to follow his lead, and in 1988—two years before she became an astronaut—she received a license to pilot small-engine planes. "I wanted to be an astronaut and I thought I should learn more about aviation," she told Andreassi. Ironically, after she began the rigorous life of an astronaut she has found little time to fly, or to devote to her other hobbies: playing volleyball and bicycling.

During the course of her career, Ochoa has always kept busy with research projects. From 1985 through 1988 she was a research engineer in the Imaging Technology Branch at Sandía National Laboratories in Livermore, California. While many scientists and inventors struggle for many years to patent their ideas, Ochoa held three patents in optical processing by the time she was in her early thirties. One of her developments was a process that implements optics for image processing, something that is normally done by computer. For instance, one method she devised removes noise from an image through an optical system rather than using a standard digital computer to do the work.

While research has always interested Ochoa, she explained that it had been difficult to decide what career to pursue. Even in college she had been unsure. In fact, while Ochoa was an undergraduate she changed her major five times: from music to business to journalism to computer science, before deciding on physics, according to the *Houston Post*. It was while she was a graduate student at Stanford, watching her friends apply to NASA, that she realized she, too, had the qualifications to be an astronaut.

It was a career that Ochoa would not have been able to consider prior to 1978, the year that NASA graduated the first six women ever selected to the program. As she told the *Houston Post,* a milestone had been reached when women were finally accepted into the program. "We realized, 'Oh, it's really open to real people, not just an elite group of test pilots,'" she recalled. Little did the twenty-year-old college student know that twelve years later she would be blazing new trails by becoming NASA's first female Hispanic astronaut.

It was a combination of Ochoa's many qualifications and her persistence that won her a spot at NASA. She first applied to the program in 1985; by 1987 she had been named as one of the top one hundred finalists. She graduated in the astronaut class of 1990, which included eighteen men and five women. In addition to graduation, 1987 marked a personal milestone for Ochoa when she married Coe Fulmer Miles of Molalla, Oregon.

Earns Spot at •

NASA

Just as she had done throughout high school and college, Ochoa made a name for herself at NASA, beginning in 1988, first as a researcher, and later as chief of the Intelligent Systems Technology Branch at National Aeronautics and Space Administration/Ames Research Center at Mountain View, California's Moffet Field Naval Air Station. Her progression through the ranks was rapid: beginning as a researcher, Ochoa was soon supervising almost forty scientists prior to her selection as an astronaut. "She was assertive," recalled deputy Nancy Sliwa to the *Houston Post*. "She defended [her] branch needs within NASA." Ochoa's accomplishments were acknowledged in 1989 when she was awarded the Hispanic Engineer National Achievement Award for most promising engineer in government. A year later she was given the Pride Award by the National Hispanic Quincentennial Commission in Washington, D.C. And 1993 marked her receipt of the Congressional Hispanic Caucus Medallion of Excellence.

Ochoa's goals have included putting her expertise to the test in space. In late 1992, as a missions specialist civilian, she prepared to go on her first flight, ATLAS 2 (Atmospheric Laboratory for Applications and Science). The shuttle mission, which was scheduled for take-off in early 1993, planned to utilize a set of instruments to measure chemical composition, temperature, and pressure of the earth's atmosphere. The astronauts task was to measure solar radiation and how it varies across different wavelengths. "What the scientists are hoping to do is measure what effect and variability the sun would have on the earth's atmosphere and determine values for concentration of chemical species in the atmosphere," explained Ochoa.

• **Prepares for**

Space Flight

Ochoa will continue to face tremendous challenges as she follows in the footsteps of Sally Ride, the first female sent on a U.S. space flight. During the ten-day ATLAS 2 mission, Ochoa was one of two scientists on board the shuttle. She was chosen to play a key role by deploying instruments into space that will enable scientists to look at the sun's corona. Ochoa was one of two astronauts operating the deployment arm, working under stressful conditions caused by the limited chances to complete all planned tasks during the short mission.

Prior to the mission, Ochoa told Andreassi that, while she is excited about reaching her goal of flying in space, she is also aware there will be a lot to learn before the ATLAS 2 take-off. "But there's nothing else I'd rather be doing," she said. Ochoa was not worried about an accident in space, even with the recent memory of the Challenger shuttle disaster of 1986. All seven Challenger crew members, including teacher Christi McAuliffe, had perished when the shuttle exploded shortly after take-off, leaving friends and family watching in horror from the ground. "I'm sure on flight day I'll think about a lot of different things, but we train for a lot of different things," Ochoa explained, adding that every precaution would be taken to make the mission as safe as possible. There are always some unknown elements and the risks they might pose are part of the equation that everyone who becomes involved with a space flight understands.

After achieving her immediate goal—flying in space—Ochoa hopes to continue her work as an astronaut for "quite a number of years and beyond that I'll have to wait and see what I will do." She plans to continue making public speeches to educate people about the job and responsibilities of being an astronaut and, most of all, to continue being a role model for young women. Her emphasis will be with school children, because they are at an impressionable age. "I think that's where I can make a difference," she told Andreassi. Ochoa is keenly aware that her achievements are most noticed by Hispanic groups. "A lot of those kids have come up to me and said, 'Wow, it's inspiring to see that you made it, because it shows what I can do.' Anything I can do along those lines is important for those people and for the country in having an educated work force." She was excited to learn that she began making a positive impact on youngsters shortly after she became an astronaut. According to the *Houston Post,* after a speech Ochoa gave at a San Francisco Bay Area Catholic school, an Hispanic youngster, who was among a group of students who surrounded her, said: "I'm glad you came. You've inspired us."

**Profile by
D. D. Andreassi**

GRACIELA OLIVÁREZ

A *lthough she herself was a high school drop-out, Graciela Olivárez*

1928–1987 •

would eventually become one of the most highly profiled Hispanic

women in the United States. As the first woman to graduate from Notre

Government •

Dame School of Law, Olivárez served as both director of the Community

official,

Services Administration during the Carter administration and as a

educator

senior consultant for the United Way, positions that paved the way for

other women, most notably fellow Hispanics.

Olivárez was born on May 9, 1928, in a town near Phoenix, Arizona, to Damian Gil Valero and his wife, Eloisa Solis. Although she left high school after her family moved to Phoenix in 1944, Olivárez did not let her lack of a degree affect her confidence. She attended business school and aggressively sought a job. By 1952 she had found a position in Phoenix as director of women's programming for KIFN, a Spanish-language radio station. There, Olivárez became locally famous as the area's first female disc jockey.

During the 1960s Olivárez became increasingly active with the social and political movements of the time. As she wrote in *New Catholic World* in 1984, it was an era when "we [her generation] believed that we could do almost anything we set out to do." Olivárez's youthful optimism and determination to help impoverished people won her an influential position as the state director of the Office of Economic Opportunity (OEO) for Arizona in 1965. With its commitment to eradicate poverty, the OEO provided a wonderful opportunity for Olivárez, who deeply cared about the plight of the underprivileged. As she reminded readers in *New Catholic World,* the OEO "created programs such as Head Start, Legal Services, VISTA volunteers, Job Corps, Community Action Agencies, programs for migrant farm workers and their families, community development corporations and the weatherization program."

Olivárez did not work in this position for long. During the civil rights movement, the president of Notre Dame University, Reverend Theodore Hesburgh, had met Olivárez and was impressed with her intelligence and her record of service. He encouraged her to attend the university's law school. Although Olivárez was already in her late thirties and did not have the usual educational qualifications, she courageously decided to take Hesburgh up on his offer. In 1970, at the age of forty-two, Olivárez graduated from the Notre Dame School of Law—she was the first woman ever to do so.

• *Fights Poverty*

Following her graduation Olivárez returned to the southwestern United States. There, she taught law and worked for various government agencies. By 1972 she had been appointed the director of the University of New Mexico's Institute for Social Research and Development. From 1973 to 1975 she was a professor at the law school at that University. Next came a position as New Mexico's State Planning Officer in 1975. Olivárez's continued efforts to decrease poverty eventually caught the attention of then-President Jimmy Carter. When he appointed her as the director of the Community Services Administration in 1977, Olivárez became the highest-ranking female Hispanic in the Carter administration.

In 1980 Olivárez left the Carter administration to return to her home in New Mexico and to run her own business, the Olivárez Television Company. That same year she began to serve as a senior consultant with the United Way of America. By 1984 Olivárez was the owner of a management consulting/public relations firm in Albuquerque. At that time she continued to voice her concern regarding the poverty situation in the United States, writing in an article for the *New Catholic World*: "To solve the nation's growing numbers of poor, we need (1) rational analysis and practical programs, (2) the cooperation of both the public and private sectors and (3) sincere concern for the future of all Americans. Short-sighted ideological and political posturing, coupled with simplistic approaches, won't do."

Olivárez received many honors for her work over the course of her career. The American Cancer Society presented her with an Outstanding Leadership Award in 1960, and during the early 1970s the League of Mexican-American Women named Olivárez an Outstanding Woman of the Southwest. Amherst College in Massachusetts awarded her with an honorary Ph.D. in 1973, and Olivárez went on to receive another honorary doctorate from Michigan State University in 1976, and still another from her alma mater, Notre Dame, in 1978. The Woodlawn Organization honored her with its Leadership Award in 1978, and she won the Mexican American Opportunity Fund Aztec Award the next year. In December of 1985 Olivárez was honored by the Mexican American Legal Defense and Educational Fund for her contributions to the Latino community.

When she died in 1987 Olivárez left a legacy of hope to a generation of young Hispanic woman who sought to achieve influential positions in the areas of scholarship, business, and politics. Just as importantly, she left a tremendous legacy of determination, ideas, and optimism to those who continue to fight poverty in the United States.

Profile by Ronie-Richele Garcia-Johnson

KATHERINE D. ORTEGA

*K*atherine Davalos Ortega came to national prominence in the fall

of 1983 when then-President Ronald Reagan nominated her for the

position of United States Treasurer. Her nomination was confirmed by

the Senate and she served as Treasurer until 1989. Ortega's role as U.S.

Treasurer was preceded by a series of no less admirable achievements,

including being the first woman bank president in the state of Califor-

nia and guiding a struggling Alamogordo, New Mexico, financial

institution to a point where it could claim $20 million in assets. In her

acceptance speech following her appointment as Treasurer, Ortega is

quoted in the New York Times *as referring to her Hispanic background*

as a source of pride and inspiration: "I am the product of a heritage that

1934- •

Former U.S. •

Treasurer,

banker

teaches strong family devotion, a commitment to earning a livelihood by hard work, patience, determination and perseverance."

Ortega was the ninth child of Donaciano, a blacksmith and cafe owner, and his wife, Catarina Davalos Ortega, residents of Tularosa, New Mexico, where Katherine was born on July 16, 1934. Her paternal grandparents had brought their family to the area from Texas in the late 1880s, and Ortega grew up in Tularosa, a tiny village of less than three thousand inhabitants, nestled in the shadow of the Sacramento Mountains not far from the Alamogordo atomic bomb testing site. It was here that Ortega learned Spanish—her first language—and then English. During her early years she excelled at mathematics and was so skilled with numbers that she was allowed, even as a ten-year-old, to use the cash register at her family's restaurant business. As she got older Ortega found special pleasure and a high measure of success in her mathematics and accounting classes at school. During her last year of high school she had a part-time job at the Otero County State Bank in Alamogordo, a hint of things to come.

• **Experienced**

Job-Related

Discrimination

After graduation from high school, Ortega took a two-and-a-half year break in her education and obtained a position at a bank where she worked in order to earn money for college. She eventually entered Eastern New Mexico State University at Portales where she majored in business and economics and graduated with honors in 1957. Ortega explained what happened after her college graduation in an interview with Marian Christy of the *Boston Globe*: "When I graduated from college, I planned to teach typing and shorthand at the high-school level. I was told by the chairman of the business school that I need not apply in the eastern part of New Mexico, where such a job was open, because of my Hispanic background. My immediate reaction was: 'That's it. I won't teach.'"

Disgusted with the discrimination that would keep her from following her chosen career path, Ortega quickly decided to create her own career opportunity. She and one of her sisters, who was a certified public accountant, started an accounting firm in Alamogordo. During the 1960s and 1970s she held several different positions in accounting in New Mexico and later in California, where she moved in 1967. From 1969 to 1972 she was a tax supervisor at the firm of Peat, Marwick, Mitchell & Co. in Los Angeles, and from 1972 to 1975 she served as vice-president and cashier at the Pan American National Bank, also in that city. In 1975 Ortega became the first woman president of a California bank when she accepted the position of director and president of the Santa Ana State Bank. By 1979 Ortega had moved back to New Mexico to help run the family accounting business, which eventually became the Otero Savings & Loan Association. She served as consultant to the firm from 1979 to 1982. Ortega also became a California-certified public accountant in 1979.

About this same time, Ortega began to intensify her involvement in politics, although she once declared to a *New York Times* contributor that, "I have often said that I was born a Republican." At first, her political work was on the local and state level, with the party calling on her to play a liaison role with Hispanic and women's organizations. She also became active in the campaigns of Pete V. Domenici, a Republican senator from New Mexico; he later returned the favor when, as chairman of the Senate Budget Committee, he suggested Ortega to then-President Reagan, who needed someone to fill the treasury position within his administration.

Ortega received her first taste of national recognition from the Republicans in April of 1982 when Reagan selected her to be part of a ten-member Presidential Advisory Committee on Small and Minority Business Ownership. Eight months later, Reagan appointed her a commissioner on the Copyright Royalty Tribunal. This five-member panel is the Federal agency that determines what royalty fees cable companies throughout the nation pay for use of copyrighted material. The tribunal, which was created in 1978, also establishes royalties paid by jukebox operators to the musicians whose music they provide. Shortly thereafter, in September of 1983, Ortega learned that she would be nominated to be U.S. Treasurer

Nominated •

Treasurer of

United States

Ortega was officially nominated as Treasurer of the United States on September 12, 1983, in a ceremony marking the beginning of Hispanic Week celebrations in the nation's capital. According to the *New York Times,* in President Reagan's nominating remarks he claimed that Ortega was "symbolic of the values the Hispanic community represents" and added that "nothing is a better influence on America than the strength and decency of the Hispanic family." On October 3, 1983, after receiving her confirmation by the Senate, Reagan again praised his appointee as she was sworn in to her post by Treasury Secretary Donald T. Regan in the Rose Garden of the White House. In the *New York Times'* coverage of the event the President is reported as saying, "It's important that key positions within an Administration be filled by people who reflect the goals and ideals for which the people voted.... And this is certainly true today." During the ceremony Ortega signed special forms that were used to add her signature to plates from which U.S. currency would be printed during her tenure, an estimated 5.5 billion bills in the first year.

The position of U.S. Treasurer has in recent years nearly always gone to a politically prominent woman. Romana Acosta Bañuelos, appointed by the late President Nixon in 1974, was the first Hispanic woman to serve in this capacity; Ortega was the second. Although the post is deemed to be, for the most part, ceremonial, the U.S. Treasurer supervises the Bureau of Engraving and Printing, the United States Mint, and the United States Savings Bond Division. Some of Ortega's duties included maintaining an account of government spending, handling claims for lost, stolen, or counterfeit Government checks, and burning unusable U.S. currency. At the time she took office, Ortega was responsible for handling the nation's $220 million budget and overseeing 5,000 employees. In 1985 she was given the added responsibility of promoting the sale of U.S. Liberty Coins, three gold and silver commemorative coins designed to raise $40 million to help pay for the restoration of the Statue of Liberty.

In 1984 alone Ortega flew more than 60,000 miles to speak at both Hispanic and Republican events. Her most important speaking engagement came in August of that year when she flew to Dallas, Texas, to deliver the keynote address at the Republican National Convention. That this important role within the convention was given to a comparatively new member of the Reagan Administration surprised a lot of long-time convention observers, who had expected to see Reagan Cabinet-member Elizabeth Dole or Kansas Senator Nancy Kassebaum fill the bill. Ortega was undaunted by the assignment; she gave a stirring speech that was later reprinted in *Vital Speeches of the Day.* In her address before the convention she referred to her Hispanic heritage several times and—to the joy of Spanish-speaking delegates—even included several Spanish phrases in the text. "To those millions of Democrats abandoned by their national leadership....," she declared, "we Republicans here in Dallas say: we welcome you to our home. Nuestra casa es su casa. Our home is your home."

Ortega's high profile at the convention served to remind those feminist groups who had complained about a lack of female appointments during Reagan's administration that he had indeed filled many positions with qualified women. Ortega mentioned in a *New York Times* article that one of her goals was "to get the message out.... There is a perception that Ronald Reagan has not named women to his Administration. When I'm out there, I talk about all the subcabinet appointments. I want to set the record straight." She also credited her father for inspiring her success in a male-dominated world: "My father taught me we were as good as anybody else, that we could accomplish anything we wanted.... He encouraged all three of his daughters to make a living for themselves so we would never have to be dependent on anybody."

Since she stepped down as Treasurer of the United States in 1989, Ortega has been, for the most, part self-employed. She has served as an alternative representative to the United Nations and is on the board of directors of several major corporations, including the Ralston Purina Company and the Kroger Company, a grocery chain, both of which appointed Ortega to their boards in 1992. She is also on the advisory boards of Leadership America and the National Park Service and is a member of both Executive Women in Government and the American Association of Women Accountants.

Ortega's distinguished career has brought her many awards and honors. In 1977 Eastern New Mexico University presented her with its Outstanding Alumni of the Year Award. She has also received several honorary degrees, including honorary doctor of law degrees from her alma mater, Eastern New Mexico University, in 1984, and from Kean College of New Jersey in 1985, as well as an honorary doctor of social science from Pennsylvania's Villanova University in 1988. Other awards include the California Businesswoman's Achievement Award and the Outstanding Woman of the Year Award from the Damas de Comercio. In February 1989 she was married to Lloyd J. Derrickson; the couple makes their home near Washington, D.C. Ortega's leisure activities include travel, reading, and golf

Ortega is quite willing to serve as an example to other Hispanics who find themselves facing the obstacle of racial bigotry. "I think of myself as a role model for my people. . .," she told a *Boston Globe* contributor. "I hope they see me and say: 'Hey, there's hope. We can accomplish.' I think people can look at me and see what I've accomplished and pursue careers for themselves. Everyone encounters obstacles. I tell people if one road is closed, take another. I'm a stubborn person."

**Profile by
Marian C. Gonsior**

ELIZABETH PEÑA

*P*erformances in movies like Down and Out in Beverly Hills, La

Bamba, *and* Jacob's Ladder *and in the television shows* I Married Dora

and Shannon's Deal *have won Elizabeth Peña growing respect and*

recognition. While Pena has always been perceived as sexy, directors are

coming to realize that she is also extraordinarily versatile: she has run

the gamut of emotions, being hilarious in some roles and serious and

somber in others. Hard work and determination, combined with a gift

for acting and a striking face, have made Peña a sought-after actress.

1959- •

Actress •

The first daughter of Cuban-born actor, writer, and director Mario Peña and producer Estella Marguerita Toirac Peña, Peña was named after the city in which she was born on September 23, 1959: Elizabeth, New Jersey. It was in this city that the family lived while Mario studied drama at Columbia University. Despite their affection for the city and the United States, the young family went back to Cuba four months after Peña's birth. The Cuban Revolution was new and promising, and they wanted to rejoin their families during what seemed to be an exciting time.

Unfortunately Mario was imprisoned when he returned home; he had written a poem that the government considered to be "antisystem." When he was able to talk himself out of prison, he found himself with no choice other that to flee the country and return to the United States. Unfortunately, Estella Marguerita, Peña, and her younger sister, Tania, were not allowed to follow him; they were detained in Cuba until 1968, when Peña was nine years old. Even as they were ready to board their plane, government officials harassed the family; their papers were in English, and no one was willing to acknowledge their authority. Finally, one official waved them through the red tape in the nick of time: as Peña recalled in a *People* interview, the plane's "motors were running."

- ***Family***

Reunited in

United States

When the family was reunited and settled in New York, the elder Peñas' careers began to take off. Mario founded New York City's Latin American Theater Ensemble with Estella, and they each became respected figures in New York's theater scene. Elizabeth owes her love of acting, as well as her determination to succeed as an actor, to her parents. "My father and mother are the biggest influences in my life," she confided to *Interview* in 1987. "They've been able to survive as actors in the theater in New York and have instilled that same sense of survival in me." While she was inspired by her parents, Peña also recalls that her mother did not want her to become an actress. When she was accepted to New York's renowned School of Performing Arts, Peña told *People,* her mother fell to her knees, wailing, "If you become an actress, you'll kill me." Peña retorted, "Well, you better start arranging your funeral." Aside from graduating from the School of the Performing Arts, Peña also studied acting with Curt Dempster at the Ensemble Studio Theater and Endre Hules at La Mama ETC. In addition to acting, she studied clowning with Mark Stolzenberg and speech and voice with Lynn Masters. Despite her initial dismay, Estella soon began to support her daughter's efforts to become an actress.

Peña's mother was not the only one to be persuaded by her daughter's determination to utilize her gift for acting. Peña aggressively pursued roles in motion pictures and on stage. In 1979 she played Aurelita in the movie *El Super,* and in 1980 she landed a part in *Times Square*. Her next role was that of Rita in the movie *They All Laughed,* which she followed with a number of stage appearances in New York. Included among these many roles were the parts of Jesse in *Dog Lady,* Maria in *Bring on the Night,* Cynthia in *Shattered Image,* Teresa in *La Morena,* Juliet in *Romeo and Juliet,* Beba in *Night of the Assassins,* and Teresa in *Italian-American Reconciliation.* By 1984 Peña had landed another movie role, that of Liz, the girlfriend of costar Rubén Blades in *Crossover Dreams*.

At this point in her career Peña felt she was ready to take on Hollywood. She moved to the famous town and began to search for roles. The casting director for *Down and Out in Beverly Hills* (1986), a movie starring Richard Dreyfuss and Bette Midler, found himself deluged with photos and messages from Peña. Although she had just arrived in town and had no agent, she was determined to get the part, and determined to do it by herself. By the time she was given a screen test, Peña was almost broke. She gave the test her best, and the casting director was impressed. He cast Peña in her first high-profile role as the Salvadoran maid, Carmen. Peña's sexy as well as funny performance in *Down and Out in Beverly Hills* received favorable attention, and she was soon an actress in demand.

This success made 1987 a very busy year for Peña. She won a role in another hit movie, *La Bamba*, portraying Rosie, the abused yet loyal wife of Richie Valens's elder brother. Later that year Peña earned a role in *I Married Dora*, a television situation-comedy about a man who marries his Central American maid so she won't be deported. While Jeff Jarvis, writing in *People,* asserted that the show should receive a grade of "D", he also acknowledged Peña's talent. "Only one small asset rescues this sludge-brained idea from an instant F: Elizabeth Peña's charm." In 1987 Peña excelled in still another movie, Steven Spielberg's *Batteries Not Included*.

Although she took a break from acting after marrying William Stephan Kibler in 1988, Peña stayed busy accepted a number of awards, including the Hispanic Women's Council Woman of the Year Award, the New York Image Award, the U.S. Congress Congressional Award, and the Nosotros Golden Eagle Award. Peña's career picked up pace again in 1990, with what *Newsweek* called a "warm and gritty" performance as Jezzie, the girlfriend of Jacob Singer (Tim Robbins) in the eerie movie *Jacob's Ladder*. That same year, she was cast as the client/secretary of a heartbroken lawyer in the television show *Shannon's Deal*. Tom Shales, writing in the *Washington Post* and quoted in *People,* maintained that Peña was "so assertive and gutsy.... Maybe the show should be about *her*."

While in her roles as supporting actress Peña brightened many productions, including the television shows *Hill Street Blues, TJ Hooker, Cagney and Lacey, As the World Turns, Tough Cookies* and *Saturday Night Live*; the made-for-television movies *Drug Wars: The Camarena Story* and *Found Money*; and the movies *Blue Steel* and *Fat Chance*, that all changed in 1995. That was the year when, with the back-to-back release of *Dead Funny* and *Free Willy II*, she at last achieved star billing. While receiving mixed reviews from critics, Peña shone alongside costar Andrew McCarthy in *Dead Funny*, a tale about a museum publicist who finds her boyfriend dead in her apartment and sets about figuring out whodunnit. Although a whale demanded top billing in the popular *Free Willy II*, Peña found the process of acting alongside such a hefty costar to be eyeopening. "You were in this beautiful set working on this sweet movie and you'd look around and see all these little kids playing in the water, running around, climbing trees, and searching for seashells, and it was like Shangri-La," she told *Hispanic*.

In addition to her acting, Peña is committed to giving something back to her community. In 1994 she combined a lifelong love of reading with drama in "Celebrando La Diferencia," a six-part series on Hispanic literature that she organized with the help of friends like Edward James Olmos. Performed at Hollywood's Met Theatre, the series attracted several hundred young viewers over its six-week run. "The irony of this is that it started out as a little idea," she said, noting that the greatest pleasure in the program was its positive effect on "tough" kids. Peña remains equally positive about her career as an Hispanic actress. "I've never thought of [being Hispanic] as an obstacle," she tells Allis. "I think it's good. There are certainly enough five-foot-seven blonds."

**Profile by
Ronie-Richele
Garcia-Johnson**

ROSIE PEREZ

1964- •

Actress, •

dancer,

choreographer

A ctress and choreographer Rosie Perez used to claim she had a

hard time sleeping—her career was not moving fast enough for her.

Anyone but the indomitable Perez would have been blown away by the

sheer speed of her rise in the entertainment industry: In just a few short

years she went from being an undergraduate science student to becom-

ing one of the most sought-after pop music choreographers in the

industry, as well as a rising actress. "I'm very happy with the way things

are going for me right now," she told Entertainment Weekly *in 1992,*

"but I still feel like they're going too slow. I want it all." Gaining roles in

noteworthy films alongside such leading men as Jeff Bridges, Nicholas

Cage, and Harvey Keitel in more recent years, Perez would seem to be

well on her way to reaching her goal.

Rosa Mary Perez was born September 6, 1964, at Greenpoint Hospital in Brooklyn, New York, the daughter of Ismael Serrano and Lydia Perez. Raised in Brooklyn's mostly Puerto Rican Bushwick district, Perez is one of ten brothers and sisters who grew up watching their parents dance "salsa" on weekends and holidays. Her mother had been a singer in Puerto Rico, and music always filled the house; along with the sounds of childish rambunctiousness. "Growing up with nine brothers and sisters was an early lesson in assertiveness training," Perez reminisced to *Entertainment Weekly*. "In a family like that, you have to compete for attention."

A good student who excelled in science, Perez moved to Los Angeles at the age of eighteen to attend Los Angeles City College, where she studied marine biology and planned to major in biochemistry. It was while dancing at a trendy Los Angeles Latin club that she was first invited to dance on the television show *Soul Train*. After doing a couple of shows, Perez quit, but while she was there she met Louis Silas Jr., senior vice-president of black music at MCA Records. Silas asked Perez if she wanted to be in a recording group, and although the college student declined, she kept in touch with him.

One day Silas asked Perez if she would be willing to choreograph one of his artists who was coming out with his third solo album. Silas wanted this artist to have a younger appeal and asked Perez to find some dancers who could dance "hip-hop" with him. Perez at first refused because she had no experience, but hearing the album changed her mind and decided to go ahead with the project. The artist's name was Bobby Brown and the project was a success.

After seeing Brown show his new moves on the television program *Soul Train,* a new Motown recording group called The Boys asked Perez to choreograph their show. With the double successes of Bobby Brown and The Boys, offers poured in. Perez and her partners, Heart & Soul, found themselves busy creating the stage and/or video choreographies for many artists, including Diana Ross and rappers Al B. Sure, LL Cool J, Heavy D & the Boyz, and for such record labels as Motown, Polygram, and Capitol. The next step was the small screen, when Perez choreographed the Fox television program *In Living Color*. When *GQ* asked her to define her dancing style, Perez—who considers herself a better choreographer than a dancer—replied, "Clearness. Quickness. Difficult combinations. I'll never do a move for a four count—usually just a two and move on. That's what earns me respect with the club people." She then laughingly added: "Here's my dancer's arrogance. I haven't seen anybody who can articulate hip-hop the way I do, in such a lean, crisp

Launches •

Choreography

Career with

Bobby Brown

way, and still be authentic. There are a lot who try and do it, and it comes off very corny. I still got the flavor." And others agreed: In 1993 Perez was the host of HBO's three-part hip-hop music show, *Society's Ride*.

- *Takes on Acting*

  in Do the Right

  Thing

In her official public relations "biography," Perez explains how her movie career was launched. "While I was choreographing The Boys, I was dancing at the Funky Reggae Club in Los Angeles. Spike Lee was having his birthday party there and the band EU was performing. The band asked me to dance on stage; afterwards Spike introduced himself to me. His partner, Monty Ross, gave me their phone number and asked me to call. I forgot all about it until I was leaving to go back to Brooklyn (the school semester had finished) and decided to call them. They were really excited and asked me if I would be in Los Angeles long. When I told them that I was returning to Brooklyn in a couple of days, they started screaming and Spike said, 'This is fate.' I didn't know what he meant by that, because he never mentioned the possibility of a movie until a month later. When I told him I had to return for the new school semester in Los Angeles, he offered me the role of Tina in *Do the Right Thing*. Instead of finishing that semester, I decided to do the movie, and it changed my life."

In an interview with *Newsweek*, Perez described her movie debut experience as possibly the best and worst thing that had ever happened to her. There was a nude scene involving an ice cube that, she has said, made her feel like she was "raped" by the camera. When Hispanic groups criticized her for promoting a stereotype, Perez defended the film, which was released to a critical uproar in 1989. "I was not portraying something that's not really out there," was her response to critics; but she also informed her agent she didn't want to play any "Tinas" in the future.

- *Film Career*

  Rapidly

  Progresses

By contrast, her role as Woody Harrelson's feisty girlfriend in the 1992 basketball-based film *White Men Can't Jump,* was originally written for a white woman who'd attended an Ivy League school. But writer/director Ron Shelton was so impressed by the instant chemistry between Perez and Harrelson that he hired her and, without making major changes to the script, the role was transformed from that of a Barnard graduate to a former Brooklyn disco queen.

In quick succession, Perez's acting credits have gone on to include the films *Untamed Heart, Night on Earth*, 1994's *It Could Happen to You*, and *Fearless*, for which she received an Academy Award nomination for best supporting actress. Surprisingly, she found the time to marry boyfriend Rocky Santiago, in September 1993. Meanwhile, television has kept Perez as busy as her film career: appearances have included the popular *21 Jump Street* and *Criminal Justice*, a recurring role in the CBS series *WIOU,* and a spot as cohost of *In A New Light,* a 1995 ABC special alerting viewers about the increasing frequency of AIDS as a killer of young people. "Minorities can play regular roles too," Perez states in a *Preview* interview, and her opinion carries the weight of her own successful acting career behind it. "And being a minority you have a responsibility to help other minorities along the way."

**Profile by
Elena Kellner**

DOLORES PRIDA

D olores Prida has been hailed as one of the most important

contemporary Hispanic playwrights in the United States. Armed with a

sharp, satiric wit and a good sense of humor, she writes plays which

bring to life on stage the problems of racism and social injustice that are

visited on the Hispanic segment of the population of the United States,

present her strong belief in feminism, and reflect the search for identity

by Hispanics torn between two cultures.

1943- •

Playwright •

Born in Caibarien, Cuba, on September 5, 1943, Prida came to the United States with her parents, Manuel Prida and Dolores Prieto, as part of the wave of exiles who fled Fidel Castro's pro-communist government. Settling in New York, she attended Hunter College from 1965 to 1969, majoring in Spanish-American literature. During her first fifteen years in the United States, Prida worked for publishing houses and periodicals as both editor and journalist. Among her jobs were serving as managing editor of the Spanish-language New York daily newspaper *El tiempo,* as New York correspondent for the Latin American magazine *Vision* from 1977 to 1980, and as executive senior editor of *Nuestro,* a national English-language magazine for Hispanics. Linked to *Revista areito,* the publication of young Cuban intellectuals who sought a new understanding with the Havana government, Prida traveled to Cuba in both 1978 and 1979 to participate in a dialogue that eventually allowed visitation of the island nation by exiles who had relatives there. Although her written work never touched upon the area of Cuban politics, Prida's involvement in this project has lead to death threats on the part of some more militant anti-Castro exiles, creating a climate that has made it impossible for her works to be presented in parts of New Jersey and Southern Florida, areas with dense Cuban-American populations.

Prida made her debut as a playwright in 1977 with her bilingual musical comedy *Beautiful Señoritas,* produced by Duo Theater in New York. The play's call for the liberation of Hispanic women from the dual repression of patriarchal males and the Catholic Church has made it a favorite; in fact, in 1980 *Beautiful Señoritas* was presented as a special performance at the National Organization for Women convention in San Antonio.

In 1981 Prida's *Coser y cantar* premiered at the Duo Theater. The play's two characters, She, the English speaker, and Ella, her Spanish counterpart—the two sides of an uprooted Latin woman—argue throughout the one-act drama, exposing the problems of living in two worlds. *Coser y cantar* has been performed on stage repeatedly since its debut. In addition, as a radio play it has been broadcast throughout the United States. Prida's first collection of plays, *Beautiful Señoritas and Other Plays,* was published in 1991 by Arte Público Press of Houston, Texas.

In addition to her work as a playwright and journalist, Prida has also taught a playwriting workshop at Hostos Community College and written scripts for documentary films. She has received a variety of recognitions, among them a Doctor of Humane Letters from Mount Holyoke College in 1989, the Cintas Fellowship Award for literature in 1976, and the Creative Artistic Public Service Award for playwriting from 1979-1980. Director of publications for the Association of Hispanic Arts since 1983, Prida continues to work in New York City where she remains active in the theater.

**Profile by
Silvia Novo Peña**

TEY DIANA REBOLLEDO

L *iterary critic and educator Tey Diana Rebolledo is renowned for*

her research on literature by Chicana and Latin American women

writers, especially the study of early work by such authors. Her interest in

19th- and early 20th-century literary works and unpublished manu-

scripts by Hispanic writers was fueled by her own mother's writings—

work that went unpublished and languished in the family trunk for

many years. The silencing of women's voices, either through neglect or

lack of publishing opportunities, has strongly influenced Rebolledo's

research.

1937- •

Critic, •

educator

Rebolledo was born April 29, 1937, in Las Vegas, New Mexico, to Esther Vernon Galindo and Washington Antonio Rebolledo. Both parents were creative writers; her father was also a professor of Spanish at Highlands University in Las Vegas and the author of a book of short

stories and other literary works. Her parents' creative influence made a mark on Rebolledo's life. She recalls accompanying her father to the local Spanish-language radio station where, as host of a talk show, he discussed Hispanic culture. The family's trips to Mexico reinforced the strong cultural roots that they had established in northern New Mexico. When Rebolledo was ten, her family moved to New London, Connecticut, where her father had taken a post teaching Spanish at Connecticut College. She remembers that the relocation was a culture shock because few Spanish-speaking people lived in the community and the New England lifestyle was so different from what she experienced in New Mexico. Her world was further disrupted when her father died in 1951.

In 1959 Rebolledo received her B.A. in Spanish from Connecticut College and began graduate work in Latin American studies at the University of New Mexico. Newly married, she obtained her M.A. in 1962, a year before her daughter was born. Rebolledo next moved to Portland, Oregon, where she chose to be a homemaker and rear her daughter; she resumed teaching Spanish at a community college after her child had reached school age. In 1974 she and her family resettled in Tucson, Arizona, where she began doctoral studies at the University of Arizona. Rebolledo received her Ph.D. in Spanish in 1979, writing her thesis on Rosario Castellanos, a feminist Mexican poet. An educator at the University of North Carolina, Chapel Hill for one year, she also served as a member of the Department of Foreign Languages at the University of Nevada in Reno from 1978 and 1984. She returned to the University of New Mexico in 1984 as director of the women's studies program, with a joint appointment in the Spanish department. In 1988 she became a full-time professor of Spanish and Chicana literature.

Rebolledo's interest in Chicana literature began when she was a graduate student in Arizona. She was introduced to Margarita Cota Cárdenas, a Chicana poet who invited the student to attend several poetry readings. Rebolledo's casual introduction to Chicana/o literature soon became a consuming interest and her first published paper was on Cota Cárdenas's work. Her continued scholarship focused on Chicana authors and trends and connections in the literature. In *Infinite Divisions: An Anthology of Chicana Writers,* which she edited with Eliana S. Rivero and published in 1993, Rebolledo presents the historical development of Chicana writing from 1880 to the early 1990s, including works by such writers as Sandra Cisneros and Alma Villanueva. And in her earlier compilation, 1988's *Las mujeres hablan: An Anthology of Nuevo Mexicana Writers,* she includes the work of emerging authors such as Marina Rivera.

Chicana Poet •

Influences

Academic Work

311 •

Such works and accomplishments have earned Rebolledo a reputation for being a respected Chicana literary critic and scholar. Acknowledged for her academic achievements, she has received the University of New Mexico Scholar award, the 1989 New Mexico Commission on Higher Education Eminent Scholar award, and grants from the New Mexico Quincentennial Commission and the National Endowment for the Humanities for her research on Chicana writing. A member of the editorial board of Arte Público Press since 1990, Rebolledo continues to work in Albuquerque, New Mexico, where she lives with husband Michael Passi, and their daughter, Tey Marianna Nunn.

**Profile by
Teresa Márquez**

CHITA RIVERA

A lthough the stagegoing public would be most likely to recognize

Chita Rivera as Anita from the musical West Side Story *and as Rosie*

from Bye Bye Birdie, *those in the business know that Rivera has the*

ability to make or break a musical. Rivera, a woman of Puerto Rican

descent, has been illuminating theaters with her energetic, explosive

dancing, her powerful voice, and her comic gestures. In addition to

headlining numerous musicals, she has starred in movies and appeared

on television. Although her long career has already inspired a new

generation of actresses, Rivera remains as popular and radiant as ever.

(1933-) •

Actress, •

dancer

The third child of Pedro Julio Figueroa and Katherine del Rivero, Dolores Conchita Figuero del Rivero was born on January 23, 1933, in Washington DC. Her father, a Puerto Rican musician who played both clarinet and saxophone in the U.S. Navy Band, died when she was only

seven years old. To provide for her family, Katherine, who was of Puerto Rican and Scots-Irish descent, found a job as a government clerk. Rivera's widowed mother, however, did more than put food on the table; she enrolled her daughter in singing, piano, and ballet classes.

Rivera was most enthusiastic about ballet. Performing in "shows" her brother Julio arranged in the basement of their home, she demonstrated so much promise in class that her instructor, Doris Jones, encouraged her to audition for a scholarship to Balanchine's School of American Ballet. She won the scholarship in 1950; in order to attend the school, which was located in New York City, she went to live with her uncle's family in the Bronx.

The young dancer graduated from Taft High School in 1951, and the very next year landed her first professional job as a dancer. Rivera had accompanied a friend from the School of American Ballet to an audition for a touring production of *Call Me Madam*, which was to be choreographed by Jerome Robbins. Deciding to audition herself, Rivera ended up with the part. Dolores, or Conchita del Rivero, as she now called herself, toured the country with the popular musical for almost a year before deciding to return to New York. She then accepted an offer to replace Onna White as a principal dancer in *Guys and Dolls*.

Makes Debut in •

Call Me

Madam

Rivera was on her way to becoming a sought-after performer. After her Broadway debut in *Guys in Dolls*, in 1953 she found herself in the chorus of *Can-Can* and then on television's *Imogene Coca Show* in 1954. Friends involved with the production of *Can-Can* persuaded the young woman—who was now referring to herself as Chita O'Hara—to change her name. As Chita Rivera she became well-known as a singer, actress, and dancer, and joined the Off-Broadway production of *Shoestring Revue* in 1955. The revue received critical praise, with Rivera singled out for special attention. It was not long before she was cast in the role of the French prostitute Fifi, in a Broadway production of *Seventh Heaven*. That same year she was chosen to tour with the Oldsmobile Industrial Show.

In 1956 Rivera captured the role of Rita Romano in *Mr. Wonderful,* a Broadway musical produced for Sammy Davis Jr. She also began to appear as a guest on variety shows, including *The Garry Moore Show, The Ed Sullivan Show, The Arthur Godfrey Show, The Sid Ceasar Show, The Dinah Shore Show,* and *The London Palladium Show.* Rivera's many successful performances led to one of her best parts ever—that of Anita in *West Side Story.*

A major musical conceived by Jerome Robbins, *West Side Story* is William Shakespeare's *Romeo and Juliet* in a contemporary setting: a

- *Wins Acclaim*

with Role in

West Side

Story

young couple falls in love despite their dissimilar and antagonistic backgrounds and their story ends tragically. In *West Side Story* Romeo is Tony, a "white, American" gang member, while Juliet is Maria, the Puerto Rican sister of a rival gang member. Anita is Maria's brother's girlfriend, a transformation of the nurse who helps Juliet marry Romeo in Shakespeare's play. Cast as the fiery Anita, Rivera sang "A Boy like That" and "I Have a Love," as well as "America," a song that has become a musical classic.

Both *West Side Story* and Rivera became instant hits in 1957. The musical ran for 732 performances and, besides an offer of marriage, the actress garnered a Antoinette Perry (Tony) Award nomination. Although Rivera did not win a Tony, she did win a husband, marrying Anthony Mordente, one of the dancers in *West Side Story*. When Rivera became pregnant with their daughter, Lisa Angela Mordente, she left the musical, but after the birth of the baby, who has grow up to become an actress herself, the acting couple resumed their roles when *West Side Story* found its way to London in 1958. When the play was adapted as a film, actress Rita Moreno reprised Rivera's role.

After *West Side Story* closed in England in 1959, Rivera starred in another hit musical on Broadway and in London. In *Bye Bye Birdie*, which ran from 1960 to 1961, Rivera was cast in the role of Rosie Grant, alongside actor Dick Van Dyke. In the musical, Rosie, a secretary who wants to save her advertising-agency employer, hatches a contest for young women that lets the lucky winner kiss a popular rock star—Birdie—goodbye as he leaves for military service. Enthralling audiences with her clever acting, Rivera's dynamic rendition of the songs "Spanish Rose," "How to Kill a Man," and "Shriners' Ballet" earned her another Tony nomination. She then went on to play Athena Constantine in a short run of the play *Zenda,* in California in 1963, and starred in a British television show with the immensely popular British rock group the Beatles in 1964. Her next appearance was as Anyanka, the gypsy princess, in *Bajour*. That performance won her a third Tony nomination, a citation from *Best Plays,* and an invitation to become the official hostess of the "World's Fair and Summer Festival Season" in New York City.

- *Develops Solo*

Cabaret Act

By this time, Rivera was a celebrated stage star; she decided to venture out on her own. With the help of Fred Ebb and John Kander, a lyricist/composer team that Rivera collaborated with throughout her career, she developed a cabaret act. In 1966 she took her new show on the road throughout the United States and Canada. Even though the cabaret was well received, she soon decided to return to the stage, going on to perform as Jenny in *The Threepenny Opera,* as Linda Low in *Flower*

Drum Song, as Charity in the national tour of *Sweet Charity,* as Nickie, Charity's roommate, in the motion picture version of *Sweet Charity,* and as Christopher Columbus's mistress in *1491.*

The early 1970s found Rivera on tour once again, appearing in *Jacques Brel Is Alive and Well and Living in Paris,* as well as performing in standing productions like *Born Yesterday, Milliken Breakfast Show, The Rose Tattoo,* and *Sondheim: A Musical Tribute.* In 1974, she performed in *Father's Day* in Chicago; Oliver Hailey, the author of the drama, had personally asked her to play the part of the divorcée. Next, she starred with Hal Linden, portraying Katherine in *Kiss Me Kate,* which toured cities in the United States. In 1975 she took her cabaret act on the road once again. "Chita Plus Two" stirred audiences at the Grand Finale nightclub in New York and at Studio One in Los Angeles. After the conclusion of her tour, Rivera played Velma Kelly in *Chicago* in New York City; for that performance with Gwen Vernon and Jerry Orbach she earned a fourth Tony nomination. Although the musical was extremely successful and ran for more performances than even *West Side Story,* Rivera left the production to begin another tour with her cabaret act. She spent the latter part of the 1970s and the first year of the 1980s traveling throughout the United States, Canada, and Europe, earning an award for the best variety performance in 1980 by the National Academy of Concert and Cabaret Arts.

During the early 1980s Rivera continued to perform on stage and screen. In 1981 she starred in two musicals, neither of which received critical attention. For her work in *Bring Back Birdie*—a sequel to *Bye Bye Birdie*—however, Rivera received her fifth Tony nomination, for her dancing in "A Man Worth Fighting For" and "Well, I'm Not." She then appeared on the 1982 PBS television special *Broadway Plays Washington: Kennedy Center Tonight,* followed by *Night of 100 Stars.* In 1983 she portrayed the Queen in magician Doug Henning's *Merlin;* while the musical was unsuccessful, Rivera won yet another Tony nomination for her performance. From 1983 to 1984 she starred in the musical *Pippin,* which was produced for the Showtime cable television network.

In the mid-1980s Rivera performed in two outstanding musicals and finally won a Tony Award. *The Rink,* was created specifically for Rivera by her friends Ebb and Kander. In the musical Rivera played Anna, a woman faced with closing a skating rink left to her by her late husband. Costarring the famous singer Liza Minnelli as Anna's daughter Angel, the musical depicted a strained mother/daughter relationship; in real life, however, the two costars had been friends since 1975, when Minnelli replaced Gwen Verdon for five weeks during the run of *Chicago.* Minnelli was quoted in *People* as saying of Rivera, "She's a

Costars with •

Liza Minnelli

force and she thinks I'm a force. It's like two grounding poles, and there's this electrical thing that goes VROOM." Rivera said of Minnelli in the same article, "I look at Liza and I see my Lisa." Partly because Rivera had just lost her mother—as Minnelli had lost her own mother, *Wizard of Oz* star Judy Garland—and partly because Minnelli had been inspired to act in musicals after seeing Rivera perform in *Bye Bye Birdie,* the two performers sang and danced with more than their usual passion.

While *The Rink* received some so-so reviews, critics raved about Rivera. Richard Corliss commented on her performance in *Time* magazine: "Packing 30 years of Broadway savvy into the frame of a vivacious teen-ager, the 51-year-old entertainer could by now sell a song to the deaf; she commands the audience like a lion tamer with a whip snap in her walk; and, by the forces of magnetism and sheer will, she eats co-stars for breakfast." While a critic from *New York* magazine was less enthusiastic, he acknowledged Rivera's talent: "Miss Rivera's performances are knowing and efficiently executed.... [She] is an able singer, authoritative dancer, and clear enunciator, with an emotional range that has gradations as well as extremes, and a projection of gags with a certain zing—more vibration than punch—that is idiosyncratic and winning." The judges for the Tony Awards recognized Rivera's achievements by naming her outstanding actress in a musical.

After releasing *The Rink,* an album recorded with Minnelli and the rest of the singers from the musical, and appearing in *Night of 100 Stars II* and in a televised coverage of *Macy's Thanksgiving Day Parade,* Rivera moved on to *Jerry's Girls,* a revue produced in New York City beginning in 1985, the year Rivera was inducted into the Television Academy Hall of Fame. Once again, Rivera was lauded. A critic for *New York* magazine commented, "the ageless Chita Rivera does some rousing things vocally and pedally." Unfortunately, Rivera suffered an accident that left her unable to finish the musical's run, and members of the chorus had to fill in for her. In April of 1986 she suffered another accident: while driving in New York City, her car collided with a taxi. Rivera had to work very hard to overcome the compound fractures in her left leg; although she was more than fifty years of age, she bounced back from her injuries, learning to deal with the twelve pins that now stabilize her leg.

In the late 1980s the indefatigable Rivera mixed television roles with theater performances, appearing in *The Mayflower Madam* and *Can-Can* on stage, and *Celebrating Gershwin* and *Broadway Sings: The Music of Jules Styne,* among other shows, on television. In 1992, at almost sixty years of age, she starred in *Kiss of the Spider Woman,* a musical written by the team of Kander and Ebb. Based on the novel written by the late Manuel Puig, *Spider Woman* deals with the dilemmas of those involved in revolutionary movements. While it speaks to the world, it is especially pertinent to situations in some politically volatile Latin American countries. In both the novel and the play—which Puig helped develop alongside director Harold Prince—two prisoners share a cell. To pass the hours, one of them describes the movie musicals he has seen. In the play, these movie-musical scenes are acted out in vignettes featuring Rivera, who portrayed Aurora, a B-movie actress who doubles as a beautiful symbol of death. It was a challenge for the actress to play such a complex character.

And it was a challenge which she met successfully: Rivera won a second Tony award in 1993, as well as receiving Entertainer of the Decade honors from the National Hispanic Academy of Media Arts and Sciences the same year. When the popular production left London and New York stages to tour the United States in 1994, Rivera continued in her role until 1995, when she turned over the part to actress Vanessa Williams. She proved to be a tough act to follow: as composer Kander told *Newsweek*, "Without her, I don't think the show could work. When you try to replace Chita, you always make a compromise."

In whatever roles the future holds for Rivera, she will continue to be worth watching: A high kick, a vivacious nod, and a soaring voice packed with emotion—all of these elements have combined in her to create an acting force who will long be remembered by those who have seen or heard her.

**Profile by
Ronie-Richele
Garcia-Johnson**

LINDA RONSTADT

1946- •

Singer •

*F*ew performers in any medium have proven more daring than

Linda Ronstadt, a singer who has made her mark in such varied styles as

rock, country, operetta, and mariachi. In the 1970s, the multi-Grammy

Award-winning Ronstadt churned out a veritable stream of pop hits

and heartrending ballads that delighted country and rock fans alike.

Just when she seemed pegged as a pop idol, however, she turned her

talents to opera—in The Pirates of Penzance and La Bohème—and to

torch songs accompanied by the Nelson Riddle Orchestra. Almost every

Ronstadt experiment has met with critical acclaim and, surprisingly,

with fan approval and hefty record sales. Newsweek contributor Margo

Jefferson attributes this success to Ronstadt's voice, which she describes as having "the richness and cutting edge of a muted trumpet." Jefferson concludes, "In a field where success is often based on no more than quick-study ventriloquism, Linda Ronstadt stands out. She is no fad's prisoner; her compelling voice wears no disguises."

Time reporter Jay Cocks calls Ronstadt "gutsy," "unorthodox," and a challenger of creeds. As the singer tells it, she developed a habit of rebellion early in life and stuck to it with singleminded determination. Ronstadt was born and raised in Tucson, Arizona, the daughter of a hardware store owner who loved to sing and play Mexican music—she later made an album of his favorite songs. Ronstadt herself enjoyed harmonizing with her sister and two brothers—she was proud when she was allowed to take the soprano notes. At the age of six she decided she wanted to be a singer, and she promptly lost all interest in formal schooling. Aaron Latham, a classmate at Tucson's Catalina High School, wrote in *Rolling Stone* that by her teens Ronstadt "was already a larger-than-life figure with an even larger voice. She didn't surprise anyone by becoming a singer. Not that anyone expected her fame to grow to the dimensions of that voice. But the voice itself was no secret."

Ronstadt attended the University of Arizona briefly, dropping out at eighteen to join her musician boyfriend, Bob Kimmel, in Los Angeles. With Kimmel and guitar player Kenny Edwards, Ronstadt formed a group called the Stone Poneys, a folk-rock ensemble reminiscent of the Mamas and the Papas and the Lovin' Spoonful. The Stone Poneys signed a contract with Capitol Records in 1964 and released a single, "Some of Shelley's Blues," in early 1965. Their only hit as a group came in 1967, when "Different Drum," a cut from their second album, made the charts. By that time, intense touring, drug abuse, and a series of disappointing concert appearances as openers for the Doors caused the Stone Poneys to disband. Ronstadt told *Rolling Stone* that her band was "rejected by the hippest element in New York as lame. We broke up right after that. We couldn't bear to look at each other."

Embarks on

Solo Career

after Breakup

of Stone Poneys

Ronstadt fulfilled her Capitol recording contract as a solo performer, turning out some of the first albums to fuse country and rock styles. On *Hand Sown . . . Home Grown* (1969) and *Silk Purse* (1970), she teamed with Nashville studio musicians for an ebullient, if jangly, country sound. The latter album produced her first solo hit, the sorrowful "Long, Long Time." In retrospect, Ronstadt has called her debut period the "bleak years." She was plagued by the stresses of constant touring, difficult romantic entanglements, cocaine use, and critical indifference. And to make matters worse, she suffered from stage fright and had little rapport with her audiences. "I felt like a submarine with depth charges going off all around me," she told *Time*. Ronstadt eluded failure by moving to Asylum Records in 1973 and by engaging Peter Asher as her producer and manager. Asher collaborated with her on her first bestselling albums, *Don't Cry Now* and the platinum *Heart like a Wheel.*

Heart like a Wheel was the first in a succession of million-selling albums for Ronstadt. By the mid-1970s, with hits such as "When Will I Be Loved?," "Desperado," "You're No Good," "Blue Bayou," and "Poor, Poor Pitiful Me," the singer had established herself as rock's most popular female star. Stephen Holden describes Ronstadt's rock style in a *Vogue* magazine profile, as combining "a tearful country wail with a full-out rock declamation. But, at the same time, her purity of melodic line is strongly rooted in folk." A *Time* contributor elaborates: "She sings, oh Lord, with a rowdy spin of styles—country, rhythm and blues, rock, reggae, torchy ballad—fused by a rare and rambling voice that calls up visions of loss, then jiggles the glands of possibility. The gutty voice drives, lilts, licks slyly at decency, riffs off Ella [Fitzgerald], transmogrifies Dolly Parton, all the while wailing with the guitars, strong and solid as God's garage floor. A man listens and thinks 'Oh my, yes,' and a woman thinks, perhaps, 'Ah, well....'"

A leap from rock to operetta is monumental; few voices could make it successfully. In 1981 Ronstadt astonished both critics and fans by trilling the demanding soprano part of Mabel in a Broadway production of *The Pirates of Penzance.* Her performance led *Newsweek* correspondent Barbara Graustark to comment, "Those wet, marmot eyes turn audiences on like a light bulb, and when her smoky voice soars above the staff in a duet with a flute, she sends shivers down the spine." Ronstadt's appearance as Mimi in *La Bohème* off-Broadway in 1984 was received with less enthusiasm by the critics, but the singer herself expressed no regrets about her move away from rock. "When I perform rock 'n' roll," she told *Newsweek,* "it varies between antagonistic posturing and to-the-bones vulnerability. I wanted to allow another facet of my personality to emerge.... I've gained confidence in knowing that now . . . I can handle myself in three dimensions, and even if never use my upper extension except in the bathtub, I've gained vocal finish."

That "vocal finish" was applied to yet another Ronstadt experiment: three albums of vintage torch songs, *What's New?, Lush Life,* and *For Sentimental Reasons,* featuring the Nelson Riddle Orchestra. Cocks calls *What's New?* a "simple, almost reverent, rendering of nine great songs that time has not touched.... No one in contemporary rock or pop can sound more enamored, or winsome, or heartbroken, in a love song than Linda Ronstadt. Singing the tunes on *What's New?,* or even just talking about them, she still sounds like a woman in love." Holden writes, "One of the charms of Ronstadt's torch singing is her almost girlish awe in the face of the songs' pent-up emotions. Instead of trying to re-create another era's erotic climate, she pays homage to it with lovely even-handed line readings offered in a spirit of wistful nostalgia." Holden adds that *What's New?* "revitalized Ronstadt's recording career by selling over two million copies, and, coincidentally, defined for her generation the spirit of a new 'eighties pop romanticism.'" Ronstadt also earned several prestigious awards for her 1986 album *Trio*, a joint country music venture with Dolly Parton and Emmylou Harris, including a Grammy award for best country performance.

• *Album Reflects*

Mexican

Heritage

Ronstadt's more recent projects have departed even further from the pop-rock vein. In 1987 the singer released *Canciones de mi padre*, an album of *mariachi* songs that her father used to sing. "When we were little, we spoke Spanish at home, but the schools pounded it out of us pretty early," she told James Brady in *Parade*. "There was an antibilingual attitude then. So my Spanish is very rudimentary—child's Spanish, really." *Newsweek* critic David Gates calls the work "Ronstadt's best record to date," noting that "its flawless production is the only conces-sion to Top 40 sensibilities. And Ronstadt . . . has found a voice that embodies not merely passion and heartache, but a womanly wit as well." *Mas canciones*, Ronstadt's follow-up to *Canciones de mi padre*, appeared in 1991. That same year, the singer starred in *La Pastorela*, an updated version of a traditional Mexican holiday play, which aired on PBS's *Great Performances*. "I loved the idea of doing a work particular to Mexico," she told Edna Gunderson in *TV Guide*. "*La Pastorela* is not found in Cuba or Venezuela. People tend to lump Hispanic cultures together. They think Ricky Ricardo would have been happy dancing the tango in a mariachi band." Ronstadt continued to explore Latin music in 1993's *Frenesí*, a collection of Afro-Caribbean mambos and boleros of the 1940s and 1950s.

Meanwhile, the versatile songstress had returned to Top 40 music in *Cry like a Rainstorm, Howl like the Wind*. The album was released in 1989, followed by a 1994 collection of pop covers under the title *Winter Light*. In 1995, Ronstadt took another foray into country-rock with *Feels like Home*, which included covers of such diverse tunes as "Morning Blues" by the great late banjoist Uncle Dave Macon, the Carter Family's "Lover's Return," and Neil Young's "After the Gold Rush."

In recent years, music has taken a back seat to more personal concern; the comfortably single Ronstadt is now the mother of two adopted children. In the time she still devotes to her music, she remains eclectic: While she will not rule out recording more rock, Ronstadt seems far more fascinated by other forms and other, more remote, historical periods. Gates finds the raven-haired artist "the most adventurous figure in American popular music," concluding that, at the very least, Ronstadt is "commendable in her refusal to bore herself." Ronstadt herself outlined her future for the *Los Angeles Times*: "My dream is to be rocking on the porch when I'm 80, sharing music with my family or just talking about something. It has been a long journey, but I feel really lucky. A lot of people in this business lose their enthusiasm for music, but I found a way to make the music I love."

Profile by
Anne Janette Johnson

ILEANA ROS-LEHTINEN

1952- •

U.S. •

Congress-

woman

*B*eing first has become something that Ileana Ros-Lehtinen does

quite well. In 1982 she became the first Cuban-born female to be elected

to the Florida State Legislature. Seven years later, after a successful

career as a state legislator, she won a special election held on August 29,

1989, to fill the seat left vacant by the death of long-time Miami political

powerhouse Claude D. Pepper. A few days after her victory, Ros-

Lehtinen was sworn in as the first Cuban American, as well as the first

Hispanic woman, ever elected to the U.S. Congress. "As the first Cuban-

American elected to Congress," Boston Globe *commentator Chris Black*

noted, "she also will be likely to become one of the most visible, most

quoted Cuban-born politicians in the nation."

Ros-Lehtinen (pronounced ross-LAY-teh-nin), who is known as Lily to her family and friends, was born July 15, 1952, in the Cuban capital city of Havana, to Enrique Emilio Ros, a certified public accountant, and Amanda Adato Ros. In 1960 she and her family—including her parents and a brother—fled to Miami from Cuba, one year after political leader Fidel Castro's revolution rocked that tiny island nation. Almost immediately, Ros-Lehtinen's parents became involved with other recent refugees in plotting the downfall of the Castro regime. But after the failure of an invasion attempt by anti-Castro forces at Cuba's Bay of Pigs in 1961, the possibility of returning to Cuba became more and more remote, and Enrique Ros vowed to raise his children as loyal Americans. His wife recalled in a *Boston Globe* article how strongly her husband felt about his decision: "He said you cannot educate two kids without a flag and a country. This is going to be their country and they have to love it."

Ros-Lehtinen earned her associate of arts degree from Miami-Dade County Community College in 1972 and her bachelor of arts degree in English from Miami's Florida International University in 1975. Eleven years later she completed requirements for a master of science in educational leadership from the same institution. Since then, she has continued her studies as a doctoral candidate in educational administration at the University of Miami. Before embarking on her political career, Ros-Lehtinen worked as a teacher and was principal for ten years at Eastern Academy, a school she founded. Her love of politics came as a legacy from her father, who had concentrated so much of his life on the hope of restoring democracy to his native land. He is said to have been the chief architect of her political career and was at her side when she announced her victory in the U.S. Congressional race.

- **Launches**

Political Career

as State

Representative

Ros-Lehtinen's first elected office was in the Florida state legislature, where she served as a representative from 1982 to 1986 and as a state senator from 1986 to 1989. While in the state legislature she met her future husband, Dexter Lehtinen, who was also a member of that legislative body. Although early in her career Ros-Lehtinen showed a tendency to focus on issues of a global nature rather than on those affecting her constituents in a personal way, Black wrote in the *Boston Globe* that she eventually became "a politician of the opposite extreme, a pragmatic legislator focused almost exclusively on the most parochial of issues. One Miami political reporter now describes her as 'a pothole kind of legislator,' much more concerned with the specific needs of individuals and businesses in her district than broader changes in public policy."

When Ros-Lehtinen resigned her seat in the state senate shortly before the August 3, 1989, primary, it appeared—much to the dismay of the Miami area's non-Hispanic voters—that the race to fill Florida's 18th congressional district seat might be a head-to-head battle between two Cuban American women. Early favorites included Ros-Lehtinen on the Republican side and Miami City Commissioner Rosario Kennedy for the Democrats. However, the opponent who emerged from the primary was Gerald F. Richman, a Jewish attorney, a former president of the Florida Bar Association. The Ros-Lehtinen–Richman campaign was marked by deep cultural and racial tensions and came to be one of the most ethnically divided congressional races in Florida's history. A highlight of an otherwise brutal contest came from President George Bush, who not only gave Ros-Lehtinen his personal endorsement, but made a special trip to Miami to deliver a speech on her behalf.

Most of the controversy surrounding the campaign grew out of a response to Republican party chair Lee Atwater's announcement that since the district was fifty percent Hispanic, electing a Cuban American to the seat was of utmost importance. Richman, the Democratic candidate, was quoted in a *Time* article as having countered Atwater's claim with the assertion, "This is an American seat." Cuban American and other Hispanic voters were deeply offended by Richman's reply and the implication it carried that Hispanics are not truly Americans. Spanish-speaking radio stations in the Miami area assured their listeners that a vote for Richman would be the equivalent of voting for Castro. Another source of division during the campaign came from the National Republican Congressional Committee (NRCC) which, according to reports in *National Review*, attempted to run Ros-Lehtinen's campaign from Washington. William McGurn explained the problem with a quote from a Republican insider: "The NRCC treated this district like a colony.... Their attitude was that they knew Florida's 18th better than the people who live here."

Triumphing over the bitterness of the campaign, Ros-Lehtinen emerged victorious from the race, capturing fifty-three percent of the vote. Post-election analysis showed that voters largely seemed to cast their ballot based on their ethnic heritage: ninety-six percent of blacks and eighty-eight percent of non-Hispanic whites voted for Democratic candidate Richman; while ninety percent of Hispanics, which accounted for sixty-seven percent of the district and who voted in record numbers, voted for Ros-Lehtinen. In her victory speech, the new congresswoman maintained that she would work to heal the wounds caused by the campaign. "It's been a terrible divisive campaign," she told the *New York Times*. "But now it's time for healing. I know that there are a lot of people out there who feel alienated." Ros-Lehtinen's win was also seen as a victory for the Republican party because the seat she had captured had belonged to the Democrats for twenty-six years. When the seat came up

Wins Turbulent •

Race for U.S.

Congressional

Seat

for reelection in 1990, Ros-Lehtinen—who insisted on debating her opponent in Spanish—received sixty percent of the vote: a decisive mandate to continue her political career.

During her tenure, Ros-Lehtinen has been a member of both the Government Operations and Foreign Affairs committee and has served on the latter's subcommittee on Human Rights and International Organizations as well as its subcommittee on Western Hemisphere affairs. She has also been involved with the subcommittee on Employment and Housing, where she is the ranking minority member. In an *Hispanic* article focusing on Hispanic political candidates, Anna Maria Arias described Ros-Lehtinen's stand on issues important to voters in her district. According to Arias, Ros-Lehtinen supports bilingual education, is "in favor of a seven-day waiting period for the purchasing of guns, and voted for a bill that would improve veterans' benefits." Also vehemently anti-abortion except to save a woman's life, she favors a constitutional amendment to ban flag burning, and advocates the death penalty for convicted organizers of drug rings. As Congress prepares to move into a new century, the issues surrounding U.S. immigration policy have been increasingly on her mind. "[I]mmigrants come to this country not to be a burden on the state but in search of freedom, opportunity, and a better life," she wrote in *Hispanic*. "I consider today's battle against an increasing anti-immigrant sentiment a crucial challenge our community has to confront and I am sure that together with my Hispanic colleagues, we will continue this fight."

True to her ethnic roots, Ros-Lehtinen remains a staunch adversary of Castro and an equally outspoken champion of a free Cuba. In 1990 she expressed her strong opposition to South-African leader Nelson Mandela's visit to Florida during his eight-city tour of the U.S., a trip which engendered a virtual hero's welcome for him in the other states to which he traveled. While there seemed to be a near unanimous outpouring of praise for Mandela and his efforts to end apartheid—racial segregation—in his native country, Ros-Lehtinen felt she could not honor a man who had not only publicly embraced such advocates of violent revolution as the Palestine Liberation Organization's Yasser Arafat and Libya's Muammar Gaddafi, but who also was on record as a strong supporter of Castro. She pointed out that Cuban Americans longing for a return to democracy in their country of origin could not forget that members of Mandela's African National Congress had received military training on Cuban soil.

Ros-Lehtinen again spoke out against Castro when she condemned participation in the Pan American Games, an Olympics-like international sports competition to be held in Cuba during the first two weeks of

August in 1991. She argued that Castro's bid to have the Games in his country was merely a ploy to bolster Cuba's ailing economy and to provide ready propaganda supporting his regime. In a *Christian Science Monitor* article on the topic, the congresswoman wrote: "Castro has his circus for now, but despite the fanfare of the Pan American Games, he is an anachronism in a world that values democracy and freedom. It will not be long till he follows the path of the dinosaurs into extinction. Cuba's economic crisis is so desperate that Castro would shave his own beard if that would give him the American dollars which he holds so dear."

The ethnic pride Ros-Lehtinen inherited from her father remains strong in the politician, and perhaps because of this, she is very conscious of her position as a role model for Hispanics. She also values the achievements made by other Hispanic women, and when presented with a special award from *Hispanic* magazine in 1992, she praised their successes. "[The Hispanic woman] is an accomplished writer, or a computer programmer, or an attorney, or a doctor, as well as a loving wife and mother." She also believes that Hispanic women will continue to make contributions in the future. "Now, more than ever," she wrote in *Vista,* "we Hispanic women must re-energize and refocus our efforts to realize the vast potential that lies within our grasp."

**Profile by
Marian C. Gonsior**

LUCILLE ROYBAL-ALLARD

*L*ucille Roybal-Allard became the first woman of Mexican Ameri-

can ancestry to be elected to the United States Congress when she joined

that house as a Democratic representative of the 33rd Congressional

District in 1992. In the years since, her political style—described as quiet

and conciliatory—has contributed to her many legislative victories,

including winning passage of what some have hailed as landmark

environmental legislation, as well as new laws in the areas of domestic

violence and sexual harassment. Roybal-Allard is especially proud of

her work to empower local communities. As she related in an interview

with Diana Martínez: "People often don't know how their lives are

impacted by what's going on in Sacramento or Washington, D.C. People

1941- •

U.S. •

Congress-

woman

333 •

can take control of their lives. They can be involved in the political process and make a difference."

Roybal-Allard was born and raised in the Boyle Heights section of Los Angeles, California, a predominately Mexican American community. She attended Saint Mary's Catholic School before earning her B.A. from California State University, Los Angeles, in 1961. The oldest daughter of a political family, Roybal-Allard's father is the highly esteemed former California Congressman Edward Roybal. After thirty years of Congressional service, Ed Roybal—often called the dean of California Latino legislators—retired in 1992. Roybal-Allard has warm memories of working on her father's campaign; he was a great example to her, but she is quick to give equal credit to her mother. "My mom has been a tremendous role model," she revealed to Martínez. "She's really the one who has helped to support and spearhead my father's career. She used to run his headquarters, which used to be our home when we were kids because they couldn't afford a headquarters. So she has always been there, helping him get elected, walking precincts, registering voters, doing all the things that needed to be done. At the same time, she'd be at his side whenever he needed to be at public events. She's worked very hard and is greatly responsible for his success, because it really does take a partnership. In politics it takes the cooperation of your family; otherwise it's almost impossible to succeed."

In an interview with the *Civic Center News Source,* Roybal-Allard says she remembers working on her father's political campaigns as early as age seven. "We used to fold and stuff and lick stamps. When I got a little bit older they used to call us 'bird dogs,' and we would do voter registration. So I was a bird dog for a few years." But there was a downside as well: "I think for me the main part of it was the lack of privacy and lack of personal identity. When my sister and I would go to a dance where people might not know who we were, we used to decide on a different last name so we could just be anonymous and have fun.... I remember as a freshman in college in a political science class I raised my hand to answer a question and after I finished the professor said 'Well, now we know what your father thinks,' and went on to the next student."

Experiences such as these led Roybal-Allard to the conclusion that she did not want to be a politician. While she continued to be involved in her father's campaigns and those of other Latino politicians, she chose a career of community and advocacy work for herself. As Roybal-Allard explained to Martínez, her decision to work in community service was a direct result of her upbringing. "When I think you have a role model like both my father and my mother, who have really dedicated their lives to the community and have taught human values and understand the value of people, it really has an impact on one's life." She served as the executive director of the National Association of Hispanic CPAs, in Washington, D.C., was assistant director of the Alcoholism Council of East Los Angeles, and worked as a planning associate for United Way. She enjoyed community work, but as time went on she became more and more frustrated by the barriers created by political policy-makers. In 1987 a combination of political opportunity and personal circumstances changed Roybal-Allard's mind about running for office.

The 1987 election of Assemblywoman Gloria Molina to the newly created seat on the Los Angeles City Council left Molina's assembly position vacant. Roybal-Allard knew Molina through their mutual community activities and she had worked on the assemblywoman's campaign. Molina asked Roybal-Allard to consider running for the vacant assembly position. Her personal situation also contributed to her decision to run. As she explained to *Hispanic,* "The timing was just right for me. My children were grown and my husband's job called for a lot of travel." Roybal-Allard's second husband, Edward Allard III, has his own consulting firm whose clients are mostly on the East Coast. Roybal-Allard told Martínez that she received no pressure from her father to run. "I'm sure that his involvement in politics ultimately was one of the reasons . . . that I wound up getting involved in politics. But he has always been one that believed that we needed to be independent and make decisions on our own, and if we need guidance he will be there." Once she decided to run for California's State Assembly, she received help from both her father and Molina. She easily defeated nine other candidates and won with sixty percent of the vote.

As a newly elected assemblywoman, one of Roybal-Allard's first tasks was to continue the fight against building a prison in East L.A., a tremendous challenge for a new politician considering that her principal foe was the Governor of the State of California. In 1986 Governor George Deukmejian proposed a site near a heavily Mexican-American residential area as the location for a new state prison. Deukmejian tried to steamroll the opposition in order to get the prison built, but his own plans flattened instead. For seven years Roybal-Allard, along with Molina and other local Latino politicians, worked with grassroots organizations, professional groups, and church leaders to prevent the prison's construction. As an expression of her philosophy of local empowerment, Roybal-Allard assisted community women in organizing "The Mothers of East L.A." which proved to be implacable in its opposition to the prison. A series of legal maneuvers halted construction of the prison but did not kill it. Deukmejian left office in 1990, but the struggle against the prison continued until September 1992, when

Decides to •

Pursue Political

Career

Governor Pete Wilson signed a bill, amended by Roybal-Allard, which eliminated the funds for the construction of the East L.A. prison. This victory, coming on the heels of Roybal-Allard's departure for the U.S. Congress, gave her cause to reflect on her own feelings and what the political struggle meant to her community. As she stated in a press release, "I started my assembly career when the East Los Angeles prison bill was approved and it feels great to be leaving the assembly on this victory note.... This is a victory for the entire community. For seven years our community has marched against the prison, we have fought in the courts and in [California State capital] Sacramento—this fight has empowered us. This community was once viewed as powerless. However, the Mothers of East Los Angeles and other community groups have served notice to the state's powerbrokers that ignoring the desires of the East Los Angeles community will no longer be accepted."

Roybal-Allard would represent the 56th District from 1987 to 1992, serving on a number of influential committees, including the Assembly Rules committee and the very powerful Ways and Means committee, which oversees the distribution of public monies. She was also the chair of the Ways and Means subcommittee on Health and Human Services. During those years, the East L.A. prison wasn't the only struggle Roybal-Allard would wage to improve the quality of life in her district. She fought against a toxic waste incinerator, again aided by the highly respected grass roots organization, Mothers of East Los Angeles. As a result of that struggle, Roybal-Allard authored a bill which entitles every community in California to an environmental impact report before a toxic incinerator is built or expanded, a protection that was often omitted prior to her efforts. This bill, along with her strong voting record on the environment, earned her the Sierra Club's California Environmental Achievement Award.

- **Takes Action on**

Women's Issues

Roybal-Allard also authored a series of laws which place her in the forefront of women's issues, including a requirement that the courts take into consideration an individual's history of domestic violence in child custody cases. She has also worked for legislation requiring colleges to provide information and referrals for treatment to rape victims and enacted two laws that strengthen the legal position of sexual assault victims by redefining the meaning of "consent." Another of her bills requires the California State Bar to take disciplinary action against attorneys who engage in sexual misconduct with their clients. This would be the first such law adopted by any state in the country. For her legislative efforts, Roybal-Allard has received a number of prestigious awards and commendations, including honors from the Los Angeles Commission on Assaults against Women, the Asian Business Association, and the Latin American Professional Women's Association. Roybal-

Allard was also honored in 1992 by the Mexican American Women's National Association (MANA) in Washington, DC, where she was presented with the "Las Primaras" Award for "her pioneering efforts in creating a better future for the community through the political process. In addition, Roybal-Allard was named in *Hispanic Business*'s 1992 list of "100 Influentials."

Ironically, when Roybal-Allard was first elected to the California Assembly many thought her to be too demure to be effective. But, as she explained to *Hispanic,* her conciliatory style is long-range effective. "People may be your enemies today on one issue, but they may be your allies tomorrow on another issue. So I've learned to work well with groups on both sides of the aisle, even with those who I oppose bitterly on particular issues." Her track record on political effectiveness in the California Assembly was impressive, and voters in the 33rd district looked forward to equal successes as she began her term in Congress. A member of the Small Business and Banking, Finance, and Urban Affairs committees, Royal-Allard continues to be committed to improving the lot of many middle-class urban neighborhoods by providing empowerment through national legislation—quietly but effectively.

**Profile by
Diana Martínez**

VICKI RUIZ

1955-

Professor of

humanities,

historian

*I*n a very short time, Vicki Lynn Ruiz has risen to the top of her

profession, fueled, she told interviewer Tom Pendergast, "by insomnia

and a drive to succeed." Ruiz, an educator and oral historian who has

attempted to understand the lives of Mexican women in the twentieth

century and to transmit that knowledge to her students, is Andrew W.

Mellon Professor of the Humanities at California's Claremont Graduate

School, a position that has allowed her the utmost flexibility as both a

scholar and a teacher since joining the school's faculty in 1992.

Chairman of the department of history since 1993, Ruiz's goals at

Claremont are to complete a groundbreaking history of Mexican women

in the United States and to build a strong graduate program.

Ruiz's interest in Mexican history springs directly from her own past. She was born on May 21, 1955, in Atlanta, Georgia, the daughter of Robert Mercer and Ermina Pablita Ruiz. Robert's parents disowned him for marrying a Hispanic woman, so when he and his wife started a family, their children took the surname Ruiz.

Ermina was proud of her heritage and enjoyed sharing it with her children. Besides recounting stories of working in the coal mines and beet fields of southern Colorado, she told them of her father, who had come to the United States during the Mexican revolution and was once an active member of the Industrial Workers of the World (a radical union that was organized between 1905 and 1920), and of her mother, a proud woman whose family had immigrated to Colorado from Mexico early in the nineteenth century.

Ruiz, however, grew up in Florida, far from her Mexican roots. Her father owned a large sport fishing boat and moved the family back and forth from Marathon to Panama City, depending on the season. Ruiz told Pendergast: "I grew up on the water, and I particularly loved the time we would spend in the Florida Keys. I loved to get lost in the different colors of the parrot fish, and squirrel fish, and angel fish." The family's nomadic existence meant that Ruiz attended many different schools as a child, but by the time she reached the eighth grade her mother insisted that they stay in one place.

Living in what Ruiz only half-affectionately calls the "Redneck Riviera"—Panama City, Florida—posed its share of difficulties. Some local parents did not want their sons dating a Mexican girl, and Ruiz was denied a Daughter of the Confederacy academic scholarship because she could not trace her ancestry to the pre–Civil War South. By the time she finished high school, she knew she wanted to escape her small town, and education provided the quickest way out.

• *Examines Role*

of Women

Cannery

Workers

Ruiz entered Florida State University believing that she wanted to be a high school teacher, but her professors eventually convinced her to pursue graduate studies instead. "I applied to Stanford University on a whim," she related to Pendergast, "and a professor named Al Camarillo called me and told me he would support my application." Camarillo proved to be a huge source of support and guidance for Ruiz, introducing her to the history of the women's cannery unions in California and to Luisa Moreno, an early union organizer who had been deported from the United States for her activism. "I went to Guadalajara, Mexico, to interview Moreno," Ruiz said, "and I came back knowing what I would study."

Ruiz received her master's degree in 1978 and her doctorate in 1982, both from Stanford. Her subsequent examination of the cannery workers was published by the University of New Mexico Press in 1987 as *Cannery Women, Cannery Lives: Mexican Women, Unionization, and the California Food Processing Industry, 1939–1950.* In a *Southwestern Historical Quarterly* review, Yolanda G. Romero called the book "an outstanding addition to the historical literature on labor," and William Flores, writing in the *Oral History Review,* deemed it "essential reading for anyone engaged in research on Chicanos and Mexicans, on cannery workers, and more broadly on issues of gender and work." Ruiz has also contributed articles and book reviews to periodicals, including *Ms.* and *Journal of American History.*

Ruiz's first academic post was at the University of Texas in El Paso. "I felt lucky that there was a job in my field," she told Pendergast, "and I kept thinking how lucky I was to be teaching, because I was learning so much from my students." She left El Paso in 1985 for the University of California at Davis, where she enjoyed the support of a community of Chicano scholars, and stayed at Davis until 1992, when she accepted a position at the Claremont Graduate School near Los Angeles.

During this entire period Ruiz broadened her work in the field of Mexican women's history, co-editing *Women on the United States–Mexico Border: Responses to Change,* 1989's *Western Women: Their Land, Their Lives,* and 1991's *Unequal Sisters: A Multicultural Reader in U.S. Women's History,* a book praised by *Ms.* magazine as "probably the best single volume in this area." In 1992 she began work on *From Out of the Shadows: A History of Mexican Women in the United States, 1900–1990,* in which she examines "the changing cultural landscape created out of the interaction of two distinct cultures, examining the different ways that Mexican women have responded to American culture."

Shifts Research •

Focus to

Mexican

Women's

History

Besides teaching and writing, Ruiz has pursued a variety of other interests. She has served as a consultant to the National Women's History Project and helped in the coordination of the Texas Sesquicentennial Oral History Workshop. In addition, Ruiz was a member of the advisory board of the Research Clearinghouse on Southern Women and Women of Color and has been a part of the executive board of the Immigration History Society since 1989. Her memberships include the Organization of American Historians, the Committee for Minority History and Minority Historians, and the American Studies Association, where she has been a member of the program committee since 1989. Since 1992, Ruiz has served as vice-chair of the Council of the Humanities in her adopted state of California.

Ruiz cites union organizer Luisa Moreno as one of her role models, citing her strength and bravery in organizing women in the California food processing industry. But the historian reserves the greatest praise for her mother, whose enthusiasm for life never wavered, despite the fact that she often had to work long hours at difficult jobs to help support her family. "My mother was a survivor," Ruiz recalled, "and she found great joy in working and helping out. She was also a wonderful storyteller."

**Profile by
Tom Pendergast**

Ruiz herself is the mother of two boys, Miguel and Daniel, from her first marriage, which lasted from 1979 until 1990. She married Victor Becerra in 1992.

CRISTINA SARALEGUI

W ith her Spanish-language talk show, journalist Cristina Saralegui

1948- •

has become Hispanic television's answer to Oprah Winfrey and Sally

Jessy Raphael. A popular writer and talk show host, she is not afraid to

Television talk •

face controversy and insists that she only has one objective: to inform the

show host,

Latino community. Saralegui emphasized her main concern during an

editor

interview with Hispanic magazine: "We do the show to help Hispanics

here. Once you cross the border you are an immigrant, not a tourist.

This is where our kids grow up and we have to be concerned about our

community."

Cristina Maria Saralegui was born January 29, 1948, in Havana, Cuba, to Francisco and Cristina Saralegui. Her grandfather, publishing tycoon Don Francisco Saralegui, was the dominant influence in her early life. Recognized throughout Latin America as "the Paper Czar," or "Don

Pancho," her grandfather introduced young Saralegui to his business. "I was four or five," Saralegui recalls in her official biography, "when I would stroll by the [side] of my grandfather, visiting the huge rotary presses and the editorial departments of our family-owned and -operated magazines, *Bohemia, Carteles,* and *Vanidades.* They were the three most successful magazines published out of the island."

In 1960, at the age of twelve, Saralegui and her family left their comfortable life in Havana and started a new life in Miami's Cuban exile community. "I remember my last day in Havana," she relates in her biography. "Looking out of the balcony at the beautiful sea, and thinking as my vision became blurry with tears, that this was probably the last time I would see my friends and this magnificent view, which I loved so much."

In Miami, Saralegui prepared herself to enter the family's traditional business by studying mass communications and creative writing at the University of Miami. During her last year at the university, she began an internship with *Vanidades Continental,* the number-one ladies' service magazine in continental Latin America. Saralegui worked hard at *Vanidades Continental:* "At the time it was a huge challenge. I had to teach myself to write in Spanish. Having attended high school and college in the United States, and receiving all my formal training in English, I was more fluent in the English language."

Saralegui, however, was determined enough to earn a position as features editor of *Vanidades Continental.* She maintained that position from 1970 to 1973, when she became an editor of *Cosmopolitan-en-Español,* the Spanish-language version of the well-known *Cosmopolitan* magazine. In 1976 she took a position as the entertainment director for the *Miami Herald* newspaper. Only a year later, Saralegui was appointed editor-in-chief of *Intimidades* magazine.

In 1979 Saralegui was named editor-in-chief of *Cosmopolitan-en-Español* magazine. Boasting an international distribution, *Cosmopolitan-en-Español* was circulated in all Latin American countries and all major cities in the United States. Saralegui held this position for ten years, until resigning in 1989 to become executive producer and host of Univision Network's *El show de Cristina.*

Host of El •

show de

Cristina

Saralegui admits it was not an easy transition adapting to the demands of television. After twenty-three years as a journalist in the print media—where her personal appearance was irrelevant—Saralegui was suddenly confronted with looking good in front of the camera. A size 18, she had never exercised, and had spent most of her time behind a desk. But good friends Emilio and Gloria Estefan sent her their personal fitness trainer. "They saved my life" she told the *Miami Herald*. Saralegui started jogging three miles a day, watched her weight, changed her hair, and shrank six dress sizes.

El show de Cristina, in the style of *Phil Donahue* and *Oprah*, became known for dealing with controversial topics—such as sex—previously considered "taboo" in Spanish-language media; Saralegui went from being dubbed "the Latin Helen Gurley Brown" to "Oprah con salsa." While she did not mind such comparisons, she was disturbed by those who voiced early objections to her blonde hair. "People would write me hate letters. How dare I try to represent Hispanics when I was so white? I tried to make them see it was racism," she told the *Chicago Tribune*. In an interview with the *Los Angeles Times,* Saralegui recalled, "At the beginning they said 'it won't work. You're a Cuban woman. You have a Cuban accent. How dare you represent us [the Hispanics] because you're so white?' I understand that brown is beautiful, but so is white, pink, or whatever you are. We're a cultural minority. We go from [the darker skin tones of] Celia Cruz to me, and everything in the middle."

Saralegui was also worried that she would have difficulty finding Hispanic guests willing to talk about personal or controversial issues. "Everybody thought the Hispanics wouldn't talk about their problems, but they just needed a forum to discuss these things," she explained to the *Chicago Tribune*. "After the first show, letters started coming in and they told me stuff that I would not tell my pastor, my gynecologist or my husband."

In Mexico in particular, rigorous opposition to *El show de Cristina* has been led by religious figures and influential conservatives alike. Viewing the show as a threat to traditional Mexican values and a potential corruptor of young people, the show was moved from its original 4 p.m. time slot to 11 p.m., when many viewers have gone to bed. "I am bringing modernity and the way people think in big cities to Mexico," Saralegui responded in the *Los Angeles Times*. "Mexico City has the same problems as New York and Miami, and they know that."

It turned out that any objections to Saralegui's complexion or morals, as well as her own worries about the show, didn't matter; *El show de Cristina* was a huge success. It has been rated the number-one daytime television show and ranked among the top ten Spanish-language programs in the United States. Moreover, the show won an Emmy Award in 1991.

In 1991 the outspoken Saralegui launched a three-minute daily radio show entitled *Cristina opina*. Prior to the debut of this nationally

- *Emmy Award*

for **El show de**

Cristina

syndicated program, distributed through the Cadena Radio Centro Network, Saralegui said in her biography, "I am very excited about *Cristina opina* because it is going to give me an opportunity to share my thoughts, my feelings, my concerns, the experiences I have gathered working hands-on with Hispanics of every country in the past 29 years, and will be a great addition to the work we have accomplished on television."

When asked by *La opinion* if there have been changes in her personal life since she began to work on television, Saralegui replied, "Yes, for good. The routine of my private life has remained almost the same. I've never been a pretentious person; since childhood I got used to leading a tranquil and healthy life. I've always dedicated myself to writing, [and] I love to read a lot, especially biographies. I consider myself a very private person and my family respects this. Even if it doesn't seem so, I am a person who likes time by herself. Be it at home, on the plane, in the hotel, at the studio, wherever I may be, I'll always find five or ten minutes to study, because I like to do so. I have always done this, with or without the programs."

Late in 1991 Saralegui launched yet another project, *Cristina la revista* ("Cristina the Magazine"). She is executive director of this monthly lifestyle magazine, which is an off-shoot of her television program. "The magazine is more trouble than the two TV shows put together. Print is always harder to do than television," the former journalist confessed to the *Miami Herald*. By 1992 Saralegui had achieved another of her professional goals by adding one more dimension to her career. She became the executive producer and host of *Cristina,* an English-language version of her Spanish talk show, making Saralegui the first Hispanic to host daily television programs in two languages. She is quick to point out that any *Cristina* show is unmistakably a Cristina production, mainly because she chooses the subjects. "I tell the producers what angles I want. I OK all the angles. I'm very hands on," she explained to the *Miami Herald*.

Saralegui is managed by her second husband, Marcos Avila, eleven years her junior, a former bass player and part-founder of the music group Miami Sound Machine. In an interview with the *Chicago Tribune* she recalled: "I got married the first time because I wanted to have a family. I thought romance was for foolish ladies. I met Marcos when I was 35, and I thought, God sent me this to show me how wrong I was before. I was eleven years older than him, I wore a suit, I was the editor-in-chief of a ladies' magazine and I had a big staff. He was a little musician with a ponytail and an earring. Imagine him at an editorial cocktail party! Everybody's family had a fit!"

They married in 1984 and Avila now heads Cristina Saralegui Enterprises, Inc., which handles all of Saralegui's operations and business ventures. "That's the secret of our marriage" she told *Más* magazine. "Being together and talking about everything twenty-four hours a day." She also told *Hollywood Latinews,* "I think the most important thing I learned from my failure in my first marriage is that you have to have the same dreams and you have to go in the same direction. It's really important you work in the same kind of job."

Today, when Saralegui is not writing, taping, touring, consulting, or exercising, she can be found with her husband, her two daughters, Cristina Amalia and Stephanie Ann, and her son, Jon Marcos, in their Miami home. Saralegui told *La opinion* that future goals include appearing in a movie, learning to pilot a plane, and deep-sea diving. "I want to have fun while I work. Life is not only work and more work; you also have to do things that appeal to you." She admits two of her virtues are being honest and consistent, but reveals her biggest flaws are being "an extreme perfectionist, much too honest, and not too patient."

The green-eyed blonde has over twenty-five years of journalism experience and has received numerous distinctions. In addition to being listed as one of *Hispanic Business*'s "100 Influentials" in 1992, she was named one of the "Legendary Women of Miami," received the Corporate Leader Award from the National Network of Hispanic Women, and has addressed organizations ranging from Women in Communications to the Union of American Women of Puerto Rico. She has served on international juries of beauty pageants, has participated as Celebrity Grand Marshal at several national parades and has been awarded the keys to many cities in the United States and Latin America.

In addition to her own television series, Saralegui has been a guest on numerous national and local television programs. She has made frequent appearances on the Spanish-language program *Sabado gigante,* acted as creative consultant for *TV mujer,* and appeared in the Univision soap opera *Amandote.* She also produced a series of television specials in the style of *This Is Your Life,* celebrating the lives of leading Latin entertainers. "The reason we do these programs," she told *Hollywood Latinews,* "is because celebrities many times are people who started off in life very poor and they don't have the opportunities that middle class people have, yet they reach such heights. And we want to see, motivationally speaking, how they have made it. They are superachievers. So, when I do these special programs, what I stress is that aspect that if they could do it, we can do it too." As to Saralegui's own secret of success? As noted in *New York Newsday:* "To be absolutely fearless and plow ahead, no matter what."

**Profile by
Elena Kellner**

SELENA

1971–1995 •

W hile it took a bullet from a deranged fan to bring the name

Selena to the attention of Anglo audiences, Hispanics throughout the

Singer •

United States and south of the border were having a passionate love

affair with the up-and-coming young Latina songstress when her life

ended on March 31, 1995, at the age of twenty-three. Known for her up-

tempo renditions of the traditional ranchera classics of the Texas-

Mexican borderlands, Selena was on the verge of being launched by her

record company as the next Latin crossover artist when she was shot and

killed by the former president of her fan club. In a gesture that

demonstrated their immense love for the singer, fans made Selena's

Dreaming of You, *the crossover album left unfinished at her death, the*

first recording by a Latina to reach the Number One spot on the *Billboard* pop music charts.

Selena Quintanilla Perez was born April 16, 1971, in Lake Jackson, Texas, one of four children of Abraham Jr. and Marcella Quintanilla. After her father, a part-time musician, was laid off from Dow Chemical, the area's major employer, the family relocated to a westside barrio in Corpus Christi and turned to music full time to make their living. Singing at weddings and dance halls in the family's Tejano band by the time she was nine years old, it was clear to both Abraham and Marcella that their daughter was destined for greatness.

Much of Selena's childhood was spent traveling from one gig to another. Thanks to the watchful eye of her father, the young singer did not have the usual adjustment problems that come with growing up on the road. Although considered by some to be overprotective, Abraham made sure that both his daughters were raised according to traditional Hispanic moral values. Education was not ignored either: Selena received her high school diploma by taking correspondence courses, finding the time to study in between performances. In 1989, at the age of eighteen, she and her band, Los Dinos—complete with her sister as drummer and her brother as guitarist and co-writer—scored a recording contract with EMI, which put them on the fast track to success as Hispanic recording artists. By the time she was twenty-one, Selena was a millionaire, attracting record crowds to her concerts, and recording top-selling albums. In 1994 her *Selena Live* album won the singer and her band a Grammy award and nation-wide attention for the best Mexican-American album of the year.

The composition of Selena y los Dinos reflected the lead singer's close ties to her family: managed and agented by her father, the band included her sister Suzette, her brother Abe, and her husband, bass player Chris Perez, whom the singer married in 1992. The family was so close, in fact, that Selena and Chris made their home—a simple two-bedroom ranch house—right next door to her parents. A down-to-earth woman with a stage show that portrayed her as "truly likeable and real—not a common characteristic in most Latino mainstream acts," according to the *Los Angeles Times,* Selena projected a unique personality both on and off stage.

The singer's release of *Entre a mi Mundo* in 1993 came on the heels of that year's Tejano Music Award honors for best female artist, best female vocalist, and best grupo album of the year. Her concerts before Hispanic audiences continued to attract record-breaking crowds; at the Houston Astrodome in her home state, Selena performed to over 58,000 fans. As a reviewer for *Hispanic* noted of *Entre a mi Mundo,* the album

Under Her •

Father's

Watchful Eye

"offers plenty of evidence to suggest that she'll become the next Hispanic artist to rival Gloria Estefan's crossover appeal.... From her stock-in-trade *ranchera* rock to pop ballads, Selena has the ability to assimilate any style and make it her own." Other popular albums by the Latina superstar included *Fotos y recuerdos* and *Amor prohibido,* which sold over 400,000 copies in the United States alone. In addition to her stage performances, she had a small role as a singer in a mariachi band in the 1994 film *Don Juan DeMarco,* which starred Marlon Brando and Johnny Depp.

- *Rise to Star*

Status Ends in

Tragedy

"Never in my dreams would I have thought that I would become this big," Selena confided to *Time* magazine in early 1995. "I am still freaking out." Just weeks later the successful singer's rise to stardom ended tragically, as the singer was murdered on March 31 by Yolanda Saldivar, a thirty-two-year-old ex-employee who had recently been fired on charges of embezzling over $30,000. The first president of Selena's fan club and later the manager of Selena's two boutiques, Saldivar was taken into custody by police after a nine-hour standoff during which she held police at bay in the parking lot of the Corpus Christi motel where the shooting took place, holding the murder weapon to her head and threatening to take her own life. Although she claimed that the shooting was an accident, Saldivar was convicted of the murder and sentenced to life in prison in November of 1995.

Although devastated by the tragedy, Selena's parents tried to remain calm, reassuring each other and the rest of their family members through their strong faith as Jehovah's Witnesses. Indeed, their main concern over the weeks and months ahead proved to be protecting their daughter's name from profiteers and tabloid journalists. Saldivar "committed a horrible act," Abraham Quintanilla stated in *USA Today,* expressing pity for his daughter's killer. "She took the life of a beautiful human being, she hurt her own family, she hurt ours, and she hurt a lot of fans who loved Selena." Equally devastated was the singer's husband, Perez, who had been looking forward to celebrating the young couple's third wedding anniversary on April 2nd. "I can be dealing with everything okay, and then they start talking about her on the radio and play her new song" he admitted to *People,* "and it's like dropping a heavy rock and squashing me. It brings back all those memories."

Shocked fans responded to the killing by reaching out to the singer's family and to each other. Hundreds gathered, many of them young Latinas who revered Selena as a role model—a fellow Hispanic "boasting of a tight-knit family and a down-to-earth personality, a Madonna without the controversy" in the words of *Time*—at the site of her death. Others passed in solemn procession past the home of the singer's parents, leaving flowers, letters, and other tokens in the front yard or on the doorstep of the family's two Selena Etc. boutiques. Memorial services were held in San Antonio, where Selena had a large audience. On the day of her burial, thousands were in attendance.

Aftershocks from the death of the "Queen of Tejano" were felt throughout the United States and neighboring Mexico. When notorious talk-show host Howard Stern made what many considered to be racist remarks concerning her murder during his nationally syndicated show, several Texas state senators took to the floor in anger. Given extensive coverage by a host of national television and radio networks, the events of Selena's tragic death served to bring Hispanics to the attention of the entire nation in a more sympathetic light. And, as Catherine Vasquez-Revilla commented in *Hispanic*: "The death of Selena Quintanilla Perez, while a great loss to the community, also brings recognition to Mexican Americans, and unity to Hispanics."

While Tex-Mex music has seen its share of star performers, many believe that Selena was truly different. "She came along as the community had reached what syndicated Tejano columnist Victor Landa calls a 'choque'—a confrontation—between the values of the immigrant generation and their Americanized children," explained Richard Willing in *USA Today*. "Selena, the star who never left home, who taught herself Spanish, who formed her music from old Mexican folk songs and modern machine-made riffs, was the bridge over this troubled crossroads." She was proof positive that Latinas could be successful, and her untimely death left a huge void in the lives of thousands of young fans.

After her death Selena was honored by a special edition of *People* magazine, which quickly sold out its run of over 900,000 copies, and numerous tributes to her rise from rags to riches appeared throughout the U.S. media. Vasquez-Revilla gave perhaps the most fitting eulogy to the singer. "For Mexican Americans," the commentator wrote in *Hispanic*, "Selena's success became their success. She inspired confidence and ethnic pride. The stage lights that shone on her also reached across to include Mexican Americans by highlighting their language, music, and culture. Her greatest gift was that her talent, beauty, and success empowered all Hispanics."

Mourned •

throughout the

Nation

**Profile by
Pamela L. Shelton**

LUPE SERRANO

A ffiliated for nearly two decades with the American Ballet Theatre

(ABT), prima ballerina Lupe Serrano has enjoyed a long and rewarding

career in the field of dance, first as a performer and most recently as a

teacher. Indeed, dancing has been the focus of her life for almost as long

as she can remember.

- 1930-
- *Ballerina,*
- *dance*
- *instructor*

Serrano's father, Luis Martinez Serrano, was a musician and songwriter from Barcelona, Spain, who was raised in Buenos Aires, Argentina. On a tour that took him to Mexico City, he met Luciana Desfassiaux, a Mexican native whose parents had come from France. The success of his tour detained Serrano in Mexico long enough for him to marry Luciana and start a family. But in 1930, Luis, eager to take his expectant wife home to meet his parents, agreed to conduct an orchestra that was traveling through South America. The group was in Santiago, Chile, when Lupe arrived on December 7. During Luciana's recovery from the birth, her husband fell ill; while the tour moved on, the Serranos remained in Chile for the next thirteen years.

Even as a small child, Lupe was oblivious to anything other than dancing. Family legend has it that she danced constantly. According to her parents, on her third birthday she made all her guests sit down while she performed for them. Luis and Luciana eventually decided their daughter should have formal lessons, and despite the rather limited educational choices available to them in Chile, they managed to find a suburban school that offered some training in modern dance, oriental, soft shoe, pointe work, and castanets.

• *Begins Formal*

Ballet Training

in Mexico City

The Serranos returned to Mexico City when Lupe was thirteen, and it was then that her formal ballet training began. "I had terrible habits by then," the dancer recalled in an interview with Peg McNichol. "But I had been in so many recitals that I had a sense of how to fill the stage." She studied seriously with a ballet company in Mexico City and soon earned a position in the Corps de Ballet—"the very last row of the corps," as she remembered. Lupe's efforts paid off, however, and at the age of fourteen she debuted in the company's production of *Les Sylphides*.

Serrano worked especially hard in high school, condensing the academic work of her last two years into one so she would be free to tour. Her devotion to ballet left no time for a college education, but she studied extensively on her own, not only to prepare for the dances themselves but to learn about the many places to which she traveled. At the Palacio de Bellas Artes, for example, Serrano broadened her knowledge of English and French and took courses in such subjects as drama, history, music, and folklore.

Around the time she was eighteen, Serrano went on a tour with Cuban prima ballerina Alicia Alonso that took her through Central America and Colombia. When she returned to Mexico City, she found that her teacher had formed a ballet company. While at first it seemed like an exciting opportunity for the young dancer, the experience would provide Serrano with a harsh lesson in the economic realities of being a dancer. "Ballet is not a self-supporting art anywhere in the world," she observed in an interview. "It has to be sponsored. A person like my ballet teacher, who was devoted to the art of ballet, of course would not have the ability to raise funds." The company folded after only eighteen months, unable to bear the weight of expenses for toe shoes, costumes, and other needs.

• *Seeks Her*

Fortune in New

York City

Serrano then joined the government-sponsored Ballet Folklorika of Mexico, but she soon felt the pull of New York City and the promise it held out to young dancers. Having saved a little money, she arrived in the United States at the age of twenty and obtained a position with the Ballet Russe de Monte Carlo, where she was featured in her first solo performances and had the opportunity to travel throughout North and South America.

But that company went bankrupt, too, and Serrano returned to Mexico City and had a starring role on a television program about the classical arts. It was 1952 and television was still fairly new, so Serrano had to make adjustments for the cameras. "We had to rearrange the way we covered space on the floor, because the cameras were not very mobile," she recalled in her interview. "And you had to be much more subtle in expression, because the camera brings you much closer to the audience. On the stage, you have to think of projecting yourself a block away. Television is much more intimate."

One day Serrano's phone rang with a long-distance call from New York. On the other end of the line was the former road manager of the Ballet Russe de Monte Carlo. He was now with the ABT in New York, and he wanted to know if Serrano was interested in auditioning for the troupe.

Serrano wasted little time returning to the United States. She took classes and auditioned for the prestigious company several times. When she was accepted in 1953 she joined as principal dancer, a position of great honor. "I remember having such respect for the company itself," she said to McNichol. The first time she led her fellow dancers in a big finale, Serrano thought to herself, "'Well, look at you now, leading this group of wonderful dancers.' I felt a great sense of pride." During the nearly two decades Serrano performed with the ABT, she appeared in more than fifty different roles ranging from classics such as *Swan Lake* and *Giselle* to a variety of contemporary works.

Auditions •

Successfully for

the ABT

One of Serrano's most memorable experiences as a member of the ABT came in 1961 when the troupe visited the Soviet Union as part of a cultural exchange. They had to deal with many cultural and linguistic barriers—many eventually settled on French or German as a common language—but when they danced, everyone understood. During their eleven-week tour, the ABT performed portions of Balanchine's *Theme and Variations* and excerpts from other American ballets such as *Rodeo*, *Fancy Free*, and *Combat* as well as classical *pas de deux* such as *La Fille Mal Gardee*. Serrano enchanted audiences in Leningrad so completely that they insisted she repeat her solo performance rather than just take a bow for it.

The tour also included dates in parts of Europe. Serrano remembers being in Athens and standing in the Acropolis under the full moon during a party hosted by the American Embassy. At one point, staff members invited the dancers to stroll around the ruins. For Serrano, it was a magical evening, "to be stepping on those stones that had been laid down so many years ago."

In 1963 Serrano and her husband since 1957, ABT conductor Kenneth Schermerhorn, welcomed their first child, Erica. The ballerina noted to McNichol that returning to dancing after having a baby was "not that difficult," but she did notice that she had "a completely different feeling, as though dancing was a wonderful self-indulgence. I had a much more relaxed approach to it then." By this time, Schermerhorn was affiliated with the New Jersey Symphony, and the family moved to New Jersey to be closer to his job. A busy Serrano now commuted to New York for classes and rehearsals.

In 1967 the ballerina experienced perhaps the most active year of her entire career. She danced excerpts from *Raiymonda* at a White House performance for then-President Lyndon Johnson, toured the Soviet Union for a second time where she was met with a reception as enthusiastic as the first, and gave birth to her second daughter, Veronica. Serrano then took a year off, returning to the ABT as a permanent guest artist and choosing her own performances. After her husband accepted a position with the Milwaukee Orchestra, the family relocated to Wisconsin.

Serrano continued to make guest appearances with the ABT and also started teaching at the University of Milwaukee and the Conservatory of Milwaukee. She found teaching to be a superb way to communicate her love for ballet; watching young dancers blossom and professional dancers refine their skills under her tutelage was, to the prima ballerina, extremely rewarding.

• **Retires from**
---
the Stage

In 1970 Serrano turned forty. The press began referring to her as a "veteran ballerina" and making references to her age before commenting on her performances with the ABT. Despite her desire and ability to perform, the remarks unsettled her so much that in 1971 she decided to retire from the stage. At the same time, her marriage ended in divorce. Serrano's family urged her to return to Mexico City, but she felt the United States was her home, especially since it was the place where she had been raising her two young daughters.

Serrano soon accepted her first full-time teaching position as assistant director at the National Academy of Arts in Illinois. Like many ballet companies, the school struggled with overwhelming financial demands before it was finally forced to close. In 1974 the Pennsylvania Ballet School named Serrano company teacher and director of the apprentice program. A year later she became school director, a position she held until 1983. Among her students during this period were her daughters; only Veronica, however, opted to continue her lessons and pursue a career in dance, eventually becoming a soloist with the ABT as her mother had before her. In addition to her duties with the Pennsylvania Ballet School, Serrano taught master classes for professional dancers. She also judged dance events and was invited to guest teach at the San

Francisco Ballet, Minnesota Dance Theatre, Cleveland Ballet, Washington Ballet, Cincinnati Ballet, Rome Opera Ballet and the American Ballet Theatre.

In 1988 Serrano left Philadelphia to become the artistic associate for the Washington (D.C.) Ballet. She continues to dance, but only within the confines of the classroom, where she concentrates on instructing advanced students aged thirteen to eighteen, and professionals. "I have never lost my love for that," she declared in her interview. "It still gives me great pleasure."

Sometimes Serrano thinks she should try choreography, or perhaps develop a dance video or write a book about ballet technique. But most of her time is caught up in her devotion to teaching. She says she has reached a point in her life where she no longer feels driven to be the best at everything she does. For now, insists Serrano, it is enough to do her best with her students, whom she works with during her three classes a day and in individual coaching sessions.

**Profile by
Peg McNichol**

MADELEINE STOWE

*H*er brunette good looks and a lucky break got Madeleine Stowe her

1958- •

first acting job. But it was almost ten years before the statuesque actress

gained star status in Hollywood's competitive movie industry. Finally, in

Actress •

1992, after her critically praised performance in the historical drama

Last of the Mohicans, *Stowe's name began appearing on cinema mar-*

quees, as well as on the lists of Hollywood directors. Despite her fragile

beauty and her penchant for being cast as a vulnerable woman in a host

of films, Stowe has a behind-the-scenes reputation for being down-to-

earth and determined to do things on her own terms. "[She's] not push-

aroundable," comments director Robert Altman of the actress, who

turned in an award-winning performance in his 1992 film Short Cuts.

Fellow director Jonathan Kaplan agrees. "Madeleine is so delicate and graceful, but she has a strong, iron will. It's unusual to have . . . her kind of fragile body language in a woman who is really tough and so utterly fearless when it comes to authority."

Born August 18, 1958, in Los Angeles, California, Stowe was one of three children born to Robert Stowe, a civil engineer, and his wife, Mireya Mora, the daughter of a well-to-do Costa Rican family. Her mother supported Stowe's early love of music by arranging piano lessons for her daughter; her father had other ideas. His possessiveness and violent outbursts of temper, which were soon diagnosed as symptoms of multiple sclerosis, kept her home life tense and, for a young girl, confusing. "Neighbors would come running, and here we were these three little kids trying to pretend that nothing was wrong," Stowe told the *Los Angeles Times,* recalling the many times her father lost control in public. "I kept wishing that my mother would stand up to him, but she was such a saint. I always felt a little bit evil compared to her." Stowe's father died in 1983.

• **Sidesteps**

College on Her

Way to

Hollywood

After graduating from high school, the quiet Stowe enrolled at the University of Southern California, inspired by a love of old movies to major in film direction. However, fate intervened, in the form of an overriding urge to cut classes in favor of haunting the local theater as a stagehand. While passing out programs at a production starring actor Richard Dreyfuss, Stowe was noticed by Dreyfuss's agent, who got the nineteen-year-old college student a bit part on *Baretta,* a popular nighttime television series. Although she looks back on these early appearances and shudders, the actress seemed to have found her niche.

Other, more challenging roles soon came the way of the strikingly beautiful Stowe. After several years of playing what she termed "ethereal" roles, however, the actress felt the need to take a break from the camera and get in touch with who she really was. "So I just stopped and traveled through Central America," she told Margy Rochlin in *Interview,* "where I have family, and I went to a couple of islands in the Caribbean. All I know is that a year and a half later, when I came back to acting, I had a different perspective on things." Stowe returned to work in projects like the miniseries' "The Gangster Chronicles" and "Blood and Orchids."

The 1987 comedy-thriller *Stakeout* was Stowe's first motion picture role; although the film receiveed mixed reviews, her performance made critics give her a second look. Other films followed, including being cast next to costar Kevin Costner in the 1990 thriller *Revenge,* and playing girlfriend to actor/director Jack Nicholson in *The Two Jakes.* It wasn't until 1992, when she hit her stride as the high-spirited daughter of a doomed British general in *Last of the Mohicans* that Stowe proved to audiences that she was capable of taking a leading role. Cast opposite Daniel Day-Lewis's Hawkeye, Stowe stood her ground in this lushly filmed frontier epic, adapted from the classic American novel by James Fenimore Cooper.

Her role alongside Lewis in *Last of the Mohicans* marked a shift for Stowe for yet another reason. Up until this point, she had mainly been cast—by virtue of her fragile looks—in the role of the imperiled, helpless girlfriend, a part which usually involved on-camera nudity. "There was a certain amount of sniggering about the amount of nudity she engaged in in her films," explained Michael Apted—who directed Stowe in *Blink*—in the *Los Angeles Times,* but Madeleine sees that as part of her ammunition. She's like the great actresses in the '30s and '40s, very beautiful but with nothing cute about her looks, a woman who is not afraid of her own sexuality." To be sure, while the nudity itself never concerned Stowe, what it represented did. "You know, they want a woman to be pretty, to be sexy, and they want her to be desirable," the actress explained to Rochlin. "What they don't want is for her to speak, to aggressively pursue anything. They can project anything they want onto her and not have her talk back. I was really shocked by that [in filming *Revenge*]. I find these characters are remarkably silent." By the time she came under Apted's direction, Stowe was determined to have a hand in balancing the role between she and her costar, Aidan Quinn, building his character into more than just the "love interest" she had been relegated to playing for so long.

Under the direction of Robert Altman in his 1993 *Short Cuts,* Stowe broke away from her typical roles and gave a performance that earned her the nod as best supporting actress from the National Society of Film Critics. As the down-to-earth, no-nonsense wife of two-timing policeman Tim Robbins, Stowe proved that her acting talents ran much deeper than mere physical presence. She followed that success with several more films, including Apted's *Blink,* a 1993 thriller in which she was cast in her first starring role as a semi-blind violinist who witnesses a murder; and *China Moon,* shot the same year as a starring vehicle for actor Ed Harris.

More recent film appearances include 1994's *Bad Girls,* and *Twelve Monkeys,* a film directed by Terry Gilliam in 1995. In *Twelve Monkeys,* Stowe is cast as a psychiatrist alongside Bruce Willis and Brad Pitt; with former Monty-Pythoner Gilliam at the helm, the cast will cross the time barrier in this off-beat thriller-romance. The actress went permanently back in time for the filming of *Bad Girls,* where Stowe and costars Mary Stuart Masterson, Andie MacDowell, and Drew Barrymore get the chance to let loose and have some fun as a pack of gun-toting, tobacco-spitting former prostitutes who head for the high country in the wild west of the 1890s. Despite the problem's she had with the film's title—"It's totally politically incorrect" she announced in the *Los Angeles Times*—*Bad Girls* was especially fun for Stowe because of the amount of time she got to spend in the saddle; an avid horsewoman, she owns a four-horse ranch near Luckenbach, Texas, with her husband, actor Brian Benben. Married since 1986, the couple was expecting their first child in 1996. In addition to looking forward to motherhood, Stowe plans to continue her acting career, seeing it as the ideal job. "I love the life of an actor," she told Hilary de Vries in the *Los Angeles Times*, "because you spend brief amounts of time with other people and then you just leave. I need to be alone a lot, and I need to be outdoors."

**Profile by
Pamela L. Shelton**

ISABEL TOLEDO

1963?- •

Fashion •

designer

"*I* *sabel Toledo is one of the most inventive American designers of*

the under-30 generation," writes New York Times *contributor Anne-*

Marie Schiro. Toledo first appeared on the New York fashion scene in the

mid-1980s, when her husband and business partner, sculptor Ruben

Toledo, showed some of her hand-sewn designs to trend-setting fashion

retailers Patricia Field and Henri Bendel. By the late 1980s, Toledo's

designs were appearing in numerous fashion magazines, including

Cosmopolitan *and* Women's Wear Daily, *and she was no longer sewing*

everything herself. Though she is now widely recognized for her innova-

tive designs that contrast fabrics and shapes to produce whimsical

effects, Toledo told Cosmopolitan: *"I design for myself. If people buy my*

clothes, they're telling me they like how I look. It's very personal."

Toledo was born in Cuba in the early 1960s. She and her family immigrated to the United States when she was five, settling in West New York, New Jersey. When her three daughters objected to going to a babysitter, Toledo's mother convinced the girls that they were actually going to sewing lessons. Toledo took her mother seriously, she told *Cosmopolitan,* and really learned to sew. She started sewing her own wardrobe, and the first clothes that her husband sold he lifted directly out of her closet. Though she never intended to become a fashion designer, Toledo took courses at the Fashion Institute of Technology and at the Parsons School of Design, both in New York City. In the mid-1980s she worked at the Costume Institute of the Metropolitan Museum of Art, where she restored and designed period clothing for mannequins and did research.

The first appearance of Toledo's designs in fashion stores attracted immediate attention: people called to place orders and to see her seasonal collections. Soon she and her husband—childhood friends who married in 1985—had enlisted the help of their parents in the effort to keep up with increasing demand for Toledo's clothes. Finally they found a financial backer who helped them get her designs sewn at a Brooklyn, New York, factory that he owned. By 1987 Toledo's designs were selling at exclusive fashion stores such as California's I. Magnin and Bergdorf's and Barneys in New York, at prices ranging from $120 to $450 an item.

Toledo and her husband continue to inspire each other to new creative heights. "Working together takes us twice as far," Ruben told Anne Rosenblum in *Harper's Bazaar.* "The process breeds mistakes, but we get two ideas out of one." She provides the inspiration and a steady stream of coffee and good advice whenever he is in the midst of an intensive project. He uses his talent as an illustrator to sketch her initial designs—Toledo herself works out the architecture of a garment from a picture in her mind—plans marketing strategies, and give some good advice of his own. "Just do it in denim," is his motto, according to Isabel.

Toledo's trademark is indeed denim, which she complements with such fabrics as linen, organza, and mohair to produce a look that *Hispanic* magazine called "young" and "energetic," and which, according to Schiro, makes "her development fascinating to fashion watchers." Behind the seeming simplicity of her styles are the small details that make her garments so unusual—and so costly. Gussetted sleeves, intricate piping, bias-cut skirts, and the creative interplay of fabric and texture characterize her designs, as well as a streak of perfectionism that prompts Toledo to personally check every garment on its way to the stores. Her stylistic trademarks are circles and curves, which she integrates into the technically intricate structures of her designs, whether a foldable mini-skirt made out of two circles or a balloonlike sleeve over a long, billowy shirt. Her designs are unusual, her style constantly evolving, but Toledo is not designing for everyone. "Women don't like to be told by other women what to wear," she told Michael Gross of the *New York Times,* but "the fact is, I'm a woman and I know what's best for me."

**Profile by
Tom Pendergast**

CHRISTY TURLINGTON

1969- •

Model •

W ith her refined good looks gracing the pages of the world's most

prominent fashion magazines since 1986, model Christy Turlington has

managed to translate her classic features into an annual income of

more than $1.5 million—all before she reached her mid-twenties. One

of the latest crop of international supermodels, which includes Claudia

Schiffer, Linda Evangelista, and Paulina Porizkova, Turlington's suc-

cess confirms the advertising truth of the 1990s: ethnic sells. With an

olive-skinned beauty that New York magazine calls "unspecified

ethnic," Turlington does, indeed, sell. "There's a suggestion of an inner

life and intelligence in those eyes," explained Linda Wells, editor-in-

chief of Allure to the New York Times. "To advertisers, she's money in

the bank."

The second of three daughters born to Dwaine and Elizabeth Turlington, Christy arrived on the scene January 2, 1969. Raised in Walnut Creek, California, a quiet suburb of San Francisco, she travelled a lot because of her father's career as a pilot for Pan-Am Airlines; her mother, a native of El Salvador, had met her husband while working as a stewardess on a flight to Hawaii. When Turlington was ten, the family moved to Coral Gables, Florida, where, like many girls her age, she caught horse-fever and began to ride competitively. It was on one of her visits to the stables to ride that Turlington was discovered by a local photographer, Dennie Cody, who, as he told *New York,* "knew right away. You don't run across many girls you know can make it to the top."

With Cody's encouragement and her supportive mother never far from her side, Turlington began modeling for local businesses, working after school for upwards of $60 an hour. Cody cautioned both the young model and her mother that the only thing that would hold her back in the fashion business would be a lack of motivation, along with beauty, but motivation was something Turlington had in abundance. In 1983, after her father suffered a heart attack and the family returned to the San Francisco area, she continued going to school and spending some of her afternoons in front of the camera. The following year fifteen-year-old Turlington and her mother visited fashion houses and photographers in Paris, but didn't get an overly enthusiastic response. Undaunted, the high school junior arrived in New York City during the summer of 1985, determined to find a place in the field of modelling. After distributing her portfolio to photographers and magazine editors throughout Manhattan, she was a day away from boarding a plane back to the West Coast when *Vogue* cast a net for the brown-eyed beauty. Although she returned home in time for school in the fall, photo shoots for the magazine took Turlington to Paris and New York throughout the school year; during the following summer she modeled for Eileen Ford, staying in a townhouse on Manhattan's Upper East Side that Ford reserved as a dormitory for young, aspiring models.

By December 1986 the soon-to-be supermodel had moved to New York City, where, at age eighteen, she rented a Soho loft next door to Katie Ford, Eileen Ford's daughter. "I got a little kitten, I had a suitcase, and Katie put a bed in my room," Turlington recalled to *New York.* "That was all I had." But by the following year things had certainly changed: In addition to working for some of New York's best fashion photographers, including Herb Ritts, Irving Penn, and Steven Meisel, Turlington could count models like Naomi Campbell among her best friends. Romance had entered her life as well, in the form of actor/screenwriter Roger

From Riding •

Trail to

Fashion

Runway

Wilson, with whom Turlington had a live-in relationship off and on over the next several years. New York City had, indeed, begun to feel like home for the West Coast native.

In 1988, as a result of her work on his notorious, sexually suggestive ad campaign for the perfume Obsession two years earlier, Turlington was hired by designer/merchandiser Calvin Klein to be the face attached to his new "Eternity" fragrance line. Although Ford herself attempted to dissuade her, the young and inexperienced model was quick to sign on the dotted line, both flattered by Klein's attention and excited by the high visibility the job would give her. By 1992 Turlington's classic profile had graced the pages of magazines world-wide in fronting the successful Eternity ad campaign, for which she would earn almost $3 million for the eighty days of work she would do before the camera during each of the next four years. Then, in 1992, she signed an equally lucrative five-year contract with Maybelline.

• **A Crash Course**

in Contract

Negotiations

In her new contract with the cosmetics giant, Turlington would be earning almost $1 million a year for two weeks' work; not only was it more money than her contract with Klein had paid, but it was also a non-exclusive contract. When a model is contracted to a particular product line, his or her face becomes associated with those products; by that same contract he or she is not allowed to appear in magazine articles, cover shots, interviews, or any other form of advertising. By signing a non-exclusive contract with Maybelline, Turlington could supplement her contract salary with work for other companies on non-competitive ad campaigns, plus several other smaller jobs—including runway jobs, which can average between $7,000 and $25,000, depending on the client. Turlington finally quit accepting runway assignments because, as she was quoted as saying in the *New York Times,* they "encourage fashion people to become critical, mean, and vicious." Fortunately, in the case of her contract with Klein, the model renegotiated the terms and got herself back in circulation on the pages of magazines nationwide.

Turlington's face continues to sell products; under the basic laws of supply and demand, she has been able to dictate her own terms. A four-time *Cosmopolitan* cover-girl by the time she was twenty-three, she feels that the fees she can charge clients are fair, considering the business she's in. "There's a tremendous amount of money that's being made," she noted of the fashion and cosmetic business in *Forbes.* "So when you think of it as being your commission, it's not that ridiculous."

And clients are more than happy to pay, and not just because of Turlington's selling power. "She can be an Indian or a mulatto or Miss Debutante," explained photographer Arthur Elgort in *New York.* "Her eyes are not on the clock. She'll drive the Jeep. She'll help with the suitcases. She's never outside herself, looking at herself, saying, 'This'll be good for my career.' You never hear 'Christy got in late' or 'Christy's tired.' She is worth every nickel."

While consistantly referred to as one of the "nicest" models in the industry, Turlington senses a different reaction to her success from the general public. "People don't want to like you," she told *New York* in a discussion of the way she, Campbell, and fellow model Linda Evangelista had been portrayed by the media during the late 1980s. "You're young and beautiful and successful. They think you don't have a skill. So when things go well for you, they aren't happy. That's just human nature." But she hasn't let her success spoil her upbeat nature; when she did the inevitable bathing-suit calendar on the heels of her success in modeling for Klein, Turlington donated her entire share of the proceeds to a relief fund to aid the citizens of El Salvador.

The months she spent as a contract model for Calvin Klein's Eternity campaign left Turlington with a lot of free time between shoots; to fill up the space she enrolled in literature and writing classes at the University of California at Los Angeles. She was also featured in the Lifetime Channel's cable-TV special *Christy Turlington Backstage,* a portrait of the daily grind of a high-fashion model that aired in February 1993. In 1994 she could be seen in a television commercial for Kellogg's cereal. Turlington joined fellow supermodels Campbell, Schiffer, and Elle Macpherson as a figurehead for the Fashion Cafe in 1995, a theme restaurant located in New York City's Rockefeller Center that caters to a tourist clientele.

Where does she plan to spend her time after her grueling modeling days are through? Attending college full-time, where Turlington would like to accelerate her part-time studies in literature and architecture. And after that? Writing. While heads may turn now at the mention of her name, she would like to translate her millions into gaining the ability to turn pages as a professional writer. Meanwhile, between modeling assignments, the successful supermodel alternates between her New York apartment and California's Bay Area, where she has been a co-partner in an acid blues club called the Up & Down Club since 1993. Her hobbies include collecting Arts and Crafts–era furniture and photographs.

**Profile by
Pamela L. Shelton**

NYDIA MARGARITA VELÁZQUEZ

*N*ydia Margarita Velázquez, the daughter of an impoverished

sugar-cane cutter, is the first Puerto Rican woman to be elected to the

United States House of Representatives. Velázquez, a Democrat, won her

seat in Congress in November 1992, after a grueling and controversial

Democratic primary that pitted her against longtime incumbent Ste-

phen J. Solarz and a crowded field of Hispanic challengers. She now

represents the 12th Congressional District in New York City, a heavily

Democratic and Hispanic district that was created in 1992 to encour-

age the election of a Hispanic representative. The district of just over

500,000 people encompasses poor and working-class neighborhoods in

Queens, Manhattan, and Brooklyn.

1953- •

U.S. •

Congress-

woman

As a Puerto Rican woman raised in a hardworking rural household with few modern conveniences, Velázquez brings a unique perspective to national politics. She was born March 23, 1953, in Yabucoa, Puerto Rico. Once famous for its sugar-cane industry, Yabucoa is located in a lush valley on the island's southeast coast. Velázquez and her twin sister were among the nine children raised by Benito and Carmen Luisa (Serrano) Velázquez, who lived at the edge of town in a small, wooden house, surrounded by sugar-cane fields and bordering the Rio Limon River.

To support the family Carmen sold *pasteles,* a traditional Puerto Rican food, to cane cutters in the fields. Benito, who had a third-grade education, cut sugar cane and later became a butcher and the owner of a legal cockfighting business. Also a local political leader, Benito founded a political party in Yabucoa and, significantly, passed on to his daughter Nydia a strong social conscience, according to the *New York Times.* During Velázquez's childhood, dinner conversations often revolved around workers' rights and other political issues. "I always wanted to be like my father," she told an interviewer in the *New York Times.*

Always eager to learn, Velázquez convinced her family to allow her to start school at the age of five. She proved to be a bright student, skipping several grades to graduate early and become the first in her family to receive a high school diploma. At sixteen, Velázquez was already a freshman at the University of Puerto Rico in Rio Piedras. She graduated magna cum laude in 1974 with a bachelor's degree in political science. After teaching briefly, she won a scholarship to continue her studies in the United States. With her family's reluctant support Velázquez left her home in Puerto Rico to enter New York University, where she earned a master's degree in political science in 1976 before returning to the University of Puerto Rico in Humacao to teach political science. Leaving Puerto Rico again in 1981, she became an adjunct professor of Puerto Rican studies at Hunter College at the City University of New York, where she taught for two years.

In a 1992 interview with *Newsday,* Velázquez revealed that she left Puerto Rico for more reasons than simply to advance her education and career. "I was harassed when I was a professor at the University of Puerto Rico, when the New Progressive Party took power in Puerto Rico," she explained. Accused by this conservative faction of being a Communist and leftist, she decided to make her home in New York, but Velázquez's career in politics and public service has subsequently included work in both the United States and Puerto Rico.

• *Political*

Climate

Prompts Move

to U.S.

She received her first taste of New York City–style politics in 1983 when she served as special assistant to former U.S. Representative Edolphus Towns, a Democrat from Brooklyn. As a special assistant, Velázquez was in charge of immigration issues, and part of her job included testifying before Congress on immigration legislation. In 1984 she was appointed to the New York City Council, filling the vacancy left when former Councilman Luis Olmedo was convicted on charges of federal conspiracy and attempted extortion. At the age of thirty-one, Velázquez became the first Latina to serve on the council.

After losing her council seat in the next election in 1986, Velázquez returned to Puerto Rico to serve as the national director of the Migration Division Office of Puerto Rico's Department of Labor and Human Resources, a post she held until 1989. In that year the governor of Puerto Rico appointed Velázquez secretary of the Department of Puerto Rican Community Affairs in the United States, a cabinet-level position that functions as a major link between Puerto Rico and the U.S. Government. Responsible for the New York City headquarters and four regional offices, Velázquez advised the Puerto Rican government on Puerto Rico's public policy and its commitment to the Puerto Rican community in the United States. She had the opportunity to prove the strength of her political influence that same year, after Hurricane Hugo devastated Puerto Rico. Velázquez personally called General Colin Powell, then head of the Joint Chiefs of Staff; shortly thereafter the Commonwealth received a promise of federal assistance. During her tenure as secretary, Velázquez also led successful voter registration drives that resulted in the registration of more than 200,000 new voters in Puerto Rican communities in the Northeast and Midwest. In 1991 she initiated *Unidos contra el sida,* "United against AIDS," a project to fight the spread of AIDS among the Puerto Rican population.

Velázquez's close ties with the Puerto Rican Government came under scrutiny during her 1992 bid for Congress. Her critics charged she was more concerned with Puerto Rican politics than with the problems of her U.S. constituents—an accusation she repeatedly denied. During the campaign it was disclosed that Velázquez, while working for the Puerto Rican Government, had personally supported a pro-Common-wealth position in the fierce, ongoing debate over the island's colonial status. During the congressional race she adopted a neutral stance on whether Puerto Rico should become a state, nation, or continue as a commonwealth. "My responsibility as a member of Congress is to support whatever pledge Puerto Ricans make to resolve the situation," she told *Newsday.* Acknowledging that she is concerned about Puerto Rico, she related to a *Newsday* reporter during the campaign: "I say that, yes, we have been oppressed and disenfranchised for too long."

Velázquez's bid for Congress came at a time of national efforts to bring Hispanics and other minorities to the polls. The 12th Congressional District was one of nine new districts created in 1992 to increase minority voting power under the Voting Rights Act. The district includes a patchwork of Hispanic neighborhoods in three boroughs, including Corona, Elmhurst, and Jackson Heights in Queens; the Lower East Side in Manhattan; and Williamsburg, Bushwick, Sunset Park, and East New York in Brooklyn. According to the *New York Times,* the average income in the district is $22,500, over $10,000 less than the state average. Some twenty-two percent of the people are on public assistance, and twenty-seven percent are non-citizens. While a majority of the district's population is Hispanic—including Puerto Ricans, Dominicans, Colombians, and immigrants from other Spanish-speaking countries—the region also includes whites, blacks, and Asian Americans.

Former Representative Solarz's Brooklyn district, which was heavily Jewish, was dissolved by the redistricting process. As a non-Hispanic, Solarz was criticized for seeking to represent a district designed for minority leadership. But he insisted that he was the best person for the job. "I categorically reject that only a black can represent a black district, or a Hispanic an Hispanic district," he told the *New York Times.* Although Solarz was a respected foreign-policy expert in Congress, he was also one of many legislators caught in the House banking scandal during the early 1990s, when it was revealed that he had written 743 overdrafts.

The 1992 Democratic primary in the 12th district was a bitter battle, pitting five Hispanic candidates against the popular Solarz, a nine-term Congressman. Velázquez ran an old-fashioned, grassroots campaign, pounding the pavement, making phone calls, and garnering support from family and friends. Although she raised just a fraction of Solarz's campaign fund of over two-million dollars—she could not afford much campaign literature or television advertisements—Velázquez gained the endorsements of New York City Mayor David Dinkins, Hispanic union leader Dennis Rivera, president of Local 1199 of the Drug, Hospital and Health Care Workers Union, and the Reverend Jesse Jackson. Dinkins's support was in part a political thank-you for Velázquez's 1989 voter registration efforts, which had helped Mayor Dinkins win the Hispanic vote in the mayoral election.

Still, with four Hispanic opponents, one of her biggest challenges was to unite the district's diverse and politically fractured Hispanic community. Not only did Velázquez have to prove that she could represent all Hispanics in her district—not just the Puerto Ricans—she also had to fight the prejudice that often separates Puerto Ricans raised on the island from those with roots on the mainland. Even Velázquez's supporters describe her as controversial. "I think that Nydia just provokes very strong opinions of love and hate from people because she's so passionate herself," commented Luis A. Miranda Jr., president of the Hispanic Federation of New York City, in an interview with the *New York Times*.

Velázquez won the September 15 primary. Soon after, she returned to Puerto Rico and her hometown, where she was given a heroine's welcome. According to an account in the *New York Times,* she rode into Yabucoa in a pickup truck, accompanied by Mayor Angel Luis Ramos and a state senator. A loudspeaker proclaimed: "She's back! Our Nydia Velázquez, who will be the first Puerto Rican woman in Congress, is back in Sugartown!" Velázquez told the crowd that she dedicated her victory to her mother and the women of Puerto Rico. In an interview with *Newsday,* Ramos commented, "She represents a good example for the children. She came from a poor family and went to public school."

A Triumphant •

Celebration in

"Sugartown"

The low point of the 1992 campaign came in early October, when an anonymous fax received by both the *New York Post* and a local Spanish-language television station detailed Velázquez's attempted suicide and hospitalization the previous year. The incident was given much attention by the *Post;* not surprisingly the story spread throughout the national media like wildfire. Velázquez never denied the charges. Instead, she held a press conference, where, surrounded by friends and family, she acknowledged that she had suffered serious depression as the result of personal problems, including her mother's illness and a brother's drug addiction. "In 1991, in a troublesome period of my life, I attempted to commit suicide," said Velázquez, as reported by the *New York Times.* "It was a sad and painful experience for me, and one I thought was now in the past." She noted that she was "appalled" and "outraged" that privileged medical information in the form of confidential hospital records had been released to the public, in violation of state law; she brought a lawsuit against St. Clare's Hospital, the source of the confidential information, in 1994.

Velázquez's supporters must have recognized their candidate as a survivor who had overcome personal adversity and proven her potential to lead their communities. Velázquez, at the age of thirty-nine, defeated both Republican and independent challengers in the November election, taking more than three-quarters of the vote. At her election-night party in Williamsburg, Brooklyn, surrounded by "Fair Housing" signs, Velázquez said, in Spanish, that her victory was important for herself, her parents, and her people in the 12th District. "For you, I'm going to

Proves Herself •

a Survivor

fight to gain better jobs, better lives, and better opportunities," she told her supporters.

As a non-traditional politician, Velázquez does not fit the standard conservative or liberal labels; instead, she has often referred to herself as progressive. She continues to concentrate her congressional career on the problems confronting her urban district, including jobs, the economy, child care, and housing, and supports federal construction projects to create jobs and government loans to help small businesses. Shortly before her election-day victory, Velázquez told the *New York Post* that she wanted to improve the educational system and stem the tide of crime and drugs. On the international front, she opposes Jewish settlements on Israel's West Bank and favors increased economic aid to Latin America.

Velázquez is also dedicated to showing that Hispanic women can serve proudly in the political arena. "We are the ones who go out and collect signatures, but when it came to the final process, we were not good enough to run for office," she noted in *USA Today*. Among only forty-seven female representatives in the 103rd Congress, she is outspoken, independent, and determined, a breath of fresh air in Washington's "politics as usual." "New blood is good," Velázquez told the *New York Times* on election day. Along with providing a new voice for Hispanics in Congress, she continues to work with other minority and progressive members of Congress to improve the quality of life for all people in the nation's inner cities.

**Profile by
Ann Malaspina**

CARMEN ZAPATA

1927- •

Actress, •

producer,

activist

*O*ften referred to as "The First Lady of the Hispanic Theater," actress Carmen Zapata has been the cofounder, president, and managing producer of the non-profit Bilingual Foundation of the Arts (B.F.A.). This Los Angeles–based performing arts organization has been dedicated to bringing Hispanic experience and culture to both English and Spanish-speaking audiences through the medium of bilingual theater since its inception in 1973. Zapata has received acclaim for her organization's productions, both from the surrounding community and critics and reviewers. Working closely with the Los Angeles Unified School District to introduce the works of great Hispanic authors to students, Zapata remained closely involved with the BFA up until her

retirement in 1993.

Carmen Margarita Zapata was born in New York City on July 15, 1927, to Julio Zapata, a Mexican immigrant, and Ramona Roca, a woman from Argentina. Zapata and Roca met and married in New York; they lived with their three daughters in Spanish Harlem. As the family spoke Spanish exclusively in their home, Zapata's early experiences in school were so traumatic that she cannot remember her first years of schooling even years later. Despite the language her family spoke and the neighborhood in which they lived, Zapata was not well informed about Mexican culture as a child.

Zapata's talents manifested themselves at an early age; as a young girl she played the piano and the violin at family gatherings, sang in the school choir, and appeared in school plays. Although she did not at first approve of her daughter's desire to have a career in show business, Ramona Zapata sacrificed much to give her young daughter dancing and music lessons. Her sacrifices were not made in vain: after studying at the Actors Studio and with noted teacher Uta Hagen, Zapata was on her way to success.

Zapata made her Broadway debut in the chorus of the 1946 hit musical *Oklahoma,* and graduated to a lead role when the play went on the road. When she finally returned to Broadway, Zapata took over one of the principal roles in *Stop the World, I Want to Get Off.* She also appeared in popular productions of *Bells Are Ringing* and *Guys and Dolls.*

Zapata performed in stage musicals for twenty years. Between plays, she worked at night clubs under the name "Marge Cameron," in a singing and comedy act she had created and, at one point, she emceed for strippers at a burlesque house in Toledo, Ohio. "At the time it was not 'in' to be Hispanic," she explained to the *Los Angeles Times.* "I had a hard time getting club owners to hire me, unless I shook my fanny and played the maracas."

A brief marriage to comedy writer Roy Freedman ended in divorce after five years. In 1967, following her mother's death, Zapata moved to California and began what would become an intensive film and television career. Her first film role was as a prostitute in the 1968 movie *Sol Madrid.* When producers claimed that the actress billed in the film's credits as "Marge Cameron" didn't look "all-American," that she looked "ethnic," Zapata began to use her real name once again. As a result, she now found herself stereotyped in roles of either a maid or a mother. This, of course, displeased her, despite the fact that she made good money and received a great deal of visibility.

Recognizing the need for change within the Hollywood entertainment industry, Zapata helped form the first minority committee of the Screen Actors Guild. She was also one of the original members of the Hispanic actors organization "Nosotros," which was begun by well-known actor Ricardo Montalban.

While television and films kept her busy, Zapata continued to be dissatisfied with the roles she was offered. She also missed the theater. When the daring Cuban director Margarita Galban offered Zapata the opportunity to return to the theater, the frustrated actress was enthusiastic. At that time, Galban's company, "Seis Actores," was producing a Spanish-language play, *Cada quien su vida* ("To Each His Own"). Galban offered Zapata the opportunity to play the lead, but the actress was hesitant. She recalled to the *Los Angeles Times,* "She invited me to do a piece in Spanish. I'd never acted in Spanish before; I was petrified." But Galban reassured her that the character was that of a drunkard, so mistakes in speech were permissible. "And after I did it, I became very interested in Spanish-language theater. Why? It's beautiful! There are some glorious pieces that non–Spanish speaking people are not aware of. When I realized that, I started doing my translations."

• **Translates the**

Work of

Federico

García Lorca

Zapata delved further into her Hispanic roots and co-translated some of the classics of Hispanic literature. Dissatisfied with the plays available in Spanish, the actress set out to create her own stage works, accomplishing the formidable task of bringing into English Federico García Lorca's Spanish trilogy: *Bodas de sangre, Yerma,* and *La casa de Bernarda Alba,* as well as Fernando de Rojas's *La celestina* and J. Humberto Robles Arenas's *Uprooted.* Zapata and her writing partner, Michael Dewell, were appointed by the Lorca estate as official translators. Bantam Books published their acclaimed translation of the noted poet and playwright's dramatic trilogy in 1986.

In 1970 Zapata, Galban, and scenic designer Estela Scarlata joined forces. With $5,000 provided by Zapata, the trio rented a theater in downtown Los Angeles and borrowed sets, lights, and costumes from the surrounding studios. They then launched a new theater which, in 1973, became the Bilingual Foundation of the Arts.

In an interview with the *Los Angeles Times,* Zapata acknowledged the new trend toward Hispanic theater, something her B.F.A. had already been doing for years. "That was always the idea—to have everyone learn about, share and become part of our literature, our tradition." This has been done at the B.F.A. theatre for over two decades, as, on different nights, performances have alternated between English-speaking and Spanish-speaking versions. "We decided in 1979 to go bilingual," explained Zapata, "because that would make us unique as a theater. We also thought it would be nice if we reached into the non-Hispanic community and had them enjoy the beauty of our literature."

Zapata, who confesses that the theater is her "baby" and that while running it she was left with little time for acting, has nonetheless accumulated extensive performance credits, which include more than 300 appearances in television programs such as *Marcus Welby, Owen Marshall, Medical Center, Mod Squad, The Rookies, The Bold Ones, Bonanza, Treasury Agent, Streets of San Francisco, MacMillan and Wife, Switch, Charlie's Angels, Chico and the Man, Barreta, Fantasy Island, Archie Bunker's Place, Trapper John, M.D.,* and many others. She appeared regularly in the Anthony Quinn series for ABC, *Man and the City,* and had recurring roles on *The Dick Van Dyke Show* and the NBC soap opera *Santa Barbara.* In 1976 she starred in her own ABC television series *Viva Valdez.* From 1981 to 1982 she had a recurring role in the series *Flamingo Road* and was featured in the 1990 show *How to Murder a Millionaire.* Zapata admitted to *Hollywood Latinews* that she is most proud of the nine seasons in which she starred as the matronly "Doña Luz" in the PBS bilingual children's television show, *Villa Alegre.*

Zapata's professional recognitions include Dramalogue's 1984 Best Actress Award for her dramatic performance in the play *Blood Wedding,* a local Emmy for her 1973 documentary *Cinco Vidas,* and a 1971 Emmy nomination for her role in the television series *The Lawyers.*

Garners Emmy •

Nominations

As a guest speaker, Zapata has addressed audiences at various California universities and at fund-raising functions for charitable groups. Her community involvement has included service on the board of the National Conference of Christian and Jews, the United Way, the Boy Scouts of America, the National Repertory Theatre Foundation, and the Mexican-American Opportunity Foundation. She counts among her many memberships the Mayor's Committee on the Arts for Los Angeles, the California Arts Council's Ethnic Advisory Minority Panel, and many other organizations. Zapata has served as a panel member of the Expansion Arts Program of the National Endowment for the Arts, the Los Angeles Special Olympics Events Committee, and other programs.

A tireless activist, Zapata's efforts on behalf of her community have earned her many awards. These honors include an Outstanding Woman in Business Award from Women in Film, the Boy Scouts of America Community Leadership Award, a Mexican-American Foundation award, and recognition as 1985's woman of the year from the Hispanic Women's Council. She was also granted an honorary doctorate in human services from Sierra University. And in 1990 Zapata received what she admits is her favorite award: the Civil Order of Merit (*El Lazo de Dama de la Orden del Merito Civil*) by His Majesty Juan Carlos I, King of Spain, which recognizes Zapata's commitment to Hispanic concerns within the arts and in the realm of community service. She is one of only a few to have been so honored by the Spanish Head of State, a ceremony that could be likened to that of the Queen of England bestowing knighthood upon Dame Judith Anderson or Sir Laurence Olivier. Finally, on November 22, 1991, in recognition of her outstanding contributions to the arts in the state of California, Zapata was among nine Californian artists, arts organizations, and patrons to receive the prestigious Governor's Award for the Arts presented by Governor and Mrs. Pete Wilson.

In her continued commitment to the B.F.A., Zapata has been closely involved with the recently developed Teen Theatre Project (*Teatro Para Los Jovenes*), an innovative theater-in-education program designed by the foundation to meet the needs of junior and high school students identified as "at risk." Play productions—which are sponsored by grants from the Seaver Institute and the Kraft General Foods Foundation—are performed in the schools by ethnically diverse professional actors chosen for their ability to relate to and communicate with students; performances are followed by an open discussion of issues affecting teenagers. Zapata feels the program is an important step towards addressing the needs of students of many urban schools. In a television interview with *Hollywood Latinews,* she pointed out that a 1990 study of New York City schools showed arts programming to be the single most effective deterrent to drop-out rates. The Teen Theatre Project was modeled after B.F.A.'s highly successful theater-in-education program for elementary students, which has served nearly one million children since its inception in 1985.

Zapata continues her involvement with both Hispanic theater and her community as commissioner of Los Angeles's Cultural Affairs Department, a position she has held since 1993. During an interview with *La opinion,* the busy actress/producer, who makes her home in Van Nuys, California, admitted, "If I stop working I die. Work keeps me alive. I need to have something to do when I get up in the morning, to have a place to go, and that place is my theater."

**Profile by
Elena Kellner**

A CLOSER LOOK

● **ISABEL ALLENDE**

Coddou, Marcelio, editor, *Los libros tienen sus propios espíritus: Estudios sobre Isabel Allende*, Universidad Veracruzana, 1986.

Boston Globe, April 23, 1993, p. 14.

Chicago Tribune, May 19, 1985; November 17, 1991, p. 3.

Christian Science Monitor, June 7, 1985; May 27, 1987; June 10, 1993, p. 14.

Contemporary Literary Criticism, Volume 39, Gale (Detroit), 1986.

Detroit Free Press, June 7, 1987.

Detroit News, June 14, 1987

Erro-Peralta, Mora, "Isabel Allende," in *Dictionary of Literary Biography*, Volume 145: *Modern Latin-American Fiction Writers, Second Series,* Gale, 1994, pp. 33–41.

Globe & Mail (Toronto), June 24, 1985; June 27, 1987.

Hart, Patricia, *Narrative Magic in the Fiction of Isabel Allende*, Fairleigh Dickinson University Press (Rutherford, NJ), 1989.

Hispanic, October 1990, pp. 12–13.

Los Angeles Times, February 10, 1988.

Los Angeles Times Book Review, June 16, 1985; May 31, 1987; June 6, 1993, p. 13; April 30, 1995, pp. 3, 8.

Mother Jones, December 1988.

Nation, July 20–27, 1985.

New Statesman & Society, July 5, 1985; July 2, 1993, pp. 38–39.

Newsweek, May 13, 1985.

New York Review of Books, July 18, 1985.

New York Times, May 2, 1985; May 20, 1987; February 4, 1988. *New York Times Book Review*, May 12, 1985; July 12, 1987; October 23, 1988; May 2, 1993, p. 13; May 21, 1995, p. 11.

Observer, July 4, 1993, p. 62

People, June 10, 1985; June 1, 1987; May 2, 1994; June 5, 1995.

Publishers Weekly, March 1, 1985; May 17, 1985.

Review, January/June 1985.

Rojas, Sonia Riquelme, and Edna Aguirre Rehbein, editors, *Critical Approaches to Isabel Allende's Novels,* P. Lang (New York City), 1991.

Spectator, August 3, 1985.

Time, May 20, 1985.

Times (London), July 4, 1985; July 9, 1987; March 22, 1989; March 23, 1989.

Times Literary Supplement, July 5, 1985; July 10, 1987; April 7-13, 1989.

Tribune Books (Chicago), October 9, 1988.

US News and World Report, November 21, 1988.

Village Voice, June 7, 1985.

Voice Literary Supplement, December 1988.

Washington Post Book World, May 12, 1985; May 24, 1987; October 9, 1988; May 23, 1993, p. 6.

World Literature Today, spring 1993, pp. 335–36.

● **MARIA CONCHITA ALONSO**

Alonso, Maria Conchita, interviews with Elena Kellner, February 1992 and May 1992.

For more ●

information

Hispanic, May 1989, pp. 14–16.

Hispanic Business, July 1992, p. 22.

Los Angeles Times, August 9, 1986.

Time, July 11, 1988, p. 72.

• *LINDA ALVARADO*

Alvarado, Linda, telephone interview with Carol Hopkins, September 15, 1992.

Hispanic Business, October 1994.

Minority Business Entrepreneur, July/August 1989.

• *JULIA ALVAREZ*

Alvarez, Julia, *How the Garcia Girls Lost Their Accents,* Algonquin, 1991.

Alvarez, J., *The Other Side/El Otro Lado,* Dutton, 1995.

American Scholar, winter 1987, pp. 71–85.

Atlanta Journal, August 11, 1991, p. A13.

Boston Globe, May 26, 1991, p. A13.

Brújula Compass (Spanish-language; translation by R. Garcia-Johnson), January-February, 1992, p. 16.

Hispanic, June 1991, p. 55; September 1992, pp. 36, 38.

Library Journal, May 1, 1991, p. 102.

Los Angeles Times, June 7, 1991, p. E4.

Más (Spanish-language; translation by R. Garcia-Johnson), November/December 1991, p. 100.

New York Times Book Review, October 6, 1991, p. 14.

Nuestro, November 1984, pp. 34+; March 1985, pp. 52+; January/February 1986, pp. 32+.

Publishers Weekly, April 5, 1991, p. 133; July 11, 1994, p. 62.

Washington Post, June 20, 1991, p. D11.

• *JUDITH F. BACA*

Artweek, October 6, 1979, p. 5; November 14, 1991, pp. 10–11; November 21, 1991, pp. 10–11.

CARA: Chicano Art-Resistance & Affirmation (1965-1985), Wight Gallery/University of California, Los Angeles, 1991.

Hispanic, May 1991, pp. 17–18.

Interview with Ann Malaspina, August 1992.

Life, December 1980, pp. 87–90.

Lippard, Lucy, *Mixed Blessings: Art for a Multicultural America,* Penguin, 1988.

Los Angeles Times, April 5, 1991, p. F16.

Telephone interview with Yleana Martinez, August 1992

Z Magazine, October 1991, pp. 70–74.

• *MAXINE BACA ZINN*

De Colores: Journal of Emerging Raza Philosophies, winter 1975, pp. 19–31.

Publishers Weekly, October 25, 1993, p. 55.

Telephone interview with Yleana Martinez, August 1992.

• *JOAN BAEZ*

Baez, Joan, *Daybreak,* Dial, 1968.

Baez, Joan, *And a Voice to Sing With,* Summit, 1987.

Christian Science Monitor, September 3, 1987, p. 21.

Los Angeles Times, February 3, 1991, p. K1.

Newsweek, July 20, 1987, p. 62.

New York Times, November 7, 1960; November 13, 1961; December 12, 1989, p. C24.

New York Times Book Review, June 21, 1987, p. 30.

Rolling Stone, November 5, 1987, p. 163. *Time,* June 1, 1962, p. 39; November 23, 1962, p. 54.

U.S. News & World Report, June 29, 1987, p. 60.

• *LOURDES G. BAIRD*

Detroit Free Press, August 6, 1992, p. 3A; August 9, 1992, p. 2F.

Los Angeles Times, November 30, 1989, p. B1; December 4, 1989, p. B6; May 15, 1990, p. B1; May 21, 1990, p. B6; July 11, 1990, p. B6; July 19, 1990, p. B1.

• *MARIAH CAREY*

Boston Globe, October 4, 1991, p. 49.

Ebony, November 1993, pp. 36–42.

Los Angeles Times, June 24, 1990, p. 62; August 4, 1990, p. F18; November 23, 1993, p. F1.

New York Times, April 14, 1991, p. 28; May 21, 1995, p. 38; June 11, 1995, p. WC18; July 23, 1995, p. 30.

USA Today, February 17, 1993, p. D14.

• *ROSEMARY CASALS*

Jacobs, Linda, *Rosemary Casals: The Rebel Rosebud*, EMC Corp., 1975.

People, May 31, 1982, p. 85.

Thacher, Alida M., *Raising a Racket: Rosie Casals*, Raintree, 1976.

• *ANA CASTILLO*

Archives, Arte Público Press, Houston, Texas.

Booklist, April 1, 1993, p. 1409.

• *LORNA DEE CERVANTES*

Dictionary of Literary Biography, Volume 82: Chicano Writers, First Series, Gale, 1989.

Sánchez, Marta Ester, *Contemporary Chicana Poetry: A Critical Approach to an Emerging Literature*, University of California Press, 1985.

• *DENISE CHÁVEZ*

Chávez, Denise, *The Last of the Menu Girls*, Arte Público, 1986.

Contemporary Authors New Revisions Series, Volume 131, Gale, 1991.

Los Angeles Times, November 9, 1994, p. F1

New York Times Book Review, October 12, 1986, p. 28.

• *LINDA CHÁVEZ*

Christian Science Monitor, December 11, 1986, p. 26.

Fortune, March 4, 1985, pp. 161–64; November 21, 1988, p. 188.

Hispanic, August 1992, pp. 11–16.

New Republic, May 13, 1985, p. 11; February 24, 1986, pp. 8–10; August 3, 1987, pp. 12–13.

New York Times, August 31, 1986, p. 58; September 10, 1986, p. 15; October 16, 1986, p. B16.

People, November 3, 1986, pp. 115–16.

Policy Review, winter 1988, pp. 46–47.

Savvy, January 1987, pp. 43–48, 75.

Transition, Number 56, 1992, pp. 112–22.

USA Today, May 1, 1995, p. 6D.

Wall Street Journal, August 15, 1986, p. 36.

Washington Monthly, June 1985, pp. 34–39.

Washington Post, July 25, 1986, p. 1; August 15, 1986, p. 17; October 24, 1986, p. C3, 5; October 28, 1986, p. 15; October 29, 1986, p. 1, August 16, 1988, p. 22; October 20, 1988, p. 18.

• *SANDRA CISNEROS*

Authors and Artists for Young Adults, Volume 9, Gale, 1992.

Cisneros, Sandra, *The House on Mango Street*, Arte Público Press, 1984.

Cisneros, S., *My Wicked, Wicked Ways*, Third Woman Press, 1987.

Cisneros, S., *Woman Hollering Creek and Other Stories*, Random House, 1991.

Cisneros, S., *Loose Woman*, Knopf, 1994.

Cisneros, S., *Hairs/Pellitos*, Knopf, 1994.

Glamour, November 1990, pp. 256–57.

Library Journal, May 15, 1994, p. 76.

Los Angeles Times, May 7, 1991, p. F1.

Los Angeles Times Book Review, April 28, 1991, p. 3.

Mirabella, April 1991, p. 46.

Newsweek, June 3, 1991, p. 60.

New York Times Book Review, May 26, 1991, p. 6.

Publishers Weekly, March 29, 1991, pp. 74–75; April 25, 1994, p. 61.

Washington Post Book World, June 9, 1991, p. 3.

• *JUDITH ORTIZ COFER*

Booklist, November 15, 1993, p. 59.

Cofer, Judith Ortiz, *Silent Dancing: A Partial Remembrance of a Puerto Rican Childhood*, Arte Público, 1990.

Contemporary Authors New Revision Series, Volume 32, Gale, 1991.

Georgia Review, spring/summer 1990, pp. 51–59.

Los Angeles Times Book Review, August 6, 1989, p. 6.

New York Times Book Review, September 24, 1989, pp. 46–47.

Publishers Weekly, June 8, 1990, p. 50.

Women's Review of Books, December 1990, p. 9.

• *MIRIAM COLÓN*

Colón, Miriam, interview with Gloria Bonilla-Santiago, February 17, 1989.

Daily News, August 7, 1982, p. 16.

Daily News Magazine, April 19, 1982, p. 20.

El Diario La Prensa, June 19, 1980, pp. 1–36; August 11, 1982, p. 4.

New York Times, September 12, 1971, pp. 1–2; April 8, 1987, p. 9.

San Juan Star, April 16, 1979, p. 5.

Soho News, April 8, 1981, p. 2.

• *GRACÍELA DANIELE*

Dance, January 1991, p. 70; March 1993, p. 90.

Nation, June 11, 1990, p. 834.

National Review, December 31, 1990, p. 49.

New Republic, November 20, 1989, pp. 30–31.

New York, September 2, 1985, pp. 57–58; November 23, 1987, pp. 115–16; October 30, 1989, pp. 101–102; May 21, 1990, p. 78.

New Yorker, December 21, 1987, pp. 103–104; May 28, 1990, p. 101; March 15, 1993, p. 122; February 21, 1994, pp. 107–108

New York Times, January 25, 1981; November 1, 1987, sec. 2, p. 5; October 20, 1989, p. C3; November 11, 1992, sec. 2, p. 5; June 16, 1995, pp. C1, 16.

Nuestro, August 1981, p. 63.

Time, July 11, 1988, p. 83; July 10, 1995, p. 61.

• *DOLORES DEL RIO*

Architectural Digest, April 1992, pp. 128–33, 254.

Hadley-Garcia, George, *Hispanic Hollywood: The Latins in Motion Pictures,* foreword by Dolores Del Rio, Citadel Press (New York City), 1990.

Hispanoamericano (Spanish-language; translation by Carl J. Mora), April 25, 1983, pp. 44–47.

Modern Maturity, February 1981, pp. 69–71.

Mora, Carl J., *Mexican Cinema: Reflections of a Society, 1896-1988,* revised edition, University of California Press (Berkeley), 1989.

New York Times, April 13, 1983, p. D23.

Shipman, David, *The Great Movie Stars: The Golden Years,* revised edition, Hill & Wang (New York City), 1979.

Woll, Allen L., *Films of Dolores Del Rio,* Gordon Press, 1978.

• *GLORIA ESTEFAN*

Boston Herald, March 7, 1990; March 14, 1990.

Detroit Free Press, August 1, 1988.

Hispanic, September 1993, pp. 102–03.

Los Angeles Daily News, September 12, 1989.

Los Angeles Herald Examiner, January 29, 1989.

Los Angeles Times, June 22, 1993, p. F1.

Miami Herald, September 30, 1988; May 7, 1989; July 9, 1989; May 27, 1990.

New York Post, July 25, 1988; February 28, 1990; March 21, 1990; March 22, 1990; March 23, 1990.

New York Tribune, September 14, 1988; December 13, 1989.

People, October 27, 1986; February 18, 1991.

Rolling Stone, June 14, 1990.

Washington Post, July 17, 1988.

• *CLARISSA PINKOLA ESTÉS*

Ballantine Books press release, 1992.

Estés, Clarissa Pinkola, *Women Who Run with the Wolves: Myths and Stories of the Wild Woman Archetype,* Ballantine, 1992.

Hispanic, October 1993, pp. 72–73.

Library Journal, June 15, 1992; May 15, 1993; June 1, 1994; January 1994.

Newsweek, December 21, 1992.

New York Times, February 28, 1993.

People, December 21, 1992.

Publishers Weekly, May 11, 1992; October 5, 1992.

San Francisco Chronicle, August 2, 1992.

USA Today, August 13, 1992.

• SANDRA MARÍA ESTEVES

Archives, Arte Público Press, Houston, Texas.

Gordils, Yanis, "Sandra María Esteves," *Biographical Dictionary of Hispanic Literature in the United States,* edited by Nicolas Kanellos, Greenwood Press (Westport, Connecticut), 1989, pp. 85–94.

• ANITA PEREZ FERGUSON

Hispanic, October 1990, pp. 26–30

Los Angeles Times, March 10, 1991, p. 6.

• GIGI FERNÁNDEZ

Hispanic, July 1988.

Los Angeles Times, July 11, 1993, p. C11.

Más (translated from Spanish by Diane Telgen), November 1992, p. 53.

New York Times, February 1985, pp. 180–181.

Sports Illustrated, February 20, 1995, pp. 157–58, 163.

• GISELLE FERNANDEZ

Fernandez, Giselle, telephone interview with Sally Foster conducted on September 14, 1992.

Hispanic, July 1994, pp. 52–53.

USA Today, December 6, 1995, p. 3D.

• MARY JOE FERNÁNDEZ

Los Angeles Times, June 25, 1986, section II, p. 1.

New York Times, September 21, 1984.

Sports Illustrated, February 11, 1991, pp. 76–79.

Tennis, June 1994, pp. 94–100.

World Tennis, February 1991, pp. 25–26.

• MARÍA IRENE FORNÉS

Betsko, Kathleen, and Rachel Koenig, *Interviews with Contemporary Women Playwrights,* Beech Tree, 1987, pp. 154–67.

Chicago, April 1990, p. 89.

Chicago Tribune, June 14, 1969; February 8, 1988, Section 5, p. 3; February 9, 1988, Section 2, p. 10; May 27, 1988, Section 5, p. 4.

Contemporary Authors New Revision Series, Volume 28, Gale, 1990.

Contemporary Literary Criticism, Volume 61, Gale, 1990.

Contemporary Theatre, Film, and Television, Volume 1, Gale, 1984.

Dictionary of Literary Biography, Volume 7: Twentieth-Century American Dramatists, Gale, 1981.

Fornés, María Irene, *Lovers and Keepers,* Theatre Communications Group, 1987.

Fornés, M., *María Irene Fornés: Plays,* PAJ Publications, 1986.

Fornés, M., Promenade and Other Plays, Winter House, 1971.

Hispanic, July 1988, pp. 44–46.

Los Angeles Times, August 2, 1989, Section 6, p. 7.

Marranca, Bonnie, and Guatam Dasgupta, *American Playwrights: A Critical Survey,* Volume 1, Drama Books Specialists, 1981.

Nation, April 6, 1985, p. 412; April 23, 1988, p. 580.

Newsweek, January 25, 1982, p. 73.

New Yorker, May 7, 1979, p. 131; January 4, 1988, p. 59.

New York Times, April 17, 1968; June 5, 1969; February 22, 1972; January 14, 1978, January 22, 1978; April 25, 1979; December 30, 1981; October 25, 1983; March 13, 1984; March 20, 1985; April 17, 1986; April 23, 1986; December 15, 1987, p. C21; October 17, 1989, p. A16.

Performing Arts Journal, Number 1, 1984. *Variety,* March 23, 1992, pp. 113–14

• DAISY FUENTES

Hispanic, August 1993, pp. 14–15

Los Angeles Times, August 17, 1993, p. F1.

New York Times, April 25, 1993, p. 8; October 10, 1993, section 9, p. 3.

USA Today, January 13, 1995, p. D1.

Vogue, August 1991, pp. 110–16.

• NELY GALÁN

Chicago Tribune, March 3, 1990, p. 10.

Hispanic, November 1988, pp. 50–51; November 1991, pp. 18–24.

Los Angeles Times, April 26, 1994, p. F1.

New York Times Magazine, December 11, 1994, pp. 59–61

USA Today, May 17, 1994, p. 3D.

Variety, March 28, 1994, p. 46.

• CRISTINA GARCIA

Ann Arbor News, April 23, 1992.

Publishers Weekly, January 13, 1992.

Time, March 23, 1992.

• CARMEN LOMAS GARZA

Booklist, June 1, 1990, p. 1907.

Caminos, November 1984, pp. 44–45, 53.

El grito, summer 1971, pp. 2, 70–73.

Houston Post, August 19, 1976, p. 7B.

Imagine, summer/winter 1986, pp. 129–32, 231–32.

Los Angeles Times, November 7, 1992, p. F1.

Publishers Weekly, July 13, 1990, pp. 54–55.

• RITA HAYWORTH

American Film, July 1986, pp. 69–72.

Good Housekeeping, August 1983, pp. 118–27; September 1983, pp. 74–82.

Harper's Bazaar, November 1989, pp. 156–59.

Ladies' Home Journal, January 1983, pp. 84–89.

Leaming, Barbara, *If This Was Happiness,* Viking (New York City), 1989.

Ms., January 1991, pp. 35–38.

New York Times, May 16, 1987.

People, November 7, 1983, pp. 112–17; June 1, 1987, pp. 72–79; November 13, 1989, pp. 129–32.

Time, May 25, 1987, p. 76.

Variety, May 20, 1987, pp. 4–6.

• ANTONIA HERNÁNDEZ

Hispanic, December 1990, pp. 17–18.

Hispanic Business, February 1992, p. 10.

Intercambios Feminiles, spring 1988.

La Paloma, December 1991.

Los Angeles Daily Journal, September 3, 1985, p. 1.

Los Angeles Times, August 5, 1985, sec. 2, p. 1; December 13, 1992, p. M3.

Parents, March 1985, pp. 96–100, 170–174.

Vista, August 1992, p. 28.

• CAROLINA HERRERA

Américas, September/October 1990, pp. 30–35.

Architectural Digest, April 1987, p. 128; September 1988, p. 178.

Boston Globe, September 15, 1988, p. 65.

Harper's Bazaar, August 1986, p. 152; September 1989, p. 380.

Hispanic, March 1989, pp. 28–30; October 1989, pp. 36–37.

Newsweek, June 30, 1986, pp. 56–57; March 1989, pp. 28–32.

New York Times, October 31, 1989, p. B8; April 9, 1991, p. B8; January 4, 1994, p. D21.

Nuestro, October 1985, p. 60.

People, May 3, 1982, p. 122.

Vogue, March 1987, p. 342; June 1990, p. 270; January 1991, p. 132.

• MARIA HINOJOSA

Hinojosa, Maria, telephone interview with Ronie-Richele Garcia-Johnson, August 1992.

Los Angeles Times, March 30, 1995, p. E1.

• DOLORES HUERTA

Bakersfield Californian, January 25, 1991, p. A1–2.

Day, Mark, *Forty Acres: Cesar Chavez and the Farm Workers,* Praeger, 1971.

Dunne, John Gregory, *Delano: The Story of the California Grape Strike,* Farrar, 1976.

Frontiers, Volume 11, number 1, 1990, pp. 26–92.

Huerta, Dolores, interviews with Margaret Rose, March 16, 1984, February 4, 1985, February 8, 1985, February 12, 1985, February 19, 1985, (La Paz) Keene, California, and February 26, 1985, Bakersfield, California.

Intercambios Femeniles, winter 1989, pp. 11–12.

Labor History, summer 1990, pp. 271–93.

Levy, Jacques, *Cesar Chavez: Autobiography of La Causa,* Norton, 1975.

London, Joan, and Henry Anderson, *So Shall Ye Reap,* Crowell, 1970.

Los Angeles Times, January 25, 1991, p. A3; February 14, p. E5.

Majka, Linda C., and Theo J. Majka, *Farm Workers, Agribusiness, and the State,* Temple University Press, 1982.

El Malcriado, July 1, 1970, pp. 16–18.

Matthiessen, Peter, *Sal Si Puedes: Cesar Chavez and the New American Revolution,* Random House, 1969.

Meister, Dick, and Anne Loftis, *A Long Time Coming: The Struggle to Unionize America's Farm Workers,* Macmillan, 1977.

Ms., November 1976, pp. 11–16.

Nation, February 23, 1974, pp. 232–38.

Progressive, September 1975, pp. 38–40.

Regeneración, Volume 1, number 11, 1971, p. 20, Volume 2, number 4, 1975, pp. 20–24.

Santa Fe New Mexican, November 10, 1938.

Stockton Record, March 2, 1986.

Taylor, Ronald B., *Chavez and the Farm Workers,* Beacon Press, 1975.

Union W.A.G.E., July/August 1974, p. 6.

• *MARI-LUCI JARAMILLO*

Jaramillo, Mari-Luci, interview with Michelle Vachon, September 20, 1992.

• *TANIA LEÓN*

Kanellos, Nicolás, editor. *The Hispanic American Almanac,* Detroit: Gale Research, 1993. p. 729.

• *NANCY LOPEZ*

Chicago Tribune, September 4, 1993, p. 6.

Hispanic, June 1989, pp. 15–16.

New York Times, March 31, 1985; May 19, 1988.

People, April 25, 1983.

Sports Illustrated, August 5, 1985; August 4, 1986; February 9, 1987; May 29, 1989, p. 65.

USA Today, March 28, 1995, p. C.

• *MÓNICA CECILIA LOZANO*

Hispanic, March 1992, p. 60.

Lozano, Mónica, personal interview with Ronie-Richelle Garcia-Johnson, conducted on August 31, 1992.

• *WENDY LUCERO-SCHAYES*

Atlanta Constitution, July 28, 1989, p. F3; August 2, 1990, p. F7.

Detroit Free Press, April 14, 1992, p. D1.

Lucero-Schayes, Wendy, interview with Diane Telgen, April 15, 1992, Ann Arbor, MI.

• *SONIA MANZANO*

Atlanta Constitution, May 10, 1989, p. B1.

Boston Globe Magazine, May 7, 1989, p. 8.

Manzano, Sonia, telephone interview with Luis Vasquez Ajmac, April 23, 1992.

• *MARISOL*

ARTNews, May 1989, pp. 147–51.

• *ELIZABETH MARTINEZ*

Chicago Tribune, February 19, 1995, p. 6.

Library Journal, November 1, 1988, pp. 35–39; November 15, 1994, p 14.

Los Angeles Times (Orange County edition), April 7, 1986, pp. V1, 3.

Martinez, Elizabeth, interview with Michelle Vachon, August 28, 1992.

Orange County Register, March 15, 1989, pp. K1, 4; September 12, 1989, p. B2.

Wilson Library Bulletin, December 1994, p. 11

• *VILMA MARTINEZ*

Los Angeles Daily Journal, January 6, 1992.

Los Angeles Times, May 6, 1994, p. B6.

Martinez, Vilma, telephone interview with Carol von Hatten, September 19, 1992.

• *NICHOLASA MOHR*

Authors & Artists for Young Adults, Volume 8, Gale, 1992.

Best Sellers, December 1975, p. 266.

Booklist, July 1994, p. 1934.

Bulletin of the Center for Children's Books, June 1976, p. 161; July/August 1977, p. 178; May 1986, p. 178.

Children's Literature, Volume 3, 1974, pp. 230–34.

Contemporary Literary Criticism, Volume 12, Gale, 1980.

English Journal, February 1978, p. 100.

Essence, May 1980, p. 25.

Horn Book, February 1976, p. 57; February 1980, p. 56; September/October 1986, pp. 591.

Interracial Bulletin of Books for Children, November 4, 1976, p. 15.

The Lion and the Unicorn, fall 1978, pp. 6–15.

Newsweek, March 4, 1974, p. 83.

New York Times, January 20, 1980.

New York Times Book Review, November 4, 1973, pp. 27–28; November 10, 1974; November 16, 1975; May 22, 1977.

Publishers Weekly, July 25, 1986, p. 190.

Sadker, Myra Pollack, and David Miller Sadker, *Now upon a Time: A Contemporary View of Children's Literature,* Harper, 1977.

School Library Journal, April 1977, p. 79; August 1986, p. 105.

Something about the Author Autobiography Series, Volume 8, Gale, 1989, pp. 185-94.

Vista, May 14, 1989, p. 3.

Weiss, M. Jerry, editor, *From Writers to Students: The Pleasures and Pains of Writing,* International Reading Association, 1979.

● *PAT MORA*

Contemporary Authors, Volume 129, Gale (Detroit), 1990.

Christian Science Monitor, July 18, 1990, pp. 16–17.

English Journal, September 1990, p. 40.

Horn Book, July/August 1990, pp. 436–37.

National Catholic Reporter, May 10, 1991, p. 24.

Nuestro, March 1985, p. 51.

Library Journal, March 15, 1993, p. 96.

● *RITA MORENO*

Boston Globe, September 5, 1986, p. 62; September 8, 1986, p. 26.

Chicago Tribune, May 3, 1988, section 5, p. 3; November 15, 1988, section 5, p. 8.

Cosmopolitan, August 1981, p. 14.

Harper's Bazaar, May 1981, pp. 160–61; September 1981, pp. 309–11.

Hispanic, October 1989, pp. 30–33; December 1989, p. 40; September 1990, p. 56.

Los Angeles Times, November 17, 1988, section 6, p. 1.

Ms., January/February 1991, pp. 93–95.

Newsweek, May 25, 1981, p. 74.

New Yorker, June 22, 1981, p. 86; June 24, 1985, p. 78.

New York Post, March 13, 1955.

New York Times, March 1975.

Nuestro, October 1981, pp. 44–46; March 1986, pp. 16–25.

People, May 3, 1982, pp. 105–07.

TV Guide, January 15, 1983, pp. 26–29; January 14, 1995, pp. 26–28.

Variety, February 26, 1986, p. 60.

Washington Post, March 19, 1990, p. C5.

● *EVELYN NIEVES*

Nieves, Evelyn, telephone interview with D. D. Andreassi, August 1992.

● *ANTONIA NOVELLO*

Detroit Free Press, October 30, 1990.

Glamour, August 1990.

Hispanic, January/February 1990, p. 20; October 1991, p. 15.

Los Angeles Times, Jun 29, 1994, p. B7.

Newsweek, October 30, 1989.

New York Times, October 18, 1989, p. A20; November 2, 1989; June 27, 1991, p. D20;

November 5, 1991, p. A16; November 6, 1991, p. A25.

Parade, November 11, 1990.

People, December 17, 1990.

Saturday Evening Post, May/June 1991, pp. 38–41, 93.

Washington Post, October 18, 1989; October 24, 1989; May 8, 1990.

• *ELLEN OCHOA*

Hispanic, May 1990, p. 19.

Houston Post, July 17, 1990, p. A9; July 22, 1990, p. A9; July 23, 1990, p. A9.

Ochoa, Ellen, telephone interview with D. D. Andreassi, August 1992.

• *GRACIELA OLIVÁREZ*

Los Angeles Times, December 5, 1985, sec. H, p. 1.

National Catholic Reporter, November 6, 1987, p. 2.

New Catholic World, July/August, 1984, p. 183.

Redbook, April 1975.

Washington Monthly, April 1980, p. 60.

• *KATHERINE D. ORTEGA*

Atlanta Constitution, May 13, 1986, p. B1.

Boston Globe, November 24, 1985, p. B25.

Ms., August 1984, p. 22.

New York Times, September 13, 1983, p. B14; October 4, 1983, p. 19; August 24, 1984, p. 20.

Vital Speeches of the Day, September 15, 1984, pp. 712–13.

• *ELIZABETH PEÑA*

Contemporary Theater, Film and Television, Volume 5, Gale, 1988.

Hispanic, November 1994, pp. 16–17.

Interview, April 1987, p. 34.

Más, fall 1990, p. 14.

Newsweek, November 12, 1990, pp. 77–78. *New York,* February 3, 1986, pp. 82–83; April 16, 1990, pp. 97–98.

People, September 30, 1985, p. 10; October 19, 1987, p. 15; May 13, 1991, pp. 107–08.

• *ROSIE PEREZ*

Biography of Rosie Perez, provided by Baker-Winokur-Ryder Public Relations.

Chicago Tribune, November 6, 1994, p. 8.

Entertainment Weekly, April 3, 1992, p. 11.

GQ, August 1992, pp. 49–58.

Newsweek, May 4, 1992, pp. 64–65.

Preview, April 1992, p. 25.

Rolling Stone, May 14, 1992.

• *DOLORES PRIDA*

Archives, Arte Público Press, Houston, Texas.

Escarpenter, Jose, and Linda S. Glaze, "Dolores Prida," in *Biographical Dictionary of Hispanic Literature in the United States,* edited by Nicolas Kanellos, Greenwood Press (Westport, CT), 1989, pp. 244–49.

Weiss, Judith, "The Theaterworks of Dolores Prida," in Dolores Prida's *Beautiful Senoritas and Other Plays,* Arte Público Press (Houston), 1991, pp. 9–16.

• *TEY DIANA REBOLLEDO*

Publishers Weekly, May 17, 1993, p. 74.

Rebolledo, Tey Diana, interview with Teresa Márquez, September 18, 1992.

• *CHITA RIVERA*

Atlanta Journal/Constitution, March 13, 1988, p. J2.

Boston Globe, March 13, 1988. p. PAR13; June 19, 1988, p. A1; July 22, 1989, p. 6.

Chicago Tribune, April 8, 1986, sec. 1, p. 4; February 7, 1988, sec. 13, p. 14; February 10, 1988, sec. 2, p. 11.

Contemporary Theatre, Film, and Television, Volume 8, Gale, 1990.

Dance Magazine, May 1984, pp. 146+.

Globe & Mail, (Toronto), February 1, 1992, p. C3.

Horizon, October 1984, p. 56.

Los Angeles Times, December 4, 1988, p. C5; December 15, 1988, sec. 6, p. 1.

Ms., December 1984, p. 34.

Newsweek, May 24, 1993, p. 63

New York, February 20, 1984, pp. 86–87; January 13, 1986, p. 50.

New York Times, November 26, 1989, sec. 1, p. 71.

People, March 5, 1984, pp. 61–64.

Time, February 7, 1983, p. 63; February 20, 1984, p. 84; April 21, 1986, p. 72; November 30, 1992, p. 78.

Variety, June 5, 1985, p. 54; December 25, 1985, p. 62; June 4, 1986, p. 47; February 17, 1988, p. 180.

● *LINDA RONSTADT*

down beat, July 1985.

Esquire, October 1985.

The Illustrated Encyclopedia of Country Music, Harmony Books, 1977.

Los Angeles Times, December 5, 1993, p. 6.

Newsweek, October 20, 1975; April 23, 1979; August 11, 1980; December 10, 1984; February 29, 1988.

Parade, December 22, 1991, p. 22.

People, October 24, 1977; April 30, 1979.

Rolling Stone, December 2, 1976; March 27, 1977; October 19, 1978; November 2, 1978; August 18, 1983.

Saturday Review, December 1984.

Stambler, Irwin, *The Encyclopedia of Pop, Rock, and Soul,* St. Martin's, 1974.

Time, February 28, 1977; March 22, 1982; September 26, 1983.

TV Guide, December 21, 1991.

Vogue, November 1984.

Washington Post Magazine, October 9, 1977.

● *ILEANA ROS-LEHTINEN*

Boston Globe, August 31, 1989, p. 3.

Christian Science Monitor, August 9, 1991, p. 18.

Hispanic, September 1990, p. S5; October 1990, p. 26; August 1992, p. 28; April 1995, p. 92.

Ladies' Home Journal, November 1991, p. 182.

National Catholic Reporter, April 19, 1991, p. 1.

National Review, November 24, 1989, p. 39.

New York Times, August 31, 1989, p. 16.

Time, September 11, 1989, p. 31.

Vista, February 4, 1992, pp. 6, 22.

Washington Post, July 30, 1989, p. 4; August 17, 1989, p. 4.

● *LUCILLE ROYBAL-ALLARD*

Civic Center News Source, January 13, 1992, pp. 1, 8, 12.

Hispanic, March 1990, p. 20.

News release from the office of Lucille Roybal-Allard, September 16, 1992.

Roybal-Allard, Lucille, interview with Diana Martínez, September 2, 1992.

● *VICKI RUIZ*

American Historical Review, April 1989.

Journal of American History, June 1988; December 1988; December 1989; December 1990.

Ms., July/August 1990; March/April 1995, pp. 68–71.

New Republic, October 22, 1990.

Oral History Review, spring 1989.

Southwestern Historical Quarterly, April 1989.

Ruiz, Vicki, interview with Tom Pendergast, September 9, 1992.

● *CRISTINA SARALEGUI*

Chicago Tribune, May 31, 1992.

Hispanic, November 1991, pp. 18–24.

Hollywood Latinews (television program), interview with Elena Kellner, October 16, 1991.

La opinion (translated from Spanish by Elena Kellner), Panorama section, October 20, 1991.

Los Angeles Times, May 25, 1993, p. 4.

Los Angeles Times Calendar, June 22, 1992; June 25, 1992.

Más (translated from Spanish by Elena Kellner), July/August 1991, pp. 43–50.

Miami Herald, June 21, 1992, pp. 11–31.

New York Newsday, April 2, 1992; June 22, 1992.

Saralegui, Cristina, official biography provided by Magikcity Communications.

● *SELENA*

Chicago Tribune, April 6, 1995, p. 30.

Hispanic, May 1995, p. 96.

Hispanic Business, July 1995, pp. 18, 20. *Los Angeles Times,* August 27, 1994, p. F1; April 8, 1995, p. F1.

People, July 10, 1995, p. 36.

New York Times, Arpil 1, 1995, p. 1

Time, April 10, 1995, p. 91.

USA Today, July 18, 1995, p. 6D; October 9,. 1995, pp. D1–2.

• *LUPE SERRANO*

Serrano, Lupe, interview with Peg McNichol, September 1992.

• *MADELEINE STOWE*

Boston Globe, January 23, 1994, p. B35.

Interview, May 1990, pp. 92–93.

Los Angeles Times, January 30, 1994, p. 7

Newsweek, February 14, 1994, p. 52.

• *ISABEL TOLEDO*

Cosmopolitan, June 1987, pp. 240–41.

Harper's Bazaar, March 1992, p. 48.

Hispanic, October 1989.

New York Times, April 16, 1987; April 6, 1990; April 13, 1991.

Women's Wear Daily, November 6, 1989; April 9, 1990; November 5, 1990; April 16, 1991.

Vogue, February 1995, pp. 108–10.

• *CHRISTY TURLINGTON*

Forbes, May 25, 1992, p. 164. *New York,* March 9, 1992, pp. 38–46

New York Times, July 2, 1995, p. 33.

• *NYDIA MARGARITA VELÁZQUEZ*

Newsday, September 21, 1992, p. 37; September 26, 1992, p. 10; September 27, 1992, p. 18; October 10, 1992, p. 13.

New York Post, November 4, 1992, p. 4.

New York Times, July 9, 1992, p. B3; September 7, 1992, pp. 21–22; September 27, 1992, p. 33; October 10, 1992, p. 25; October 29, 1992, p. B7; November 2, 1992, p. B1, 4; November 4, 1992, p. B13; May 14, 1994, p. 24.

Noticias del Mundo, November 4, 1992, pp. 1, 4.

USA Today, October 27, 1992, p. 2.

Washington Post, October 9, 1992, p. 12.

• *CARMEN ZAPATA*

Hollywood Latinews (television program), interview with Elena Kellner, February 1992.

Los Angeles Times, Calendar section, February 5, 1989.

La opinion (translated from Spanish by Elena Kellner), Panorama section, December 29, 1991.

Zapata, Carmen, biography provided by the Bilingual Foundation of the Arts, 1992.

SUBJECT INDEX